JOURNAL FOR THE STUDY OF THE OLD TESTAMENT
SUPPLEMENT SERIES
43

Editors
David J.A. Clines
Philip R. Davies

Department of Biblical Studies
The University of Sheffield
Sheffield S10 2TN
England

JOURNAL FOR THE STUDY OF THE OLD TESTAMENT
SUPPLEMENT SERIES

43

Editors
David J.A. Clines
Philip R. Davies

Department of Biblical Studies
The University of Sheffield
Sheffield S10 2TN
England

THE CULT OF
MOLEK
·
A REASSESSMENT

George C. Heider

Journal for the Study of the Old Testament
Supplement Series 43

BL
1605
.m6
H4
1986

Copyright © 1985 JSOT Press

Published by
JSOT Press
Department of Biblical Studies
The University of Sheffield
Sheffield S10 2TN
England

Printed in Great Britain
by Redwood Burn Ltd.,
Trowbridge, Wiltshire.

British Library Cataloguing in Publication Data

Heider, George C.
    The cult of Molek : a reassessment.—(Journal
for the study of the Old Testament supplement
series, ISSN 0309-0787; 43)
1. Judaism—History—To ca.100 A.D.
2. Idols and images—Israel—Worship
3. Moloch (Semitic deity)
I. Title   II. Series
296   BM170

ISBN 1-85075-018-1
ISBN 1-85075-019-X Pbk

TABLE OF CONTENTS

Appendix

APPENDIX:

PREFACE

Both scholars and popular writers have long been fascinated with
the Old Testament's Molek and with the cult associated with that term.
Writers from Milton (<u>Paradise Lost</u>) to Dickens (<u>The Haunted Man</u>) to
James Michener (<u>The Source</u>) have been tantalized by the awful (and awe-
full) rite of child sacrifice to this "horrid king besmeared with blood"
(<u>Paradise Lost</u> I.392). Scholars have, no doubt, been attracted for the
same reason, but they have concentrated their research on the meaning of
"Molek" (which occurs but eight times in the MT) and the nature of the
cult. Unfortunately (in Johannes Simons's words concerning the Jerusalem <u>millô'</u>), "as usual, the great number of theories claiming to have
solved these problems is inversely proportional to the amount of clear
data" (<u>Jerusalem in the OT</u> [Leiden: Brill, 1952] 131). Nevertheless,
two scholars have come "to bestride the narrow world [of Molek studies]
like a Colossus" by challenging the traditional understanding (as in
Milton) of the term and cult, respectively: Otto Eissfeldt and Moshe
Weinfeld. This study essays a new evaluation of these issues, not merely vis-à-vis the proposals of these scholars (and many others), but with
an eye toward new (and newly-applied) comparative evidence and a complete reevaluation of the Biblical evidence regarding the significance
of Molek in the history of Israel's religion. The following investigation cannot and does not claim to represent the "solution" to the Molek
problem; after all, the latter may well be, as Adolf von Harnack be-

lieved, "die <u>grösste</u> Frage--ohne Zweifel--der vergleichenden Religionsgeschichte" (Agnes von Zahn-Harnack, <u>Adolf von Harnack</u> [2d ed.; Berlin:
W. de Gruyter, 1951] 46). This study can claim, however, to present a
paradigm for understanding Molek which can be defended as accounting
more adequately for the full body of evidence now available than have
previous efforts.

A word of explanation is in order for the transliteration of MT m<u>ō</u>-
<u>lek</u> as "Molek" throughout this study. Previous scholars (and dictionar-
ies) have often employed "Moloch" (the LXX form) or "Molech" (which reflects the older practice of transcribing the Hebrew spirantized <u>kaph</u>
with /<u>ch</u>/; cf. Baruch). "Molek" is now to be preferred since modern
transcription does not show spirantization, except where it is at issue.
In general, the transliteration of the Hebrew in the following pages is
in accordance with the rules prescribed by the Society of Biblical Literature (SBL). Biblical abbreviations and citations also follow SBL
style. Other Semitic languages are rendered in keeping with standard
scholarly practice.

The conclusion of the following study brings with it the happy duty
of acknowledging the contributions and assistance of many others.
First, my thanks go to Prof. Marvin H. Pope of Yale University, who not
only suggested the topic to me as one worthy of reexamination, but
served as a constant source of fresh insights and constructive criticism. Secondly, I acknowledge the help of Prof. Pope's colleagues in
the Department of Near Eastern Languages and Literatures, particularly
Profs. Gary Beckman, Benjamin Foster, William Hallo and Franz Rosenthal,
who gave of their time and expertise in particular facets of the compar-

Preface

ative portion of this study. My fellow students Mark S. Smith and Elizabeth Bloch-Smith were especially helpful in the Ugaritic (2.3) and Syro-Palestinian archeology (3.3) sections, respectively. Outside of Yale, I am pleased to thank: Prof. Baruch Levine of New York University, for a stimulating conversation on matters Molek; Prof. Lawrence Stager of the University of Chicago, for sharing the results of his excavations at Carthage; Prof. Charles A. Kennedy of the Virginia Polytechnic Institute and State University, for providing me with a copy of his essay on the discoveries at Pozo Moro, Spain, and with photographs of the same; and, especially, Prof. Paul Mosca of the University of British Columbia, whose kindness in making available a copy of his dissertation far outweighs the differences with its conclusions which I have felt compelled to express. Above all, my thanks go to my director, Prof. Robert R. Wilson, for his suggestions and willing engagement with my thoughts as they developed into their present form. The shortcomings of the latter are, of course, solely my responsibility.

On a more personal level, I acknowledge the support of the members of Cheshire Lutheran Church, Cheshire, CT, of my family and especially of my wife, Carolyn, who rightly felt herself to be on occasion (in her words) "Molek's latest snack," and to whom this study is dedicated with respect and affection.

LIST OF ABBREVIATIONS

(A)ASOR (Annual of the) American Schools of Oriental Research

AB   Anchor Bible

AbS   Abu Şalabikh (tablet inventory number)

ADAJ   Annual of the Department of Antiquites of Jordan

AfO   Archiv für Orientforschung

AHW   Wolfram von Soden, Akkadisches Handwörterbuch

AIPHOS   Annuaire de l'Institute de Philologie et d'Histoire Orientales et Slaves (Brussels)

AJBA   Australian Journal of Biblical Archaeology

AJSL   American Journal of Semitic Languages and Literatures

ANET   J. B. Pritchard, ed., Ancient Near Eastern Texts (3d ed.)

AnOr   Analecta Orientalia

AntJ   Antiquaries Journal

AOAT   Alter Orient und Altes Testament

ARET   Archivi Reali di Ebla Testi

ARM   Archives royales de Mari

ArOr   Archiv orientální

ARW   Archiv für Religionswissenschaft

ATD   Das Alte Testament Deutsch

BA   Biblical Archaeologist

BASOR   Bulletin of the American Schools of Oriental Research

BDB   F. Brown, S. R. Driver and C. A. Briggs, Hebrew and English Lexicon of the Old Testament

BHK   R. Kittel, Biblia hebraica

Abbreviations

BHS	Biblia hebraica stuttgartensia
Bib	Biblica
BibOr	Biblica et orientalia
BKAT	Biblischer Kommentar: Altes Testament
BO	Bibliotheca orientalis
BSOAS	Bulletin of the School of Oriental and African Studies
BZ	Biblische Zeitschrift
BZAW	Beihefte zur ZAW
CAD	The Assyrian Dictionary of the Oriental Institute of the University of Chicago
CBQ	Catholic Biblical Quarterly
CIS	Corpus inscriptionum semiticarum
CRAIBL	Comptes rendus de l'Académie des inscriptions et belles-lettres
CT	Cuneiform Texts from the Babylonian Tablets in the British Museum
CTA	Andrée Herdner, Corpus des tablettes en cunéiformes alphabétiques (MRS 10)
D	The Deuteronomic Literature (Deuteronomy and Dtr)
DBSup	Dictionnaire de la Bible, Supplément
DISO	C.-F. Jean and J. Hoftijzer, Dictionnaire des inscriptions sémitiques de l'ouest
DSS	Dead Sea Scrolls
Dtr	The Deuteronomic History (Joshua through Kings), or the Deuteronomic Historian
EAEHL	M. Avi-Yonah and E. Stern, eds., Encyclopedia of Archaeological Excavations in the Holy Land
EI	Early Iron Age
GKC	Gesenius' Hebrew Grammar, ed. E. Kautsch, trans. A. E. Cowley
H	The Holiness Code (Leviticus 17-26)
HAT	Handbuch zum Alten Testament

Abbreviations

HKAT	Handkommentar zum Alten Testament
HSM	Harvard Semitic Monographs
HTR	Harvard Theological Review
HUCA	Hebrew Union College Annual
IB	Interpreter's Bible
ICC	International Critical Commentary
IDB	G. A. Buttrick, ed., Interpreter's Dictionary of the Bible
IDBSup	Supplementary volume to IDB
IEJ	Israel Exploration Journal
JA	Journal Asiatique
JANESCU	Journal of the Ancient Near Eastern Society of Columbia University
JAOS	Journal of the American Oriental Society
JBL	Journal of Biblical Literature
JCS	Journal of Cuneiform Studies
JNES	Journal of Near Eastern Studies
JNSL	Journal of Northwest Semitic Languages
JPOS	Journal of the Palestine Oriental Society
JSOT	Journal for the Study of the Old Testament
JTS	Journal of Theological Studies
K	Ketib
KAI	H. Donner and W. Röllig, eds., Kanaänaische und aramäische Inscriften
KAT	Kommentar zum Alten Testament
KAV	Otto Schroeder, ed., Keilschrifttexte aus Assur verschiedenen Inhalts
KB	L. Koehler and W. Baumgartner, Lexicon in Veteris Testamenti Libros
KB3	W. Baumgartner, Hebräisches und Aramäisches Lexikon zum Alten Testament

Abbreviations

KJV	King James Version
KTU	M. Dietrich, O. Loretz, J. Sanmartín, eds., *Die keilalphabetischen Texte aus Ugarit* (AOAT 24)
LB	Late Bronze Age
LCL	Loeb Classical Library
LXX	The Septuagint
MA	Middle Assyrian (ca. 1500-1000 B.C.)
MB	Middle Babylonian (ca. 1530-1000 B.C.), or Middle Bronze Age
MEE	Materiali Epigrafici di Ebla
MRS	Mission de Ras Shamra
MT	Masoretic Text of the OT
MVAG	Mitteilungen der vorderasiatisch-ägyptischen Gesellschaft
NAB	New American Bible
NCB	New Century Bible
NEB	New English Bible
NESE	Neue Ephemeris für semitische Epigraphik
n.s.	new series
NT	New Testament
OA	Old Assyrian (ca. 1950-1750 B.C.)
OB	Old Babylonian (ca. 1950-1530 B.C.)
OECT	Oxford Editions of Cuneiform Texts
OIP	Oriental Institute Publications
OLZ	Orientalistische Literaturzeitung
Or	Orientalia (Rome)
OrAnt	Oriens antiquus
OT	Old Testament
OTL	Old Testament Library
P	Priestly (source or tradition in Pentateuch)

PEQ	Palestine Exploration Quarterly
PRE	Realencyklopädie für protestantische Theologie und Kirche (followed by edition number: 1 [1858]; 2 [1882]; 3 [1903])
PRU2	C. Virolleaud, ed., Le Palais Royal d'Ugarit II (MRS 7)
PRU5	C. Virolleaud, ed., Le Palais Royal d'Ugarit V (MRS 11)
Q	Qere
QDAP	Quarterly of the Department of Antiquities in Palestine
RA	Revue d'assyriologie et d'archéologie orientale
RAI	Rencontre assyriologique internationale
RB	Revue biblique
REJ	Revue des études juives
RES	Répertoire d'épigraphie sémitique
RestQ	Restoration Quarterly
RGG	Religion in Geschichte und Gegenwart (followed by edition number: 2 [1930]; 3 [1960])
RHR	Revue de l'histoire des religions
RivB	Rivista biblica
RLA	Reallexikon der Assyriologie
RS	Ras Shamra (tablet inventory number)
RSF	Rivista di studi fenici
RSO	Rivista degli studi orientali
RSP	L. R. Fisher and S. Rummel, eds., Ras Shamra Parallels
RSV	Revised Standard Version
SB	Standard Babylonian (ca. 1000-500 B.C.)
SBLDS	Society of Biblical Literature Dissertation Series
SBLMS	Society of Biblical Literature Monograph Series
SBT	Studies in Biblical Theology
SEb	Studi Eblaiti

SMS	Syro-Mesopotamian Studies
TDOT	G. J. Botterweck and H. Ringgren, eds., Theological Dictionary of the Old Testament
TLZ	Theologische Literaturzeitung
TM	Tell Mardikh (tablet inventory number)
TSSI	J. C. L. Gibson, Textbook of Syrian Semitic Inscriptions
TWAT	G. J. Botterweck and H. Ringgren, eds., Theologisches Wörterbuch zum Alten Testament
UF	Ugarit-Forschungen
Ug4	Claude F. A. Schaeffer, ed., Ugaritica IV (MRS 15)
Ug5	Claude F. A. Schaeffer, ed., Ugaritica V (MRS 16)
Ug7	Claude F. A. Schaeffer, ed., Ugaritica VII (MRS 18)
VAT	Tablet numbers of the Vorderasiatischen Abteilung der Berliner Museum
VT	Vetus Testamentum
VTSup	Vetus Testamentum Supplements
WMANT	Wissenschaftliche Monographien zum Alten und Neuen Testament
WO	Die Welt des Orients
WZKM	Wiener Zeitschrift für die Kunde des Morgenlandes
ZA	Zeitschrift für Assyriologie
ZAW	Zeitschrift für die alttestamentliche Wissenschaft
ZDMG	Zeitschrift der deutschen morgenlandischen Gesellschaft
ZDPV	Zeitschrift des deutschen Palastina-Vereins

CHAPTER I
HISTORY OF SCHOLARSHIP

The issues of the meaning of Molek and of the nature of the cult associated with that term have generated an enormous quantity of scholarly literature. Although several reviews of the relatively recent discussion are available, notice is only sporadically taken of the extensive literature prior to the present century.[1] Indeed, as we shall see, there are those who argue that the history of interpretation (if not of scholarship per se) on matters Molek must be traced back to the scribes involved in establishing the MT.[2]

Such a full history would be unnecessarily tedious for our purposes. Our study will begin, rather, with the scholars of the seventeenth-century Enlightenment. This is not to dismiss with an arrogant wave of the critical hand all who went before, but only to limit the scope of our review in recognition of the fact that much that was believed about Molek was held nearly universally and without change for the first sixteen centuries of the Christian era and that the disputes which had arisen were taken over by the early critical scholars and so can be covered with them. Thus, our present objective is not a history

---

[1] E.g., Henri Cazelles, "Molok," DBSup 5 (1957) 1337-1340; and Alberto R. W. Green, The Role of Human Sacrifice in the Ancient Near East (ASOR Dissertation Series 1; Missoula, MT: Scholars, 1975) 179-187. (A comprehensive list of abbreviations used in this study may be found in the preliminary matter.)

[2] This refers to the dispute over the original vocalization of MT mōlek, discussed below (1.2).

of interpretation for its own sake, but a review of those persons and positions which contributed to the present status quaestionis. Specifically, it will be the purpose of this chapter to note those assumptions and debates which were carried over from medieval sources by the early representatives of modern Biblical scholarship; to show how what was assumed and what was considered crucial to debate changed with new insights and evidence (and how certain issues and arguments recurred from time to time); and to suggest that further study of this topic is indicated both by the shortcomings of past proposals and by the availability of new insights and evidence.

1.1 SEVENTEENTH- AND EIGHTEENTH-CENTURY SCHOLARSHIP

While Molek was discussed from time to time by certain of the church fathers,[3] it was for the most part from the medieval rabbis that scholars of this period adopted the issues they considered crucial to the question. With the rabbis, they assumed that Molek was derived from the Semitic root meaning "king," that it referred to an idol god and that the various "mlk gods" of the Old Testament (e.g., Molek, Milkom, Adrammelek, Anammelek) were closely related, if not identical. The rabbis' crucial point of controversy was also directly taken over, viz., whether the act of dedication of children to Molek entailed actual child sacrifice by burning, or was rather in some way symbolic. Like their rabbinic counterparts, the early modern proponents of the former alternative assumed that the classical accounts of Carthaginian and Phoenician child

---

[3] E.g., Origen, Chrysostom and Ambrose, as cited by Andreas Beyer in his "Additamenta" to J. Selden, De Dis Syris (Amsterdam: Lucam Bisterum, 1680) 261.

sacrifice by fire were accurate historically and bespoke a cultic practice held in common with Israelite Molek worship.[4] The major developments of this period were an increased interest in comparative religion (specifically, with what gentile gods Molek might be equated) and a strong focus on Amos 5:26 (likely because it is the sole reference to Molek in the NT, being quoted in Acts 7:43 according to the LXX).

The views of the scholars under discussion were not monolithic, of course, nor were they without change over the two centuries involved. The first major contribution was the essay of Johannis Selden in 1617, in which he defended the view of numerous rabbis that the Israelites' h‘byr b’š lmlk ("making to pass over by the fire to Molek") entailed a "februation," rather than an actual burning of children.[5] The growing interest in comparative religion is illustrated by Selden's comparison of the midrash of the seven "conclavia" into which the Israelites were admitted by presenting increasingly precious sacrifices with Mithric rites, as well as his citation of personal names containing mlk from Tyre and the aforementioned effort to identify Molek with one or more gentile gods (Selden so designated Saturn).[6]

---

[4] The corpus of classical accounts of child sacrifice in Phoenicia and the Punic colonies is collected by Paul Mosca as chapter I of his 1975 Harvard Ph.D. dissertation, "Child Sacrifice in Canaanite and Israelite Religion: A Study in Mulk and mlk," to be published by Scholars Press.

[5] Selden, De Dîs Syris, 93-94. Thomas Goodwin's slightly earlier work (Moses et Aaron: seu Civiles et Ecclesiastici Ritus Antiquorum Hebraeorum [4th ed.; Ultrajecti: Balthasaris Lobé, 1698 (orig. 1616)]) cites the usual (for these scholars) classical and medieval authors and takes the opposite side from Selden on the "burning" issue, but apparently had far less impact on the later debate, perhaps because it was originally published in English!

[6] The midrash is discussed at length, and its sources detailed, in G. F. Moore, "Biblical Notes: 3. The Image of Molek," JBL 16 (1897)

It is of much interest (but little comfort) to this student of the Molek question that several dissertations on the subject appeared in the century and a half following Selden's work.[7] Valentin Greissing's may be taken as representative.[8] It exhibits a careful assemblage of philological data concerning Lev 20:2 (on which it focuses) and an interest in the issues of comparative religion and the nature of the cult (i.e., burning vs. februation), complete with a listing of prior proposals. The result is a brief discussion of the topic which both adumbrates the later debate at several points, and yet betrays its place in the early stages of critical sensitivity.[9] Of particular interest, so far as the anticipation of the later debate is concerned, is Greissing's suggestion that the MT mōlek was vocalized with hōlem to distinguish it from melek ("king"). This presaged the highly-influential proposal of Abraham Geiger, to be discussed below (1.2), that the vocalization was a dysphemism of the original melek using the vowels of bōšet ("shame").[10]

161-165.

[7] Besides that of Greissing (discussed immediately following), see J. G. Schwab, De Moloch et Remphan (1667); Christiani Sam. Ziegra, De crudelissima liberorum immolatione Molocho facta (1684); and Daniel Dietzsch, De cultu Molochi (n.d.). These latter three may be found in vol. 23 of Blasio Ugolino's Thesaurus antiquitatum sacrarum (Venice: Joannem Gabrielem Herthz et Sebastianum Colletti, 1760).

[8] zbḥ bnym lmlk h.e. Immolatio Liberorum Molocho Facta (Wittenberg: Christian Schrödter, 1678).

[9] E.g., in the very title of the dissertation: zbḥ never occurs in the same verse as Molek (Lev 20:2 included) and is found with reference to child sacrifice no earlier than Ezek 16:20 (or perhaps Hos 13:2; see further the discussion in chap. IV).

[10] "Dysphemism" (the antonym of "euphemism") refers in OT studies to the alleged practice of the redactors or scribes of the MT in substituting vowels or even whole words for those present in the received text, so as to indicate contempt for the term so treated. Thus, in Geiger's view, occurrences of melek as the name of a foreign god were

The second highly influential effort of this period was the chapter "Lex transitum per ignem, in honorem <u>Molechi</u> prohibens" in John Spencer's seminal work on comparative religion, <u>De legibus Hebraeorum ritualibus et earum rationibus</u>.[11] Like his predecessors, Spencer was much concerned with the identity of Molek. His contribution was to move the focus of the search outside of the Greek-Roman pantheon as such to categories more congenial to Semitic religions; his identification of Molek with the sun has drawn adherents down to the present century.[12] With nearly all scholars who followed him, Spencer favored the interpretation of the Biblical references to the Molek cult as involving actual burning (not even citing the rabbis, in fact). Nevertheless, the influence of medieval logical categories had not entirely disappeared from Spencer's work, as can be seen in his enumeration of both "more remote" (<u>remotior</u>) and "near" (<u>proxima</u>) causes for the Biblical laws forbidding Molek worship.[13]

---

revocalized to <u>mōlek</u> to associate "shame" with the very mention of the god's name.

    Another adumbration worth noting is the proposal of Andreas Beyer in his 1680 "Additamenta" to Selden, <u>De Dis Syris</u>, 255, that Molek might have been derived from <u>hlk</u>; recent scholars usually attribute the suggestion to Alt (1949) or to de Vaux (1964)!

[11] (2d ed.; Hagae-Comitum: Arnold Leers, 1686) 284-296. Brevard Childs observes: "Spencer is rightly judged the father of modern comparative religion, at least in respect to Old Testament law" (<u>The Book of Exodus</u> [OTL; Philadelphia: Westminster, 1974] 494).

[12] E.g., W. W. Baudissin in his article "Moloch" in <u>PRE3</u> (discussed below). Others, to be sure, had suggested a solar identity for Molek (e.g., Petitus), but it was Spencer who really made the case in the eyes of modern scholars who accepted the proposal.

[13] The extent of Spencer's influence on others may be seen in the degree to which his arguments are simply repeated by Hermann Witsius in his "De Cultu Molochi" (<u>Miscellaneorum Sacrorum</u> [Trajecti ad Rhenum: Franciscum Halman, 1692] 1.608-617), although Witsius was virulently

While it was not the last of the seventeenth-eighteenth century contributions on the subject, the 1720 dissertation of Martin Friderick Cramer may be seen as a transitional point between the works described above and those which were published in the nineteenth century, when the matter of Molek once again drew intensive scholarly effort.[14] As with Greissing's dissertation forty years earlier, the essay proceeds from a philological concern with the meaning of the name "Molek" to the februation vs. burning question. Even the argumentation employed regarding the latter shows the transitional character of Cramer's work: the author appeals to classical authors and to the Holy Spirit (noting the parallel use of h'byr and śrp in Jer 32:35 and 7:31) in favor of the actual burning interpretation, yet also cites the use of h'byr b'š in Num 31:23, the very verse used over 250 years later by Morton Smith as his clinching datum in controversy with the "februationist" Moshe Weinfeld.[15] Like his predecessors, Cramer takes great pains with interpreting Amos 5:26 (especially the meaning of sikkût and the replacement of MT kîyûn with LXX Raiphan), but he anticipates the chief nineteenth-century debate by insisting that, although the verse shows that Israel practiced the Molek cult already in the wilderness, Moses had nothing to do with it.[16]

---

opposed to Spencer on other occasions (so Childs, Exodus, 494). It is worth observing that Witsius anticipated de Vaux's argument that a regular cult of the sacrifice of human firstborn was unlikely at any time in Israel's history.

[14] *De Molocho Ammonitorum Idolo* (Wittenberg: Officina Vidua Gerdensiae, 1720).

[15] "A Note on Burning Babies," JAOS 95 (1975) 478. The controversy will be discussed below (1.8).

[16] Later eighteenth century efforts by Daniel Dietzsch (cited above) and

1.2   NINETEENTH-CENTURY SCHOLARSHIP

The first two scholars of note in the nineteenth century focused on what
we might call the "Phoenician connection." This line of research had
been undertaken long before (cf. Selden's collection of mlk names from
Tyre). But in the work of Friedrich Münter and F. C. Movers considerable further investigation was made of personal and divine names with the
alleged theophoric element mlk and of what was assumed to be the relevant cult of child sacrifice in the Phoenician colony of Carthage (still
on the basis of ancient literary, not yet archeological, evidence).[17]
Both concluded that Molek was in some 'way equivalent to Baal and was,
more importantly, a fire god. Like most writing on the Phoenicians before the advent of the finds from Ugarit, such conclusions resulted
largely from a combination of information from the Bible and relatively
late ancient sources (e.g., Philo of Byblos) with judicious speculation.[18]

The terms of the debate in the nineteenth century were, however,
set above all by a pair of works published in the year after Movers's
book. Their thesis is well-summarized by the title of one: Der Feuer-

---

by Salomon Deyling ("Tabernaculum Molochi," Observationum Sacrarum
[Leipzig: Haeredum Frider. Lanckisii, 1737] 2.444-456) did little
more than review prior proposals.

[17] Münter, Religion der Karthager (2d ed.; Copenhagen: Johann Heinrich
Schubothe, 1821); Movers, Die Phönizier (Bonn: Eduard Weber, 1841).

[18] Münter's suggestion that Carthaginian (and Phoenician) religion was
essentially star- or fire-worship (p. 5) apparently resulted from a
combination of hints that the recipient of child sacrifice was Kronos
(the Phoenician El and Roman Saturn, i.e., a star or planet), as Philo says, with other clues that the god involved was the sun (so
Spencer's influential voice, reinforced by the fiery nature of the
rite). Movers, on the other hand, seems more influenced by the parallels drawn with Mesopotamian fire-worship (pp. 324-325).

und Molech-dienst der alten Hebräer als urväterlicher, legaler, orthodoxer Kultus der Nation.[19] Both scholars attempted, like many of their contemporaries, to discern in the Biblical accounts attenuated signs of the evolution of Israelite religion from the times before Yahwistic orthodoxy became normative for the people and their literature. Specifically, both contended that patriarchal and Mosaic religion practiced human sacrifice to Molek and, indeed, that Yahweh was distinguished from Molek only later.[20] Especially significant methodologically was the attempt of both scholars to find references (allegedly often "cleaned up" later) to human sacrifice inside or outside of the Molek cult in a wide variety of religious activities (e.g., festivals like Passover and practices like circumcision) and deaths with some connection to God as cause or recipient (e.g., Jepthah's daughter, Agag and the ḥerem, Uzzah at the ark and Saul's sons at the hands of the Gibeonites). But above all, Daumer and Ghillany alleged that it was the laws requiring all firstborn human males to be "consecrated" (qdš) or "given" (ntn) to Yahweh in Exod 13:2 and 22:28 (respectively), without the (supposed) later modification of the redemption provisions, which showed the antiquity of human sacrifice (and Molek worship) in Israel. These two

---

[19] G. Fr. Daumer (Braunschweig: F. Otto, 1842). The second work is F. W. Ghillany, Die Menschenopfer der alten Hebräer (Nuremberg: Johann Leonhard Schrag, 184 2).

[20] Thus Ghillany contended that Abraham actually sacrificed Isaac (pp. 660-678) and Moses and Aaron their sons (pp. 683-687 and 694-699, respectively). Ghillany's thesis that the "orthodox" view of Yahweh as separate from Molek was established only with Josiah's reform both shows the influence of de Wette's dating of Deuteronomy and anticipates the later suggestion of Eissfeldt's parvum opus (Molk als Opferbegriff im Punischen und Hebräischen und das Ende des Gottes Moloch [Beiträge zur Religionsgeschichte des Altertums 3; Halle: Max Niemeyer, 1935], discussed at length below [1.5]) that child sacrifice was licit in Israel until the Deuteronomic reform.

scholars thus both radicalized the terms of the debate and greatly expanded the Biblical material which their successors had to consider. That some of their arguments now seem almost incredibly crude (such as Daumer's linking of "Yahweh" with an ostensible Iroquois verb "jawoheje" meaning "to die" [p. 11]) in no way diminishes the force which their underlying thesis had in their own and succeeding generations.

The reaction to Daumer and Ghillany was not entirely "scholarly" or "academic." Rabbi M. Löwengard's attack on their thesis, for instance, was clearly motivated by a desire to prevent its use to support the anti-Semitic "blood accusation" then still lingering in Europe.[21] But most significant in its impact on later investigators was the extensive review of the books by Ernst Meier.[22] Meier contended that all ancient oriental mythology was essentially dualistic, that in the case of Palestine Baal was the god of fortune and Molek of misfortune, and that the Daumer/Ghillany thesis was untenable because no people would worship solely a god of misfortune (p. 1020). To be sure, the argument lends a taste of irony to Meier's complaint that Ghillany's deductions betrayed "ein crasssinnlichen, rohen Rationalismus" (p. 1049), but it does show the relevance which continued to be ascribed to the issue of Molek's identity vis-à-vis the rest of the known gods (especially, now, Yahweh).

A second major expansion of the relevant Biblical data was attempted in 1857 by Abraham Geiger.[23] Geiger argued not only that the occur-

---

[21] Jehova, nicht Moloch, war der Gott der alten Hebräer (1843), cited by Baudissin in "Moloch," PRE3 13:269, where Baudissin terms the work "an historischem Urteil wertlos."

[22] Theologische Studien und Kritiken 16 (1843) 1007-1053.

[23] Urschrift und Übersetzungen der Bibel (2d ed.; Frankfurt am Main: Madda, 1928) 299-308.

rences of MT mōlek were a dysphemistic revocalization (see discussion in 1.1,9 and in chap. IV below), but also that some twenty-five instances of MT melek were references to the old idol King god which had been missed by the correctors. Geiger's theory of Molek as dysphemism has found more adherents among scholars since his time than this proposed expansion of data, but one suggested instance has met common approval (Isa 30:33), while others have been seriously considered.[24]

Until the very end of the nineteenth century, the scholarly debate over Molek and the related child sacrifice in ancient Israel was almost exclusively conducted not in monographs or journals, but in Bible dictionary and encyclopedia articles and in histories of Israelite religion.[25] Of these, the most noteworthy were certainly the articles (all entitled "Moloch") by J. G. Müller in the first edition (1858) and by W. W. Baudissin in the second and third editions (1882 and 1903) of the Realencyklopädie für protestantische Theologie und Kirche.[26] Müller's

---

[24] Another, less often accepted idea of Geiger's requires mention, viz., that the much-debated h'byr used in reference to the cult of Molek is but an old correction for hb'yr, as found unchanged in 2 Chr 28:3.

[25] A significant exception to this statement is the writings of a series of Dutch scholars: Henricus Lucas Oort (Het menschenoffer in Israel, 1865); Claudius Henricus van Herwerden (Het menschenoffer in Israël, 1868); Abraham Kuenen (Jahveh en Molech, 1868); C.-P. Tiele (De Egyptische en Mesopotamische Godsdiensten, 1872); and Bernardus Dirks Eerdmans (Melekdienst en vereering van hemellichamen in Israël's Assyrische periode, 1891). All affirmed with Daumer and Ghillany the place of ritual human sacrifice in pre-Josianic Yahwism, although they differed with the earlier scholars (and with one another) on numerous fine points and were in general more sophisticated than the two earlier scholars on matters of philology and source criticism. An accessible summary position is that of Kuenen in his The Religion of Israel (trans. Alfred Heath May; London: Williams and Norgate, 1874) 1.250-252.

[26] The preeminence of the PRE as a whole in this period contributes to this judgment, in addition to the intrinsic merits of the articles. Significant, contemporary articles and histories include those of

article, published in the year after Geiger's Urschrift, represents what was at the time a careful, "middle of the road" summary of others' views and his own (the latter clearly shaped by his interest in pre-Columbian Mexican religion). Thus, Müller is non-committal on Geiger's bōšet proposal (p. 714) and opposed to Daumer and Ghillany (p. 720), while, on the basis of his work with ancient "nature cultures," he attempts a compromise on the "februation" issue (he suggests that hʻbyr refers to the purification of the victim before the child was sacrificed, although the term could mean the entire cultic act by synechdoche [p. 718]). Müller's most influential contribution, however, was likely his suggestion that the traditional association of Molek with Kronos and Saturn was not a testimony to their cross-cultural equivalence,[27] but simply a result of the cults of child sacrifice associated with each and of the myths of Kronos and Saturn consuming their own offspring.[28]

Winer (cited below); Konrad Schwenck (Die Mythologie der Semiten [Frankfort am Main: J. D. Sauerländer, 1849] 277-318); Adalbert Merx ("Saturn" in Bibel-Lexicon [ed. Daniel Schenkel; Leipzig: F. A. Brockhaus, 1875] 5.191-200); Max Duncker (Geschichte des Alterthums [5th ed.; Leipzig: Duncker und Humblot, 1878] 1.330-336); Konstantin Schlottmann ("Molech" in Handwörterbuch des Biblischen Altertums [ed. E. C. A. Riehm; Bielefeld: Velhagen und Klasing, 1884] 2.1010-1013); Bernhard Stade (Geschichte des Volkes Israel [Berlin: G. Grote, 1887] 1.609-611); Friedrich Baethgen (Beiträge zur semitischen Religionsgeschichte [Berlin: H. Reuther, 1888] 37-40,145-146); and Eduard Meyer and Alfred Jeremias ("Moloch [Melech]," Ausführliches Lexicon der griechischen und römischen Mythologie [ed. W. H. Roscher; Leipzig: B. G. Teubner, 1890-7] 3106-3110).

[27] As the first of the great German Bible dictionaries of the nineteenth century had held, for instance: George Benedict Winer, ed., "Molech," Biblisches Realwörterbuch (Leipzig: Carl Heinrich Reclam, 1838) 2.118-120.

[28] "Which came first, the myth or the cult" has, to be sure, been debated loud and long; see Green, The Role of Human Sacrifice, chap. II, for a recent review.

For Wolf Wilhelm Baudissin the subject of Molek was the cornerstone
of a scholarly career which saw him become the premier representative of
the nineteenth century's "history of religions school."[29] His inaugural
dissertation was a reexamination of the relationship of Yahweh and Molek
that attempted to refute the widely-accepted hypothesis of Daumer and
Ghillany.[30] His two PRE articles expanded on this and related matters of
Biblical interpretation, but focused above all, as one might expect of a
leading comparativist, on the alleged foreign provenance of the god and
his cult. Indeed, Baudissin's investigations of Molek continued well
into the present century, receiving prominent mention in his two great
opera on ancient Semitic deities, Adonis und Esmun (1911) and the
posthumously-published Kyrios (1929).[31] While, as will be seen, his
ideas on both the god and the cult developed somewhat over the half-
century he wrote on them, his position remained sufficiently constant to
be best treated at once, even though this will require some backtracking
afterwards. What is clear beyond doubt is that his arguments form a
contribution to this issue second only to that of his student, editor
and successor as leading scholar of the history of Semitic religions,

---

[29] Hans-Joachim Kraus calls Baudissin the "hervorragende Sprecher" of
the "ältere religionshistorische Schule" (Geschichte der historisch-
kritischen Erforschung des Alten Testaments [2d ed.; Neukirchen-
Vluyn: Neukirchener, 1969] 379).

[30] Jahve et Moloch: sive de ratione inter deum Israelitarum et Molochum
intercedente (Leipzig: Fr. Guil. Grunow, 1874). The arguments in
favor of an "orthodox Molek cult" had, to be sure, come a long way
since those proposed by the above-named pair of scholars, which Baudissin termed "oberflächlich und verständlos" (PRE2 10:175): cf. the
Dutch scholars listed above.

[31] Adonis und Esmun (Leipzig: J. C. Hinrichs, 1911); Kyrios als Gottesname im Judentum und seine Stelle in der Religionsgeschichte (4
vols.; ed. Otto Eissfeldt; Giessen: Alfred Töpelmann, 1929). (Baudissin died in 1926.)

Otto Eissfeldt.

As for the source of Israel's Molek (or "Melek," following Geiger),
it was Baudissin who made the classic case for looking to Phoenicia. He
himself admitted that the evidence was more cumulative and inferential
than direct: Phoenicia had no god named "M-l-k" as such; nor, from the
Biblical side, is there a tradition of specifically Phoenician origins
(i.e., not including the Canaanites). Rather, Baudissin arrived at his
conclusion by eliminating Israel itself and Assyria as contenders.
Countering the former possibility was a function of his argument against
the Daumer/Ghillany hypothesis: Baudissin held that Amos 5:26 concerned
the time of the prophet, not the wilderness period, and that Ezek
20:25-26 (the other passage widely alleged to show an early, orthodox
Molek cult in Israel) does not have to do with legal acts, commanded by
Yahweh.[32] As for Assyria, Baudissin noted the ease with which Ahaz's
syncretistic proclivities (2 Kgs 16:10-16) might be associated with what
Baudissin believed was the earliest reference to the Molek cult (16:3),
and with the similar cult of child sacrifice attributed to the Sepharvites (17:31) to their _mlk_ gods, all to suggest an Assyrian origin.
Baudissin's rejoinder was that the Assyrian god Malik was at no time an
important enough deity to serve as the impulse for the Judean cult, that
Sepharvaim was not in Assyria, and that in any event there is no evidence for cultic child sacrifice in Assyria-Babylonia. On the other

---

[32] PRE2 10:169, and PRE3 13:272-273, respectively. The laws of the
firstborn, alluded to above, were falsely generalized to include humans only late in the monarchy, he claimed. Baudissin also stressed
that, while both Yahweh and Molek may have had both beneficent and
destroying sides (_pace_ Meier, above), Yahweh was not "specialized" as
a force of nature, as Molek was as the sun, nor did Yahweh have a
consort corresponding to Meleketh, the alleged counterpart of Molek.

hand, in favor of a Phoenician source he stressed the confluence of known, major mlk gods (chiefly Melqart of Tyre) and classical reports of child sacrifice in Phoenicia and especially in the Tyrian colony of Carthage.[33]

However, Baudissin did not contend that Israel (or, more precisely, Judah) simply borrowed Molek and his cult, bag and baggage, from Phoenicia. Rather, in view of the mlk gods of the peoples from all over the Syro-Palestinian littoral (e.g., Ammon's Milkom), he suggested that Melek had been a divine name in Canaan since before the Israelite occupation, but that the worship of the Tyrian Baal (Melqart) imported by the Northern King Ahab had spurred a revival of this god's worship, first in the North, then in the South.[34] Thus, Baudissin's position was a nuanced one. He credited Phoenicia not with the origin of Israel's Molek or cult, but with providing the impetus for the revival of "altväterlich" worship, first mentioned in the Bible under Ahaz.

As for the cult of child sacrifice, some development in Baudissin's thinking is evident. At all points he was certain that real sacrifice was involved. Furthermore, as with the god itself, Baudissin would not contend that the idea of human sacrifice burst new upon Israel at some point in the monarchy; the various proofs of orthodox Molek worship adduced by Daumer, Ghillany et al. (above all, Genesis 22) were seen by

---

[33] The references to such activity in Phoenicia are chiefly Quintus Curtius Rufus, History of Alexander 4.3:23; Sanchuniathon in Philo of Byblos's Phoenician History, quoted in Eusebius, Praeparatio Evangelica 1.10:40c; and Porphyry, De Abstinentia 2:56.

[34] The god was worshipped as Melek, not Melqart, because the latter name actively retained its meaning, "king of the city" (i.e., Tyre), and was therefore inappropriate in Israel. Baudissin made no comment on the apparent inconsistency of the Greek adaptation of the full name as "Melikertes" for the sea-god (PRE3 13:288).

Baudissin only as proofs of human sacrifice in early Israelite cult, either before Yahwism took full hold or in some mixtus form. But whence
and when the cult connected with Molek came to Israel was less clear to
him. In PRE2 he suggested that the cult had come to Israel along with
Melqart, in the time of Ahab. To meet the objection that the Greek and
Roman authors speak only of a cult of human sacrifice to El (the Greek
Kronos), and not to Melqart (the Greek Heracles),[35] Baudissin held then
that the classical writers had often confused the Phoenician gods and
had likely lumped together reports of this sort of cult under Kronos,
given the myths of that god's filiophagy (p. 173). On the other hand,
nearly twenty years later in PRE3, Baudissin suggested that the deadly
cult was borrowed later than Melqart: Melqart had come from Tyre in
Ahab's time, while later, at the time of Ahaz or perhaps Manasseh, there
had come the cult of child sacrifice, dedicated to El-Kronos, who bore
the title melek; this older god's cult had then been mixed with that of
the younger Melqart, who bore the name (though not the title), "king"
(pp. 289-290).

Baudissin was not unaware of the weaknesses in his theory. For one
thing, it is notable that the allegations of child sacrifice in Phoenicia and its colonies are uniformly from non-Phoenician sources, most of
them writing from a perspective of centuries after the alleged events,
raising the possibility that they are unhistorical propaganda. (It must
be recalled that, at least before Adonis und Esmun in 1911, Baudissin
had no access to archeological support from Carthage for his ancient
sources, and that such information as he could claim from surface finds

---

[35] Pliny the Elder, Naturalis Historia 36.4:39, is the sole exception
Baudissin notes.

later turned out to be irrelevant.)[36] Furthermore, as to his theory's Biblical implications, Baudissin explicitly admits the weakness noted by every critic of the Phoenician-source hypothesis: one must account for the influence of the cult on the Southern Kingdom without similar (recorded) effect on the geographically intervening North.[37] Further problems with Baudissin's suggestions have become evident to more recent scholars, above all, the quantity of sheer guesswork, however ingenious, involved in drawing conclusions about Phoenician deities and cult from the relatively late accounts and few inscriptions then available.

Baudissin's position in his later writings was essentially unchanged, although he did place more emphasis on Yahweh as a <u>mlk</u> god (though not ever the same as Molek) from earliest times, because of his resemblance to the Aramean storm god, Hadad,[38] and on the specifically Phoenician origin of the cult of child sacrifice to Molek.[39]

---

[36] One must recall that even the term "archeology" (or "archaeology") long meant the study of <u>all</u> antiquities, and not merely <u>realia</u>, as can be seen in the treatment of the Molek question in W. Nowack's <u>Hebräische Archäologie</u> (Freiburg: J. C. B. Mohr, 1894) 2.305-306. Baudissin himself admits (<u>Kyrios</u> 3:101, n. 2) that the Jerusalem jar handles inscribed with <u>lmlk</u>, which he took in <u>PRE3</u> 13:272 as evidence of Israelite idolatry, refer simply to royal property.

[37] <u>PRE3</u> 13:290. Baudissin had earlier (p. 271) rejected the clearest Biblical suggestions of Northern cultic child sacrifice, 2 Kgs 17:17 and Ezek 23:37, as late and tendentious (cf. discussion in chap. IV below).

[38] <u>Adonis und Esmun</u>, 33-35. The connection with Hadad remains a matter of great interest: Moshe Weinfeld's article favoring a non-sacrificial understanding of the Molek cult ("The Worship of Molech and of the Queen of Heaven and its Background," <u>UF</u> 4 [1972] 133-154) suggests identifying Hadad with Molek, a proposal which meets the approval of his otherwise sharp critic, Morton Smith (cited above).

[39] Even at the last, however, Baudissin had to admit that his proof was indirect: "Ich wüsste nicht, wo anders man den Ursprung dieses Kultus suchen sollte als in Phönizien" (<u>Kyrios</u> 3:101).

As the discussion to this point of nineteenth-century scholarship on the Molek question has implied, most writing on the issue was done by German (and Dutch) scholars. An examination of the great English and American Bible dictionaries and encyclopedias of the late nineteenth and early twentieth centuries shows the varying degree of impact which the German interest in comparative religion had, as opposed to the earlier approach of exegesis alone, supplemented by the classical testimonies of child sacrifice. Thus, James Strong's article, "Molech," is almost entirely occupied with sorting out relevant Biblical references from irrelevant and with midrashic and classical accounts,[40] while the lectures by the great British mediator of critical German scholarship, W. Robertson Smith, abound in parallels to Phoenician myth and cult.[41] In any event, a fundamental concern with foreign parallels to and sources of Israel's Molek worship was well-established in Anglo-American scholarship by the early years of the present century, as may be seen in the pertinent articles of both the Encyclopedia Biblica and Hastings's Dictionary of the Bible.[42]

---

[40] Cyclopaedia of Biblical, Theological, and Ecclesiastical Literature (ed. J. McClintock and J. Strong; 2d ed.; NY: Harper and Brothers, 1894) 4.437-440. An extremely similar article is "Molech," A Dictionary of the Bible (ed. W. Smith; Hartford, CT: S. S. Scranton and Co., 1899) 575-576.

[41] Lectures on the Religion of the Semities (2d ed.; London: A. and C. Black, 1894) 358-377.

[42] George Foot Moore, "Molech, Moloch," Encyclopedia Biblica (ed. T. K. Cheyne and J. S. Black; NY: Macmillan, 1902) 3.3183-3191; and W. H. Bennett, "Molech, Moloch," A Dictionary of the Bible (ed. James Hastings; NY: Charles Scribner's Sons, 1903) 3.415-417.

Even these articles made no claim to present the definitive answer
to the interpretive confusion surrounding Molek, however. Bennett's article, for instance, does explicitly declare the "februationist" position wrong, but does not take a stand on the matter of the original vocalization of the god's name (the "bōšet issue") and contents itself
with presenting four options of greater or lesser probability for explaining the provenance of Molek and his relationship to Yahweh. Clearly, the nineteenth century had succeeded in bringing new perspectives
and methodologies to bear on Molek, which raised new questions, but the
shortage of new evidence and continuing differences over the interpretation of the old made solutions appear as elusive as ever.

1.3   SCHOLARSHIP AT THE TURN OF THE CENTURY

Following a half-century in which the debate had been dominated by dictionary and encyclopedia articles, the decades at the turn of the century, 1890-1910, saw three monographs and a journal article published
which attempted to answer once and for all prior questions and proposals
which have been discussed above. As will be seen, their force lay not
in any overall solution to the Molek question, but rather in showing either in those prior works or (ironically) in themselves the unlikelihood
of further progress without a dramatic breakthrough in either methodology or evidence. At the same time, they proved transitional by pointing,
however obliquely, to the shape of the investigation to come.

The first of these works was Adolf Kamphausen's brief monograph,
Das Verhältnis des Menschenopfers zur israelitischen Religion.[43] Kamp-

---

[43] (Bonn: Röhrscheid und Ebbecke, 1896).

hausen addressed himself specifically to refuting two positions which he considered extreme in the interpretation of the story of Jepthah's daughter in Judges 11: on the one hand, Kaulen's proposal that Jepthah had not really sacrificed his daughter, but had dedicated her, à la Samuel, to a life of cultic service; on the other hand, the view of Meinhold that human sacrifice as typified by this story was demanded by Yahweh. Thus, Kamphausen said little on the nature of Molek (he refers the reader to Baudissin's PRE2 article for this), but he had much to say about the nature of the related cult and its place in the history of Israel's religion.[44] Specifically, Kamphausen argued (following Sellin) that the daughter's two-month period of mourning would have been unnecessary, and the alleged festival in her memory senseless, if the daughter were merely headed for life as a priestess (which, he argues, could not have been all that extraordinary). On the other hand (and at far greater length), Kamphausen reviewed one by one the passages alleged to show an orthodox cult of human sacrifice in ancient Israel. Despite his ostensible focus on Meinhold's interpretation of Judges 11, it is clear that his main concern was with Wellhausen's reconstruction of the evolution of Israel's religion: Kamphausen insisted that the laws against Molek worship in Leviticus must go back (at least in their content) to the age of Moses, and that, indeed, Genesis 22 shows that human sacrifice was excluded from Israelite orthodoxy even before Moses. However, Kamphausen was no Keil or Hengstenberg: he had his doubts about the historicity of Judges 11 (while insisting that the story is about real

---

[44] By now the reader should have little difficulty in seeing the two refuted positions as but transpositions of the februation and Daumer/Ghillany hypotheses, respectively.

sacrifice) and contended that by denying the reliability of the prophets
as historians he had taken away the nearest thing to proof of orthodox
child sacrifice in the hands of his opponents, Ezek 20:25-26. In sum,
Kamphausen's contribution was to provide a critical, exegetically-based
response to the dominant nineteenth-century proposal (Daumer/Ghillany),
just as Baudissin had done from the perspective of comparative religions.

Secondly, the brief but highly-influential 1897 _JBL_ article by G.
F. Moore must be mentioned. As noted above, the article dealt with the
midrashim concerning the manner of Molek worship in ancient Israel. Besides being a fine specimen of source criticism, by analyzing the medieval descriptions into two underlying midrashim, the article was the
first to make a convincing case for moving beyond the commonplace observation that the rabbinic stories bore a remarkable resemblance to the
classical accounts of Carthaginian child sacrifice (especially that of
Kleitarchos), to the suggestion that the rabbis had borrowed from such
accounts.[45] While some would differ with Moore's suggestion that even
the Carthaginian accounts might be "pseudo-historical variation of the
older myth" (p. 164), his underlying argument won immediate acceptance,
and reconstructions of Israel's Molek cult based on the midrashim are
notable by their absence thereafter.[46]

---

[45] As Eissfeldt notes (_Molk als Opferbegriff_, 68), Oort had hinted at
this in 1865, but only with Moore did it find general acceptance.

[46] Mosca, for instance, calls Moore's challenge to the existence of a
Carthaginian statue upon which children were offered "hypercritical"
("Child Sacrifice," 35).

The second monograph, Carl Mommert's <u>Menschenopfer bei den Alten</u> <u>Hebräern</u>, merits but brief notice.[47] The book attempts, essentially, to see a <u>Heilsgeschichte</u> of human sacrifice in Israel, contending that Old Testament bloody sacrifices, including those of firstborn humans, were commanded by God as "Vorbilder" of the sacrifice of Jesus, which was a Jewish "Ritualmord" (pp. 87-88). The book goes on to accuse the Jews of continuing such practices (i.e., the infamous "blood accusation"), even though since Jesus' death such sacrifices have been "verabscheuungswür-diger Unfug." The Molek cult is involved here since Molek (and Baal and Jupiter) are but alternate names used by different peoples for Yahweh. Thus, while Mommert lists and criticizes some of Daumer's cruder argu-ments (pp. 7-9), he defends and even goes beyond the latter's hypothe-sis. While some later scholars would see merit in the thesis of ortho-dox Molek worship (above all, Eissfeldt), Mommert's arguments were uniformly rejected (when they were even mentioned) as an untenable, ex-treme extension of the nineteenth century's most-debated hypothesis.[48]

No one was a more strident critic of Mommert than the author of the third turn-of-the-century monograph, Evaristus Mader.[49] Mader begins with a thorough, if highly tendentious, history of scholarship on the

---

[47] (Leipzig: E. Haberland, 1905).

[48] It must be emphasized that Mommert's views were extreme, but they were an extension, not advanced <u>ex</u> <u>nihilo</u>. Ghillany had written in his Foreword: "Der vorliegende Theil behandelt die Menschenopfer der a l t e n Hebräer; ob ein zweiter Band folgen werde, der den Gegen-stand bis auf die neueste Zeit heraufführt, möge dahin gestellt blei-ben" (p. v). Fortunately, this "agenda" does not seem present for most other scholars who favored the "orthodox Molek cult" view.

[49] <u>Die Menschenopfer der alten Hebräer und der benachbarten Völker</u> (Bi-blische Studien 14:5/6; Freiburg: Herder, 1909).

Molek question from Daumer/Ghillany through Mommert.[50] Despite their
agreement on the basic issue of whether orthodox Yahwism had included
human sacrifice, Mader scores Kamphausen for denying the historical
worth of passages like Ezek 20:25-26 and, above all, for not going beyond the negative statement that human sacrifice was not native to Israelite religion. It is the positive side, the question of foreign
provenance, which is the primary burden of Mader's work. Specifically,
Mader collects evidence from mythology, inscriptions and classical writers to show the existence of human sacrifice throughout the ancient Near
East, including Egypt, which he contends on the basis of Egyptian archeology and Bible passages such as Ezek 20:25-26, Amos 5:25-26 and the
Pentateuchal prohibitions must have been the source of the Israelite Molek cult. He is therefore at great pains to counter the literary-
critical arguments of Wellhausen et al. and the comparative arguments of
Baudissin. Regarding the latter, Mader insists that a Phoenician provenance is unlikely since the classical authors testify that Phoenician
child sacrifice was to Kronos, not Melqart (the Bible verses cited above
presumably overcome the similar lack of an Egyptian mlk god). Concerning the place of the Molek cult in Israelite religion, Mader opposes
Daumer and Ghillany both in methodology and in content. As for methodology, he objects to the attempted expansion of relevant Biblical evidence by insisting that God's claims on the firstborn in Exodus do not

[50] He even mentions a late eighteenth-century forerunner of Daumer and
Ghillany, Weihbischof Zirkel of Würzburg, although he cites only a
late biography, and that work says only that Zirkel believed that human sacrifice was practiced in pre-exilic Israel, not that it had a
place in Yahwism (August Friedrich Ludwig, Weihbischof Zirkel von
Würzburg: in seiner Stellung zur theologischen aufklärung und kir-
chlichen Restauration [Paderborn: Ferdinand Schöningh, 1904]).

require an interpretation as child sacrifice, and that activities such as the herem were not sacrifices at all. As for content, Mader revives Meier's argument against the equation of Yahweh and Molek (that no people would worship solely a destroying god) and that of Baudissin (that the term mlk was not applied to Yahweh before Isaiah's time), adding a strong attack on the subjectivity of rewriting early accounts to find Molek worshippers in Abraham, Moses, Aaron and David. Mader's work has proved a useful summary of the nineteenth-century debate and of the conservative (here, Roman Catholic) perspective on the issues raised therein. His insistence that not all killing in the Old Testament with a connection to Yahweh can be construed as sacrifice (much less Molek worship) has found widespread support, while his suggestions on the Egyptian provenance of Israelite child sacrifice have been rejected by nearly all succeeding scholars, because of differences over the interpretation both of key Bible verses and of the archeological evidence cited by Mader to show human sacrifice in Egypt. Still, in placing the strong emphasis which he did on the latter sort of evidence, Mader betrays his presence in the new century by adumbrating the debate soon to erupt full force on the Molek question. Ironically, although this new phase of the discussion received its first impulse from finds in Palestine itself, it was discoveries from the far end of the Mediterranean which would play the greatest role in setting the terms of the present debate.

1.4   TWENTIETH-CENTURY SCHOLARSHIP BEFORE EISSFELDT

The excavations of R. A. S. Macalister at Gezer from 1902 to 1909 most
obviously mark the new phase in the study of Molek. Of greatest interest was a "high place" replete with jars containing the bones of infants
buried head-down, along with vessels for food and dirt. Macalister dated the find to his "Second Semitic period" (encompassing the Middle
Bronze to Late Bronze Ages) and suggested that here, at long last, was
incontrovertible proof that child sacrifice was a custom among the Canaanites before the Israelite conquest.[51] Similar finds at Taanach by E.
Sellin and at Megiddo by G. Schumacher led a series of scholars to suggest that here was support for the Biblical view that the Israelites had
adopted the practice from the prior inhabitants.[52] Indeed, the main
point of contention among these scholars was the further question of
whether or not the skeletons were indicative of a regular cult of the
sacrifice of firstborn sons, relevant to the provisions of Exod 13:2 and
22:28-29.

Such claims of archeological proof did not by any means go unchal-
lenged. Ernst Sellin, for example, denied that he had unearthed any
such evidence at Taanach (at least until he heard of Macalister's
finds). Friedrich Schwally, for another, scored Macalister et al. for
gross eisegesis:

---

[51] The Excavation of Gezer (London: J. Murray, 1912) 2.402. Macalister
reasoned: "That these infants were all the victims of sacrifice is
suggested by their close association with the high place and confirmed by the fact that two at least displayed marks of fire."

[52] G. B. Gray, "The Excavations at Gezer and Religion in Ancient Palestine," The Expositor 7 (1909) 430-436; Rudolf Kittel, Geschichte des
Volkes Israel (5-6th ed.; Stuttgart: Friedrich Andreas Perthes,
1923), sub "Kinderopfer"; and Paul Volz, Biblische Altertümer (Stuttgart: Calwer, 1925) 171-181.

In diesem Falle ist aber jeder Gedanke an ein Opfer ausge-
schlossen. Denn auf dem ganzen Erdkreise gibt es keine Analo-
gie dafür, dass Opfer beigesetzt, oder dass beigesetzte Lei-
chen geopfert wurden.[53]

Candidates for analogous finds (albeit not Palestinian ones) would soon
be plentiful enough. But a second criticism would prove more enduring.
Schwally objected to claims to have located foundation sacrifices on the
grounds that it had not been shown that the bones and the wall were from
the same stratum (p. 354). In general, challenges to the digging and
recording techniques of archeologists of this period, but especially Macalister, have rendered their conclusions suspect, although they are,
tragically, beyond review.[54] Nevertheless, for over a third of the present century, Gezer was accepted by most as a literal <u>locus</u> <u>classicus</u> for
ritual child sacrifice.[55]

Archeologists throughout the Near East were by this time alert to
the possible implications of finds showing human sacrifice. In Mesopotamia C. L. Woolley claimed to have found such evidence in the "royal
tombs" of Ur, but his interpretations were rejected by most and, in
fact, it was generally agreed that human sacrifice was, at most, exceedingly rare in the "land of the two rivers."[56]

---

[53] "Berichte: Semitische Religion im allgemeinen, israelitische und jüdische Religion," <u>ARW</u> 19 (1919) 352-353.

[54] See, for example, the scorching critique of Macalister by W. G. Dever
in "Gezer," <u>EAEHL</u> 2 (1976) 432-434.

[55] Adolphe Lods so cites it in <u>La religion d'Israel</u> (Paris: Hachette,
1939) 102.

[56] Woolley, <u>Ur Excavations: 2. The Royal Cemetery</u> (London: Kegan, Paul
Trench and Co., 1954). The extensive study of Friedrich Blome (<u>Die
Opfermaterie in Babylon und Israel</u> [Rome: Pontifical Biblical Insti-
tute, 1934] 413) was especially influential in showing the rarity of
Mesopotamian human sacrifice.

Far more fruitful were those campaigns which looked westward from Palestine, above all, those which dug in the area of ancient Carthage.[57] Beginning in 1921, a series of French (and later also American) archeologists excavated the "Salammbo" temenos (sacred area) within the walls of the Punic city, called at first the "precinct of Tanit" and later (with an eye toward the Biblical parallels) the "tophet." As Lawrence Stager notes, the results of their efforts have not been reported with either the speed or the quality commensurate with the finds' significance.[58] As early as 1923, however, the scholarly world was apprised that a large quantity of urns had been exhumed, containing a mixture of the bones of sheep, goats, birds and children with ashes and earth.[59] Furthermore, at levels above the lowest, these burials were often marked by stelae, the most significant of which was found at Poinssot-Lantier stratum C (which they dated to the fourth century B.C.). Depicted thereon was a robed, standing figure, bearing what appeared to be a child; René Dussaud, who discussed the inscriptional finds in an article parallel to that of Poinssot-Lantier on the realia, suggested from similar portrayals of animals being borne that the stele showed a priest bearing a child to be sacrificed.[60]

---

[57] Mosca summarizes the finds at the several Punic sites in the western Mediterranean area from 1922 through the mid-1970's on pp. 38-55 of "Child Sacrifice," which may be consulted for further details.

[58] "The Rite of Child Sacrifice at Carthage," New Light on Ancient Carthage (ed. John Griffiths Pedley; Ann Arbor: The University of Michigan Press, 1980) 1.

[59] Louis Poinssot and Raymond Lantier, "Un sanctuaire de Tanit à Carthage," RHR 87 (1923) 32-68.

[60] Poinssot and Lantier ("Un sanctuaire de Tanit," pl. 4/2) present a line drawing of the stela. A high-quality photograph may be found in Gaalyah Cornfeld and David Noel Freedman, Archaeology of the Bible:

Similar sacred precincts have been excavated at other Punic sites in the western Mediterranean, as discussed by Mosca; these, together with the finds of more recent campaigns at Carthage and elsewhere, will be more fully discussed in chap. III below. As we have seen above in the summary of the dispute over the finds at Gezer, Taanach and Megiddo, however, the interpretation of bare *realia* will always be the occasion for much disagreement. Some scholars challenged the sacrificial reading of the western Punic finds on the same grounds as the scholarly consensus eventually rejected such a reading for Gezer, etc.: that the archeologists may have found nothing more than a cemetery for young children.[61]

Yet unlike the archeological situation in Palestine (in general, not merely regarding Molek or child sacrifice), the realia of the Punic sites were clothed in evidence of other sorts. Besides the classical testimonies and iconographic representations mentioned above, Punic and Neopunic epigraphic evidence, especially from North Africa, had been coming to light already in the previous century. These inscriptions have, if anything, led to more intense scholarly disputes than the (other) objects unearthed by archeologists, as a significant number of the inscriptions contain the letters "mlk." But taken together with the

---

Book by Book (San Francisco: Harper and Row, 1976) 52. Dussaud presented his views on the stela in "Trente-huit textes puniques provenant du sanctuaire des portes à Carthage," *Bulletin Archéologique* (1922) 245. Poinssot and Lantier agree with Dussaud's interpretation (pp. 61-62).

[61] An early doubter was J.-B. Chabot in "Seance du 13 Juin," *CRAIBL* (1924) 192-193. The remarks of Claude Schaeffer (*CRAIBL* [1956] 67) represent more recent objections. Both Weinfeld ("Worship of Molech," 136) and Mosca ("Child Sacrifice," 49) quote Schaeffer at length, the former with approval.

ashes and bones, the epigraphic stelae provided invaluable correlative evidence which demanded consideration by interpreters, including those who sought a link with the Biblical god or cult. We turn now to a review of the history of the inscriptions' interpretation, culminating in the revolutionary proposal of Otto Eissfeldt in 1935.

The inscriptions which began the debate were published in the great collections <u>Corpus Inscriptionum Semiticarum</u> (<u>CIS</u>) and <u>Répertoire d'Épigraphie Sémitique</u> (<u>RES</u>).[62] The items of interest were dedicatory inscriptions including the letters <u>mlk</u>, plus certain others which were alleged to deal with child sacrifice. The former sort almost always contained <u>mlk</u> in a compound with other letters, such as <u>mlk'štrt</u> (e.g., <u>CIS</u> 1.8) or <u>mlk'mr</u> (<u>CIS</u> 1.307); only one instance with <u>mlk</u> alone (or <u>lmlk</u>, with Lidzbarski) entered the discussion, the Neopunic text 30 from Constantine.[63] The <u>mlk</u> element was usually interpreted either as "king" or as a divine name (Malik, or the like), although as early as 1897 Berger had suggested that <u>mlk'dm</u> just might be "non pas un titre divin, ni un titre royal, ni un ethnique, mais la désignation de l'objet offert en

---

[62] Some of the inscriptions, notably those discovered in 1875 by Lazare Costa in Constantine, Algeria, were also published in smaller groups in journal articles by Philippe Berger and J.-B. Chabot and in a collection by Mark Lidzbarski (Berger, "Les inscriptions de Constantine au Musée du Louvre," <u>Actes du onzième Congrès international des Orientalists</u> [1897], 4th section [reprint; Nendeln/Liechtenstein: Kraus, 1968 (orig., 1898)] 273-294; Chabot, "Punica XI: Les inscriptions néopuniques de Guelma [Calama]," <u>JA</u> 11/8 [1916] 483-520, and "Punica XVIII: Stèles Puniques de Constantine," <u>JA</u> 11/10 [1917] 38-79; Lidzbarski, <u>Handbuch der Nordsemitischen Epigraphik</u> [2 vols.; Hildesheim: Georg Olms, 1962 (orig., 1898)]). These publications remain significant not only for their attempts to interpret the inscriptions (summarized below), but also because they occasionally provide alternate readings of the texts.

[63] Chabot, "Punica XVIII," 72.

sacrifice."[64] As will be seen, Berger's hunch proved to be more than a little prophetic.

As for the inscriptions without mlk, here also there were sharp disputes over the import of alleged references to child sacrifice. The best example is the differences over the interpretation of the "Salammbo inscription," first published in 1922 by Chabot.[65] The crucial letters are mś'bn, which, Chabot says, are clearly written divided as mś 'bn and are to be rendered "stèle de pierre" (relating mś to the Hebrew maśśā', "gift," from nś', "to lift, offer"). The inscription is, on this reading, an innocuous reference to the donation of a stele to Tanit. Dussaud responded by insisting that the letters should be divided mś' bn, as they are, in his opinion, in the mutilated text CIS 1.408 (a parallel which Chabot also noted). Thus, he would read "offrande du fils" (also taking the first word from the root nś'). For Dussaud, therefore, the inscription was the long-sought native admission of the practice alleged by classical writers: ". . . pour le première fois, nous trouvons dans un texte punique la mention du sacrifice humain, du sacrifice d'enfants bien attesté à Carthage par les auteurs classiques."[66] Furthermore, Dussaud unhesitatingly applied this reading to the interpretation of Biblical passages containing forms of nś' with children as the object (e.g., Ezek 24:25). Taken together with the contents of the sacred precincts

---

[64] The reading of mlk as "king" may be seen in Chabot's understanding of the text in "Punica XVIII," 49-50, no. 58; that of the divine name in Lidzbarski, Ephemeris für semitische Epigraphik (Giessen: Alfred Töpelmann, 1908) 2.56. The quotation is from Berger, "Les inscriptions de Constantine," 291.

[65] "Note sur une inscription punique de Carthage," CRAIBL (1922) 112-114.

[66] "Trente-huit textes puniques," 244-245.

and the iconographic evidence noted above, this inscription left Chabot fighting a scholarly rear-guard action. Although he would not be the last to attack the interpretation of the Punic finds as showing child sacrifice, most succeeding efforts to avoid applications of these finds to the Biblical data necessarily focused on establishing some discontinuity between the cult of the Phoenician colonies and that of the Israelites.[67]

As the later excavations of Ugarit, Mari and Ebla would show, it is the nature of the discovery and interpretation of ancient texts to proceed slowly, from excavators, to those who edit and publish, through debators of the correct reading of the original, to those who suggest some continuity with Biblical material which, at its best, can illuminate both the epigraphic finds and the Scriptural text. Such was the progress of those inscriptions which revolutionized the study of Molek at the hands of Otto Eissfeldt. The crucial texts were on three stelae discovered in 1930 by Jeanne and Prosper Alquier near Ngaous, Algeria, and published with two previously-known inscriptions in the next year by Stéphane Gsell.[68] The inscriptions were in Latin, from the late second or early third centuries A.D., and concerned votive offerings to Saturn. The crucial insight (for present purposes) came in a supplementary note to Gsell's article by Chabot (pp. 26-27), which suggested that the terms which appeared in Latin as morcomor, morchomor, mochomor and molchomor

---

[67] See the discussion below of Schaeffer and Weinfeld. Chabot was joined at the time in rejecting a child-sacrifice reading of the finds by another scholar, working from the side of the texts: H.-I. Marrou, "La collection Gaston de Vulpillière à el-Kantara," *Mélanges d'archéologie et d'histoire* 50 (1933) 42-86.

[68] "Stèles votives à Saturne découvertes près de N'Gaous (Algérie), par Jeanne et Prosper Alquier," *CRAIBL* (1931) 21-26.

were variants of the last, which, in turn, was but a transcription of
the <u>mlk'mr</u> to be found in two known Punic inscriptions (<u>CIS</u> 1.307 and <u>JA</u>
11/10 [1917] 49-50, no. 58). He divided the latter into two morphemes:
<u>mlk</u>, related to the Semitic root meaning "to rule, advise, and (in Ara-
maic) promise"; and <u>'mr</u>, "lamb" in the list (or "tariff") of sacrifices
from Marseilles (<u>CIS</u> 1.165). While wary of being too definite given the
meager contexts, he proposed that the entire term meant "la promesse, ou
l'accomplissement de la promesse d'un agneau."

A year later, in 1932, Jérôme Carcopino refined Gsell's readings of
the Latin stelae and, more importantly, suggested that Gsell had rightly
seen the inscriptions as records of substitutionary sacrifices, but had
failed to press the issue of what the lambs were being substituted
<u>for</u>.[69] Carcopino insisted that the inscriptions' "Concessa" and "Dona-
tus" were children whose names reflected the gift of life they had received through the sacrifice of a lamb in place of themselves.

With Carcopino's proposal the stage was set for Eissfeldt. Before
we turn to him, however, we must realize that not all contributions on
the Molek question in the period 1910-1935 were made by those working
from the fruits of archeology. The encyclopedia articles of the time
did little more than summarize the conclusions of Baudissin and Moore,
although George A. Barton in <u>The Jewish Encyclopedia</u> did well to emphasize the seldom-considered, though obvious reason that scholars had so
often looked past a prime candidate for the source of Molek from the
Biblical perspective, namely, Ammon: so little is known of the language

---

[69] "Survivances par substitution des sacrifices d'enfants dans l'Afrique
romaine," <u>RHR</u> 106 (1932) 592-599. Gsell had written: "l'agneau est
le remplaçant de ceux que le voeu a liés au dieu et que Saturne a
daigné conserver en vie" ("Stèles Votives," 26).

or culture of any of the Transjordanian states.[70]

Far more important in the long run was the suggestion of Marie-Joseph Lagrange already in 1903, that Molek (originally Melek) was a chthonic deity, equivalent to the Babylonian Nergal.[71] Lagrange's argument was, in essence, that Milk (the alleged Phoenician form of Melek) might be equated with the (El-)Kronos of Byblos to whom child sacrifice was offered according to classical authors, because Kronos is derived from the Greek verb krainō, "to rule," just as Milk/Melek is from the Semitic root of the same sense. Furthermore, a tabella devotionis showed that the latter god's consort, Milkat, was also called Allat, and Allatu was the Semitic name for the Babylonian infernal goddess, Ereshkigal, whose consort was Nergal. This, in Lagrange's estimation, explained the relative scarcity of Babylonian references to a god Malik: the god's nature and cult were developed rather under the name Nergal.

Lagrange recognized that his theory was not conclusive. He explicitly acknowledged that showing Kronos of Byblos to be a chthonic deity would be a desideratum.[72] He called attention to the presence in 2 Kings 17 both of Nergal (v. 30) and of the gods Adrammelek and Anammelek, to whom the Sepharvites burned their sons in the fire (v. 31). However, he stressed, it is Syrians in v. 31 who are sacrificing to their gods; the

---

[70] "Moloch (Molech)," The Jewish Encyclopedia (NY: Funk and Wagnalls, 1916) 8.653-654. See also our presentation of the Transjordanian evidence in 2.5 below. Other significant articles at the time were by Kurt Galling, "Moloch," RGG2 4 (1930) 154-155; and by Anton Jirku, "Moloch," Paulys Real-Encyclopädie (ed. by W. Kroll; Stuttgart: J. B. Metzler, 1933) 16/1.8.

[71] Études sur les Religions Sémitiques (2d ed.; Paris: Victor Lecoffre, 1905) 99-109.

[72] It should be noted that Lagrange explicitly rejected any attempt to equate Nergal with Kronos-Saturn (p. 108).

Babylonian practice was not under discussion. A more revealing passage for Lagrange was Isa 57:9, where he saw a practice of sending "messages" to the King of the Underworld via infant victims. Yet not all human sacrifice was to infernal deities: the sacrifice of companions and servants (as in Woolley's finds) he saw as a separate matter.

Baudissin lost no time in marshalling arguments against Lagrange's proposal.[73] He argued that Malk (the Phoenician original, rather than Milk) was indeed equivalent to Kronos of Byblos and possibly the origin of the Old Testament Molek (although he rejected the connection using krainō). But Malk-Kronos was also known as Baal (since the high goddess of Byblos was called b'lt), who was no underworld deity by any means. Therefore, any connection of Malk with a Babylonian or Assyrian chthonic god had to be a later merger. Finally, although Baudissin conceded that melek in Isa 57:9 was a divine name, he disputed the equation of the "messages" with burned babies; possibly only unrelated necromancy was involved.

The proposed equation of Molek and Nergal was approached from the other side in 1934, when the Assyriologist Peter Jensen offered evidence that the Old Testament Melek, Ammon's Milkom and Moab's Kemoš were all equivalent to one another and to Nergal.[74] He claimed that Melek's infernal character is established by the practice of his fiery cult in the gê' hinnōm, later a name for hell, while a connection with fire is established for Nergal, the god of hell, by an ideogram for his name which means "Haus mit dem reinen (heiligen) Ofen." Furthermore, Jensen cited

---

[73] ZDMG 57 (1903) 812-837, especially 819-820.

[74] "Die Götter kĕmôš und melek und die Erscheinungsformen Kammuš und Malik des assyrisch-babylonischen Gottes Nergal," ZA 42 (1934) 235-237.

Akkadian texts which list Kammuš as a manifestation of Nergal and equate
the latter with a god Malik (to be translated "king" or "advisor").
Since the Sumerian n e r - g a l means "king" (according to Jensen), the
Akkadian god Malik may be but a translation, suggesting an East Semitic
origin for the deity. Finally, Jensen cites Mālikun of the Quran (Sura
43:77) as an angel set over the damned by Allah.

As will be seen, it is the thesis of this entire study that Lagrange and Jensen were fundamentally on the right track regarding the
chthonic character of Molek, whatever one may say of their argumentation
or corollary proposals. Yet, in their own time they were only sporadically engaged, with the notable exception of Baudissin's attempt to refute Lagrange. Their thesis was certainly not forgotten, but the publication of a slim, seventy-one page monograph in the year after Jensen's
article so fundamentally redefined the terms of the debate that few
scholars engaged in the Molek question had time for anything but build-
ing on it or refuting it for nearly four decades thereafter. Otto Eissfeldt, the leading scholar of comparative Semitic religion in his day,
stood on the shoulders of giants before him, of course, but his proposal
had the potential to render most of their work simply beside the point.
It is to that proposal that we now turn.

1.5 OTTO EISSFELDT

In 1934, on the basis of the work of Gsell, Chabot and Carcopino, Albrecht Alt had called for a reexamination of the Punic mlk in the context of cultic terminology: "doch bedarf das Wort mlk, das vielleicht
auch in anderen kultischen Termini der punischen Inschriften wiederzu-

kennen ist, noch einer genaueren Untersuchung."[75] With Eissfeldt's <u>Molk</u> <u>als Opferbegriff im Punischen und Hebräischen und das Ende des Gottes</u> <u>Moloch</u>, Alt got his wish with a vengeance.[76]

As mentioned above, earlier interpreters of the Punic inscriptions had read the <u>mlk</u>-references either as the name of a deity or as a title, "King," in either case referring to the divine recipient of the offering commemorated by the inscription. Eissfeldt's crucial observation was that such references occurred at widely different places in the word order of the inscriptions, whether right after the name(s) of the god(s) to whom the gift was made (which regularly occur first in the texts), or after the name(s) of the human offerer(s), or near the end of the entire inscription (pp. 14-15,23). This presented a syntactical conundrum, so long as one assumed that in all cases the <u>mlk</u>-references were in apposition to the divine names with which the inscription began. If, however, these references were rather technical terms for sacrifice, the variation in word order could be accounted for.

It was then up to Eissfeldt to propose what these references might signify, given that, as mentioned before, almost all of them were found in a compound with another element, like 'mr.[77] Eissfeldt accepted Cha-

---

[75] "Zur Talionsformel," <u>ZAW</u> 52 (1934) 304.

[76] Eissfeldt himself provided a handy summary of his proposal in "Molochs Glück und Ende," <u>Forschungen und Fortschritte</u> 11 (1935) 285-286.

[77] Much of Mosca's second chapter ("Child Sacrifice," 55-96) is organized around the Punic <u>mlk</u>-references listed immediately following this note. Rather than providing a history of scholarship organized like this one (chronologically), Mosca collects the Punic, Neopunic and Latin texts grouped by the form each contains, and then gives a critical review of the interpretations suggested by Eissfeldt and by his supporters and opponents. (The reason for this schema will be clear below, when Mosca's contribution is discussed.) As a result, there will be some overlap between Mosca's work and my own at this

bot's suggestion that the Punic (and resulting Latin) mlk'mr meant "Ge-
lübde, Opfer eines Schafes" (p. 12). He then discussed several other
compounds including mlk which were found far more often than the two occurrences (known at the time) of mlk'mr: mlk 'dm, mlk bśr (which Eissfeldt suggested was short for mlk 'dm bśr[m] btm), bmlk 'zrm 'š, mlk
b'l, mlk 'sr, mlkt bmṣrm and lmlk. For some, he expressed confidence
that, despite the limited evidence, his thesis provided a reliable rendering; mlk 'dm, for instance, was surely "Versprechen, Opfer eines Menschen," either in a human sacrifice (objective genitive) or, more likely, as an offering by a (common, not royal or priestly) man (subjective
genitive) (p. 19). In other cases he made his proposals more tentative-
ly, as with bmlk 'zrm 'š, where he suggested 'š might mean "sheep" (cf.
Hebrew śeh) or perhaps "fireoffering" (cf. Hebrew 'iššeh), while 'zrm
had several potential cognates (p. 25). Finally, it is to Eissfeldt's
great credit as a scholar that he included evidence which he was unable
to subsume under his theory, such as mlk b'l, where he believed mlk
likely meant either "king" or, perhaps, "messenger" (p. 28). Yet most
important for comparative purposes were clearly the final two items
listed above, in which mlk occurs without a compounding element, and
above all in the last (lmlk), whose syntactical position in the one occurrence known to Eissfeldt (Constantine Neopunic text 30) suggested its
use as a technical term for sacrifice and which, most notably, matches

---

point and in my second chapter (where the epigraphic evidence will be
handled as such), so that it will not always be necessary to describe
each position in the detail which otherwise would be required. The
scholars and proposals involved cannot simply be skipped over, however, both because of the requirements of coherence in this study and
because of the fundamental disagreements I have with Mosca's approach
and conclusions (which, again, will become clear below).

letter for letter the consonants of Molek as it occurs in seven of eight
instances in the Old Testament (i.e., with the preposition l) (p. 30).

With this point made, Eissfeldt presented the other half of his
thesis, the "im Hebräischen" of his title. After eliminating 1 Kgs 11:7
from consideration, on the grounds that its Molek is an error for Milkom
(a common enough suggestion), Eissfeldt argued that the remaining seven
occurrences of the word were best read as technical terms for some form
of child sacrifice, on analogy with the Punic dedicatory inscriptions,
and using the same vocalization as the Latin form known from Ngaous,
molc-.

He began by arguing from the LXX's rendering of the five occurrences in Leviticus. First, he held, the translation archōn suggests that
the original Hebrew had not read melek (which the LXX usually renders
with basileus), but rather mōlek, which the LXX (mis)understood as
"rule" or (the participle) "ruler" (thus, rejecting Geiger's bōšet hypothesis). Secondly, he contended that the LXX's care in employing or
omitting the article elsewhere was a reliable sign that it had not originally been present in the MT's lammōlek (thus, setting up parallels
with the Punic lmlk and with Hebrew usage such as lə'ōlāh in Gen 22:2,
"as a burnt offering"). He proposed that this original *ləmōlek, "as a
molk-sacrifice," had been reinterpreted as an idolatrous divine name as
a result of the Deuteronomic reform under Josiah. Such revisionism was
necessary, in Eissfeldt's view, because until then child sacrifice had
been permitted as a legitimate element of the Yahweh cult, devolving especially from Yahweh's claim on the firstborn in the earliest strands of
Exodus.

Slightly over half of the book is given over to arguing the case
for interpreting the Old Testament Molek as a sacrificial term and to
suggesting how various passages either betray their Deuteronomic Tendenz
or hint at the original state of affairs. According to Eissfeldt's reconstruction, child sacrifice in Israel was allowed, but only occasionally practiced, in the time from the patriarchs until Josiah, as shown
by such narratives as Genesis 22 and Judges 11, and by the neutral mention of such offerings in Mic 6:7 and Isa 30:33. He insists that Israel
did not learn child sacrifice from the Canaanites or Phoenicians, but
may have been influenced in specific matters of praxis by them (leaving
open the possibility, never stated, that the molk-sacrifice per se was
borrowed). The near-silence of the historical and prophetic accounts
regarding child sacrifice in Israel from the rise of the monarchy to
Ahaz's sacrifice (2 Kgs 16:3) he would attribute either to the incom-
pleteness of the traditions or to the concern of the prophets of that
period with more widespread and dangerous abuses; in any event, accounts
such as that of Meša's sacrifice (2 Kgs 3:27) show that Israel was acquainted with the practice. Thus, while the Deuteronomists might rage
against child sacrifice as something external to pure Yahwism, the contemporary prophets knew better and betrayed the real state of affairs
with such statements as Jer 32:35 and Ezek 20:25-26. Yet, whatever
their sins as historians, it redounds to the credit of the Deuteronomists that by their "humanitarian" program, Israel succeeded in eliminating the molk from within (rather that being compelled to do so from
without, as the Carthaginians were by the Romans).

In Eissfeldt's view, then, the Biblical god "Molek" is a creature of Deuteronomic <u>Tendenz</u>, nurtured by the rabbinic imagination, as it was inspired by the classical accounts of a Carthaginian idol's statue which clasped babies in its fiery embrace. That both such accounts and the inscriptions which led to his solution of the problem described the same Punic practice manifested for him a remarkable irony:

> Das Merkwürdige dabei ist, dass die punische Religion, die dem Moloch zu seinem Aufstieg verholfen hat, ihm nun auch den To-desstoss versetzt. Denn Urkunden dieser Religion, die Texte, von denen die vorliegende Untersuchung ihren Ausgang nahm, sind es ja doch, die seinen Stern nun vollends zum Erlöschen bringen. (p. 71)

As the remainder of this chapter will demonstrate, Eissfeldt cast a long shadow over the work of nearly every scholar who has since confronted the Molek problem. This study can be no exception. In the end this entire project must represent a confirmation, modification or rejection of Eissfeldt's proposals and supporting arguments (although it may, and will, deal also with aspects of "Molek" which Eissfeldt did not choose to address). Many potential weaknesses in his position will become apparent as we examine the scholars who worked in Eissfeldt's wake; yet it will also be clear that he has not lacked for defenders (Eissfeldt himself not having chosen to address himself to the matter of Molek at any length again). For these reasons, the full, critical review to which the significance of Eissfeldt's work in the history of scholarship entitles him must be postponed until we see how the shape of the question has developed since he so radically re-formed it, and until we have examined both old and new evidence ourselves, with an eye toward testing his thesis against it.

1.6   EISSFELDT REVIEWED: SCHOLARSHIP FROM 1935 TO 1938

Numerous reviews of Molk als Opferbegriff appeared in the years immediately following its publication. While a couple of them were no more
than summaries of Eissfeldt's main points,[78] most chose up sides in
strong terms, especially in regard to the book's treatment of the Biblical evidence. Eissfeldt's most enthusiastic supporter was René Dussaud,
who had himself adumbrated the proposal to eliminate the god Molek already in 1904.[79] Dussaud attempted in his review to place the advocates
of Molek as a special god's name on the horns of a dilemma, using the
parallel wording of Jer 19:5 and 32:35. If one followed the MT in the
latter verse and read lammōlek, then that word was parallel to labba'al
in the former and presumably equivalent. On the other hand, if one read
(with Eissfeldt) ləmōlek, the parallel term in 19:5 would be 'ōlôt labba'al, a sacrificial term.[80] W. F. Albright also responded with effusive
praise and philological support for Eissfeldt's rendering of mlk'mr.[81]
On the other hand, while Wolfram von Soden accepted Eissfeldt's view of
Molek as a sacrificial term, it was precisely on the matter of philology
that von Soden saw room for improvement, arguing for a derivation not
from the root mlk (so Chabot and Albright), but from hlk.[82] A fourth re-

---

[78] E.g., J. de Groot, Nieuwe Theologische Studiën 18 (1935) 295; and H.
[sic; read F.] Blome, Theologie und Glaube 28 (1936) 227.

[79] "Milk, Moloch, Melqart," RHR 49 (1904) 163-168. Dussaud had argued
that there never was any distinct Phoenician god Milk (apart from
Melqart or El-Kronos), although he did not suggest that OT Molek was
anything other than a divine title.

[80] Syria 16 (1935) 407-409.

[81] JPOS 15 (1935) 344. He termed the interpretation of the other mlk-
references "very doubtful," but could suggest nothing better.

[82] TLZ 61 (1936) 45-46. Molek would then be a *maqtil form, he claimed,

viewer, Leonhard Rost, expressed what became a common modification of Eissfeldt's views among Old Testament scholars: he found the argument for Molek as a sacrificial term persuasive, but denied the claim that child sacrifice had been legitimate in Israel until the Deuteronomists, on the grounds that the references to actual sacrifices were too few and that the oldest laws concerning the firstborn always provided for their redemption.[83]

We may well begin the examination of the negative reviews of Eissfeldt's book by noting the scholar who was probably his most persistent critic and whose position was nearly the exact inverse of Rost's. Eduard Dhorme supported Eissfeldt's reconstruction of the history of child sacrifice in Israel, but he defended the traditional reading of Molek as a divine name (actually, as a deformation of melek, à la Geiger).[84] First, Dhorme expressed discomfort with the progress "insensible-ment" from the various Punic mlk combinations to a morpheme ostensibly meaning "sacrifice" or "offrande." More explicitly, he cited Lev 20:5 and 2 Kgs 23:10 as instances where the Hebrew Molek could be read as "sacrifice" only with great difficulty: the former Eissfeldt himself

---

like other sacrificial terms from verbs of motion, such as môpēt and 'ôlāh. Albrecht Alt made essentially the same proposal in 1949 on the basis of the Phoenician Karatepe inscriptions. It is seldom pointed out, however, that he saw a small problem here: "Man sollte dann in dieser Nominalbildung allerdings zwischen dem zweiten und dem dritten Radikal einen Vokal erwarten, den aber die Wiedergabe des Status constructus des Wortes in lateinischen Inschriften mit molch nicht aufweist" ("Die phönikischen Inschriften von Karatepe," WO 1 [1949] 282-283). Indeed, by the next year he withdrew the proposed connection with hlk ("Die Opfer in den phönikischen Inschriften von Karatepe," TLZ 75 [1950] 573, n. 2).

[83] Deutsche Literaturzeitung 57 (1936) 1651-1652.

[84] RHR 113 (1936) 276-278.

had admitted was his hardest case; while Exod 13:12 showed that h'byr with the preposition l should be presumed to take a divine name as object (as in 2 Kgs 23:10).

Even more detailed critiques came from two Roman Catholic scholars, Roland de Vaux and Augustin Bea.[85] De Vaux attacked Eissfeldt's reading of the evidence on both the Punic and the Biblical sides. While he accepted Eissfeldt's rendering of mlk'mr, he discussed extensively the one phrase bśrm btm, which Eissfeldt had read as "das Fleich in Vollkommenheit" (p. 20); de Vaux held that the Punic for "flesh" was š'r, and that the phrase should be translated "en bonne santé, en integrité" (p. 279). More importantly, this implied for de Vaux that the phrase which often was linked with bśrm btm, namely mlk 'dm, could not be translated as Eissfeldt wished, either. As for the Biblical material, de Vaux argued: "Quelle que soit la valeur de son explication de molchomor, mlk'mr, des textes africains, l'exégèse biblique ne semble pas devoir en être affectée" (pp. 281-282). Specifically, he noted that the earliest Punic evidence came from the fourth century B.C. and that the sense of mlk as "promettre" was restricted to the relatively late Syriac, so that applications to Biblical Hebrew were hardly secure. Within the Bible itself de Vaux concentrated on Eissfeldt's attempts to refute the "bōšet hypothesis" and the original presence of the article in lammōlek. He appealed largely to parallels within the Bible (e.g., 'aštōret) and outside it (the mlk gods of other Semitic peoples) to show that the original Hebrew was lammelek, "to the (divine) Melek." Hence, in his opinion, Israel had used Melek to refer to some Canaanite deity, likely

---

[85] De Vaux, RB 45 (1936) 278-282; Bea, "Kinderopfer für Moloch oder für Jahwe?," Bib 18 (1937) 95-107.

Melqart.

Bea, on the other hand, chose to focus solely on the religionsgeschichtliche question of whether child sacrifice in Israel had been to
Yahweh, as Eissfeldt claimed, or to Molek. His strongest arguments
dealt with the instances of Molek in Leviticus. He asked why, if the
Deuteronomists had changed the interpretation of Molek to a divine name,
the ostensibly later Holiness Code had retained the original term as if
it were self-explanatory. Further, he argued that the hmlk in Lev 20:5
was clearer evidence for the original presence of the article with
(l)mlk than the LXX was against it, and that the phrase znh 'hry in that
same verse took as its object only gods or things which might be worshipped (like the ephod in Jud 8:27, which Eissfeldt had cited in his
favor). The remainder of Bea's arguments tended to be psychological,
such as his contention that Isaiah's silence in the face of Ahaz's practice of the cult is understandable since Isaiah had already broken with
Ahaz in Isaiah 7, or that "es ist psychologish undenkbar" that Jeremiah
would say nothing if all did not know that child sacrifices were to a
foreign deity (effectively begging the question in verses like Jer 7:31
and 19:5). His ultimate argument was that, given that neither Josiah
nor Jeremiah had effectively altered the religious practice of his day,
it is ludicrous to suppose that they had left their mark so clearly on
the identity of the recipient of child sacrifices; only one solution
fits the historical evidence, that the Molek cult was a Canaanite practice which revived in Israel's times of religious decay.

Anton Jirku's review in the following year largely matched Bea's
exegetically-based approach, although he did add the proposal, later to

be developed by Albright, that Eissfeldt had been right about there being a shift in meaning between <u>molk</u> as god and as sacrifice, but dead
wrong about the direction of the shift: <u>Molk</u> had first been a god.[86]
Nivard Schlögl also contributed a review which was notable mostly for
its idiosyncratic defense of the traditional reading (using free emendations and questionable attributions of authorship) and for its invec-
tive:

> Es [Eissfeldt's theory of orthodox child sacrifice] beruht
> alles auf der falschen Evolutionstheorie, die man auf die Re-
> ligionsgeschichte anwendet, der doch, sollte man meinen, das
> moderne Heidentum und noch mehr die moderne Gottlosigkeit den
> Todesstoss versetzt.[87]

Thus, the battle was joined. In fact, Dussaud had responded to the
first volleys even before all of the negative reviews cited above had
been published.[88] Answering Dhorme, Dussaud claimed that any problems
which Eissfeldt's theory may have with Leviticus 20 resulted from late
redactors, who transformed the sacrificial term into the name of a "mau-
vaise génie." Responding to de Vaux's difficulties with reaching to
Syriac for "promise" as the sense of Molek, Dussaud agreed with de Vaux,
but took back any meaningful concession by insisting that the term does
mean "sacrifice." It was the evidence he cited in support of this last
point, however, that was important, as it opened up a new era in Molek
studies: Dussaud claimed to have evidence for "<u>molk</u> = sacrifice" from
the texts of Ras Shamra-Ugarit. Dussaud argued that a phrase from the
tablets of the first campaign at Ras Shamra, [d]bḥ mlk lprgl (<u>CTA</u>

---

[86] "Gab es im AT einen Gott Molek (Melek)?," <u>ARW</u> 25 (1938) 178-179.

[87] "Das Wort <u>molek</u> in Inschriften und Bibel," <u>WZKM</u> 45 (1938) 203-211
(quotation from 207-208).

[88] In a second review of Eissfeldt's book in <u>AfO</u> 11 (1936) 167-168.

35:50), meant "sacrifice <u>molk</u> à Prgl," a reading confirmed for him by parallel phrases from two other texts, <u>mlk</u> <u>dn</u> (<u>CTA</u> 12.2:59) and <u>dbḥ</u> <u>dnt</u> (<u>CTA</u> 4.3:19-20).[89] The merits of these interpretations are best left for the next chapter, where the Ugaritic occurrences of <u>mlk</u> will be discussed. For now, however, it should be noted that Virolleaud and Dhorme had already offered translations of the first phrase which, given the nascent state of Ugaritic studies at the time, were at least equiprobable with that of Dussaud.[90] In fact, it would be the mid-1950's before Ugaritic studies could be brought to bear on the Molek question with sufficient control to make a real contribution. But it remains to Dussaud's credit that he opened the door.

1.7 EISSFELDT REFUTED AND REFINED: SCHOLARSHIP FROM 1939 TO 1975

Ras Shamra was not the only new trove which promised access to the age under study, untroubled by the possible distortions of tradition and textual transmission. Four years after the first campaign at Ugarit, Tell Hariri on the middle Euphrates was discovered to be the ancient Mari, complete with a large store of tablets in an Akkadian dialect. Georges Dossin called attention to one which bore the place name AN-$\underline{\text{Mu}}$-$\underline{\text{lu-uk}}^{\text{ki}}$ (=$\underline{\text{Ilum-muluk}}$), thus demonstrating the presence of <u>mlk</u> as a genuine Semitic divine name at Mari.[91] Furthermore, variants of the name

---

[89] For the sake of uniformity, early Ugaritic texts will be cited from Andrée Herdner's <u>CTA</u>, even where her reading differs from that of the scholar in question (here Herdner agrees with Dussaud's reading). Numbers following volumes in the MRS series (including <u>CTA</u>) refer to texts, unless otherwise indicated.

[90] Virolleaud: "offre un sacrifice, (ô) roi, à Pergel" (<u>Syria</u> 15 [1934] 152, n. 1); Dhorme: "sacrifice du roi à Prgl" ("Première Traduction des Textes Phéniciens de Ras Shamra," <u>RB</u> 40 [1931] 41).

showed that Muluk was but a variant of the more common Akkadian Malik.
To Bea, who popularized Dossin's observation among Biblical scholars,
this suggested the antiquity of the god known in the Bible as Molek, so
that the popularity of his cult in eighth-seventh century Judah was but
a resurgence.[92] It was Albright, however, who made the most of the new
data. Noting the similarity in vocalization to Eissfeldt's Punic molok
[sic], "vow, pledge," as well as to the Biblical *ləmōlek, "as a sacrificial vow," Albright proposed that the Mari tablets showed that Muluk
(from mulku, "kingship") had been the north Mesopotamian-Syrian patron
of vows, from whose name the Syriac and Punic word for a vow of special
sanctity had been derived.[93] Thus, as noted above under Jirku's review
of Eissfeldt, Eissfeldt's suggestion for the development of mulk-/molc-
was, in a sense, reversed (although Albright still agreed that in Israel
the word changed from sacrificial term to divine name). Since human
sacrifice may be seen as "the harshest and most binding pledge of the
sanctity of a promise" (p. 163), 2 Kgs 17:31 provided the crucial link
of proof for Albright: child sacrifice had been offered by Syrians to
Adrammelek (really Adad-milki). Albright then surmised: "It is thus
possible that Ahaz was one of the first to borrow the Syrian custom of
sacrificing children to confirm a solemn vow or pledge" (p. 163).

---

[91] "Signaux Lumineux au Pays de Mari," RA 35 (1938) 178, n. 1.

[92] "Moloch in den Maritafeln," Bib 20 (1939) 415. Bea also made much of
the earlier research of Nikolaus Schneider, who claimed to have found
in Ur III texts of the twenty-fourth century B.C. a god
(d)Ma-al-ku-um, whom he identified with the Ammonite Milkom, as well
as Molek. The discoveries of Dossin and Schneider will be discussed
further below (2.2.1 and 2.4.1, respectively).

[93] Archaeology and the Religion of Israel (3rd ed.; Baltimore: Johns
Hopkins, 1953) 162-163.

For Eissfeldt and his leading supporter, Dussaud, the focus of the investigation remained on the Punic materials which, in their eyes, increasingly confirmed Eissfeldt's original hypothesis. A 1946 article by Dussaud resolved the problems which Eissfeldt had had in his book with two mlk-references, mlk 'sr and mlk b'l. Dussaud claimed that the /s/ in mlk 'sr was, in fact, really an archaic /m/, so that the phrase in the text in question (CIS 1.123b) was really the familiar mlk 'mr, and the mlk b'l in the parallel CIS 1.123a, was, therefore, also a reference to a molk-sacrifice of some sort.[94] Eissfeldt gratefully accepted Dussaud's assistance and stressed that the stelae in question were from the seventh-sixth centuries B.C., contemporary with the ancient Israelite practice of the cult.[95] Dussaud found further confirmation for a sacrificial interpretation of mlk b'l in the results of Gilbert Picard's excavations at Carthage: "pour la première fois et d'un façon incontestable, cette formule est mise en relation directe avec les sacrifices d'-enfants, sur le terrain même du dépôt de leur cendres."[96]

---

[94] "Précisions épigraphiques touchant les sacrifices puniques d'enfants," CRAIBL (1946) 376-377. Giovanni Garbini rejected the reading "'mr" and the conclusions concerning mlk b'l in "mlk b'l e mlk 'mr: A proposito di CIS I 123B," RSO 43 (1968) 5-11. See, however, Mosca's refutation of Garbini in "Child Sacrifice," 71-73.

[95] "The Beginnings of Phoenician Epigraphy according to a Letter written by William Gesenius in 1835," PEQ 74 (1947) 84-86. Thus, Eissfeldt was able to refute the criticism of de Vaux (presented above), that the sense of the Punic mlk was irrelevant to Old Testament studies because of the gap of at least two centuries between the Israelite practice and the earliest Punic inscriptional references.

[96] "Précisions épigraphiques," 382. Picard's finds had been reported in "Le sanctuaire dit de Tanit à Carthage," CRAIBL (1945) 443-452.

One should not get the impression, however, that by the late 1940's scholarship on the Molek question had become a matter of a refinement here or a confirmation there of Eissfeldt's hypothesis. On the contrary, beginning in 1949 a series of scholars presented alternate hypotheses or complete refutations of Eissfeldt.

The first major alternative to Eissfeldt was proposed by John Gray.[97] Like many of that scholar's contributions to ancient Near Eastern and Biblical studies, Gray's hypothesis is at once highly creative and, in the view of his colleagues, highly idiosyncratic. Gray suggested that one can equate Molek (or Milkom) with Kemoš of Moab through Gideon's comment in Jud 11:24. Furthermore, Kemoš is either identical or easily assimilated to the Venus star-god Attar by their occurrence as a "double-barrelled" divine name in the Meša inscription.[98] Finally, a further equation may be made with the Ugaritic deity of the evening star, Šalem.

The point of all this equating is to tie the Biblical Molek both to known cases of child sacrifice (Kemoš in 2 Kgs 3:27; Attar in the Narratives of St. Nilus)[99] and to a broader range of Biblical references than

---

[97] "The Desert God Attr in the Literature and Religion of Canaan," JNES 8 (1949) 72-83. Gray summarized his proposal, essentially unchanged, in two considerably later publications: "Molech, Moloch," IDB 3 (1962) 422-423; and The Legacy of Canaan (VTSup 5; 2d ed.; Leiden: Brill, 1965) 171-173.

[98] On this point Gray's suggestion is by no means original: Cyril of Alexandria and Theophylact had already proposed an identification of Molek with Venus in the patristic era. Moreover, Ditlev Nielsen (Ras Šamra Mythologie und Biblische Theologie [Abhandlungen für die Kunde des Morgenlandes 21/4; Leipzig: Die Deutschen Morgenlandischen Gesellschaft, 1936] 43-44) had proposed the equation of Attar, Milkom, Kemoš and Malik in the modern era.

[99] See "The Desert God Attar," 80, for citations. J. Henninger protested against the historical reliability of the Narratives ("Ist der so-

Molek alone involves (Milkom and, more controversially, the Ugaritic Ša-lem). The real impact of the proposal is in that last equation (with Šalem): Gray used it to suggest that the names Jerusalem, Absalom and Solomon all imply that Šalem (-Milkom-Kemoš-Aṯṯar) had been the local god of the city since pre-Israelite times, and that the "king's garden" of 2 Kgs 25:4, located near the juncture of the valleys Kidron and Hin-nom (so Gray), may have been the "precinct" of the god.

Given that Gray's "easiest" equation (of Molek with Milkom) is much-debated, the theory has found little support, or even response. The chain of equations is, indeed, a long one, and its verisimilitude is least enhanced, in my view, by the attempt to establish the Moabite Aṯṯar as the Venus star from much later Arabic myth, and then to bring in the much earlier Šalem to explain the problematic original sense of "Jerusalem." Gray's thesis is not so much impossible as it is ill-supported.

A second scholar's contribution was not so much a fresh approach as a summary of arguments which had been brought against Eissfeldt's use of both Punic and Biblical evidence. Walter Kornfeld's 1952 article repre-sents, in its own way, a backhanded tribute to Eissfeldt: after seven-teen years, Eissfeldt's seventy-one page book was still able to draw a twenty-seven page article devoted exclusively to its rebuttal.[100] Korn-feld relies most heavily on the work of Martin Buber and to a lesser ex-

---

genannte Nilus-Bericht eine brauchbare religionsgeschichtliche Quelle?," Anthropos 50 [1955] 81-148), while Albright supported Gray, at least in the use of the Narratives for historical purposes (Yahweh and the Gods of Canaan [Garden City, NY: Doubleday, 1968] 239).

[100] "Der Moloch: Eine Untersuchung zur Theorie O. Eissfeldts," WZKM 51 (1952) 287-313.

tent on the reviews of Bea and de Vaux, discussed above.[101] It is, therefore, essentially Buber's contribution which needs to be summarized here.[102]

Buber objected to Eissfeldt's theory at Punic root and Palestinian branch, from the interpretation of mlk'mr to the alleged orthodoxy of child sacrifice in Israel. He disputed Eissfeldt's (actually, Chabot's) reading of 'mr as "lamb," on the grounds that the cognates had an i/e vowel after the 'aleph, and the reading of mlk as "promise, vow" because of the restriction of that sense to the relatively late, distant Syriac. Buber preferred to see the crucial Punic phrases as cultic ejaculations: "[the god] Malk has spoken!" (for mlk 'mr); "Malk is Lord!" (for mlk 'dn ['dm]); and "Malk announces good!" (for mlk bšr, using the Akkadian bussuru). Buber's objective, following his initial objections to mlk 'mr, was to show that, given the failure of Eissfeldt's interpretation on his "best case," there was an alternative explanation for all of the mlk-references. As for the Biblical evidence, Buber contended that Eissfeldt was right in rejecting Molek as a divine name; rather it was a title (melek) used by syncretists who advocated child sacrifice to

---

[101] Buber, Königtum Gottes (2d ed.; Berlin: Schocken, 1936). An English translation of the third (1956) edition is Kingship of God (trans. Richard Scheimann; NY: Harper and Row, 1967).

[102] Buber's position is presented here, rather than in the previous section, because his proposal on the Molek issue per se made what impression it did largely through Kornfeld's mediation (to judge by later citations, at least). An exception to this is the work in the 1970's of Moshe Weinfeld, who cites Buber from the Hebrew translation and who, like Kornfeld, follows Buber closely vis-à-vis Eissfeldt (see below). Buber's proposals made an impression of a different sort on Eissfeldt's recent defender, Paul Mosca ("Child Sacrifice"), who expends considerable energy on refuting him in his chapters II (on the Punic evidence) and III (on the Biblical data).

Yahweh.[103] His main quarrel with Eissfeldt was over the latter's claim
that child sacrifice was licit in the Yahweh cult before the Deuteronomists. To counter the main evidence cited for this proposal, the laws
of the firstborn in Exodus, Buber put a new twist on an argument at
least as old as Witsius (1.1), that universal sacrifice of the firstborn
could not have been practiced at any time: the very impracticability of
the command shows that the actual sacrifice of the firstborn was never
intended. In fact, Buber insisted, Lev 20:5 shows that Eissfeldt was
wrong about the absence of the article and about the sense of Molek (an
argument also made by Bea); furthermore, the preceding three verses show
the latter point as well, because l following h'byr or ntn uniformly
means "to" or "for" (i.e., a dative) when only one l is used. In sum,
we should note, Buber's arguments regarding the Punic evidence made few
converts (except for Kornfeld and Weinfeld), while those concerning the
Biblical material were often repeated (whether or not those who used
them agreed with the conclusion that Molek was Yahweh).

Kornfeld himself went against this tendency, following Buber almost
slavishly on the Punic data, while citing Bea and de Vaux more often on
the Biblical. In his own conclusion, Kornfeld insists that mlk was
originally a human title, projected onto the divine as an epithet, and
eventually concretized to a particular god with a special cult (pp.
308-309). In the end he supports the hypothesis discussed above under
Lagrange and Jensen, that Molek was a chthonic deity and that the fire

---

[103] Buber does not favor Geiger's bōšet hypothesis, however. Rather,
the OT was stigmatizing the syncretistic use of the title by employing the Phoenician pronunciation (known from the Latin molchomor!).
He also admits that actual killing may not be entailed in all of the
references before Jeremiah, where it is clear (Kingship of God,
183-184).

sacrifices were designed to bring the victim into the realm of that god. Kornfeld's place in the history of scholarship, however, was largely as a summarizer of the anti-Eissfeldt position to date. His own positive position (albeit a derivative one) was not to receive close attention again for almost two decades.

A more original rebuttal of Eissfeldt was attempted by René Charlier on the basis of Punic and Neopunic stelae newly discovered at Constantine, Algeria.[104] Charlier addressed himself exclusively to the interpretation of the Punic evidence (i.e., he did not take up the Biblical evidence). He essentially followed Buber on mlk 'mr, adding that such an explanation would account for the ex viso et voto and ex viso capite to be found on some of the later Latin stelae (viz., assuming that "The King has spoken" had been heard in a vision of the offerer). Eliminating the lamb interpretation would also dissolve the incongruity of knowing that that animal was a typical sacrifice (so the "tariffs"), while having in hand only three Punic inscriptions containing mlk 'mr. Charlier concentrated his attention, however, on the phrase mlk 'dm bšrm btm. As for the first two elements, he claimed complete refutation of Eissfeldt's "sacrifice of (i.e., by) a common man" by pointing to Neopunic text 29, in which such a sacrifice is made by a priest. He suggested as alternatives either "king of mankind" or "king of the earth," both of which had been proposed long before. The last two elements, he had to admit after much discussion, remain a mystery.

---

[104] "La nouvelle série de stèles puniques de Constantine et la question des sacrifices dits 'Molchomor', en relation avec l'expression 'BSRM BTM'," Karthago 4 (1953) 3-48. The stelae themselves are published, along with a brief summary of Charlier's position, in André Berthier and René Charlier, Le sanctuaire punique d'El-Hofra à Constantine (Paris: Arts et métiers graphiques, 1955).

He favored a place name, however. In sum, he argued that <u>mlk</u> in Punic cannot possibly be a sacrificial term, both because of the specific texts and because of the complexity, unique among the Semites, of the sacrificial system which the variety of <u>mlk</u>-references would imply.

Because he chose to restrict his attention to the Punic evidence, Charlier's proposals were not always engaged by Biblical scholars at work on Molek. More importantly, despite the new evidence with which he was working, most of his efforts were directed at disproving Eissfeldt, rather than at establishing a new paradigm for understanding the texts. Thus, while we must take account of his arguments when considering Eissfeldt's position, his contribution will not require much independent review beyond this summary.

The most prolific of the scholars who offered alternatives to Eissfeldt in the 1950's was surely James G. Février, who wrote some five articles from 1953 to 1964 dealing with various aspects of Punic sacrificial practice and the Molek question as a whole.[105] His most provocative suggestion was certainly that <u>'dm</u> in <u>mlk</u> <u>'dm</u> meant "sacrifice of blood" (i.e., as opposed to a cereal or incense offering), with a prosthetic <u>'aleph</u> appearing before the common Semitic root for "blood," <u>dm</u>. But he also stirred controversy by seeing "sacrifice in exchange for an infant" in <u>mlk</u> <u>b'l</u> (citing Hebrew <u>'wl</u>, "suckling") and in <u>mlk</u> <u>bš'r</u> (Hebrew <u>š'r</u>, "flesh," specifically, "blood-relation"),[106] and by proposing "lamb" as

---

[105] "Molchomor," <u>RHR</u> 143 (1953) 8-18; "Le Vocabulaire Sacrificiel Punique," <u>JA</u> 243 (1955) 49-63, especially 52-56; "Essai de reconstruction du sacrifice Molek," <u>JA</u> 248 (1960) 167-187; "La rite de substitution dans les textes de N'Gaous," <u>JA</u> 250 (1962) 1-10; and "Les rites sacrificiels chez les Hébreux et à Carthage," <u>REJ</u> 123 (1964) 7-18.

[106] As for the <u>b(n)tm</u> which commonly accompanies <u>bš'r</u>, Février followed

the sense of 'zrm, with '$ or '$t specifying the gender. Dussaud's review of the 1955 article accepted all of the proposed translations (except for b$'r, which he did not mention), but objected to Février's sup-
position that all specify substitutionary sacrifices.[107] Jacob
Hoftijzer, on the other hand, not only opposed the substitutionary understanding, but also many of Fevrier's interpretations.[108] He claimed
that the translation "blood" for 'dm was impossible, since the prosthetic 'aleph was used to break up consonant clusters, whereas there is none
in 'dm. Also, he insisted that della Vida's "de sua pecunia" could not
explain all occurrences of btm; rather, btm should be rendered "in perfect condition," while the common "variant" (as usually supposed), bn
tm, meant "a perfect son," both referring to actual child sacrifices.[109]

Such criticism did not daunt Février, however. By his 1960 article
he felt able to reconstruct the evolution of the molk-sacrifice: at
first, the dearest children, even grown ones, were sacrificed; then,
successively, newborns, aborted fetuses or purchased children of the
poor, and finally lambs (pp. 176-177). He stressed that these were not

---

G. Levi della Vida, who had demonstrated from bilingual inscriptions
that Punic btm equalled the Latin d(e) s(ua) p(ecunia) ("Inscrizioni
neopuniche di Tripolitana," *Rendiconti dell' Accademia Nazionale dei
Lincei* [1949] 8.4.400-405).

[107] *Syria* 34 (1957) 393-395.

[108] "Eine Notiz zum Punischen Kinderopfer," *VT* 8 (1958) 288-292.

[109] Some years later, in 1967, Garbini entered the discussion once more,
this time proposing a solution to the variant forms following b$'r.
He suggested that bt meant "daughter," and bn(')t, "daughters," so
that the whole phrase referred to the substitution of one or more
daughters in sacrifice for a son ("Une nouvelle interpretation de la
formule punique B$RM BTM," *Comptes rendus du group linguistique d'é-
tudes chamito-sémitiques* 11 [1967] 144-145). In an appended response ("Observations") Maurice Sznycer rejected the proposal as in-
ferior to other options which had been suggested.

discrete stages, but that substitution had begun as early as the sixth century B.C. (i.e., at the first mention of mlk 'mr); yet, he insisted, this was the sequence.[110] His emphasis on substitution for human sacrifice continued in 1962, when he proposed a new interpretation for mol-chomor: it entailed a complex rite designed to obtain a birth, in which the future mother offered a "vision sacrifice" with the vow to "consecrate" the child to the god. Upon the child's birth, a lamb was sacrificed instead, and the god dissuaded from taking umbrage at the switch by the Talionsformel (anima pro anima, etc.). Lest anyone accuse him of overly-inventive Formgeschichte, Février stressed the similarities between his proposed rite and the birth narratives of Samson and Samuel in the Bible (pp. 6-7). His final article (1964) was less venturesome, but it did make clear that despite the points of commonality between the molk-sacrifice as practiced at Carthage and in Israel, there was an alternative to Eissfeldt's supposition that the two had obtained the rite from a common source at an early date. The molk was imported during the late monarchical period as "un rite étranger" in Israel, rightly condemned by the prophets as "une practique abominable et comme une infidélité au dieu national" (p. 18). Thus, for all their agreement on the core sense of mlk in Punic and Hebrew, Février was far apart from Eissfeldt both on other matters of Punic interpretation and on the reconstruction of the place of Molek in the history of Israelite religion.

---

[110] As we shall see, the proposition that the direction of the development of child sacrifice was toward substitution, i.e., attenuation of the rite, has been held with virtual unanimity, including de Vaux and Mosca (below). See chapter III, however, for evidence to the contrary.

Nevertheless, Février's views seem nearly congruent with Eissfeldt's in comparison with those expressed by a third scholar, whose first work on Molek appeared in 1953. Karel Dronkert's dissertation of that year agreed with Eissfeldt on precious little more than that the MT vocalization mōlek was original.[111] And even there one may find the nub of the controversy between them: Eissfeldt argued for the originality of the o-vowel because of its presence in the Latin molchomor; Dronkert favored the MT reading on principle, and in the case of Molek as a divine name, as supported by the finds from Ur III Drehem and Mari (see Schneider and Dossin, above). Dronkert scarcely disputed Eissfeldt's interpretation of the Punic evidence, challenging only the use of a meaning from Syriac for the Punic molk (p. 43). He did argue at great length, however, against the methodology of Eissfeldt (as well as Baudissin and Eerdmans) in allegedly giving precedence to extra-Biblical evidence and in reading the Old Testament material in its light. Thus, in his own work he proceeds first with an extensive chapter on the relevant Biblical material, then with the extra-Biblical, before proposing a six-stage reconstruction for the history of Molek worship in Israel. Dronkert insists on applying each Biblical passage to the time of which it speaks (e.g., Leviticus and Amos 5:26 to the wilderness period), rather than to the time at which one might critically date the material (with the curious, and unexplained, exceptions of Ezekiel 16 and 20). There is no doubt, therefore, that Judah's Molek cult was but the recrudescence of ancient Canaanite practice. Dronkert then examines the

---

[111] De Molochdienst in het Oude Testament (Leiden: Brill, 1953). Dronkert presented his views in more popular form in Het Mensenoffer in de oudtestamentische Wereld (Baarn: Bosch & Keuning, [1955]).

surrounding lands for signs of child sacrifice or the worship of a mlk
god. He finds both nearly everywhere he looks; only the Hittites evidence neither, while the Ugaritic texts were still too sketchy to draw
any conclusions. Nevertheless, he concludes that no external evidence
can compel a change in the Biblical view that Israel borrowed child sacrifice (and Molek) from the Canaanites, that the "theocratic" kings sup-
pressed the cult, and that under the "non-theocratic" kings (such as
Jeroboam I and Ahab) Molek worship reappeared, first as idolatry and
then, after Ahaz and Manasseh, combined with Yahweh worship.

As late as 1975, A. R. W. Green referred to Dronkert's work as "the
latest and most comprehensive on the [Molek] question."[112] Without a
doubt, Dronkert has assembled a vast amount of data, especially extra-
Biblical, and has mounted a serious effort to comprehend the phenomenon
under examination without being caught up in what all too often appear
the vagaries of Biblical criticism. However, as H. A. Brongers noted in
a generally favorable review, the tragedy of all this effort is that it
yielded nothing new: one might have hoped for more than a demonstration
that Israelite Molek worship was probably borrowed from the Canaanites.[113] His other two reviewers, H. H. Rowley and de Vaux, objected
strenuously to Dronkert's rejection of the bōšet-dysphemism hypothesis
by relying heavily on the LXX (a matter of eternal debate among text
critics, to be sure) and to his failure to mention the seventh-sixth
century B.C. stelae from Malta discussed in 1946 by Dussaud (since the
stelae answer one of the major challenges to Eissfeldt's use of the Pun-

---

[112] The Role of Human Sacrifice, 351, n. 163.

[113] Nederlands Theologisch Tijdschrift 8 (1954) 243-245.

ic molk to interpret the Biblical Molek, the time-gap allegedly between them).[114] We might add that, while the order of presentation of material is not necessarily a cause for argument, Dronkert's own approach constantly risks petitio principii with the assumption that the relevant Biblical texts, rare and scattered as they are, are a perspicuous, "fixed point" (p. 138) to which other classes of evidence can be related. Therefore, while Rowley may not have been entirely fair (or kind) in claiming that "the author is too concerned to defend tradition to examine it impartially," subsequent research has clearly proved him out in his conclusion that "it is unlikely to be regarded as a definitive study."

We may mention briefly a more creative alternative to Eissfeldt, published in 1954 by N. H. Tur-Sinai.[115] Tur-Sinai objected to Eissfeldt's interpretation of both the Punic and the Biblical evidence. His proposal was to take molk as a ritual (with Eissfeldt), but, with due attention to the sense of the common Semitic mlk, as a specifically royal one: "the kingship of some god, that is, the ceremony of his enthronement, which was associated with a human sacrifice or with that of a lamb as a substitute."[116] The interpretation has had little impact, largely, perhaps, because it remains in modern Hebrew. What has attracted far more attention than the hypothesis as a whole is Tur-Sinai's proposed emendation of Amos 2:1, so as to have it refer to the molk-

---

[114] Rowley, BO 10 (1953) 195-196; de Vaux, RB 62 (1955) 609-610.

[115] "mlk wśrym," Ha-Lashon ve-ha-Sefer (Jerusalem: The Bialik Institute, 1954) 1.61-101.

[116] The summary is that of Weinfeld ("The Worship of Molech," 137), who terms the idea "highly improbable" (in favor of Buber's explanation).

rite.[117]

The scholar whom we named above Eissfeldt's most persistent critic entered the debate again, twenty years after he had reviewed Molk als Opferbegriff, with further objections.[118] Dhorme's objective in this short article was to show the presence of a god Moloch (King) alongside of Ba'al (Master, Owner) in the ancient Semitic pantheon attested by the Bible (p. 57). To this end he stressed the similar ways in which both names had been subject to dysphemism. Secondly, he contended that both Molek and Milkom were forms of the original Melek, the former changed by dysphemism, the latter by mimation for emphasis ("le Roi par excellence"). Most importantly, however, he brought into direct conflict with Eissfeldt's thesis a Ugaritic text (PRU5 4 = RS 19.15), in which the words dbḥ mlk, which, as we have seen, Dussaud read as "molk-sacrifice" in CTA 35:50, were clearly parallel to dbḥ ṣpn, suggesting that in both cases the word following dbḥ designated the divine recipient of the sacrifice.[119] Dhorme concluded the article with more familiar arguments from Biblical Hebrew usage, stating that a change in the interpretation of la-molék [sic] in Leviticus 20 from a divine name to "en offrande, en sacrifice" was "au prix de subtilités exégètiques infinies" (p. 61).[120]

---

[117] "mlk wśrym," pp. 84-87. W. F. Albright adapted the suggestion in Yahweh and the Gods, 240. We shall deal with the passage in chapter IV below.

[118] "Le dieu Baal et le dieu Moloch dans la tradition biblique," Anatolian Studies 6 (1956) 57-61.

[119] "Le dieu Baal," 60. See 2.3.7 for further discussion of this text.

[120] It is at once intriguing and ironic that Eissfeldt's most durable supporter and opponent employed the same Biblical datum as the clinching argument against the other. Dussaud had written (AfO

Henri Cazelles's study (cited in n. 1) has remained standard for its superb history of scholarship in the twentieth century through its publication in 1957. His own analysis of the question places him essentially in Eissfeldt's camp. He accepts the sacrificial sense of the Punic molk, specifically refuting Charlier. While he acknowledges that Malik was a divine name in Mesopotamia, he insists that it was but an epithet at Mari and that mlk referred to Ba'al at Ugarit (when it was not a city name or the sacrificial term). The rite itself entered Israel (i.e., the North) under Tyrian influence at the time of Elijah and Elisha and penetrated the South during the rule of Ahaz with the popularity of Syrian worship. The adoption of the practice was natural enough, however, since it meshed smoothly with the Passover, originally a propitiatory rite of spring. The Israelites quickly forgot the proper sense of the Phoenician sacrificial term and applied it to the King god to whom they made their offerings, a god of the same sort as Milkom of the Ammonites, whose cult had been in Israel at least since the time of Solomon.

With Cazelles's summary the debate stalled for a brief time, allowing for assimilation of the proposals of the 1950's and for further research. The next scholar to make a major presentation on the subject was Roland de Vaux, whose brief statement in 1961 and more extended re-

---

11:167): "Nous pensons que Eissfeldt a vu juste parce que, en dehors des sacrifices d'enfants, il n'est jamais question dans l'Ancien Testament d'un dieu Moloch." Dhorme turned the argument on its head ("Le dieu Baal," 61): "Ce qui devrait faire réfléchir les partisans de cette théorie, c'est que cet abstrait molék ne se retrouve nulle part dans la Bible, en dehors des cas où il s'agit de Moloch." While Dhorme does add the point that the Pentateuch is well enough supplied with sacrificial terms without Molek, we might observe that this is as good a case as any of how scholars of Molek have seen their own views assured in ambiguous data.

flections in 1964 dominated the debate in the 1960's.[121] Given our earlier discussion of Albright's position in <u>Archaeology and the Religion
of Israel</u>, we can see much truth in Mosca's trenchant comparison of the
two men's developing views:

> It is at once ironic and highly suggestive of the great com-
> plexity of the whole <u>mulk-mōlek</u> debate that in succeeding
> years Albright moved gradually away from his initial enthusi-
> astic, whole-hearted acceptance, while de Vaux found himself
> forced to accept more and more facets of Eissfeldt's basic po-
> sition.[122]

For de Vaux this meant much greater stress than in his 1936 review of
Eissfeldt on the fundamental correctness of the latter's reading of the
Punic evidence: "Uncertainties manifestly remain. One conclusion seems
established: <u>molk</u>, in Punic, is a ritual term used of the sacrifices of
children, for whom it was admitted an animal victim could be substituted."[123] He was convinced of this not only by nearly thirty years' discussion of the inscriptions, but also by the stream of archeological
finds of sacrificial pits ("precincts" or "tophets"). Especially impressive to his mind was the study of the "precincts" of Carthage and
Sousse by Jean Richard.[124] Richard studied the ratio of human child to
animal bones by stratum at the two sites and concluded that the ratio of
human to animal bones decreased with time. Thus, according to de Vaux,

---

[121] <u>Ancient Israel: 2. Religious Institutions</u> (NY: McGraw-Hill, 1961)
443-446; and <u>Studies in Old Testament Sacrifice</u> (Cardiff: University of Wales, 1964) 52-90.

[122] "Child Sacrifice," 117.

[123] <u>Studies</u>, 79.

[124] "Étude médico-légale des urnes sacrificielles punique et leur con-
tenu. Thèse pour le Doctorat en médecine" (unpublished dissertation, Institut Médico-Légal de Lille, 1961), cited in <u>Studies</u>,
82-83.

substitution had been practiced from the earliest times in the colonies
and had increased as the rite became attenuated away from literal child
sacrifice. De Vaux then struggled to establish the "Phoenician connection" between Carthage and Israel, pointing to the testimony of Quintus
Curtius and to the Ugaritic mlk references in ritual contexts (although
he admitted there were many lacunae in the latter, making certainty of
application impossible). In the end he had to concede: "Both about the
name which child sacrifices received in Phoenicia and about the rite observed in these, the indigenous texts leave us uncertain."[125]

Still more complicated for de Vaux was the question of how to evaluate Eissfeldt's thesis as it applied to Israel. On the one hand, both
from the texts dealing with the consecration of the firstborn and from
those having to do with the Molek cult, he was as adament as ever that
child sacrifice was never licit in Israel. Nevertheless, the great similarities of the Israelite cult with that known from the Punic colonies
compelled him to state: "It thus becomes more likely that they [the Israelites' sacrifices] had the same name as at Carthage: they were molk
sacrifices."[126] So was Eissfeldt correct in declaring "das Ende" for Molek? De Vaux takes note of the wide Semitic use of mlk as a divine ap-
pellative and concedes that all of the Biblical occurrences can be understood as referring to the god (and that Lev 20:5 must be). De Vaux's
solution is to suggest that the term must have been misunderstood already when it was borrowed from Phoenicia by the Judahites, who no doubt
associated the term with the King god to whom children were being burned

---

[125] Studies, 87.

[126] Ibid., 88.

at Samaria even before the fall of the North.[127]

De Vaux's 1964 monograph drew a multitude of reviews, many of which did not deal in any detail with his discussion of human sacrifice (although one declared his treatment "by far the most brilliant analysis of the subject in recent times").[128] By far the most significant in the on-going history of scholarship, however, was a review which dealt with neither the Punic nor the Biblical evidence at any length.[129] K. Deller began with an attempt to demonstrate that the god Adrammelek of 2 Kgs 17:31 is, in fact, more correctly Adad-melek, or "König Wettergott." The core of his article, however, was an examination of neo-Assyrian contracts which provided for the burning of the children of defaulters in the ḫamru ša Adad outside of the city. Deller contended that the children were not really burned, but rather were made the property of the god: "Gemeint ist doch die Aussonderung eines Menschen als fortan Gottes ausschliessliches Eigentum" (p. 385). The only literal burning was of spices, to enhance the solemnity of the ritual. Thus, in Deller's view, 2 Kgs 17:31 censures the Sepharvites not for child sacrifice, but for dedicating to a false god children who were due to the real and living God. There was, to his mind, no connection with the Phoenician-Punic "Moloch-Kult" (p. 386).[130]

---

[127] Ibid., 89. De Vaux gives no Biblical citation for this latter claim. For him, as for Eissfeldt and all his supporters, timing the switch in the understanding of Molek was a most difficult matter.

[128] J. B. Segal, *JTS* 17 (1966) 419.

[129] K. Deller, *Or* n.s. 34 (1965) 382-386.

[130] The importance of Deller's contribution will become manifest in the discussion of Weinfeld's proposal below.

With de Vaux's adoption of his hypothesis to so great an extent, Eissfeldt might fairly be said to have carried the day by the late 1960's. As we have seen, his program had set the agenda for the debate for over thirty years. By 1968, in a discussion of the Punic and Palestinian archeological evidence concerning "tophets," W. F. Albright could say: "There are probably few competent scholars who now believe that a god Moloch is intended in any biblical passage referring to human sacrifice."[131] In the very next year, however, the Israeli scholar Moshe Weinfeld would not only join Eissfeldt's opponents on the ground chosen by Eissfeldt, but would open (or rather, reopen) an entirely different field of debate. In terms of Albright's statement, quoted above, Weinfeld would not only believe that a god was intended, but would ask (again) what cultic practice was envisioned in the Biblical passages.

Before we move to this new phase of the history of scholarship, however, we must take brief note of two other, slightly later contributions along the lines of the debate as defined by Eissfeldt. Both reflect the increasing uneasiness of the (by then) "old order." The first, in a manual on ancient Near Eastern religions, accepts molk/Molek as a sacrificial term in Punic and Hebrew, as well as the parallels in cultic practice suggested by literary sources and archeology.[132] Nevertheless, the authors are aware of the presence of Mlk as a divine name in several newly-published texts from Ugarit (in Ug5), and they speculate: "Möglicherweise kommen ihm Totenopfer zu" (p. 170). But they

---

[131] Yahweh and the Gods, 236.

[132] Hartmut Gese, Maria Höfner, and Kurt Rudolph, Die Religionen Altsyriens, Altarabiens und der Mandäer (Die Religionen der Menschheit 10/2; Stuttgart: W. Kollhammer, 1970) 175-176.

pass by on the other side of any Biblical implications of this newer data.

The second such transitional work is the dissertation of A. R. W. Green (cited in n. 1). Like most of the scholars whose positions we have reviewed in this section, Green is convinced that Eissfeldt is correct in his interpretation of the Punic evidence (p. 182). Nevertheless, while acknowledging the many contacts between the Punic and Israelite practice, he is not positive that Israel got its cult form Phoenicia and is correspondingly leery of too easy a move from Punic molk to Hebrew Molek:

> . . . it is possible that the introduction of this rite, which involves the burning of children, need not be interpreted as the Punic "molek" sacrifices, though there may be an etymological similarity between molek and Muluk. The phrase "to pass through the fire" need not be equated with the Punic sacrificial cremations, and the offerings to the gods Molek, Baal, Adrammelech, and Anammelech may actually be another type of ritual. This, of course, need not rule out some idea of burning. (p. 186)

However, despite such uncertainties, Green's approach is to work largely within the framework built by Eissfeldt and his successors.[133] Yet by 1975 not merely Eissfeldt's position, but the framework itself was in dispute.

---

[133] In Green's defense it should be stated that the Molek issue is included in his study only because of its possible bearing on the general topic of human sacrifice in the ancient Near East, and with some reluctance, it would appear, given the quantity of the literature (p. 179).

1.8   MOSHE WEINFELD AND "FEBRUATION" REDIVIVUS

While the preceding discussion has shown that the debate over Molek and
the Molek cult, conducted under the terms proposed by Eissfeldt, had by
no means reached an impasse by the 1970's, a vastly different, though
hardly new, front was opened in 1969 by Moshe Weinfeld. In a lecture to
the Fifth World Congress on Jewish Studies in that year (in Hebrew) and
in an article based on that lecture three years later (in English),
Weinfeld proposed not only that Eissfeldt had been wrong in his interpretation of the Punic molk (as Charlier and others had already
claimed), but that the very notion of a regular cult of actual child
sacrifice in ancient Israel was wrongheaded.[134]

In this latter claim he was, of course, standing with the preponderance of medieval Jewish interpreters (and before them, the Talmud)
and with such early modern scholars as Selden. In the present century
others had raised the issue, including S. R. Driver (who thought a fire
ordeal of some sort was entailed), Fritz Wilke and Norman H. Snaith (who
emphasized Talmudic suggestions that the children were ritually handed
over to become temple prostitutes) and Theodore H. Gaster (who focused
on anthropological instances collected by Frazier of rites of purification involving passage over or through fire).[135] But it was Weinfeld who

---

[134] "The Molech Cult in Israel and Its Background," Proceedings of the
Fifth World Congress on Jewish Studies (ed. Pinchas Peli; Jerusalem:
World Union of Jewish Studies, 1969) 37-61 (Hebrew) and 227-228
(English summary); and "The Worship of Molech." A more irenic sum-
mary of his position is his article, "Moloch, Cult of," Encyclopedia
Judaica 12 (1971) 230-233.

[135] The Talmudic discussions are especially those in Sanhedrin 64 and
Megillah 25a (of the Babylonian Talmud). Driver, A Critical and Ex-
egetical Commentary on Deuteronomy (ICC; NY: Charles Scribner's
Sons, 1903) 222-223; Wilke, "Kinderopfer und kultische Preisgabe im
'Heiligkeitsgesetz'," Festschrift der 57. Versammlung Deutscher Phi-

brought full energy to bear on the question from the non-sacrificial perspective and with whom, for now at least, the proposal stands or falls.

Weinfeld made two methodological distinctions which were crucial to his case. First, he insisted that one must distinguish extraordinary instances of human sacrifice from those occurring in a regularly-practiced institution with a fixed location. The former include the ḥerem, Meša of Moab's sacrifice (2 Kgs 3:27), the "substitute king" (šar puḫi) ritual of Assyria, sacrifices for magical and apotropaic purposes or in extraordinary, extra-institutional devotion (Genesis 22 and Judges 11) and, especially, the classical accounts of child sacrifice in Phoenicia and the Punic colonies. Coupled with a rejection of Eissfeldt's interpretation of the Punic stelae (largely following Buber) and of North African archeological evidence purporting to show a regular cult of child sacrifice (along with Schaeffer), Weinfeld sought to undercut not only Eissfeldt, but Baudissin before him. Indeed, Weinfeld insisted, the strongest argument against looking for a "Phoenician connection" as the source of Israel's Molek cult is in the Bible itself: how is one to explain the movement of the cult to the Southern Kingdom (Judah), when there is no evidence of its existence either in the North or in Phoenicia and, moreover, at the very time when Phoenicia was allegedly stopping the practice?[136]

---

lologen und Schulmänner in Salzburg vom 25. bis 29. September 1929 gewidmet (Vienna: Rudolf M. Rohrer, 1929) 138-151; Snaith, "The Cult of Molech," *VT* 16 (1966) 123-124; Gaster, *Myth, Legend, and Custom in the Old Testament* (NY: Harper and Row, 1969) 2.586-588.

[136] The dating of Phoenicia's giving up the cult is Eissfeldt's in his *Ras Schamra und Sanchunjaton* (Beiträge zur Religionsgeschichte des Altertums 4; Halle: Max Niemeyer, 1939) 69-70.

The second crucial methodological distinction had to do with the Biblical material. Besides eliminating from any relevance the evidence cited above, Weinfeld sought to disqualify as historiographically suspect the "moralizing literature whose tendentiousness and poetical fantasy tend to blur the authentic picture of the reality to which it refers," i.e., the (latter) prophets and writings, in favor of the "laws and historical information which generally relate to actual conditions" (in the Torah and Kings).[137]

In these "more reliable" sources, Weinfeld attempts to demonstrate, the verbs for "sacrifice" are carefully avoided in verses containing Molek in favor of ntn and h'byr, which Pentateuchal usage shows mean merely to "dedicate." Weinfeld then cites as support for his non-sacrificial view interpreters as early as the pseudepigrapha (Jub. 30:7-11), the Mishnah and the halakhic midrashim. Although these sources differ as to the nature of the "dedication" (whether it was of children to an idolatrous priesthood or sect, or of the male Israelite's semen ["seed"] to a gentile woman), he observes that all agree that h'byr lmlk means "the transference of sons and daughters to the authority of idolatry."[138] Furthermore, Weinfeld finds support in comparative evi-

---

[137] "The Worship of Molech," 141. Weinfeld expands on his view of Tendenz in Jeremiah (with Ezekiel, the book whose accuracy he most challenges) in his The Book of Deuteronomy and the Deuteronomistic School (Oxford: Clarendon Press, 1972) 27-32.

[138] "The Worship of Molech," 143. In supporting these earlier interpretations Weinfeld was, as noted above, reviving what had earlier become known as the "februation" position (since the medieval rabbis and Selden had seen the rite as one of purification). While Weinfeld insists with them on a non-sacrificial interpretation, he does not restrict it to a ritual of purification proprie dicta; hence, my references to him as a "februationist" are in quotation marks in the title of this section and elsewhere.

dence from Assyria, in contracts of the ninth to seventh centuries B.C.
which threaten the defaulting party with the burning of his children to
Adad, Adadmilki and Bēlet-ṣēri in the ḫamru outside of the city. Weinfeld subscribes wholeheartedly to K. Deller's interpretation of these
contracts, that such "burning" actually meant the children's "dedication
to the idolatrous [sic] priesthood."[139]

It is not by accident that Weinfeld places such store in the Assyrian evidence. Rather, in conjunction with the rabbinic tradition, it
provides the foundation for his historical reconstruction of the Molek
cult in Israel. Noting that the cult is first mentioned in the Bible in
the reign of Ahaz (2 Kgs 16:3) and that Ahaz was not only a vassal of
Assyria, but actively imported elements of the Aramean (if not Assyrian)
cult (16:10-15), Weinfeld proposes that Judah's "Molek cult" was, in
fact, an established institution of the dedication of children to
Adad(milki) and Ištar, the King (melek, with Geiger) and Queen of Heav-
en, practiced in the Tophet (like the ḫamru, outside of the city).
Thus, Weinfeld also might speak of "das Ende des Gottes Moloch," but by
no means in the sense Eissfeldt intended. This cult allegedly reached
its climax under Manasseh, before being eliminated under Josiah.

It remained to Weinfeld to find collateral Biblical evidence for
his reconstruction. In this connection he cites Zeph 1:4-5 and Amos
5:26 as references to the worship of the King and Queen of Heaven in Israel (the latter verse, if genuine to Amos, even showing such worship in
the North under Jeroboam II). The cult as practiced in the North after
722 is witnessed to in 2 Kgs 17:31, in the Sepharvites' "burning" (śrp

---

[139] "The Worship of Molech," 145.

b'š) their children to Adadmelek (MT Adrammelek) and 'Anatmelek (MT Anammelek).[140] He also discusses at some length the passages from Zephaniah, 2 Kings and Jeremiah which speak explicitly of the worship of the queen or the host of heaven, associating the burning of incense there with that ostensibly part of the Molek ritual.

If we begin from a "traditional" position whose essential elements are that Molek refers to a god to whom children in ancient Israel were sacrificed, it is clear that if Eissfeldt represents one extreme revision (by proposing a non-divine meaning for Molek), Weinfeld stands for the other (by positing a non-sacrificial ritual). As stated above, it is Eissfeldt's proposal which has shaped the debate ever since its publication and which, in my judgment, must be confirmed, refined or refuted if the study of Molek is to be advanced by this effort. Enough questions have been raised by the scholars discussed above to suggest that a thorough reexamination is in order. But what of Weinfeld's solution? Does Weinfeld's alternative offer a challenge to the "traditional" position of equal importance with that of Eissfeldt, and does it require an examination of equal breadth and depth? While it is every bit as learned and serious a solution as Eissfeldt's, I think not. Its fatal flaws have, I believe, been shown by previous commentators, and it is therefore possible to respond to it in the present chapter on the history of scholarship (rather than postponing treatment until later in our study, as was necessary with Eissfeldt).

---

[140] Weinfeld never quite explains whether this report, from the "generally precise language" of a historical book, reflects the "polemics" of passages like Deut 12:31, or is historically accurate.

This is not to say that Weinfeld is to be here dismissed and not heard from again. On specific points he will have much to offer. For example, his proposed identification of Molek with Adad(milki) must remain, for now, an open question. His most important contribution, however, may have been on the larger matter of showing scholarship that not only were Eissfeldt's answers subject to dispute, but his study surely did not ask every important question relevant to the Molek issue. Given the history of Molek studies for the past half-century, that is no mean feat.

Two scholars have challenged Weinfeld's 1972 _UF_ article: Morton Smith, in a "Brief Communication" in _JAOS_ (1975); and Paul Mosca in his dissertation of the same year.[141] In addition, Morton Cogan's dissertation, while not in response to Weinfeld as such, presents an alternative which asks many of his questions, but suggests quite different answers.[142] Smith accepts Weinfeld's identification of Molek with Hadad/Adad and states that his only argument is with Weinfeld's attempt to "explain away the evidence for infant sacrifice, especially by burning, in ancient Israel and neighboring peoples" (p. 477). Smith makes four points in support of his argument:

1. The distinction between Israelite practice as regular and Carthaginian as occasional is false and irrelevant.
2. Carthaginian and OT texts specify animal sacrifices as substitutes for children.

---

[141] Both are cited above (in 1.1 and 1.2, respectively).

[142] _Imperialism and Religion: Assyria, Judah and Israel in the Eighth and Seventh Centuries B.C.E._ (SBLMS 19; Missoula, MT: Scholars, 1974) 77-83. On p. 78, n. 64, Cogan calls attention to Weinfeld's 1969 essay in Hebrew (cited above), but states that his own work was done independently.

3. le ha'avir ba'esh means "to pass through fire and so burn."
4. Assyrian documents that refer to burning children as sacrifices mean what they say.[143]

Concerning the first point, Smith notes that by Tertullian's account (Apologeticum 9:2) the Carthaginian cult was "regular," complete
with temple and sacred grove, but that, in any event, temporal regularity of the ritual's performance is not a known fact in either Israel or
Carthage, nor is it required for the existence of an established cult.

Here, it seems, Smith makes a valid point. He might have added the
earlier (than Tertullian) testimony of Diodorus of Sicily (20:14), that
on the occasion of the great emergency sacrifice of children in Carthage
in 310 B.C., the people were consciously returning to a neglected custom
("as in former times they had been accustomed to sacrifice to this god
[Cronus] the noblest of their sons"). He might also have brought in the
extensive archeological finds at Carthage, dismissed by Weinfeld with
the quotation by Schaeffer (cited in 1.4 above).[144]

Secondly, Smith clashes with Weinfeld over the hermeneutics of
dealing with passages which are not clearly for or against the sacrificial interpretation: "it [Weinfeld's position] rests on the false supposition that if a text is not explicit there is no justification for an
interpretation." Insofar as it concerns the Punic evidence employed by
Eissfeldt, Smith's complaint has merit, although it must be said that
Smith's own position over against Eissfeldt remains vague.[145] But when

---

[143] "A Note," 477.

[144] The translation of Diodorus is by Russel M. Geer, Diodorus Siculus:
Library of History (LCL 10; Cambridge, MA: Harvard, 1954) 179.

[145] Smith accepts Weinfeld's view that the Old Testament Molek was Adad
(hence, not a sacrificial term), but insists that the evidence of
the Punic stelae points to real child sacrifice in Carthage.

it comes to the Old Testament texts, Smith's comment is unfair to Weinfeld: Weinfeld rests his case not on such a priori principles as Smith
suggests, but on the usage of key words in other texts for which Weinfeld mounts an argument of historical reliability.

This leads immediately to Smith's third point, concerning the sense
of h'byr b'š. Smith's citation of Num 31:23, the only instance of the
phrase which does not refer to the Molek cult, both answers Weinfeld's
call to clarify meaning through the study of usage and resolves the
sense of the phrase, but to Weinfeld's disadvantage: whether one reads
"dedicate" or "pass through," the passage clearly envisions contact with
the fire! As for Weinfeld's distinction of historically reliable from
"poetic" books, Smith insists on the usefulness at least of Jeremiah as
a commentary on the sense of Deuteronomy. In my view he could have gone
further still in emphasizing that Weinfeld has been far too gross in his
classification: very little of the Bible is not "tendentious" in some
way; what one must decide in each case is whether Tendenz has resulted
in historical distortion. In any event, as for the post-Biblical material, Smith claims that the rabbis are "notoriously apologetic" and their
interpretations "worthless except as a source of amusement" (p. 478).
One need not agree with Smith in either the degree or the tone of his
remarks to appreciate the danger in historical research to which he
points.

Finally, Smith opposes Deller as much as Weinfeld in challenging
the non-sacrificial reading of the Assyrian contracts. Indeed, as Smith
says, the contracts are open to a sacrificial interpretation, while the
Deller/Weinfeld reading lends itself to a reductio ad absurdum, if all

of the priests, priestesses and prostitutes to be provided by the de-
faulter (up to twenty-eight!) were indeed to be from his own children.

Before proceeding with Cogan's alternative, or with Mosca's attempt
to refute Weinfeld, we should note that Weinfeld himself responded
briefly to Smith in 1978.[146] The response is largely a reiteration of
arguments from his 1972 article that Weinfeld believes were misread or
ignored by Smith, evidencing the polemical spirit to which Smith gave
vent in his comment about the rabbis' reliability, quoted above. Weinfeld emphasizes that by distinguishing ad hoc from institutional practice, he is not disputing the existence of human sacrifice in Israel or
its neighbors (except, as it turns out, Assyria), only denying that the
Molek ritual as it is known to us in the legal and historical books entailed such activity. But in any event, he protests that "we have no
details about this [child] sacrifice [in the ancient world] or about the
way of its implementation" (p. 411), and so can neither prove nor dis-
prove its existence (thus simply avoiding Smith's objection to his distinction of the Israelite and Carthaginian practices). He rightly notes
that Smith had ignored his evidence for a non-sacrificial rendering of
ntn (1 Sam 1:11 and Num 8:16-17), but begs the question in responding to
the challenge of Num 31:23: "the possible outcome of the 'passing' does
not change the basic meaning of the phrase h'byr b'š which is 'to pass
through fire' and not 'to burn'" (p. 412). Furthermore, he contends
that Smith's rejection of the rabbis' witness is premature since the
contexts of forbidden sexual activity in Leviticus 18 and illicit divi-

---

[146] "Burning Babies in Ancient Israel: A Rejoinder to Morton Smith's
Article in *JAOS* 95 (1975), pp. 477-479," *UF* 10 (1978) 411-413.
Weinfeld also makes passing mention of Cogan's study, as we shall
see below.

nation in Deuteronomy 18 offer a textual basis for the later readings. Finally, he asks why the Assyrians, whom he claims knew neither burnt offerings nor blood sacrifices, should have had a practice of child sacrifice. His summary statement is "bloodied but unbowed," but it is a concession:

> To conclude: we still do not know what exactly was involved in the Molech ritual. However, to present it simply as "burning babies" and nothing else, in spite of the difficulties, philological and historical, involved, is a gross simplification. (p. 413)

As a postscript to his 1978 rebuttal, Weinfeld notes with some irritation the article of Domenico Plataroti, which also concludes that the Molek rite was not a sacrifice (although he claims one cannot tell what god was its focus), but which does not mention Weinfeld (or, for that matter, Driver, Wilke, Snaith or Gaster).[147] He adds little to Weinfeld's case, other than to deal directly with Num 31:23: he points to the connection between h'byr b'š and the ḥerem as purification without further comment on the fire (pp. 293-294). He concludes, like Driver before him, that the rite was essentially a form of soothsaying, or an ordeal (p. 299).

Like Weinfeld, Morton Cogan posits crucial distinctions in the Biblical material. His, however, are more inductive in nature. Cogan observes that different terminology is employed by the priestly Holiness (H) code concerning the Molek cult (ntn, h'byr), as compared with the description in Deut 12:31 of Canaanite child sacrifice (śrp). From this Cogan proposes "two separate rituals identifiable within legal litera-

---

[147] "Zum Gebrauch des Wortes MLK im Alten Testament," VT 28 (1978) 286-300. The article was abstracted from the author's doctoral dissertation, presented to the University of Rome.

ture: (1) a divinatory fire cult of Molech that did not involve child sacrifice, and (2) a common Canaanite cult of child sacrifice" (p. 77). He then claims that this distinction is obscured by the polemics of Jeremiah and Ezekiel, who use both sets of verbs indiscriminately and add terms like zbḥ and šḥṭ. According to Cogan, the story of these prophets is the story of nearly all scholarship on the question: "The one difference which separates investigators is the question, Which of the two rituals, the divinatory or the sacrificial, is to be read into all texts?" (p. 79). Cogan proceeds to trace just this practice in a series of sacrificial and non-sacrificial interpretations. He is unconcerned with refuting Eissfeldt's interpretation of Molek as a sacrificial term, although he does score the "somewhat cavalier approach to biblical evidence exhibited by the proponents of Eissfeldt's view" (p. 80). Also, he spends no time trying to identify the god Molek, other than as distinct from the Ammonite Milkom. Far more important to him is to show that Judah emphatically did not borrow its "Molech-type sacrifices" from the Syrians or Assyrians, although contact with them "may have awakened dormant superstitions among Judahites" (p. 83).[148]

Cogan's crucial proposal for our purposes is clearly that of the "two separate rituals" which the legal material keeps distinguished, but which Jeremiah, Ezekiel and nearly every scholar since have allegedly confounded. There is no question that Cogan's inductive approach to necessary distinctions within the Biblical literature is to be preferred

---

[148] He argues that the neo-Assyrian texts, such as those cited by Deller, suggest that the penalties of child burning were threats, not intended to be carried out. (Deller's thesis that they were carried out, only not literally, he labels "speculative.") One must recall that one of Cogan's central hypotheses is that Assyria did not impose its cult on tributaries such as Judah.

to Weinfeld's largely deductive method. But one must ask whether Cogan has not historicized or reified a distinction which can be more simply and adequately explained as varying perspectives on a single cult.[149] Cogan's challenge, as well as this possible flaw, will have to be kept in mind as we examine the Biblical material in chapter IV.

The other major response to Weinfeld's proposal is the 1975 dissertation of Paul Mosca. Like Morton Smith, Mosca is responding basically to Weinfeld's 1972 UF article (although he does also cite the Encyclopedia Judaica article from 1971). Early on he counters Weinfeld's attempt to eliminate from consideration the archeological evidence from the Punic colonies through an extensive study of that evidence (and of the stelae inscriptions), concluding: "any attempt to eliminate or deny the sacrificial element results in a wholly unsatisfactory reconstruction" (p. 49). His most intensive effort, however, is dedicated to showing that, contra Weinfeld, the evidence of the H code and of the rabbinic tradition does not establish a non-sacrificial interpretation, while that of Deuteronomy and the Deuteronomistic History (Dtr) excludes it.[150]

---

[149] Naturally, should this be the case, one is not "reading" either the divinatory or the sacrificial "into all texts." For his own reasons, Weinfeld parts company with Cogan on this point also ("Burning Babies," 413).

[150] Mosca apparently makes no distinction between "Deuteronomic" and "Deuteronomistic"; see "Child Sacrifice," 159, where he uses both terms in reference to the History. This study will use "Deuteronomic" in recognition of the difficulties inherent in distinguishing those responsible for Deuteronomy from the authors/editors of the History.

It is no surprise, therefore, when Mosca begins his study of the H material (Lev 18:21 and 20:2-5) by challenging Weinfeld's distinction of legal and historical material as "generally precise," while the prophets display "prophetic exaggeration." This, to Mosca's mind, is "oversimplified," because the very precision of the former can work to the disadvantage of the interpreter: words such as ntn and h'byr can take on specialized meanings whose sense is discernable only from context. Thus, in the case of the two lexical items noted, there is no question that "dedication" is meant; what remains to be determined is the manner of dedication. Arguing much along the lines of Morton Smith, Mosca observes that, while passages like Numbers 8 (the dedication of the Levites) may exclude a sacrificial interpretation for ntn, nothing in the context of Exod 22:28b-29 does so. In the case of the H material, Mosca suggests that lmlk originally provided the clarifying context, but that it now, lamentably, is itself the focus of dispute. However, it may be said that if Eissfeldt is right about lmlk, a sacrificial interpretation is assured, while if lmlk refers to a deity, such a reading is still permitted. Therefore, the evidence of H "neither supports nor undermines Weinfeld's understanding of the outlawed rite" (p. 147).

As for the rabbinic evidence, Mosca attempts to show that the rabbinic traditions display a far greater diversity than Weinfeld indicates. In Mosca's view the crucial flaw in Weinfeld's use of this material lies in the greatest common denominator which he can factor out of these traditions, that all entail the transference of children to idolatry: "the common feature that he discerns in the non-sacrificial traditions is general enough and vague enough to include the sacrificial traditions as well" (p. 149). In addition, the sacrificial reading of the Biblical material is no innovation, being found already in Chronicles and Josephus; rather, both interpretations "existed side by side . . . from at least the Persian period on" (p. 150).

Thus, Mosca proposes two principles for any reconstruction of the original sense of ntn mzr'w lmlk: first, that only Biblical materials produced before the rise of the aforementioned diversity (and, necessarily, misunderstanding) be used, i.e., materials "in existence by the end of the exile"; and second, that any reconstruction be judged (in part) on its ability to account for the rise of that diversity (p. 152). The second suggestion is methodologically unobjectionable; the first, however, is both difficult to achieve (given the notorious problems involved in dating the contents of Biblical books) and, in my opinion, something of a counsel of despair. We cannot be so easily relieved of considering the materials produced (and those older ones possibly altered) by a community which did, after all, stand in historical and cultural continuity with the pre-exilic and exilic one.

If Mosca believed that he had fought Weinfeld to a standstill over the H evidence, that from Deuteronomy and especially Dtr provided him with what he saw as the decisive argument: "here in Dtr it can be shown that the sacrificial interpretation is implicit in the editorial process itself and is therefore preferable" (p. 166). Since all references in Deuteronomy and Dtr (together, D) have b'š (h'byr b'š or śrp b'š), he considers it crucial to show that the phrase means "into the fire," not "through the fire" in some sort of non-sacrificial dedication ritual. The best evidence for this is Morton Smith's best evidence, Num 31:23.

But Mosca goes further, arguing that, in fact, the point is made by Wis 12:2-8, which apparently conflates Deut 12:31 (which reads śrp b'š) with Deut 18:10-11 (which has h'byr b'š). Mosca believes that this offers proof that from the earliest times the interpreters of the D corpus understood all such references (i.e., including those with h'byr) as entailing the victim's going into the fire. Mosca also offers the later development of the concept of "Gehenna" (as fiery) as evidence.[151]

In the end, Mosca says, Weinfeld has correctly perceived that there is a Tendenz in D in the use of h'byr for Israelite worship, but śrp for the same practice when done by gentiles. But he has misread its meaning. It is not a matter of exaggerated polemic against the non-Israelites (nor of two different rituals in Israel, as Cogan claims), but a theological statement: both Israelites and gentiles burned their children, but the latter did so to idols (hence, for nothing), while the former made their offerings at least to the true God, "as if he were an idol" (p. 173).

We shall respond to Mosca's own synthesis below, in the review of his position and, more thoroughly, in the examination of the Biblical material in chapter IV. For now, it seems clear enough that Mosca and Smith have between them countered Weinfeld's proposal, at least to the point of showing the limitations of his crucial methodological distinctions and the likelihood that any tendentiousness on the part of the prophets was not in the direction of falsely presenting an idolatrous ritual practiced by their countrymen as a deadly one as well. As stated above, this is not the end of Weinfeld's contribution to our study of

---

[151] Why appeals to post-exilic understandings are permitted with reference to D material but not H material is not explained.

Molek. What is evident, however, is that, if Eissfeldt's position is to be found vulnerable, Weinfeld's thesis is no high ground from which to attack it.

1.9   EISSFELDT NEWLY DEFENDED: ONCE MORE, MOLEK AS MOLK

One major contribution to the study of Molek and cultic child sacrifice in Israel remains to be examined, Paul G. Mosca's "Child Sacrifice in Canaanite and Israelite Religion: A Study in <u>Mulk</u> and <u>mlk</u>." While it antedates two of the articles cited above (Plataroti's dissertation article and Weinfeld's response to Smith, both of 1978), it cannot be subsumed under a consideration of Weinfeld's proposal, as they could. Rather, it is an attempt to reconsider the merits of Eissfeldt's "controversial theses in the light of the new evidence that has been steadily accumulating" (Introduction).

Mosca approaches the evidence in what he contends is the order of its clarity. The first chapter is, as noted above, a collection of the classical testimonies to cultic child sacrifice in Phoenicia and the Punic colonies, listed in chronological order, from Sophocles (fifth century B.C.) to Dracontius (fifth century A.D.), with the translated text of each reference followed by Mosca's evaluation of the information to be gleaned from it and his estimation of the reference's historical accuracy. He stresses that while all of the witnesses are writing from the vantage of a non-Phoenician worldview, their testimony is not automatically to be rejected for that reason; indeed, several wrote as contemporaries of the events they described. He notes that the authors almost unanimously ascribe the sacrifices to Kronos-Saturn (the Punic

Baal-Hammon, or Phoenician El), while there is less agreement as to the occasions on which the sacrifices were offered, whether in communal crises, or annually, or in private need. Several of the writers state or imply that the children were of the upper classes, while neither male gender nor primogeniture seems to have been a prerequisite for service as a victim. The rite itself focused on the fiery pit and the bronze statue of the god and seems to have been practiced in the Phoenician homeland until the period of Persian or Greek rule and in North Africa until the third century A.D. (pp. 24-27).

In his second chapter, on the Phoenician and Punic evidence obtained through archeology, Mosca finds a high degree of confirmation for the conclusions of his first chapter in the evidence found at the "sacrificial precincts" of several Punic settlements in the western Mediterranean. Unfortunately, no such holy places have been located in Phoenicia, where continuous occupation of the sites likely to be candidates has made similar finds difficult. (Thus, we might note, Mosca, like all those before him who stressed the Punic evidence, must argue that the known cults in Carthage and in Israel must somehow connect in Phoenicia, despite the absence of evidence for such a cult in the latter area.) He contends that the established "precincts" and sheer quantity of calcinated bones show that child sacrifice was an institutionalized element in the cult of the Punic colonies from their founding through to the Roman period. He follows de Vaux in arguing from the study of Jean Richard (cited above) that the increasing proportion of animal bones admixed with the children's bones indicates a growing tendency toward substitution as time passed. The finds also support the conclusion, noted

above, that child sacrifice continued long after the destruction of Carthage in 146 B.C., although there is no archeological confirmation for
the claim (by Tertullian) that it was practiced as late as A.D. 200.

It is only with the treatment of the epigraphic evidence, however,
that Mosca feels able to bring some precision to bear on his reconstruction of the (Phoenician-)Punic cult. He examines five phrases from the
stelae, largely those discussed by Eissfeldt: mlk 'mr; mlk 'dm; mlk
b'l; 'zrm 'š(t); and bšrm (bntm). Much as he did with the classical evidence, he collects the occurrences of each (printing out the texts) and
then comments, in this chapter stating his case over against the history
of scholarship on each given phrase.

Of special importance to Mosca is the dating of the inscriptions
gathered under each phrase; this enables him, once he has proposed an
interpretation of the items, to suggest how the mulk-sacrifice may have
developed, at least on Punic soil. Thus, the earliest (seventh-century)
attestations suggest to him that the mlk 'mr (mulk of a lamb) existed
side by side with the mlk b'l (mulk of a noble child); Mosca suggests
that these were the original forms of the mulk-sacrifice, with the former not a matter of substitution for a living child, but the expected
offering of those (nobles) who lacked a suitable child-candidate (p.
100). The mlk 'dm, on the other hand, does not appear until the second
century B.C. (and even then not at Carthage), only slightly after the
'zrm (later mlk 'zrm). Mosca suggests that the former means "mulk of a
lower-class child," as a substitute for a mlk b'l (clearly with an eye
toward Diodorus 20:14), while the latter would refer to the offering of
a child with some abnormality (either physical, perhaps a premature or

sickly infant, or by situation, perhaps an orphan), an offering which
only later was properly considered a mulk (p. 101). He proposes that
the absence of mlk 'dm at Carthage reflects a more conservative cultic
situation in the metropolis than in the other cities and outlying areas,
as does the failure of the full phrase mlk 'zrm to appear there (p. 85).
As for bšrm (bntm), no solution is yet convincing, although Mosca favors
a liturgical formula of some sort (p. 97).

Thereupon, Mosca turns to "our only other major source of evidence
for the mulk-rite, the Hebrew Bible" (p. 103). Again, he clearly follows the path laid out by Eissfeldt by disposing first of readings which
would prove fatal to Eissfeldt's thesis if they were to be sustained.
Thus, he immediately rejects as a textual corruption the MT's mōlek in 1
Kgs 11:7, which would clearly equate Molek with the Ammonite deity Milkom, arguing from the occurrences of Milkom in parallel verses (11:5,33)
and from the evidence of the LXX. A more serious challenge is Geiger's
theory of bōšet dysphemism in the (re)vocalization of Molek. As Mosca
admits, the consequences of proving Geiger's thesis would be disastrous
for Eissfeldt's:

> If Geiger and his followers are correct in reconstructing an
> original melek in place of MT's mōlek, the formal similarity
> underlying Eissfeldt's proposal is destroyed. Any sacrificial
> explanation of the Hebrew word is immediately eliminated; an
> original melek must be understood as a title or epithet refer-
> ring to a human or divine "king." (p. 123)

Mosca develops three arguments against Geiger's hypothesis. First, he
holds, while dysphemism is known in the Old Testament, this ostensible
instance would be qualitatively different from all other known examples.
That is, it is neither the free substitution of a negative term for a
neutral one (e.g., šiqquṣ for 'ĕlōhê in 1 Kgs 11:5), nor the substitu-

tion of a negative term associated with the original by sound (e.g., bō-šet for ba'al in Jer 3:24). In any event, the replacement must be unambiguous and entail an alteration of consonants; Geiger's Molek fails this test: "The theory that a form mōlek would immediately suggest to the reader or hearer the word bōšet (rather than qōdeš or even 'ōhel) is the product of nineteenth century ingenuity, not of Massoretic or pre-Massoretic tendentiousness" (p. 127). In this connection, he also provides alternate explanations for the other MT forms usually held to evidence the same dysphemism as Molek: tōpet and 'aštōret. Secondly, Mosca expands on Eissfeldt's argument that the LXX's archōn in place of the expected basileus in Lev 18:21 and 20:2-5 implies that its Vorlage read Molek, not melek. Instead of conceding, with Eissfeldt, that in twelve cases the LXX does indeed have archōn for original melek, Mosca seeks to show that in ten of the instances an original mōlek is probable and that the other two cases are ambiguous. He concludes that without "a single piece of concrete evidence to bolster Geiger's hypothesis," the theory "is superfluous and should be abandoned" (p. 134).

Mosca then begins his review of the relevant evidence from Leviticus, Deuteronomy and Dtr. In addition to his refutation of Weinfeld, Mosca considers objections to Eissfeldt by other scholars discussed above. As for the Leviticus material, Mosca is at particular pains to defend Eissfeldt on three points: his reading of lmlk without the article; his explanation of the troublesome 20:5 as "to whore after a type of sacrifice"; and his interpretation of ntn/h'byr lmlk as "give/dedicate for a mulk-sacrifice."[152] He concludes the discussion of the

---

[152] "Child Sacrifice," 153. Mosca cites Eissfeldt, Molk als Opferbegriff, 36-40, for the original presentation.

Leviticus material by observing that one cannot, on the basis of it alone, reject either the traditional interpretation or the "extremes" of Eissfeldt and Weinfeld (p. 158).

Mosca begins his discussion of the evidence from D by clarifying his understanding of Dtr (he accepts Cross's two-edition theory) and by eliminating as irrelevant the accounts of Jepthah's vow, Hiel's rebuilding of Jericho and (momentarily) Meša's sacrifice, all of which had played leading roles in the earlier debate. He examines the remaining passages,[153] and adds an intensive study of Isa 30:27-33 and a discussion of other prophetic passages from Micah (6:7), Jeremiah (2:23; 3:24; 7:30-32; 19:3-6; 32:34-35), Ezekiel (16:20-21; 20:25-26; 23:36-39) and (Third) Isaiah (57:5-6,9), plus Ps 106:34-35. He concludes that the picture which emerges is of a cult of child sacrifice "tolerated and even sanctioned by the official Yahwism of the eighth and seventh centuries B.C." and likely "borrowed" from the Canaanites or Phoenicians either at the time of the Conquest or in the tenth century (pp. 238-239). This "Yahwistic rite" was then practiced in the North until 722 and in the South until Josiah's reform. He also believes that he can account not only for the Tendenz of the sort discussed above under his response to Weinfeld (on the use of h'byr vs. śrp), but also for the development of the rabbinic-sexual and the "traditional" understandings of the cult of Molek:

> On the one hand, the ambiguity of ntn, the use of zr', "seed, semen," and the possibility of equating Hebrew h'byr with Aramaic 'br, "impregnate," all no doubt contributed to the later, sexual interpretation of mōlek, as did the prophetic association of child sacrifice with adultery and prostitution . . . .

---

[153] Deut 12:29-31; 18:9-12; 2 Kgs 16:3; 17:8,17-18,28-29,31; 21:2,6-9; 23:10,24-25.

> On the other hand, the equation of child sacrifice and idola-
> try that we find in Jeremiah and Ezekiel furthered the growth
> of "Molech" as an idol in his own right. (p. 240)

Finally, outside of the overlap in terminology (ntn, h'byr), Mosca sees

no connection betwen the "law of the firstborn" in Exodus and the cult

of mulk-sacrifice.

In his general conclusion (pp. 271-274) Mosca notes the high degree

to which, according to his study, the Punic and Biblical evidence are

congruent, suggesting a common origin in Phoenicia. He concedes, how-

ever, that tracing that origin is far more difficult, especially once

one attempts to do so back into the Late Bronze Age. On the other hand,

he feels confident in reconstructing an original form *mulkuM [sic],

"kingdom, royalty," and in suggesting that the word was first applied to

the rite because it entailed sacrifice by kings of their own children to

gods bearing the title "king," or, as he puts it, "the offering of roy-

alty, by royalty, to royalty."

Mosca's contribution has been considered here at some length be-

cause of its recency and, more importantly, because it represents a tho-

roughgoing, well-argued attempt to defend the essentials (and more) of

Eissfeldt's pivotal hypothesis. Thus, if, as we have said, this study

must engage Eissfeldt at length as we proceed, the same holds true, or

even truer, for Mosca's effort, which includes so much more, and more

recent, evidence from the Punic side and which is far more sophisticated

in its treatment of the Biblical material.

The necessity to postpone detailed discussion thus holds in this

case, even as it did with Eissfeldt. Some preliminary observations are,

however, in order. First, while the order of the presentation of evi-

dence is not a matter for cavilling, one must be cautious about attempts
to interrelate the material presented, lest one prematurely posit connections or even cross the line from mutual illumination to argument in
a circle.[154] Thus, whether or not one ultimately considers the story of
Jepthah's vow relevant to the study of cultic child sacrifice in Israel,
one of Mosca's reasons for rejecting it is clearly circular: "despite a
chance overlap in terminology, such a use of Jud 11:29-40 is methodologically untenable, for it contradicts much of what we know about
Phoenician-Punic mulk-sacrifices" (p. 161). But it is precisely the applicability of the Punic evidence which must be demonstrated! A more
arguable case is Mosca's crucial suggestion in his chapter II, that the
Punic b'l and 'dm denote the upper and lower classes. Mosca concedes
that the distinction is only an attractive guess:

> Clear epigraphic evidence for this new contrast is unfortu-
> nately lacking in Punic. It does, however, find indirect sup-
> port in a number of the classical texts dealing with child
> sacrifice. (p. 76)

Here, the risk of premature restriction of options seems more the danger.

Secondly, the crucial assumption throughout, as Mosca readily admits, is that of a "Phoenician connection" between the Punic colonies
and Israel, despite the paucity of Phoenician evidence of a mulk-rite.
The origins of the rite, at least insofar as Phoenicia is concerned,
"must extend back into the early Phoenician Iron Age and presumably beyond that into the Canaanite Bronze Age" (p. 273). It is therefore disappointing that the evidence from Ugarit is summarized and dismissed in

---

[154] It will be recalled that this is the problem we observed, from the
other side of the debate, in Dronkert's work.

a footnote (and that in the general conclusion to the study), ignoring, moreover, the material published in 1968 in <u>Ugaritica V</u>. Naturally, if Eissfeldt is right, such evidence may well not be relevant.[155] But given the importance of Phoenicia for Eissfeldt and Mosca as a link between the evidence of cultic child sacrifice in the eastern and western Mediterranean, and the current absence of relevant Iron Age material from Phoenicia, it seems that at very least a careful look at the Bronze Age remains of nearby Ugarit, which have made a demonstrable contribution to our understanding of ancient Israelite belief and practice in other dark corners of OT study, is called for. Such an examination would, of course, require us to consider the whole range of possibilities for the meaning of OT Molek, lest we find (or fail to find) only what we are looking for. Such a study might well lead one to ask as well if the whole range of Israel's neighbors do not need close reexamination, and not merely the relatively remote Semites of the Punic colonies.

Both of the cautions above relate to what is my central concern with Mosca's study. By announced intention it is a reexamination of Eissfeldt's theses, that is, a study of the Molek issue to see if Eissfeldt's analysis can satisfactorily account for more recent archeological and epigraphic evidence and for the Biblical material, given refined critical tools. This objective lends the study great coherence. But it also runs the great risk of overlooking entirely different paradigms which may account for the evidence as well or better than Eissfeldt can.

---

[155] As we shall see, however, Mosca's claim that the mere refutation of Geiger's <u>bōšet</u> hypothesis makes the study of (other) ancient Near Eastern <u>mlk</u> gods irrelevant and Eissfeldt's hypothesis all-but-certain ("Child Sacrifice," 137) is unjustified. Cf. Baruch Levine's observation in 1.10 below.

As will be seen, I believe that this has been the case here.

The concluding section of this chapter will point to suggestive studies done since Mosca's work, to prepare for what will be, at least in spe, a new examination of the cult of Molek.

1.10 TOWARD A NEW EXAMINATION OF THE EVIDENCE

The concern expressed above with Mosca's swift dismissal of the Ugaritic evidence is not based on purely theoretical considerations. In the years since the completion of his study, several scholars of Ugaritic have offered contributions on the Molek question which, whether or not they ultimately are to be accepted, at least present a strong argument for a reconsideration of Molek incorporating a close examination of the texts from Ras Shamra. While no one, including they, would contend that Ugaritic alone can somehow provide a solution to this problem which has proved so intractable, their work commends it as a source which dare not be passed by.

The first contribution was a 1975 article by John Healey.[156] Working from a god-list found at Ugarit, written in syllabic cuneiform (i.e., Akkadian), he argued that the name ^{d}MA.LIK^{meš} was equivalent to the alphabetic cuneiform (i.e., Ugaritic) mlkm and that the former should be read malikū, the plural of malkum/malikum, "prince, king" (p. 235). Accepting the suggestions of J. Aro and M. Birot that the usage of the plural form in texts from the Ur III and Old Babylonian periods and from Mari identifies the malikū as "infernal deities or spirits," Healey suggested that the Ugaritic mlkm meant the same.[157] He also noted

---

[156] "MALKŪ : MLKM : ANUNNAKI," UF 7 (1975) 235-238.

that both the maliku of Mari and the Anunnaki of Babylonia (called malku
in the first millennium, when they were specialized as underworld gods)
received kispum (cultic funeral feast) offerings, suggesting a further
association between Ugarit's maliku and the "spiritual or demonic powers" (p. 237), with possible links to the Ugaritic Rpum, whom variant
forms of the Šamas Hymn place in parallel with the Babylonian malku/
Anunnaki. The brief article is a probe and nothing more, but it is suggestive of the possibilities should we look north and east, as well as
north and west, and to known practices, such as the cult of the dead, to
explain the amazing persistence of the Molek cult in Israel.

A second article focused even more tightly on the possible contribution of Ugaritic studies to the Molek question: the 1981 contribution
by Alan Cooper on "Divine Names and Epithets in the Ugaritic Texts."[158]
In the entry under "mlk, mlkm," Cooper (who took over the project begun
by Marvin Pope) noted Pope's suggestion that there was a Ugaritic deity
with the epithet mlk, to be identified with the Ugaritic god of death,
Mot, and the Biblical Molek (p. 446). Cooper's article is largely a
collection of brief statements excerpted from the publications of other
scholars on Molek, organized by the Bible verses on which they were commenting. Thus, it is, above all, a bibliographical tool. However, the
article does point the way to much intriguing evidence from Ugaritic
(and elsewhere). Standing as it does in the the tradition of Lagrange
and Jensen, the proposed equation of a Ugaritic deity Mlk with the god
of Death invites consideration as an alternative to Eissfeldt, should

---

[157] See 2.2 for further discussion of the arguments of Aro and Birot and
for full citations.

[158] RSP 3 (1981) 333-469.

his thesis be found wanting in the weighing. At the very least, it demands that this close neighbor of Israelite religion (closer by far than
the Biblical writers surely would care to admit) must be included as we
turn to consider what extra-Biblical evidence may properly be brought to
bear on the Molek issue. The preceding has at minimum provided us with
reasonable cause to investigate whether reports of "das Ende des Gottes
Moloch" are not a bit premature.[159]

---

[159] One further brief contribution to this same end must be noted, "The
Cult of Molech in Biblical Israel," the excursus to chapter 20 in
Baruch Levine, *Leviticus Commentary*, forthcoming from the Jewish
Publication Society of America. Levine's chief point in the excursus is over against Weinfeld: "The ambiguity of such verbs as na-
tan, 'to offer, devote,' and he'ebhir, 'to hand over, pass through,'
cannot be construed to mean that child sacrifice is not the target
of the Levitical prohibitions of chaps. 18 and 20." He also notes,
however, that the Ugaritic god, whose name he vocalizes as "Mulku,"
"might suggest that the vocalization molekh, in the Hebrew Bible, is
original." In any event, while Levine admits that much remains unknown about this cult, his study has clearly led him to reject Eissfeldt's proposal, which is not even mentioned.

CHAPTER II
COMPARATIVE LITERARY AND EPIGRAPHIC EVIDENCE

It is by now axiomatic in Biblical studies that the investigation of Biblical phenomena, especially when done toward the end of historical reconstruction, must take into account the evidence available from the surrounding ancient Near Eastern civilizations. The present chapter will address the verbal component of such evidence, the literary and epigraphic material which impinges on our understanding of the Biblical Molek and the associated cult. (Chapter III will examine the non-verbal, archeological evidence.) This written evidence is presented as follows: first, the material from those civilizations of the Syro-Palestinian area which flourished earlier than the commonly-accepted time of the establishment of the Israelites in Canaan (i.e., through the thirteenth century); secondly, the evidence from Mesopotamia; and thirdly, the Syro-Palestinian evidence contemporary with the Old Testament Israel. Thus, while avoiding (at least initially) the controverted categories of West and East Semitic, we shall attempt to present the relevant data not merely chronologically, but with some attention to the geographical (and, arguably, cultural and linguistic) proximity of the source civilizations to Biblical Israel.[160]

---

[160] Our investigation, at least as it pertains to the meaning of Molek, is limited to Semitic civilizations, as there seems little question that the term is derived from the Semitic root mlk.

2.1   THE EBLAITE EVIDENCE

The most ancient Semitic epigraphic material from the Syro-Palestinian area is also that most recently discovered: the tablets from Tell Mardikh, Syria (ancient Ebla).[161] The vast majority of the writing on the tablets consists of Sumerian logograms, but it is generally agreed that they were read in the language of the city (conventionally, "Eblaite") since prepositions and proper names are spelled out syllable-by-syllable.[162] Thus, as is the case with the later Amorite language, our data for the reconstruction of Eblaite (especially of its grammar and syntax) are almost exclusively restricted to proper names. Furthermore, it must be noted that to this point the published texts have been almost entirely economic, administrative and lexical (i.e., with reference to our interests, not cultic or mythological).[163]

A growing consensus of scholars dates the Ebla tablets which have been published, or at least cataloged so far (mainly from the "royal palace archives," L. 2769), to the Pre-Sargonic period of the third mil-

---

[161] For further discussion of the Tell Mardikh expedition in general, see Paolo Matthiae, Ebla: An Empire Rediscovered (trans. Christopher Holme; Garden City, NY: Doubleday, 1981 [Italian orig., 1977]). For further discussion of the discovery and initial interpretation of the tablets, see Giovanni Pettinato, The Archives of Ebla (Garden City, NY: Doubleday, 1981 [Italian orig., 1979]).

[162] There are now also some lexical texts available, published by Pettinato. The monolingual texts (whether in Sumerian or Eblaite) are in Testi lessicali monolingui della Biblioteca L. 2769 (MEE 3; Seminario di Studi asiatici, Series maior 3; Naples: Istituto universitario orientale, 1981); the bilingual texts are in Testi lessicali bilingui della Biblioteca L. 2769 (MEE 4; Seminario di Studi asiatici, Series maior 4; Naples: Istituto universitario orientale, 1982).

[163] Karl Hecker stresses the present limitations of our data to personal names and non-religious genres in "Eigennamen und die Sprache von Ebla," La Lingua di Ebla (ed. Luigi Cagni; Seminario di Studi asiatici, Series minor 14; Naples: Istituto universitario orientale, 1981) 165-167.

lennium B.C.[164] There is, however, no consensus whatever on the classification of Eblaite within the Semitic family of languages. The initial
epigrapher of the Ebla expedition, Giovanni Pettinato, assigns Eblaite
to Northwest Semitic, while, according to Gelb, some Assyriologists
claim (at least privately) that Eblaite represents a dialect of Old Akkadian (East Semitic).[165] For now, given the large amount of unpublished
material, the most prudent course is certainly that of Gelb, who refuses
to categorize Eblaite within the Semitic group (although he does believe
that it is closer to Akkadian and Amorite than to the Northwest Semitic
languages).[166] Similarly, Edward Lipiński suggests that Eblaite supports
the existence of a type of dialects in northern Syria and the Euphrates
valley which was intermediate between Canaanite and Akkadian (contra
Gelb, however, he emphasizes the resemblance of Eblaite to West Semitic,
including Amorite, vis-à-vis Akkadian).[167] Regardless of the linguistic
classification of the Eblaite language, however, the location of the
city in the Syro-Palestinian area is secure, and its cultural and economic connections seem closest with cities generally west and north of
the Sumero-Akkadian "heartland," such as Kish, Abu Ṣalabikh and Mari.[168]

---

[164] See the essays in La Lingua di Ebla, noted above, especially I. J.
Gelb, "Ebla and the Kish Civilization," 57-59.

[165] Pettinato, Archives, 65-66; Gelb, "Ebla and the Kish Civilization,"
52.

[166] See Gelb's initial statement in Thoughts about Ibla: A Preliminary
Evaluation, March, 1977 (SMS 1/1; Malibu, CA: Undena, 1977) and his
more recent formulation in "Ebla and the Kish Civilization," 52.
Gelb's reluctance to classify Eblaite is well-taken, whether or not
one agrees that the very categories East and West Semitic are to be
abandoned.

[167] "Formes verbales dans les nomes propres d'Ebla et système verbal
sémitique," La Lingua di Ebla, 209.

2.1.1   The Evidence of the Personal Names

Granted all of the uncertainties resulting from the Ebla tablets' antiquity and recent discovery, there is, nevertheless, considerable Eblaite evidence of interest to our study. Of the approximately five hundred deities which have so far been identified at Ebla, one of the two most common theophoric elements in personal names is ma-lik.[169] Given the nascent state of the study of Eblaite, it seems worthwhile to list the personal names so far identified with the ma-lik element. Appendix A presents a collection of over one hundred such names.

But is Eblaite ma-lik a divine name? The strongest confirmation would, of course, be the presence of the divine determinative, Sumerian AN = d i n g i r. Three personal names may be read as containing the divine determinative: Dar-^{d}ma-lik; Bù-AN-ma-lik; and Ìr-^{d}ma-lik. Unfortunately, as Appendix A shows, the first two are so far attested only once each, while the third, although it is the most common of all Eblaite ma-lik names (with seventy occurrences), can also be read Ìr-an-ma-lik.[170]

Nevertheless, however one adjudicates these three cases, the interpretation of ma-lik as a divine name is assured by the presence of the names of known deities (not always with the determinative!) as the theophoric element in otherwise identical names: I-ti-^{d}Enki, I-ti-^{d}Ra-

---

[168] Gelb, "Ebla and the Kish Civilization," 52-60.

[169] Pettinato, Archives, 260. The other common theophoric element is da-mu.

[170] Dietz Otto Edzard (Verwaltungstexte verschiedenen Inhalts [aus dem Archiv L. 2769] [ARET 2; Rome: Missioni archeologica italiana in Siria, 1981] 108) argues that the reading of AN as the divine determinative is "unmöglich," because otherwise ma-lik appears without the determinative.

sa-ap (cf. I-ti-ma-lik); En-na-^dUtu, En-na-^(d)Da-gan (cf. En-na-ma-lik); and Bù-da-Ba-al, Bù-da-Ìl (cf. Bù-da-ma-lik).[171]

We may add at this point that Abu Ṣalabikh, a civilization contemporary with and (following Gelb and Biggs) closely related to that of Ebla, has furnished two additional names with ma-lik as a likely theophoric element: Ì-lum-ma-lik and Il-sù-ma-lik.[172] In favor of taking ma-lik as the divine name in these two cases is the consistent appearance of ma-lik in final position in the Eblaite names listed in Appendix A and, in the case of Il-sù-ma-lik, the pronominal suffix attached to Il.

Further indication that ma-lik as a theophoric element was not limited to Ebla proper comes from the Ebla tablets themselves, as shown by Hecker.[173] Listing four persons bearing Malik names, along with their places of origin, he cites: En-na-ma-lik from Ì-ra-ar and from Munu₄-wa-tù; Ru₁₂-ṣi-ma-lik from Ar-ḫa-tù; A-si-ma-lik from GUB-lu; and I-dì-ma-lik from Igi/I-gi.[174]

---

[171] All of these examples are taken from ARET 3.

[172] The names are in texts AbS 250 (catalog 298) and AbS 229 (catalog 513), respectively (R. D. Biggs, Inscriptions from Tell Abū Ṣalābīkh [OIP 99; Chicago: University of Chicago, 1974]). Gelb and Biggs present their arguments for the connection between Ebla and Abu Ṣalabikh in their essays in La Lingua di Ebla: "Ebla and the Kish Civilization" and "Ebla and Abu Salabikh: The Linguistic and Literary Aspects," respectively.

[173] "Eigennamen," 171-172.

[174] Examination of the ARET and MEE volumes produces many more examples. One must note, however, that the location of very few of these places in known, so that the occurrence of names with ma-lik at Abu Ṣalabikh remains the best evidence that Malik was not a local Eblaite deity.

Thus, we have overwhelming evidence that by the middle of the third millennium, a deity Malik was well-established, at least in the popular religion (as reflected by personal names) of the civilization(s) represented by Ebla and Abu Ṣalabikh. The question of whether Malik played a similarly important role in the official cult must await the publication of additional texts of appropriate genres.

2.1.2 The Nature of Malik at Ebla

What, if anything, do these many names tell us about the Eblaites' conception of Malik? The ma-lik element itself provides some information. Both Matthiae and Pettinato employ the commonly-accepted etymology of the name Malik to suggest that the god's "particular nature must have had something to do with royalty."[175] They might now cite the bilingual text which equates Eblaite ma-li-gú-um with Sumerian n a m - e n.[176] This suggests that Eblaite ma-lik is lexically closer to the West Semitic meaning of the root mlk (to rule), than the East Semitic (to advise). But "something to do with royalty" is about as far as the ma-lik element will take us.

What, then, may the non-theophoric portions add? The restrictions on our knowledge of Eblaite which were detailed above make the analysis of the names in Appendix A risky, at best.[177] Still, the meaning of some

---

[175] Matthiae, Empire Rediscovered, 187; Pettinato, Archives of Ebla, 247 (where he gives the divine name as Milk without comment).

[176] Pettinato, MEE 4, 318. The usual term for the king of Ebla in the tablets is e n.

[177] Nevertheless, we can look forward expectantly to the analysis now in progress under the leadership of G. Buccellati, M. L. Jaffe and J. R. Paul, to be published under the title, Repertory of Ebla Onomastics. Only sample pages have appeared to date, with none impinging

names appears clear enough from their use of non-theophoric elements
well-known from other Semitic sources, e.g., A-ba-ma-lik ("Malik is father"), A-píl-ma-lik ("Heir of Malik"), Eb-du-ma-lik ("Servant of Malik"), Rí/Ré-i-ma-lik ("Malik is my shepherd"). Pettinato analyzed several personal names containing the theophoric elements Malik, Damu, Il
and Ya, and concluded: "These names grant an insight into the intimate
relationship between the common man and his god; he is the servant of
the god but in recompense the god watches over him, indeed, he is like a
father who protects, provides, and listens."[178] However, because Pettinato was examining the personal names containing four different divine
names, it is impossible to say that his analysis revealed anything about
the popular conception of Malik in particular.

A more promising approach is that of H.-P. Müller.[179] Müller observes that only two personal names from the list known to him were
found only with the element ma-lik (and no other divine name):
A-kà-al-ma-lik ("verzehrt hat M.") and Ip-ḫur-ma-lik ("vereinigt hat
M.").[180] He suggests that both were "Ersatznamen," given a child born
into a family recently diminished by death. The former name may show

on our study.

[178] Archives of Ebla, 260.

[179] "Religionsgeschichtliche Beobachtungen zu der Texte von Ebla," ZDPV
96 (1980) 11-14. Müller's claim (p. 14) that the Semitic mlk gods
(from Ebla, Mari and Ugarit) have "keiner Verbindung zu dem umstrit-
tenden Terminus mōlek [in der Welt des Alten Testaments], der nichts
mit einem Totenopfer zu tun hat" is another matter altogether, dependent on his analyses of the evidence from Mari and of the OT term
(the latter apparently explicated in the forthcoming TWAT article on
mōlek). The value of his work on the Ebla material may be assessed
independently.

[180] The latter, he concedes (p. 12), does also occur a few times with
other theophoric elements.

that Malik already had at Ebla the underworld character known to be his from the Akkadian texts which identify him with Nergal (see 2.4.3,4); the latter indicates Malik's capability to make a family "whole" again. Thus, the names show "eine Tod-Leben-Ambivalenz des Gottes" (p. 12). Naturally, this is making much of little evidence; one might object immediately that the uniqueness of Malik's appearance in A-kà-al-ma-lik may be by sheer accident of our discoveries to date, and that, once again, definitive interpretation of most Eblaite names is presently beyond our capabilities. Nevertheless, given our limitation to the evidence of personal names, Müller's methodology seems the only possible means of discerning Eblaite beliefs concerning Malik using only Eblaite evidence. His conclusions are therefore not so much conclusive as suggestive of hypotheses to be tested against the evidence of the civilizations we have yet to examine. Should later evidence point to a chthonic-fertility character for the god, we may well suspect that the Eblaite names stand in continuity with such a later conception. However, lest we press the Eblaite material too much, let it be stated clearly: all our present knowledge will permit is the conclusion that a god Malik, "having something to do with royalty," played a significant role in the popular cultus of mid-third millennium Ebla and its environs.

2.1.3 Evidence of Cultic Child Sacrifice at Ebla

Before we proceed with other Semitic civilizations, however, we must also ask whether the excavations at Ebla have produced any written evidence of cultic child sacrifice. Unfortunately, very little is yet known about any aspect of the conduct of the cult: "The documents amply report what was offered to the gods but are totally silent about the manner and the rite of the sacrifice itself."[181] Furthermore, it may be stated without reservation that no text listing those offerings (i.e., a "tariff") has so far suggested that a child (or any human) was sacrificed. However, Pettinato does speculate that the name of a month in the "new calendar" of Ebla may indicate that such sacrifices were known:

> To these a third feast may be added, called i z i - g a r in Sumerian and ḫul/rumu, literally "consecration" in Eblaite, which, as observed by my colleague M. Dahood, could well refer to the sacrifice of children, a widespread practice among the Punic peoples of the first millennium B.C.[182]

Unfortunately, whatever the comparative evidence might suggest, the Sumerian i z i - g a r means nothing more than "setting fire."[183] Without further evidence, especially of archeological realia, to bring the Punic material to bear on the Sumerian and Eblaite terms is, at best, to run the substantial risk of eisegesis.

We turn now to the far richer evidence of a second civilization which lay on the western periphery of Mesopotamia, at Tell Hariri, ancient Mari.

---

[181] Pettinato, Archives of Ebla, 255.

[182] Ibid., 257.

[183] P. Anton Deimal, Šumerisches Lexikon (Rome: Pontifical Biblical Institute, 1930-1950) 2.400,1098. Dahood is presumably relating the Eblaite term to the Akkadian ḫarāmu, "to separate" (CAD 6.89-90), or to Hebrew ḥrm, "consecrate, devote."

2.2   THE AMORITE EVIDENCE (MARI)

The decision to turn immediately from Ebla to Mari produces not an arbitrary juxtaposition based strictly on chronology, but a transition between closely related cities. Gelb, in fact, has been bold enough to suggest that Ebla, Abu Ṣalabikh and Mari shared a single language, at least through the post-Ur III period at Mari.[184] We cannot, of course, retroject our understandings of the evidence from Mari onto Ebla.[185] But we may reasonably expect much continuity, also in religious conceptions and practices, as Mari takes us from the Early Dynastic to the Old Babylonian periods.

With the material from Mari we move from a language of yet-undetermined classification (Eblaite) to the somewhat better-known, but mixed speech of Mari. Just as was the case in Babylon in the Old Babylonian period, Mari's population included both Akkadian and Amorite elements, with the latter making up the ruling class. Amorite is a West Semitic language, known to this point almost entirely through personal names, including many from Mari. This section will present the relevant evidence from Mari and other Amorite sources, especially Tell Alalakh (a contemporary Syrian site with a large Amorite population), from those personal names. Mari also provides a different sort of evidence which will, for the first time, give us a context in which we can begin to de-

---

[184] "Thoughts about Ibla," 12. Gelb has detailed some of the similarities in "Ebla and the Kish Civilization," 63-64.

[185] Gelb, for one, has stressed the discontinuity in the language of the Mari texts between the post-Ur III and Old Babylonian periods ("Thoughts about Ebla," 9). On the other hand, G. Garbini ("Considerations on the Language of Ebla," La Lingua di Ebla, 81-82) emphasizes the continuity between Eblaite and Amorite: while they are separate languages, the latter developed in an Eblaite "linguistic milieu."

scribe the character of the god Malik with some assurance.

2.2.1 The Evidence of the Personal Names

The personal names from Mari have been collected by three scholars: Herbert Huffmon, Giorgio Buccellati and I. J. Gelb.[186] As was the case in Eblaite, one cannot always be sure that the divine name is involved, rather than the epithet, "king," or (if one prefers an Akkadian derivation) "counselor."[187] The epithet seems clearly to be in use where the name also contains a known god name, such as ^{d}Na-bu-ú-ma-lik.[188] On the other hand, we can be sure that the Amorites did acknowledge a deity Malik: not only are there names where Malik occupies the theophoric position held in other cases by a known god (as at Ebla), but the divine determinative clearly occurs.[189] Furthermore, the divine name occurs alone, marked by the determinative: ^{d}Ma-al-ki and ^{d}Mi-il-kum.[190]

---

[186] Huffmon, Amorite Personal Names in the Mari Texts: A Structural and Lexical Study (Baltimore: Johns Hopkins, 1965); Buccellati, The Amorites of the Ur III Period (Pubblicazioni del Seminario de Semitistica, Ricerche 1; Naples: Istituto orientale di Napoli, 1966); Gelb, Computer-aided Analysis of Amorite (Assyriological Studies 21; Chicago: Oriental Institute, 1980). Since Gelb's work includes the lists of the other two scholars, one may refer to it for the full list of names (pp. 321-323 for the root mlk).

[187] Huffmon, Personal Names, 230. However, Huffmon's characterization of Malik as a "well-known Akkadian divine name" [my emphasis], which "appears also in Amorite names" needs revision in the light of the Eblaite evidence.

[188] It is also possible that such names are equating the two deities, but the wide variety of deities coupled with ma-lik and the tendency of such "equation names" to be late and in cultic contexts (reflecting efforts at systemization of the pantheon) militate against this.

[189] As an example of the former, see Ḫa-ab-du-ma-lik (cf. Ḫabdu-(d)Ami, Ḫabdu-Ištar). The latter is represented by Ia-šu-ub-(d)ma-[lik].

[190] Appendix B contains a list of Amorite personal and divine names, drawn from Gelb's collection (Computer-aided Analysis, 321-323),

This last pair of names raises the most difficult problem of our comparative study: how to account for the variety of ways in which the consonants m-l-k are vocalized. As this pair further illustrates, the solution is not simply to say that Malik is the vocalization reserved for the god's name, while other forms have other meanings. Indeed, as Dossin recognized already in 1938 (1.7), the place name ^{d}Mu-lu-uk^{ki} proves that a god Muluk was known at Mari. Appendix B shows that this vocalization is not limited to the name of one village, but occurs also in personal names, such as A-bi-mu-lu-ki, I-tar-mu-lu-uk and La-ar-mu-lu-uk.

How can the form Muluk be explained? First, we note that Muluk seems limited to Mari.[191] Secondly, the place name given above appears in four different spellings: ^{d}Mu-lu-uk^{ki}; I-lu-um-mu-lu-uk^{ki}; ^{d}Mu-lu-ka-yi^{ki}; and I-lu-ma-li-ka-yi^{ki}. The last form was known already to Dossin, who suggested that it proved that Muluk was a variant of Malik in use at Mari.[192] That is certainly a possibility, as is the chance that Muluk was originally a local deity, who had become assimilated to the more widespread Malik by Old Babylonian times. In any event, Muluk is, so far as we know, restricted to Mari and therefore of only passing

---

which may be relevant to our study. That is, they do not (1) contain the name of another god, as in the example above, or (2) contain an apparent verbal use of mlk, such as imlik.

[191] There are two occurrences of the name Ili^{li}-mu-lik at Ugarit (PRU4 17.288:27 and PRU6 17.242:16). As we shall argue below (2.3), Mulik in this name is probably not related to Mari's Muluk.

[192] Dossin does not say whether he has in mind a dialectical variant (as seems most likely), or a phonetic change. The latter would find the first /u/ in Muluk hardest to explain, as the second could have resulted from vowel assimilation or a variant similar to the Arabic for "one-third," thulth/thuluth (my thanks to Prof. Franz Rosenthal for this last example).

interest for our purposes.[193]

Such a limitation of attestations to Mari is not the case with other vocalizations. As Appendix B shows, one may roughly divide the names
between those with an /a/ vowel in stem position (malik, malki) and
those with an /i/ vowel (milku, milki). The following observations are
in order:

(1) the form malki occurs only twice, in ^d Ma-al-ki and
Bi-it-ta-ma-al-ki, both in a late stratum at Tell Alalakh;

(2) the milku/i forms occur either alone or in first position in
all but three cases, while malik occurs both at the beginning and
the end of names (but predominantly, as at Ebla, at the end);

(3) far more consistently than the malik or muluk names, the
milku/i forms preserve what appear to be case endings, which, however, do not always function as expected, i.e., the -ki(m) form is
used in all instances where Gelb marks the whole name as genitive,
but milki also appears to be used where the theophoric element is
nominative, e.g., Mi-il-ki-lu-i-la, La-i-la-mi-il-ki (assuming that
the /a/ on ila is the predicative ending, as in Akkadian);

(4) to anticipate the later discussion, the Mesopotamian (Akkadian)
evidence employs the /a/ forms nearly exclusively (2.4), while that
from Phoenicia (when vocalized) shows the /i/ forms (2.6), except
for Ugarit, which has both (2.3).

---

[193] Dossin's observation, subsequently repeated by many scholars, that
the vowels of Muluk and the LXX's version of Molek (i.e., Moloch)
are the same, seems best explained as a coincidence, given the span
of time between them. (We shall return to the evidence of the LXX
in chapter IV.)

How, then, can we account for the variation between forms with stem vowel /a/ and those with /i/? Again, as with Muluk, we can only present and comment upon the possible explanations. First, while we find a milki name in Amorite as early as the Ur III period at Isin (Mi-il-ki-li-il[MAR.TU]),[194] the Eblaite evidence shows that Malik is the oldest form of the root mlk used as a divine name. The problem, then, is to account for the forms with /i/. It is possible that a phonetic shift from /a/ to /i/ in the name is in process at Mari, although such a shift would not follow any regular phonetic law. Although it cannot be proved, a more satisfactory solution is to take note of Mari (and, indeed, the Amorites in general) as a frontier between Syria-Palestine and Mesopotamia. If we also observe that the later Phoenician-Punic vocalization of "king" was with an /i/,[195] it is possible that population elements originating in the Phoenician area simply translated the name of the Syrian king-god, Malik, with their word for king, complete (at the time) with case-endings, "Milku/i."[196] The two forms, Malik and Milku/i, would then have become established as alternates in Amorite (especially in the more eastern Syro-Palestinian cities like Mari), with some preference for one or the other possibly based on the position of the theophoric element in one's name.[197] Alternatively, of course, the Milku/i

---

[194] Buccellati, Amorites, 173.

[195] To judge by the neo-Assyrian spellings of Phoenician royal names and later Greek transcriptions, for instance.

[196] The consciousness of the original function of the case-endings would then have faded as the word was used as a proper name.

[197] Compare the variations in the divine name YHWH in personal names, depending on whether it occurs first or last in the name (see Michael David Coogan, West Semitic Personal Names in the Murašu Documents [HSM 7; Missoula, MT: Scholars, 1976] 49-53).

form may not be the result of any "translation," but simply the form used by a more western group, i.e., an originally separate deity, who then was brought to Mari. While this is a tempting possibility from a phonetic standpoint, it may be that to distinguish Malik and Milku/i as originally separate gods is overly subtle, granted that both appear to have the notion of "king" at their etymological base and that they seem to be interchangeable. It is our restriction to the evidence of personal names which makes further certainty so elusive. The names themselves give little indication of how the natures of Malik and Milku/i may have differed, and the context in which the names appear does not permit us to classify their bearers according to population sub-group or place of origin.[198] Regardless of what explanation one prefers for the observed phenomenon of variant forms of the divine name, the Amorite evidence provides conclusive proof that the god Malik continued to play a significant role in the popular religion of Syria-Palestine through the first half of the second millennium B.C.[199]

---

[198] On the other hand, as Biggs ("Semitic Names in the Fara Period," *Or* n.s. 36 [1967] 57) warns, one cannot press such evidence too hard, even when it is available.

[199] This role continued even after the conquest and destruction of Mari by the Kassites in the mid-eighteenth century, as is shown by the fifteenth century personal name from Tell Alalakh, Ili-ma-lik (D. J. Wiseman, *The Alalakh Tablets* [London: British Institute of Archaeology at Ankara, 1953] 132:21).

2.2.2 The kispum and the maliku

While the personal names in Eblaite and Amorite have established the existence of a god Malik, they have shed precious little light on the
god's nature. Our first solid clues come from Mari texts which speak of
offerings a-na ma-li-ki(-im), "to [the] Maliks (Malik)."[200] The phrase
occurs in some twenty-four texts, twenty-one times immediately following
a list of offerings ana kispim ša šarrāni(LUGAL^{meš}), "for the kispum of
the kings."[201] The texts specify how much of what foodstuffs are to be
offered. While the amounts vary somewhat, a typical list provides for
the kispum, 20 qa of NINDA.KUM, 4-5 qa NINDA-emṣu, 15 qa NINDA-mersu, 10
qa sipku and 2 qa oil, and for the maliku, 3 qa NINDA.KUM, 2 qa NINDA-
mersu and 15 shekels of oil.[202] Furthermore, the offerings ana maliki
were apparently made monthly, at the new moon, while the kispum feast
was held twice-monthly. Thus, it is apparent that the two offerings are
in some way related and that of the two the kispum is the more important.

---

[200] Of the twenty-four occurrences of this phrase, three include the mimation ending (-im): ARM 9.121.5:43; 9.123:12 (restored); and
12.85:10. Since the texts are from the Old Babylonian period, the
absence of the ending in the preponderance of cases presumably indicates that they are plural, i.e., mālikī or malikī (we shall discuss
the length of the /a/ below, 2.4.5). The spelling below, without
macrons (maliku/i) is meant to include all twenty-four cases.

[201] The evidence has been collected and analyzed by two scholars: Ichiro Nakata, "Deities in the Mari Texts: Complete inventory of all
the information on the deities found in the published Old Babylonian
cuneiform texts from Mari and analytical and comparative evaluation
thereof with regard to the official and popular pantheons of Mari"
(unpublished Ph.D. dissertation, Columbia University, 1974), especially pp. 354-363; and Phillippe Talon, "Les offrandes funéraires à
Mari," AIPHOS 22 (1978) 53-75.

[202] The determination of the "typical" offerings is that of Nakata, "Deities in the Mari Texts," 357. NINDA is apparently a general term
for flour or bread, while the meaning of sipku is unknown.

But to what or whom do kispum and maliku refer? While offerings ana maliki are hitherto unknown outside of Mari, references to kispum offerings are present in Mesopotamian sources. Already in 1966, J. J. Finkelstein concluded that the Akkadian kispum was a funeral feast in honor of the deceased members of the royal dynasty and, at least in the case of the text he studied most thoroughly, also for the benefit of those dead who had no one else to honor them.[203] Talon adds that the funerary and royal character of the kispum is also clear at Mari, and that the rite apparently consisted of a meal in which the offered flour/bread and oil were consumed together by the royal family and the dead, the latter perhaps represented by statues.[204]

The first scholarly attempts to understand the maliku relied almost entirely on the meanings of the root, mlk. Thus, Jean Bottéro proposed that they were the "conseillers du roi," while Maurice Birot was torn between that derivation from the East Semitic meaning and the West Semitic "prince, king."[205] It was J. Aro who first suggested a connection

---

[203] "The Genealogy of the Hammurapi Dynasty," JCS 20 (1966) 95-118. We may add that the line between the Akkadian material (to be treated in 2.4) and the Amorite is admittedly blurred in this portion of the evidence. While the kispum was certainly an Akkadian institution (CAD 8:425-427), Hammurapi's ancestors were, of course, Amorite. We are treating the kispum and (more importantly) the maliku at this point in order to consider the evidence from Mari together and because the rite under examination clearly featured the royal family, which was Amorite, at least under Zimri-Lim, to whose reign fifty-four of the fifty-nine Mari references to the kispum can be dated (Talon, "Les offrandes funéraires," 60). Whatever the origin of the kispum may have been, it is most important for present purposes to repeat that the juxtaposition with the maliku is restricted to Mari.

[204] "Les offrandes funéraires," 64.

[205] Bottéro, Textes économiques et administratifs (ARM 7; Paris: Imprimerie Nationale, 1957) 190; Birot, Textes administratifs de la Salle 5 du Palais (ARM 9; Paris, Imprimerie Nationale, 1960) 286.

with the mal(i)kū of some Old Babylonian omen texts, and concluded on that basis: "Es liegt also nahe, in den mal(i)kū etwas wie Totengeister oder Unterweltsgötter zu sehen."[206] The omen texts, which will be treated in detail below (2.4.2), do present an appealing parallel, since the mal(i)kū in them are clearly chthonic entities, as would befit the objects of offerings at a funerary feast. Aro's proposal, therefore, has met with wide acceptance. We must caution, however, that the evidence of the omen texts is from the Mesopotamian heartland, and that the conception there of a divine being or beings need not be the same as that at a "peripheral" site such as Mari, even in the same period. Specifically, the maliku of Mari need not have borne the fully negative connotation which, as we shall see, the mal(i)kū did in the omens.[207] This is particularly likely if, as we shall argue, Malik and the maliku were of Syro-Palestinian origin and borrowed by the Mesopotamians as foreign divinities.

In any event, Aro and his successors (including Nakata and Talon) have presented strong evidence that the maliku of Mari are not living participants in the kispum, but shades of the dead or underworld deities. That they were recipients of offerings in the cult of the dead as practiced by Mari's royal house suggests that they were perceived as having power, albeit not as great as that of the deceased kings. Thus, it is likely that we have to do either with the lesser departed (perhaps

---

[206] Review of ARM 9, OLZ 56 (1961) 604.

[207] A preliminary indication in favor of this hypothesis is the popularity of Malik names at Mari. It is unlikely that the name of an entirely evil deity (or deities) would have been popular in personal names (indeed, we shall see a swift decline in Mesopotamian Malik names once this entirely negative view becomes established.)

the "all souls" invited to the kispum, as described by Finkelstein) or
with minor chthonic deities (with the important proviso that these two
categories are not necessarily mutually exclusive!).

But what have the maliku to do with Malik? As was noted above, in
three instances the offerings are made a-na ma-li-ki-im, "to [the] Malik." While these cases could be scribal errors, it is tempting to see
in them exceptional instances where the offerings were made to a single
being, just as there is a single instance where the kispum was offered
to one king, Yaḫdun-Lim (ARM 3.40). If so, a clear connection would be
established between Malik and the maliku. But the proof of such a relationship must await our examination of the evidence from Ugarit (2.3).

2.2.3 The Pantheon Lists from Mari

Before turning to that evidence, we note that the god Malik does not appear in the four pantheon lists which have been published to date from
Mari.[208] Nakata would explain this omission by downgrading the status of
Malik: "Malik is a spirit or ghost and might not have been counted
among the deities."[209] The presence of Malik as the theophoric element
in numerous personal names (including the twelve listed by Nakata) would
argue against this conclusion, however. Moreover, Malik's importance in
Mari is strongly indicated, if not proved, by a later, Standard Babylonian list of underworld deities and their addresses, which calls ^{d}Malik,
"šarru ša má-ri^{ki}."[210] Outside of the chance that Malik's name may have

---

[208] See Phillippe Talon, "Un nouveau panthéon de Mari," Akkadica 20
(1980) 12-17, and the literature cited there.

[209] "Deities in the Mari Texts," 475.

[210] See 2.4.4 and Erich Ebeling, Tod und Leben nach den Vorstellungen

appeared in one of the several lacunae in the pantheon lists, it seems probable that we are dealing with a discontinuity between the official pantheon (in the lists) and the popular one (in the names), as appears to be the case at Ebla. Nakata attributes other deities' omission from the pantheon lists to the influx of the Amorite population.[211] Based on his more general conclusions, then, it is logical to suggest that the Amorites brought Malik to Mari, where the god is found in names, but not in the older, fixed lists in which only the most important West Semitic deities (such as Addu) have achieved mention.

There is, however, another possible explanation for Malik's absence from the pantheon lists. Talon presents evidence to suggest that Malik was identified with one of the prominent deities at Mari who is in the lists, Dagan.[212] Talon observes that Dagan received funerary offerings at Mari under the name bēl pagrê. He suggests that the latter term means "cadaver," and that the offerings ana maliki are the same as Dagan's niqê pagrā'i. Indeed, the proper name Dagan-malik may point to the equation.[213] In response, we may call attention to Healey's thorough study of the evidence for Dagan's connection with the netherworld, in which he concludes: "We have seen that both in Ugarit and Mesopotamia the evidence for Dagan's underworld interest is circumstantial rather than conclusive. It certainly does not warrant the ascription to him of 'clear' underworld connections."[214] Even granting Dagan's chthonic

---

der Babylonier (Berlin: W. de Gruyter, 1931) 12.

[211] "Deities in the Mari Texts," 483.

[212] "Les offrandes funéraires," 69-70.

[213] See, however, the cautions concerning "equation names," above.

aspects, it is important to recall that many other deities also had netherworld connections and that all of them could not possibly have been originally identified with Malik (or one another). Talon's proposal is suggestive, although his understanding of pagrā'u is, by his own admission, open to challenge. Even given the hypothesis of Roberts that Malik was initially an epithet of Dagan in Akkadian (which we think unlikely; see 2.4.1), Talon's proposed identification seems at best a local phenomenon, like Muluk, not of abiding interest as we continue to trace Malik through the centuries in Syria-Palestine.

2.2.4 Evidence of Cultic Child Sacrifice at Mari

Finally, we may add that there is no literary or inscriptional evidence of cultic child sacrifice at Mari.

2.3 THE UGARITIC EVIDENCE

As was the case in our transition from the Eblaite to Amorite evidence, our movement from Mari to Ugarit is not an arbitrary one, dictated simply by geographical proximity and chronological sequence. On the contrary, there were clearly trade links between the cities (at least, until the destruction of Mari, ca. 1746 B.C.), as well as cultural and religious ties.[215] With Ugarit, however, we come to the end of our study

---

[214] J. F. Healey, "The Underworld Character of the God Dagan," JNSL 5 (1977) 51.

[215] One of the texts which we shall examine below, for instance, Ug5 7, assigns the goddess 'ttrt to the place mr, surely Mari. (Texts not to be found in Herdner's CTA [i.e., those discovered after 1939] will be cited by the place of their first publication, with the RS number provided with the first reference to each text. Texts from Ug5 are from chapter 3, "Nouveaux textes mythologiques et liturgiques" [edited by Virolleaud], unless otherwise indicated.)

of Syro-Palestinian civilizations before the establishment of the Israelites in Palestine: Ugarit was not finally destroyed until the early
twelfth century B.C.

The Ugaritic material is written in two ways, alphabetic cuneiform
(Ugaritic) and syllabic cuneiform ("Akkadian"),[216] with a few tablets
containing parallel lists of words in both. The texts written in Ugaritic are at the same time the most interesting and the most challenging:
interesting, because for the first time they provide us with literary
evidence of a god Mlk per se (not pluralized) in a context which allows
us to know something of the god's nature; challenging, because they are
unvocalized and thus open to greater ambiguity at the most fundamental
level of interpretation, the establishment of the correct reading.
Thus, the name of the god under study is written in the same way as the
relatively common word for "king," mlk.

We shall examine the evidence from Ugarit in the following sequence. First, we shall treat those texts in which the use of the divine name Mlk (or of a plural form, Mlkm) is beyond dispute. Secondly,
we shall take up a series of texts in which the god Mlk may not be mentioned by name, but which do illuminate the texts in the first category.
After reviewing the evidence provided by personal names, we shall consider Mlk's place in the Ugaritic pantheon, especially vis-à-vis gods of
like nature. We shall then turn to the Ugaritic cult, dealing first

---

[216] We place "Akkadian" in quotation marks, because texts written in
syllabic cuneiform at Ugarit were not necessarily read in Akkadian
(any more than the tablets at Ebla were read in Sumerian). Moreover, it is likely that Ugarit's Akkadian was, like that at Mari,
"peripheral," in that other language elements were freely mixed in.
For example, Gelb (Computer-aided Analysis, 322) lists an Amorite
name from Ugarit, spelled Qu-ú-LUGAL.

with certain passages which have been alleged to show the practice of
molk-sacrifices similar to those which Eissfeldt claimed to have found
in the Punic material (1.5), then with evidence pertaining to the possible practice of cultic child sacrifice and of the cult of the dead.

2.3.1 The Ugaritic God Mlk

Only two texts provide indisputable references to a divine being named
Mlk: Ug5 7 and 8 (RS 24.244 and 24.251). Both texts contain lists of
divine names which demonstrate both that Mlk is a deity and that the god
by that name is distinct from the best known Ugaritic deities who bore
mlk as a title, El and Baal. In addition, the first list provides the
"address" of each god. Thus, Ug5 7:41 has mlk.'ttrth ("[the god] Mlk at
[the place] 'ttrt"). Comparison with the other divine names and addresses shows that the second term contains the directive-h suffix (in
all cases except ll. 3 and 9, the addresses of El and Baal) and that it
may refer either to a strictly mythological place (e.g., inbb [l. 20]
and šmm [l. 52]) or a historical one (e.g., ttl [l. 15] and ḥryt [l.
36]).[217] In fact, as the first detailed examination of the text (by Astour) showed, a reference to Ashtaroth (modern Tell 'Ashtarah) in the
Transjordanian Bashan region is a distinct possibility. In any event,
the reading of 'ttrth as some place name is much to be preferred to Virolleaud's initial effort in Ug5 ("[le dieu] Mlk [tourné] vers [la
déesse] 'Aštart"), which overlooks the structure of the text.

---

[217] The judgments are those of Michael C. Astour ("Two Ugaritic Snake
Charms," JNES 27 [1968] 19-21). Astour also emphasizes that the ḥ-
suffixes on the addresses are more properly called locative, rather
than directive.

The other sure instance of M̲l̲k̲ as a divine name, U̲g̲5 8:17, also occurs with ʿ̲t̲t̲r̲t̲, although in this case M̲l̲k̲ is the only name accompanied by an address: m̲l̲k̲.̲b̲ʿ̲t̲t̲r̲t̲.[218] Otherwise, the divine names, largely in the order of U̲g̲5 7, are paired. The inclusion of b̲ʿ̲t̲t̲r̲t̲ in U̲g̲5 8:17 is usually explained metri causa (i.e., as providing a second member corresponding to the second divine name in the pairs).[219] One might also suggest that the address has been added to specify that the god named M̲l̲k̲ is intended, not a god bearing that epithet, or even a human king.[220]

The statement above that only two texts have M̲l̲k̲ in contexts which indisputably show it to be a divine name is the truth, but not the whole truth. In addition, there are four texts which have forms of m̲l̲k̲ which are also clearly divine names.[221] Two of these texts are written in syllabic cuneiform, while two are in alphabetic cuneiform. All four are

---

[218] In fact, this anomaly has led some scholars to treat this ʿ̲t̲t̲r̲t̲ as a divine name. M. Dietrich, O. Loretz and J. Sanmartín ("Einzelbemerkungen zu RS 24,251," U̲F̲ 7 [1975] 127) read "Milku und Aṭtoret," although they do not explain the extraordinary use of b̲ as a conjunction. J. Gray ("Canaanite Religion and OT Study in the Light of New Alphabetic Texts from Ras Shamra," U̲g̲7, p. 83) reads a compound divine name, "Malik-with-Aṭtart," which accounts more satisfactorily for the b̲, but not for the identical form in U̲g̲5 7, where ʿ̲t̲t̲r̲t̲ is clearly an address.

[219] Astour, "Two Charms," 32; Paolo Xella, I̲ t̲e̲s̲t̲i̲ r̲i̲t̲u̲a̲l̲i̲ d̲i̲ U̲g̲a̲r̲i̲t̲ (Pubblicazioni del Centro di Studio per la Civiltà fenicia e punica 21 [Studi semitici 54]; Rome: Consiglio nazionale delle Ricerche, 1981) 248.

[220] Sergio Ribichini and Paolo Xella ("Milkʿaštart, m̲l̲k̲(̲m̲)̲ e la Tradizione siropalestinese sui Refaim," R̲S̲F̲ 7 [1979] 148) hint at this.

[221] Andrée Herdner ("Nouveaux textes alphabétiques de Ras Shamra--XXIVe campagne, 1961," U̲g̲7, pp. 8,35) suggests a fifth case in which m̲l̲k̲m̲ may be a divine name: U̲g̲7 (RS) 24.266:(rev.):8. (Since Herdner did not number the U̲g̲7 texts, the RS number is used.) K̲T̲U̲ 1.119, however, reads the word as m̲l̲k̲t̲.

divine lists, or "pantheons." The first, Ug5 1.3-e-2:81, has the known
Akkadian god name with the divine determinative, ^{d}MA.LIK, although, unfortunately, it is so far down in the long list which contains it that
the lists which run parallel to earlier parts of this text have no parallel for this item.[222] At the least, however, this text (and Ug5
1.18:32, below) establishes a connection between the Ugaritic god and
the Malik we have found at Mari (and will hear more of in Mesopotamia).
It may even provide the Ugaritic vocalization (although, as we shall see
in discussing the personal names, this is not certain).

The other three texts are the two discussed by John Healey in his
1975 UF article (summarized in section 1.10), CTA 29:(rev.):11 and Ug5
1.18:32 (RS 20.24), and a text almost identical to the former, Ug7 (RS)
24.264+280:32.[223] While some scholars initially read mlkm in CTA 29 as a
singular (Milkom, or Mlk with an enclitic-m), the Akkadian version in
Ug5 1.18, ^{d}MA.LIK^{meš}, shows clearly that the form is a plural. What remains in dispute is the interpretation of that plural noun and its relationship to the singular divine name, Mlk. Two of the first interpreters of the texts containing mlkm, Astour and Cazelles, argued that the
context favored interpreting mlkm as divinized molk-sacrifices:

> The "canonical list of the Pantheon" in all three versions
> ended in deified personifications of certain cult objects and
> sacrifices. RS 1929 No. 17:rev. 9-12 has utẖt, knr, mlkm,
> šlm: "censer, lyre, molk-sacrifices, peace-offering."[224]

---

[222] The text is RS 20.121. See Ug5, pp. 212-224, for the parallel
lists.

[223] Nougayrol (Ug5, p. 64) claimed that Ug5 9:9 (RS 24.643) also contained mlkm (where, indeed, as Healey ["MALKŪ," 235] says, one would
expect it). No collation of the text agrees, however; KTU 1.148 has
a*l*pm.

[224] Astour, "Two Charms," 280-281. Cazelles's version of the argument

This interpretation had the disadvantages of reading back from
Eissfeldt's Punic evidence across a gap of nearly a millennium (or half
that, if one begs the question of the sense of the Bible's Molek) and of
assuming that šlm was necessarily a cultic term here and not the known
goddess Šalimu (CTA 23).[225] With Healey's article most scholars have
come to prefer a comparison with the mal(i)kū of Mari and Mesopotamia.
This connection will be most fruitfully pursued after we have examined
the second category of texts mentioned above, those which do not contain
the divine name Mlk as such, but which do help explicate the texts already presented.

2.3.2 Rpu of ʿṯtrt and Hdrʿy

The most significant "explicatory" text (see immediately above) is one
of the most widely-disputed texts in the Ugaritic corpus, Ug5 2 (RS
24.252). Since it is not the stichometry which is at issue, the text is
presented according to its accepted arrangement:

A (1) [--]n.yšt.rpu.mlk.ʿlm

B wyšt (2) [il][226] gtr.wyqr.

C il.yṯb.b.ʿṯtrt

---

is in "Encore un texte sur Mâlik," Bib 38 (1957) 485 (where he reads
mlkm as a singular); see also his review of Ug5 in VT 19 (1969) 500.

[225] Jean-Michel de Tarragon (Le Culte à Ugarit: D'après les Textes de
la Pratique en Cunéiformes alphabétiques [Cahiers de la Revue Biblique 19; Paris: Gabalda, 1980] 159) declares the divinized-sacrifice
interpretation impossible on the latter grounds.

[226] Marvin Pope ("Notes on the Rephaim Texts from Ugarit," Essays on the
Ancient Near East in Memory of J. J. Finkelstein [ed. M. Ellis; Hamden, CT: Archon, 1977] 169) omits [il] (although its inclusion
would not materially affect his position).

D (3) il.ṭpṭ.bhd r'y.[227]

E dyšr wydmr. . . .

Three issues are especially prominent in the current debate: the
identity of the figure Rpu mlk 'lm; the identity of il in lines B, C and
D; and the interpretation of 'ṭtrt and hd r'y in lines C and D. The
last of these points is the most significant for us (since reading 'ṭtrt
as a place name would provide a connection with Ug5 7 and 8), but our
decision on the first two issues both cannot be divorced from that on
the third and will say much about what we can do with this text, should
we find it applicable to our study by way of our decision on 'ṭtrt.

To begin, then, with the interpretation of 'ṭtrt/hd r'y: scholarly
opinion lies divided between two positions. The first reads both items
as divine names, 'Aṭtart and Haddu the Shepherd (i.e., Baal); the other
takes them as known place names, 'Ashtaroth and 'Edrei.[228] The arguments
made by the proponents of each position have been widely aired elsewhere
and need not be repeated in detail here.[229] We are obliged to defend the

---

[227] Some scholars place r'y in the next line: J. C. de Moor, "Studies
in the New Alphabetic Texts from Ras Shamra, I," UF 1 (1969) 175; M.
Dietrich, O. Loretz and J. Sanmartín, "Der 'Neujahrspsalm' RS 24.252
[=UG.5, S. 551-557 NR. 2]," UF 7 (1975) 175.

[228] The interchange of /h/ and /i/ in the latter form is explained as
either a scribal error (since Ugaritic /h/ and /i/ differ only by a
small wedge) or as a development known elsewhere in West Semitic, as
shown by Edward L. Greenstein, "Another Attestation of Initial h/'
in West Semitic," JANESCU 5 (1973) 157-164. M. Görg ("Noch Einmal:
Edrei in Ugarit?," UF 6 [1974] 474-475) argues that this does not
solve the problem since one would expect an initial u-vowel in the
place name on the basis of Egyptian evidence. Margalit ("The Geographical Setting of the AQHT Story and Its Ramifications," Ugarit
in Retrospect [ed. G. D. Young; Winona Lake, IN: Eisenbrauns, 1981]
153) responds that "the Egyptian -iw- can correspond to West Semitic
['i] or ['a], as well as to ['u]" in transcribed Canaanite place
names.

[229] In addition to the bibliography given by Conrad E. L'Heureux (Rank

position adopted in this study, however, given the importance of this text for our use of the Ugaritic evidence.

The dispute might well be considered at an impasse, were it not for the careful concordance work done by the proponents of the latter option. Led by Pope, these scholars have shown that ytb b does not occur in Ugaritic in the sense "sit with/by," but only meaning "sit/dwell in."[230] Thus, the reading of place names rather than divine names as the objects of b commends itself. Secondly, the interpretation of hd r'y as a cognomen of Baal fails "since the element hd occurs in Ugaritic poetry only following mention of b'l in the preceding stich."[231]

To be sure, as William J. Horwitz has observed, such arguments from usage are based on relatively little evidence and may well be overthrown by future discoveries.[232] Candidates for such contrary evidence have, indeed, been proposed: ytb.il.[b(?)]at[rt] in Ug5 1:14-15 (RS 24.258); and hd.r(?)['y] in Ug5 3:1 (RS 24.245).[233] In the case of Ug5 1, however, later collations (and even Virolleaud's original hand copy) show

---

among the Canaanite Gods: El, Ba'al, and the Repha'im [HSM 21; Missoula, MT: Scholars, 1979] 169, n. 114 and 173, n. 124), see especially A. J. Ferrara and S. B. Parker, "Seating Arrangements at Divine Banquets," UF 4 (1972) 37-39; and M. Dietrich, O. Loretz and J. Sanmartín, "Der 'Neujahrspsalm'," 115-117 (favoring the divine name reading); and M. H. Pope, "Rephaim Texts," 169-170 (favoring the place name reading).

[230] Pope, "Rephaim Texts," 170. This point was convincing to the author of the only thorough study of Ugaritic prepositions to date: Dennis Pardee, "The Preposition in Ugaritic," UF 8 (1976) 245.

[231] Pope, "Rephaim Texts," 170.

[232] "The Significance of the Rephaim: rm.aby.btk.rpim," JNSL 7 (1979) 40. Horwitz also presents a more serious challenge: that hd appears to occur before b'l in one place, Ug5 14.B:2. In any event, hd has not been shown to appear without b'l in close proximity.

[233] In both cases the restorations are Virolleaud's in Ug5.

that the reading b after il is incorrect. As for Ug5 3, even strident

defenders of reading divine names in Ug5 2 admit that its presence here

is unlikely.[234] In sum, although one can by no means speak of a scholar-

ly "consensus," a significant body of scholars now seems to favor the

"locative" interpretation of 'ttrt and hd r'y.[235]

We have not yet even mentioned the datum which led Baruch Margulis

to propose the place name reading in the first place: the Biblical col-

location of Ashtaroth and Edrei in Josh 12:4 and Deut 1:4 (and else-

---

[234] De Moor, "Studies," 180-181; M. Dietrich, O. Loretz and J. Sanmartín, "Stichometrische Probleme in RS 24.245=UG.5, S. 556-559, NR.
3VS.," UF 7 (1975) 534-535.

[235] So Henri Cazelles, "Ugarit," Annuaire de l'École Pratique des Hautes
Études, Ve Section: Sciences Religieuses 88 (1979-80) 233. The remaining defenders of the other position seem increasingly hard
pressed. The strongest arguments of L'Heureux (Rank among the Gods,
172-173) in favor of reading divine names are a passage from the material Eusebius attributes to Sanchuniathon (Praeparatio evangelica
1.10.31), in which Astarte and Hadad are said to rule over a place
"with the consent of Kronos [=El]," and the observation that one
would not expect "the first mythological text which mentions the
city of Ugarit" to deal with "a god who is found in Bashan." The
former argument is, in my view, the stronger, since the Eusebius
passage does provide an otherwise rare link between Astarte ('ttrt)
and Hadad (hd), albeit some centuries after the time of Ugarit.
Still, it is forcing the sense of the passage to claim that El is
depicted as reigning with the other two gods at either hand (as does
Frank M. Cross, Canaanite Myth and Hebrew Epic [Cambridge, MA: Harvard, 1973] 21); the two reign by El's permission, not necessarily
at his side (thus, the passage cannot be said to argue for reading
il as El in Ug5 2). Indeed, the pairing of the divine names in this
single passage must be set against the repeated pairing of the place
names in the Bible (see immediately below); at best this would result in an impasse, to be resolved on the other grounds already presented. L'Heureux's second argument evaporates when, as we shall
see in chapter IV, it is realized that Bashan (and, thus, Ashtaroth
and Edrei) can be employed in a sense other than the strictly
historical-geographical one. On the other hand, J. C. de Moor
("Rāpi'ūma--Rephaim," ZAW 88 [1976] 338) is driven to invent an inscription ostensibly written on 'Og's bed (Deut 2:11), in which the
pair 'ttrt/'dr'y originally meant the divine names, but were later
misunderstood as places.

where, with variations).[236] This information was not included in the above discussion since we intend to make use of it below and wish to avoid the danger of circular argument.

The other two issues mentioned at the outset of our discussion of this text (viz., the identities of Rpu mlk 'lm in line A and of il in lines B, C and D) are linked with one another and with one's decision on the matter of 'ttrt/hd r'y. Both issues have called forth a wide variety of proposed solutions, only the essential features of which will be reviewed here. Il in lines B, C and D may be taken either as the common noun for "god" (in this case, used in apposition with Rpu mlk 'lm) or as the proper name of the head of the pantheon, El. On the other hand, the identification of Rpu mlk 'lm has proved far more open-ended: El, Baal, Mot, Molek and the personification of the Rpum have all been suggested. The resulting matrix of combinations of options possible among these three issues finds a representative at almost every position.[237]

---

[236] "A Ugaritic Psalm (RS 24.252)," JBL 89 (1970) 293. Indeed, both of the Biblical passages note that a certain 'Og dwelt in (yšb b) the two cities. The difficulties of such dual dwelling, which even Margulis has found insoluble ("Geographical Setting," 152), will be dealt with below in chap. IV.

[237] Thus, L'Heureux (Rank among the Gods, 169-172) reads il as El and equates Rpu with El. Parker ("The Feast of Rāpi'u," UF 2 [1970] 243-244) reads il as El, but denies that Rpu is El (or Baal). (He later ["The Ugaritic Deity Rāpi'u," UF 4 (1972) 104] nominated Mot.) De Moor ("Studies," 175-176) reads il as "god" and suggests that Rpu is "the chthonic aspect of Ba'lu" (who "is judging with Haddu"!). Healey ("Death, Underworld and Afterlife in the Ugaritic Texts" [unpublished Ph.D. dissertation, University of London, 1977] 178) agrees that Rpu is Baal, but not that he is chthonic (despite Rpu arṣ in Ug5 2:8-9). Pope ("Rephaim Texts," 170-171) renders il as "god" and suggests the identity of Rpu and Molek. Caquot and Sznycer (Ugaritic Religion [Iconography of Religions 15/8; Leiden: Brill, 1980] 19) take no position on il, but propose that Rpu is "the personification of the Rpum."

The position which we find most convincing is that of Pope (cited in the last note), that Rpu is a deity distinct from El or Baal and that in this text il is simply the general term for deity ("god"). Indeed, there seems no reason to bring El or Baal into lines A-D: mlk 'lm need not involve El,[238] and Baal would seem to be a candidate only because of his prominence elsewhere (however one reads hd r'y in line D).[239] The equation of Rpu with Molek is more problematic, and yet obviously of crucial interest to this study.[240] The shared address of 'ttrt provides the sedes doctrinae for this proposal. The very limited evidence for the Ugaritic deity Mlk makes further arguments in favor of the equation with Rpu difficult to adduce. But there are additional indications (if by no means concrete proof) in favor of such an identification. Unfortunately, the most suggestive are bound up with a debate among scholars of Ugaritic (which never lies far from questions about Ug5 2) over the nature of the Rpum.

---

[238] Even L'Heureux (Rank among the Gods, 171) concedes: "both elements in the epithet mlk 'lm are in line with what we know about El, though they could, of course, be appropriate to other gods too."

[239] Healey's best evidence for the equation of Rpu and Baal is in CTA 22.2:8: Rpu B'l ("Death, Underworld and Afterlife," 176-179). However, such compound divine names at Ugarit are generally joined with the conjunction when written together (e.g., Ktr-wHss), and Rpu B'l can satisfactoriy be understood as the Rpum (see below), in parallel with mhr B'l and mhr 'nt.

[240] The further equation with Mot, attributed to Pope in section 1.10 above, will be treated below.

2.3.3   Rpu <u>and the</u> Rpum

The <u>Rpum</u> (conventionally, "Repha'im," using the Biblical vocalization) become involved in our study because of their *prima facie* connection with <u>Rpu</u> and because of the similarities in content alleged by Healey ("MALKŪ") between the plural forms <u>mlkm</u> and <u>rpum</u>. The former reason entails the whole matter of how one understands the <u>Rpum</u>, itself a topic worthy of detailed study.[241] That there is a connection between <u>Rpu</u> and the <u>Rpum</u> is generally conceded, whether one holds for a genetic relationship or a "secondary approximation of the two at Ugarit."[242] Also, whatever their view of <u>Rpu</u>'s identity, most scholars suggest that he is the divine head of the <u>Rpum</u>.[243]

For our purposes, the most interesting aspect of the <u>Rpum</u> is the chthonic character of at least a large portion of them.[244] Robert Good

----

[241] Indeed, at least three dissertations focus at length on the <u>Rpum</u>: L'Heureux's from Harvard (now the book, <u>Rank among the Canaanite Gods</u>); Healey's (cited above); and Gary Tuttle's, now in progress at Yale University.

[242] The latter is advocated by Parker ("The Ugaritic Deity," 104).

[243] Caquot and Sznycer, as noted above, prefer to think in terms of a "personification of the <u>Rpum</u>."

[244] See L'Heureux (<u>Rank among the Gods</u>, 111-127) for a history of scholarship on the nature of the <u>Rpum</u>. The relevant texts are especially the so-called "Rephaim Texts" (<u>CTA</u> 20-22); the hymn to Shapash at the end of the Baal-Mot myth (<u>CTA</u> 6.6); a blessing pronounced on Keret in <u>CTA</u> 15.3:2-3,13-14; and a relatively new text, RS 34.126 (<u>KTU</u> 1.161). Essentially, the current debate concerns whether all references to the <u>Rpum</u> can be explained as the dead, now-deified ancestors of the royal house (or the nobility), or whether some indicate a group of the living (usually held to be a guild of chariot warriors, also known as the <u>maryannu</u>). Inevitably mixed in with this discussion is the question of how to understand the Biblical occurrences of the Rephaim, some of which seem virtually synonymous with the "shades" and others of which refer to "a gigantic race which inhabited parts of Palestine and Jordan before Israelite times" (see L'Heureux [<u>Rank among the Gods</u>, 111] for OT references). L'Heureux, B. Margalit ("Geographical Setting," 154) and Healey

has recently proposed an etymological explanation for the form Rpum/Rephaim which stresses this point: the Rpum are the "healed," that is, the embalmed in the sense of Gen 50:2.[245]

The Rpum were not, however, simply disembodied spirits relegated to the netherworld. As the ancestors of the living (again, at least in large part), the Rpum were conceived of as having considerable power, especially in the realm of fertility: "The Rephaim, the deified ancestors, were considered the source of fertility, as life eventually returns to earth whence it came."[246] This conception is shown clearly by text RS 34.126, where the Rpum are invited to share in a ritual meal and implored to bless the ruling dynasty (see further in 2.3.4 below). Such

---

("Death, Underworld and Afterlife," 195-197) argue that the chthonic sense of Rpum developed from a living group, whether of chariot warriors (L'Heureux) or of an early Amorite tribe whom the rulers of Ugarit counted as ancestors (Margalit and Healey). Caquot/Sznycer (Ugaritic Religion, 19-20) and Pope ("The Cult of the Dead at Ugarit," Ugarit in Retrospect [ed. G. D. Young; Winona Lake, IN: Eisenbrauns, 1981] 174-175) hold that there is no need to posit a living group of Rpum.

This study will deal with the Biblical evidence concerning the Rephaim (and related beings) below, in chapter IV. While I am inclined to accept the position of Caquot/Sznycer and Pope on the Ugaritic Rpum, a full discussion is beyond the scope of this study. For our purposes, it is sufficient to note the the Rpum had a clear chthonic connection at Ugarit.

[245] "Supplementary Remarks on the Ugaritic Funerary Text RS 34.126," BASOR 239 (1980) 41-42. This explanation is clearly superior to the traditional active participle, "Healers" (one would then expect Hebrew *rōpĕ'im) and to L'Heureux's stative understanding, "Hale Ones" (since the verb rp' is otherwise consistently transitive [Rank among the Gods, 216-218]). However, the expected form of the Hebrew passive participle would be *rĕpū'îm, so that there is clearly some problem in the history of the Hebrew vocalization. One may, therefore, continue to argue for an active participle, "Healers," later altered, and point to 2 Chr 16:12 for a cognate, still chthonic usage (so M. H. Pope, oral communication).

[246] Pope, "Rephaim Texts," 167.

an understanding also undercuts the use of the blessing of Keret in CTA 15.3:2-3,13-14 as a proof text in favor of a living body of Rpum.[247] The blessing (mid rm krt / btk rpi arṣ: "May Keret be greatly exalted / In the midst of the Rephaim of Earth") need not imply that Keret is at that moment one of the Rephaim, only that he is to be blessed by them with fecundity (a major concern in the story).

Assuming, then, that Rpu mlk 'lm is the divine head of the Rpum, we can easily appreciate why numerous scholars see a chthonic dimension to this deity (indeed, this explains why de Moor proposed Rpu as specifically the chthonic aspect of Baal). To this evidence will be added in chapter IV indications of the underworld connotations of Bashan, the region containing both Ashtaroth and Edrei, the residences of Rpu and of the Biblical Rephaim. For now, we shall examine additional texts concerning the Rpum which individual scholars have alleged contain further references to the divine Mlk(m). The interpretation of these texts cannot claim the degree of certainty (or even scholarly approbation) which the views so far accepted on Ug5 7, 8 and 2 can boast. But insofar as this study hopes to serve as a prod to further investigation, their inclusion here is essential.

Given the preceding discussion, it should come as no surprise that a prime source for such further references is the "Rephaim Texts," CTA 20-22. The most provocative alleged occurrence of the god Mlk is that suggested by Pope in CTA 22.2:9-10 (and, by implication, 22.1:11-12, which is usually restored using 22.2:9-10). He translates tm yhpn hyl(10)y / zbl mlk 'llmy as "There comes the Mighty One, Prince MLK the

---

[247] L'Heureux, Rank among the Gods, 201-202.

Wise."[248] The key to understanding the couplet is clearly how one takes the pair ḥyly / ʻllmy. Pope and L'Heureux agree that the first, at least, is a nomen professionis (Pope holds that both are). Given this analysis, L'Heureux's "retainers" might appear preferable to the adjective "mighty." Unfortunately, L'Heureux is then at a loss to understand ʻllmy. Both also agree that ḥyly is parallel to the entire following colon. However, only Pope can make sense of the latter. One might object from the perspective of content that the sudden appearance of Mlk is intrusive in the text. However, if one accepts the identification of Mlk with Rpu (or at least their close association), the appearance of Mlk in a "Rephaim Text" cannot be protested on such grounds.

Despite the best efforts of scholars, certainty with respect to the interpretation of CTA 20-22 cannot yet be claimed. For this reason, this alleged occurrence of the god Mlk can be accounted possible or even probable (as we believe), but not established. One provocative implication of Pope's analysis does deserve attention, nevertheless. If ʻllmy, "wise," was indeed a stock epithet of "Prince MLK," one might well ask if the same adjective is not concealed under scriptio defectiva in Ug5 2:1: Rpu mlk ʻlm, that is, "Rapiu, Mlk the Wise."[249] For now, unfortu-

---

[248] "Rephaim Texts," 167. Pope adduces as a cognate the Arabic ʻallāmiyy, "(very) wise" (p. 170). L'Heureux (Rank among the Gods, 153), by contrast, renders: "There are stationed my retainers, Royal princes of (?)."

[249] My fellow student, Mark S. Smith, suggested this as a possibility to me. Healey ("Death, Underworld and Afterlife," 178) also asks concerning mlk ʻlm: "Could mlk have an added significance here?" The alleged reference may stand, even if one disagrees with Pope on the sense of ʻllmy (as does Alan Cooper, "MLK ʻLM: 'Eternal King' or 'King of Eternity'," Love and Death in the Ancient Near East: Essays in Honor of Marvin H. Pope [ed. J. Marks and R. Good; Guilford, CT: Four Quarters, in press]), so long as ʻllmy is held to be a stock epithet associated with Mlk. See Healey's suggestion that the

nately, no further adjudication of the issue is possible.

2.3.4   The Mlkm and the Rpum

The second reason which we adduced above for the importance of the Rpum to our study was the similarities in content between the Rpum and the Ugaritic Mlkm, as alleged by Healey. The discussion of the Mlkm has been delayed until this point, after the presentation concerning the Rpum, in order to allow us to consider Healey's proposal. As observed above, Mlkm occurs in two of the pantheon lists in parallel position with ^{d}MA.LIK^{meš} in a third. Thus, both the plurality of the Mlkm and their connection with Malik are established. Questions remain, however, concerning the nature of that connection and the relationship of the Ugaritic Mlkm to the plural mlk-entitites we found at Mari (malikū) and those we shall find in Mesopotamia. In addition, the foregoing argument that the Ugaritic gods Rpu and Mlk are very closely associated, if not identical, raises the question of whether the same may not be said of the Rpum and Mlkm.

Healey's initial development of the pantheon lists' equation has already been summarized (1.10). In subsequent studies he has cautioned that the Mlkm cannot simply be interchanged with the mal(i)kū of Mari and Mesopotamia, going so far as to say: "The equation of . . . mlkm and malikū is a matter of similar sound, remotely related meaning, but not historical or essential connection."[250] His use of the evidence from

----

term is a gentilic ("Ritual Text KTU 1.161--Translation and Notes," UF 10 [1978] 86), as well as the occurrences of ‘llmn (a variant of ‘llmy?) in CTA 1.4:5 and RS 34.126:7.

[250] "Death, Underworld and Afterlife," 89.

Mari and Mesopotamia, however, suggests that the meaning of the two terms is really not very remote, after all. Indeed, while one must be careful in comparing religious concepts, especially between Ugarit or Mari and Mesopotamia (as we have already argued in 2.2), the Akkadian version of the pantheon list clearly was an attempt at expressing in Mesopotamian terms the meaning of the Ugaritic Mlkm. (That the two members of the equation are similar in sound no more shows that the equation was based on sound than does the pairing of Špš and Šamaš, which Healey calls "close.")[251] The Ugaritic pantheon lists are claiming that the Ugaritic Mlkm may most closely be compared in Akkadian terms with a pluralization of the god Malik, presumably the mal(i)kū. Healey is rightly reluctant simply to impose on the Ugaritic Mlkm the later, Standard Babylonian usage of mal(i)kū for the Anunnaki gods (by then a chthonic group).[252] But "no historical or essential connection" is far too strong, if, as we shall argue, both Mlkm and mal(i)kū find their ultimate source in the Syro-Palestinian Malik, and both refer to the denizens of the netherworld, whose power to affect the living was a cause for concern and propitiation.

Healey is less hesitant about the direct connection with the malikū of Mari: "The similarity of the forms at Mari and Ugarit together with the sacrificial/offering context of their use both in the Mari texts and in the Ras Shamra (cultic?) pantheon make a direct connection between the two almost certain."[253] What Healey has in mind by positing a "di-

---

[251] Ibid.

[252] "MALKŪ," 238.

[253] Ibid., 237.

rect connection" is hard to say, given his earlier cautions. Nevertheless, two Ugaritic texts supply additional evidence for the legitimacy of using the evidence of Mari to understand the Mlkm of Ugarit. Specifically, both link the Ugaritic Mlkm with a funeral feast for the Rpum.

The first is one of the "Rephaim Texts," indeed, the same text which speaks of zbl mlk 'llmy, CTA 22.2. Following the description of several sacrifices to the 'brm,[254] the text reads: dpr tlhn bq'l bq'l / mlkm (ll. 16-17). Ribichini and Xella, who take dpr with the preceding stich, translate: "The table (is set) on the heights, on the heights (are) the mlkm.[255] Similarly, de Moor (followed by Healey) reads: ". . . among the fruit on the table in the hall, in the hall of the kings" (i.e., according to Healey, the deified, dead kings).[256] Pope is more cautious, translating, "Redolent the table with fig cake, with fig cake royal," but adding, ". . . the term [mlkm] here may be freighted with multiple entente."[257] As has already been emphasized, this text is most difficult, and one dare not speak of "assured results" in understanding it. Nevertheless, it clearly does envision a gathering of the

---

[254] Which, we shall argue in chapter IV, on the basis of Ezek 39, are those who have "passed on."

[255] "'La Valle dei Passanti' (Ezechiele 39:11)," UF 12 (1980) 437. The original Italian: "La tavola (è posta) sull'altura, sull'altura (sono) i mlkm."

[256] De Moor, New Year with Canaanites and Israelites (Kampen: J. H. Kok, 1972) 2.12-13 (citing post-Biblical Hebrew and Aramaic qela' and qil'ā, and assuming a metathesis); Healey, "Death, Underworld and Afterlife," Postscript--iv.

[257] "Rephaim Texts," 168,176. If Pope's understanding of q'l is correct (based on Arabic qu'âl/qa'l), we might well have a parallel to the Mari lists of bread/flour offerings for the malikū.

Rpum with certain gods for a seven-day feast, at which a funerary milieu is indicated by several terms for the dead (besides Rpum: mtm [1. 6] and 'brm [1. 15]). In such a context living "kings" are clearly out of place; Mlkm, unless one believes it is not a noun, is best taken as the kings past.

The second text confirms that departed kings were expected at the feasts held for the Rpum. The text is the last one listed above as important for the study of the Rpum, RS 34.126 (KTU 1.161). If one accepts the KTU reading, the title (1. 1) reads: spr.dbḥ.ẓlm, "Account of the sacrifice for the shades."[258] Healey (following de Moor) notes the resemblance of the ritual described in the text to the kispum in which the "Genealogy of the Hammurapi Dynasty" was used.[259] Indeed, the text recounts the invitation of the rpi.arṣ, including the names of several unknown figures and then those of two known kings of Ugarit, 'Ammiṭtamru and Niqmaddu (ll. 11-12), both designated as "mlk." That the last two, at least, are dead kings is shown by l. 31, where the beneficiary of the ritual is named: 'Ammurapi, who, as the last king of Ugarit, reigned after all of the kings who bore either of the above pair of names. Fur-

---

[258] Pace Wayne T. Pitard ("The Ugaritic Funerary Text RS 34.126," BASOR 232 [1978] 68), who writes: "The word ẓl appears in Ugaritic, meaning 'shadow, shade' (but not 'shade-of-the-dead')."

[259] M. Dietrich and O. Loretz ("Totenverehrung in Māri [12803] und Ugarit [KTU 1.161]," UF 12 [1980] 381-382) argue that dbḥ in l. 1 of RS 34.126 may be equivalent to kispum. Therefore, although the term kispum itself has not yet appeared at Ugarit, we shall refer to the royal funeral feast there as the kispum. Healey ("Ritual Text KTU 1.161," 85) calls attention to a Ugaritic dynastic list, now published as KTU 1.113, in which each king's name is preceeded by the determinative il, suggesting the divinization of dead Ugaritic kings. Healey speculates that the list was used in the Ugaritic kispum, just as the Akkadian list examined by Finkelstein (2.2.2) was used in Mesopotamia.

thermore, ll. 15-16 show that a feast was involved. The resemblance of this ritual to the kispum of Mari is striking: the living king feasts with his ancestors in hopes of obtaining their favor (šlm) toward the royal family and the city.

It will be recalled, however, that at Mari the malikū were a distinct group from the main recipients of the kispum offerings, the šarrānu(LUGAL^meš), and that the gifts to the malikū were considerably smaller and about half as frequent. The available evidence does not permit us to say whether a similar division obtained at Ugarit. RS 34.126 provides a possible solution, however. Line 8 summarizes the list of invitees whose names we do not recognize with the designation rpim.qdmym, "the Rpum of old." Only the more recently departed pair are called mlk. Since we do not recognize the earlier group, it is hard to determine the nature of the contrast. If, however, they are much earlier kings, as the nature of the ritual would suggest, it may well be that the Mlkm were the most recently departed, and therefore, at Ugarit, the most important recipients of the kispum.

The evidence already presented shows that we are on firm ground in suggesting a close relationship between the Rpum and Mlkm. Healey speculates that the two are co-terminus, even if not of the same origin, and that the pantheon list used Mlkm, because "it is evidently more prosaic."[260] Elsewhere, he lists their common characteristics: "royal/noble, 'divine', powerful, ancestral dead, invoked in the cult."[261] Although we

---

[260] "MLKM/RP'UM and the kispum," *UF* 10 (1979) 91.

[261] "Death, Underworld and Afterlife," 272. Healey's early articles also call attention to Aisleitner's comparison of Ugaritic Rpum with Akkadian rubû (Wörterbuch der ugaritischen Sprache [Berlin: Akademie, 1963] 295), suggesting an etymological meaning, "prince." Most

must constantly recall that usage, not etymology, determines meaning, it is most tempting to suggest that the Rpum and Mlkm are either identical (the dead kings), or that the Rpum are a somewhat larger group of the dead, even if not so large a group (i.e., all the dead) as the Bible means in, e.g., Ps 88:11.[262]

2.3.5 The Evidence of the Personal Names

While the evidence presented to this point certainly reduces our reliance on personal names for information on the Ugaritic deity Mlk (over against the situation at Ebla and Mari), we cannot afford to pass by the names, either. Fortunately, the task of collection has already been performed, at least through the texts published in Ugaritica V.[263] Nevertheless, for the convenience of the reader, the list of names appears in this study as Appendix C (for specific text references, see Gröndahl). Gröndahl presents some thirty-nine personal names containing the root mlk, twenty-one written in alphabetic cuneiform and eighteen in syllabic cuneiform. As was the case at Mari, several are most unlikely to contain a divine name with that root, as they also contain the name of a known deity (e.g., Ktrmlk, Špšmlk, dIM-ma-lak). As Gröndahl notes, the names written in alphabetic cuneiform pose an additional problem: one cannot always tell whether a given instance of mlk is a verb form,

---

recently, however, he recognizes that "it is preferable to see it as related to the divine name Rapi'u" ("MLKM/RP'UM," 91).

[262] There is one Ugaritic text which suggests such a "democratized" view of the Rpum, the "Hymn to Šapaš" in CTA 6.6 (especially 1. 45). Healey ("Death, Underworld and Afterlife," 196) would date the hymn as a late addition to the Baal epic on form-critical grounds.

[263] Frauke Gröndahl, Die Personennamen der Texte aus Ugarit (Studia Pohl 1; Rome: Pontifical Biblical Institute, 1967).

the common noun or epithet ("king"), or the divine name.[264] On the other hand, just as at Ebla and Mari, the occurrence of forms of mlk with non-theophoric elements which elsewhere appear with known god names provides additional proof (if any is needed) that there was indeed a god Mlk at Ugarit (e.g., Abmlk/Abrpu, Nûrī[NE]-^{d}ma-lik/Nûrī-^{d}rašap).

As Appendix C shows, quite a few of the names are found in both Ugaritic and Akkadian forms. Unfortunately, there is no indication from the context in which the names occur that any single person's name appears spelled both ways.[265] Also, most of the names occur in judicial and economic texts, but in only a few cases is there any clear indication that the individual is not a native of Ugarit (e.g., ^{I}Ilu-milku mâr uz-zi-na amîl ^{al}la-ib-ni-ma).

Nevertheless, the names in syllabic cuneiform may be helpful in suggesting how the Ugaritians pronounced the name of their god Mlk. At first glance, Appendix C seems to settle the issue overwhelmingly in favor of the vocalization Milku (which would be no surprize, if our suggestion in 2.2 is correct, that the /i/ vowel in stem position is characteristic of the Phoenician area). However, a closer look reveals that the vast majority of the cases read simply LUGAL in the original; thus, Milku is a scholarly surmise, however much it may have been sanctified by the customary modern vocalization of Ilmlk as "Ilimilku."[266] Of the

---

[264] Ibid., 157.

[265] The best candidate is Ilu-milku the scribe, who appears in two judicial documents in Ug5, and whose name is identical in its consonants with the famous scribe (Ilmlk) of the Baal-'Anat and Keret texts. Nougayrol (Ug5, p. 13) insists, however, that we are not presently justified in identifying them.

[266] One can argue, on the basis of the evidence from the El Amarna tablets (below) and from Phoenicia, that milku is the correct reading

names in which the mlk element is spelled out syllable-by-syllable, three have the stem vowel /i/ (milki/a), two, including the only one with the divine determinative, have /a/ (malik), while one has /u/ (mulik). Some additional evidence may be offered by Ug5 1.18:32, the pantheon list which reads ^{d}MA.LIK^{meš} where the parallel in Ugaritic, CTA 29:(rev.):11, has mlkm. As we have seen, however secondary this equation may have been in a religio-historical sense, the author of the Akkadian text clearly had in mind the plural form of a deity named Malik.[267]

In sum, it is apparent that at Ugarit, just as at Mari, the original pronunciation Malik coexisted with the declined form Milku/i/a. If so, it is likely that the names written in alphabetic cuneiform were also pronounced in various ways, depending either on laws of phonetic conditioning or syntax within the names, or, as seems more promising, on ethnic divisions within cosmopolitan Ugarit. With relatively few personal names from Ugarit (in comparison with Mari), it is difficult to go beyond the possible solutions suggested in 2.2. In any event, the Ugaritic evidence is not fatal to either of them.

Just as we found it convenient to incorporate in the discussion of the Eblaite personal names those few from Tell Abu Ṣalabikh, so this is the most fitting place to include the names from the tablets discovered at Tell El Amarna. The tablets are contemporary with the evidence from

---

of LUGAL because it was the Ugaritic word for "king." See, however, the lexical list in Ug5 (137.2:32), which reads LUGAL (Sumerian logogram):šarru (Akkadian):ma-al-ku (Ugaritic).

[267] One may object, of course, that the author of the text had in mind a deity from the East who was equivalent to the god Mlk (however pronounced) at Ugarit. But this is hardly certain.

Ugarit, and many originated in nearby Byblos. Knudtzon's authoritative edition of the tablets includes but a few mlk-names: ^{I}abdi-milki(LUGAL); ^{I}abi-milki/mil-ki; ^{I}ili/i-li-milku(LUGAL); and ^{I}milkili (various spellings).[268] A comparison of this short list with the names already discussed shows that Milku/i was a divine name in the El Amarna correspondence, and that the vocalization with /i/ was uniform there. In anticipation of the examination of the Phoenician evidence, we may call particular attention to ^{I}abi-milki as the "Fürst von Tyrus (1245)."[269]

One peculiar form remains at Ugarit: mu-lik. Gröndahl suggests that it should be normalized mūlik and taken as a rare example of the Canaanite vowel shift (from mālik) at Ugarit.[270] Naturally, the validity of the hypothesis depends directly on the length of the /a/ in Malik. As stated above (2.2.2), we shall take up this latter issue after having examined the Mesopotamian evidence. The significance of Gröndahl's suggestion can hardly be overstated, however: mūlik is the closest we have yet come to the OT mōlek (to which, indeed, it corresponds). If it can be shown that the Biblical form resulted from the ancient Syro-Palestinian divine name Malik, via the Canaanite vowel shift, then the connection of the OT Molek with the evidence concerning Malik, as treat-

---

[268] J. A. Knudtzon, Die El-Amarna Tafeln (2 vols.; Leipzig: J. C. Hinrichs, 1910-1915).

[269] Also worthy of note is the occurrence of ma-lik(meš) in EA text 131:21 as a gloss to (amêlût)rabiṣi = "Vorstehern" (so Knudtzon, Die El-Amarna Tafeln, 1.557) or "königlicher Kommissär" (AHW 2:935). However, it is unlikely to be related to the Ugaritic form examined above, which bears the divine determinative and is, we have argued, derived from the West Semitic sense of mlk, "king."

[270] Die Personennamen, 18.

ed in the present chapter, will be firmly established. While we shall
argue that the relevance of this chapter to the study of Molek does not
stand or fall with the length of Malik's /a/, it surely would stand
firmly with Mālik.

2.3.6 Mlk in the Ugaritic Pantheon

What, then, can we say about the Ugaritic god Mlk? The two texts which
include the name with assurance supply only his address: Ashtaroth.
Careful attention to other texts, however, fleshes out this meager information. The likelihood of a close association (if not identity) with
Rpu mlk ʿlm (and of the Mlkm with the Rpum) adds a decidedly chthonic
coloring to the portrait. Can we go further in integrating Mlk with the
known Ugaritic pantheon? Two proposals deserve our close attention.
Both work from Mlk's chthonic character to suggest a link with another,
better-known Ugaritic god of like nature.

The first proposal is that of Alan Cooper, who suggests the identity of Rpu mlk ʿlm and Ršp (conventionally, Resheph) in his article in
the Pope festschrift ("MLK ʿLM"). Cooper observes that the Ugaritic Rpu
and Resheph (in Egyptian and Akkadian) share both characteristics and
titles. As to characteristics, both are associated with healing, with
the netherworld and "as mighty patron[s] of the king." As to titles,
Resheph (and Osiris) are called in Egyptian ḥq3 d.t and nb nḥḥ ("Lord of
Eternity"), while Nergal (Resheph's presumed Mesopotamian equivalent;
see immediately below) bears the title šar erṣeti ("King of the Earth
[i.e., the Netherworld]"). Both Egyptian and Akkadian titles are, in
Cooper's view, "the nearest thing to an . . . equivalent" of Ugaritic

mlk 'lm. Indeed, he concludes: "We may now speak of Rpu mlk 'lm as a title of Resheph/Nergal: 'The Healer, Eternal King of the Nether-world'."

The advantages of this proposal are many. Linking Rpu (and there-by, we argue, Mlk) to the well-known Semitic god of pestilence would provide an explanation for the relative paucity of references to Rpu and Mlk in any of the Semitic literatures and would allow considerable fleshing-out of our understanding of the god under study.[271] Further-more, the equation of Resheph with Nergal in the pantheon lists dis-cussed above (CTA 29:[rev.]:5 = Ug5 1.18:26) would merge neatly with an Old Babylonian god list (2.4.3), in which Malik is equated with Nergal. Indeed, the equation Mlk = Rpu = Resheph = Nergal would confirm our chthonic understanding of the Ugaritic references to Mlk and Rpu and would, in addition, sustain the link with fertility noted above with reference to the Rpum since such overtones are clearly present in the cults of Resheph and Nergal.[272]

There are, however, some obstacles in the way of such a break-through in our study. First, as Pope has observed, Ršp occurs in both Ug5 7 and 8 alongside of Mlk, but at a different address, viz., bbt.[273]

---

[271] It should be noted that Cooper explicitly rejects the equation of Rpu and Mlk. What follows, therefore, is a discussion of his propo-sal per se only insofar as it treats the merits of Rpu = Resheph/Nergal.

[272] One might also call attention to the occurrence of Ršp.mlk in Ug5 12.2:7 (RS 24.249) (along with 'ttrt šd), and of the same name, probably used by a person, in PRU2 106:58 (RS 15.115). Mlk is like-ly the title "king" in these cases, however.

[273] "Cult of the Dead," 172-173. On bbt see Dennis Pardee, "A Philolo-gical and Prosodic Analysis of the Ugaritic Serpent Incantation UT 607," JANESCU 10 (1978) 108. The marginal note in Ug5 7 (atr ršp.'ttrt . . .), it seems to me, in no way links Ršp with the

Secondly, the mere fact that a god is of a chthonic character and even of the highest rank in the underworld does not necessarily imply its identity with all gods of that description. This caution, which tempered our certainty in equating Mlk and Rpu above, applies all the more fully to an ostensible further equation of Mlk or Rpu with Resheph and Nergal. In addition, the equivalence established between the latter two gods on the basis of the pantheon lists cannot be considered absolute:

> However, considering the character of the Akkadian list [Ug5 1.18], which, whatever about the Ugaritic [CTA 29] is certainly a secondary and speculative attempt to find Mesopotamian equivalences for the Ugaritic, it should not be concluded that there is an historical genetic connection. . . .[274]

Healey cites in particular Ršp/Nergal as a clear instance of this "secondary and speculative attempt." Secondly, one must bear in mind that Nergal himself became lord of the Mesopotamian underworld only by becoming the consort of the infernal queen, Ereshkigal (so the myth of Nergal and Ereshkigal [ANET 103-104,507-512]). We know of no such development in the character of Resheph. We shall have to pay further attention to Nergal below, as we consider the Akkadian evidence. For now, these several difficulties should temper our enthusiasm for the apparent advantages of the four-part equation above.

---

place (or goddess) 'ttrt. Rather, the entire note is a scribal memorandum, that the stanza concerning 'ttrt at mr was omitted and should be inserted "after" (atr) that concerning Ršp (so already Astour, "Two Charms," 22).

[274] John F. Healey, "MLKM/RP'UM," 89. For further discussion of the problems in equating Resheph and Nergal, see Michael Astour, "The Nether World and its Denizens at Ugarit," *Death in Mesopotamia* (RAI 26; Mesopotamia 8; ed. B. Alster; Copenhagen: Akademisk, 1980) 231-232. For a more sanguine view, see William J. Fulco, *The Canaanite God Rešep* (New Haven: American Oriental Society, 1976) 37, and the literature cited there.

The second proposal for integrating Mlk with the better-known
Ugaritic pantheon is that mentioned above (1.10) as Pope's suggestion
that Mlk might be identified with the Ugaritic god of death, Mot.[275]
While Pope himself has not explicated this position in print, one can
see why such an idea might arise. Mot in the Ugaritic corpus of myths
is the chthonic deity par excellence, Death personified. But outside of
the myths, Mot is scarcely to be found (only in CTA 23 and in the liver
omen RS 24.277:29, outside of the Baal-'Anat cycle). Mot's absence is
especially remarkable in the pantheon lists and the texts having to do
with cult and ritual. It is possible, of course, that so fearsome a god
was not part of the cult (although other chthonic deities are listed and
mentioned).[276] It is also possible that Death was conceived of as a god
only in myth, as the countervailing force to Life represented by Baal,
although Baal was certainly not so restricted.[277] It is therefore tempting to search for Mot under the guise of other chthonic deities, such as
Mlk and Rpu. The former name would fit well the god who was Ugarit's
King of the Underworld;[278] the latter would commend itself as befitting

---

[275] Two other scholars propose the identification of the Biblical Molek
with Mot and draw on Ugaritic evidence: Manfred R. Lehmann ("A New
Interpretation of the Term šdmwt," VT 3 [1953] 361-371); and Martin
Jan Mulder (Kanaänitische Goden in het OT [Exegetica: Oud- en
Nieuw-Testamentische Studiën 4-5; The Hague: Voorheen Van Keulen,
1965] 57-64,70). Since both argue primarily with and concerning the
Biblical evidence, their views will be considered in chapter IV.

[276] J. C. de Moor ("The Semitic Pantheon of Ugarit," UF 2 [1970] 222)
suggests: "Probably [the Nether World gods] formed a separate group
of Nether World deities who were dreaded, sometimes invoked for magical purposes, but never worshipped in the cult."

[277] André Caquot ("Nouveaux documents ougaritiens," Syria 46 [1969] 261)
claims: "cette divinité [Mot] est une pure personnification drama-
tique de la mort et . . . elle ne recevait aucun culte à Ugarit."

[278] To be sure, Mot is never called "king" as such, but we do hear of

the ruler of the royal shades.

Two cautions need to be raised, however. First, we must acknowl-edge that if Ugaritic evidence on Mlk is scarce, the evidence on Mot is so concentrated as to present its own difficulties in comparisons even within the Ugaritic corpus. More importantly, if one holds that Mlk is to be identified with Rpu as the head of the Rpum, problems quickly arise in attempting to recognize any fertility dimension in Mot, while such a side to the Rpum (and, one assumes, to their head) seems assured by such texts as RS 34.126 (discussed above). Paul Watson has demon-strated that the text commonly held to show just such a fertility aspect in Mot, i.e., the description of Mot's annihilation by 'Anat (CTA 6.2:30-35), cannot support such an interpretation.[279] A second text, CTA 4.7:50, might be adduced in favor of a fertility dimension in Mot, if lymru were understood as related to mr' II (fatling), rather than mr' I (to command): "[I am he who] fattens gods and men," rather than "rules." But the likely parallelism with dymlk makes the latter trans-lation preferable.[280] This does not mean that Mot lacked any powers of fertility, only that this cannot be shown from the texts we now possess.

---

his "kingship" (CTA 6.6:28) and of his "throne" (CTA 4.8:12; 5.2:15; 6.6:28). (References are from Mulder, *Kanaänitische Goden*, 70.)

[279] "Mot, the God of Death, at Ugarit and in the Old Testament" (unpub-lished Ph.D. dissertation, Yale University, 1970) 172-187. This point is summarized in Watson's article, "The death of Death in the Ugaritic Texts," *JAOS* 92 (1972) 60-64. Watson's dissertation also shows the difficulties inherent in attempting to equate Mot with Resheph (he does not deal either with Rpu or Mlk).

[280] Even if one takes lymru with the following dyšb['], it is possible that the latter verb is being used ironically: "who satisfies the crowds of earth" could well refer to the action of Mot vis-à-vis the shades (since, as a concordance study shows, all occurrences of hmlt arṣ may be read as referring to the dead).

2.3.7   Molk-<u>sacrifices</u> at Ugarit?

A full treatment of the relevant occurrences of <u>Mlk</u> in the Ugaritic texts would not be complete without at least brief mention of certain other texts which at an earlier stage of scholarship were alleged to contribute to our question. One of these was <u>CTA</u> 35:50, used by Dussaud already in 1936 to show the existence of <u>molk</u>-sacrifices at Ugarit (see section 1.6 for fuller discussion). For a time this interpretation was widely accepted, but it has steadily lost adherents since the development of accepted philological and form-critical controls for Ugaritic beginning roughly in the mid-1950s.[281]

In 1955, at the very time when the interpretation of Ugartic <u>mlk</u> references as <u>molk</u>-sacrifices was most popular among scholars, another text was discovered which seemed to reinforce this interpretation. Both in his initial reports and in the <u>editio princeps</u>, Charles Virolleaud was so bold as to entitle <u>PRU5</u> 4 (RS 19.15): "Texte liturgique concernant le sacrifice <u>mlk</u>."[282] This interpretation met with the enthusiastic approval of Otto Eissfeldt.[283] Unfortunately for such an interpretation,

---

[281] Dussaud's interpretation was accepted without discussion by Andrée Herdner ("Un nouvel exemplaire du Rituel," <u>Syria</u> 33 [1956] 112) and Cyrus Gordon (<u>Ugaritic Handbook</u> [AnOr 25; Rome: Pontifical Biblical Institute, 1947] 246; and <u>Ugaritic Manual</u> [AnOr 35; Rome: Pontifical Biblical Institute, 1955] 289). Gordon effectively recanted his support, however, by 1965, when he removed all references to <u>molk</u>-sacrifices from the glossary of his <u>Ugaritic Textbook</u> (AnOr 38; Rome: Pontifical Biblical Institute, 1965) 433-434. (The same development obtained for alleged references to <u>molk</u>-sacrifices in <u>CTA</u> 36:10 and 138:[rev.]:4.)

[282] The initial publication of the text was in "Les nouvelles tablettes alphabétiques de Ras Shamra (XIXe Campagne, 1955)," <u>CRAIBL</u> (1956) 61-62.

[283] <u>Neue keilalphabetische Texte aus Ras Schamra-Ugarit</u> (Sitzungsberichte der deutschen Akademie der Wissenschaften zu Berlin 6; Berlin: Akademie, 1965) 15.

however, two objections have been raised, one debatable, but the other
fatal for the Virolleaud/Eissfeldt reading. Paolo Xella has argued that
the text is not liturgical or religious (as held by most scholars), but
administrative or economic, dealing with consignments of wine used in
royal sacrificial ceremonies.[284] Xella observes elsewhere that with the
disqualification of this text, "the hypothesis of a connection with
molk-sacrifices attested in the Punic world and perhaps, as recently
proposed, also in the Phoenician motherland, seems now desititute of
foundation. . . ."[285] What is worse for the Virolleaud/Eissfeldt reading, however, is that the context of the mlk reference has been ignored:
dbḥ mlk in line 2 is followed immediately by dbḥ ṣpn in line 3; if anything, this would point to the use of mlk as a divine entity.[286]

---

[284] "KTU 1.91 (RS 19.15) e i sacrifici del re," UF 11 (1979) 833.

[285] I testi rituali, 336. (Xella's original: "le ipotesi sulla connes-
sione col sacrificio-molk attestato nel mondo punico e forse, come
proposto di recente, anche nella madrepatria fenicia, paiono ormai
destituto di fondamento. . . .") The alleged evidence for molk-
sacrifices "also in the Phoenician motherland" is discussed below in
2.6.3.

[286] As Dhorme suggested (see discussion in 1.7). Considerations such as
those raised by Xella, however, make the occurrence of the divine
name Mlk here unlikely. The possibility of a "divinized sacrifice,"
discussed above with regard to CTA 29, would seem an act of despera-
tion in this case, without support elsewhere in the text. The rendering "royal sacrifice" or "sacrifice by the king" appears to be
the most prudent. See, however, Loren R. Fisher ("A New Ritual Calendar from Ugarit," HTR 63 [1970] 492) for the suggestion that the
king here is Baal.

2.3.8   Evidence of Cultic Child Sacrifice at Ugarit

So far we have concentrated almost exclusively on the existence and nature of a possible Ugaritic counterpart to Molek. The other issue to be
pursued at each step of our comparative examination is that of the cultic sacrifice of children, even as such sacrifices are the most distinctive feature of the Biblical cult of Molek. This concern has not been
lost on previous scholars of Ugaritic. In addition to those who thought
they had found literary indications of Punic-style molk-sacrifices, some
scholars have alleged that there are explicit references to child sacrifice in the cult. Although no such proposal has proved convincing to a
substantial number of scholars, the texts involved need to be presented,
along with the suggested interpretations and their shortcomings. Unfortunately, from the viewpoint of this study, no such text provides a link
to the god Mlk.

One of the scholars who has been most interested in literary indications of cultic child sacrifice at Ugarit has been Andrée Herdner.
Besides her attempts to interpret several occurrences of mlk as molk-
sacrifices (discussed above), she proposed to find in Ug7 (RS) 24.266:14
a reference to the sacrifice of a firstborn son in time of danger.[287]
The word in question occurs in a series of offerings promised to Baal:
[b]kr b['ñ]l.nšqdš, which Herdner rendered, "[Un pre]mier-né(?), Ba['a]l,
nous (te) con[sa]crerons."[288] Herdner argued that the restoration [b]kr
(firstborn) was to be preferred to [d]kr (male [animal], Hebrew zkr),

---

[287] Herdner's initial proposal was in "Une prière à Baal des Ugaritains
en danger," CRAIBL (1972) 693-703, which contained a preliminary
publication of the text.

[288] Herdner revised her translation in Ug7, p. 36, to "[des
pre]miers-nés(?) . . ." without explanation.

because otherwise Ugaritic evidences only dkr (and that only in personal names) so far. Given the restoration [b]kr, she held for the understanding "human firstborn" since any other kind would, in her view, have been specified. Finally, she observes that such sacrifices may not have been carried out, but rather, as in Israel (Exod 34:20), the firstborn may have been redeemed.[289]

The response to Herdner's proposal, as found in two short articles at the end of her 1972 presentation, did not advance the debate substantially. Claude Schaeffer maintained the position of his article in Ugaritica IV, that there was no evidence, literary or archeological, for any kind of child sacrifice at Ugarit.[290] André Dupont-Sommer, on the other hand, enthusiastically supported Herdner's reading on the basis of the Punic and Biblical cults and observed that archeology had not yet located the tophet at Jerusalem, although its existence was not in doubt. Herdner's interpretation was also accepted by Caquot and Sznycer in their semi-popular booklet.[291]

Paolo Xella, on the other hand, mounted a concerted attack on Herdner's position on the basis of the text itself.[292] He argued for the reading [d]kr as better fitting the parallel member of the prayer (11. 12-13), which contains ibr (bull). In fact, whether one prefers to read

---

[289] "Une prière," 697.

[290] "Sacrifice à M-l-k, Molech ou Melek," Ug4, pp. 77-83. In his Ug4 article Schaeffer is particularly concerned to refute the Virolleaud/Eissfeldt reading of PRU5 4 (discussed above) as referring to molk-sacrifices.

[291] Ugaritic Religion, 18.

[292] "Un Testo Ugaritico Recente (RS 24.266, Verso, 9-19) e il 'Sacrifico dei Primo Nati'," RSF 6 (1978) 127-136.

bkr or dkr, one must concede that the reading "human firstborn" or "human male" is by no means demanded either philologically or by the context. Indeed, it is ironic that Herdner asserts that npš in Ug5 12.1:11 (RS 24.249) "doit désigner un animal," when Astour had suggested that "one strongly suspects a human sacrifice" here.[293] By her own logic, one might have expected the argument that had an animal life (npš) been intended, the type of animal would have been specified.

Nevertheless, it must be emphasized that the existence of cultic child sacrifice at Ugarit has not yet been proved and that the cultural context does favor the likelihood of such a cult, at least under certain circumstances. Thus, while A. Spalinger certainly made too much of the Ugaritic evidence as presented by Herdner, he has succeeded in showing that Egyptian temple reliefs from the New Kingdom depict children in Syro-Palestinian cities under Egyptian attack being sacrificed.[294] Further evidence of cultic child sacrifice in the Semitic world will be presented and discussed in chapters III (archeological evidence) and IV (Biblical evidence).

What is beyond dispute insofar as Ugarit is concerned is the existence of an active cult of the dead ancestors. Indeed, the discovery which led to the excavations at Ras Shamra was of a Mycenean-age tomb, complete with drainpipe (knkn) from the surface for the pouring of liba-

---

[293] Herdner, Ug7, p. 7; Astour, "The Nether World and its Denizens," 235.

[294] "A Canaanite Ritual found in Egyptian Reliefs," *Journal of the Society for the Study of Egyptian Antiquities* 8 (1978) 47-60. For his part, Spalinger admits the seminal value of Ph. Derchain, "Les plus anciens témoignages de sacrifices d'enfants chez les Semites occidentaux," *VT* 20 (1970) 351-355. See also O. Keel, "Kanaanäische Sühneriten auf ägyptischen Tempelreliefs," *VT* 25 (1975) 413-469, for many additional examples.

tions.[295] Literary evidence of such a cult is provided by RS 34.126 (discussed above) and a passage in the Aqht epic, repeated four times, in which the father, Danel, lists the duties of a faithful son toward his father (CTA 17.1:27-34,45-48; 2:1-8,13-23), including some clearly posthumous tasks. It comes as no surprise that the Aqht epic is closely related to the "Rephaim texts," if we accept the position presented above, that the Rpum were the deified dead ancestors, who were the objects of the cultic devotion (RS 34.126). If we further accept the identity, or at least the close connection, of Mlk and Rpu (and the involvement of the Mlkm and Rpum), the importance of such a cult for our study becomes obvious. To be sure, the role of the cult of the dead in the Biblical cult of Molek remains to be demonstrated, but the Ugaritic evidence provides a most suggestive lead in that direction.

2.3.9   Summary of Evidence from Ugarit, Ebla and Mari

In sum, it must be stated that the Ugaritic evidence provides far more by way of such suggestive hints than conclusive demonstration. That is to be expected from a corpus and, indeed, a civilization which still present so many unsolved issues to those who seek to be their interpreters. What is clear is that the Ugaritic evidence on the existence and nature of a god Mlk and of his cult is integral to any complete study of the Biblical Molek and the practices connected with that term. This is especially the case, given the close relationship between Ugarit and Israel both linguistically and culturally, a relationship which has at nu-

---

[295] Further details may be found in C. F. A. Schaeffer, *The Cuneiform Texts of Ras Shamra-Ugarit* (Schweich Lectures, 1936; London: British Academy, 1939) 51-53 and plate 38, fig. 1.

merous points proved closer than that of Israel to any other ancient Near Eastern civilization.[296]

As we leave the environs of Canaan just as the Israelite tribes were coalescing into Biblical Israel, we note that the god Malik was well-established in the popular cult of Syria-Palestine and had been for well over a millennium. Without claiming that even within this region Malik was always, everywhere and by all conceived of in the same way, we have noted the strong indications that the god was seen as a chthonic deity. Yet, with the exception of the Ugaritic Rpu, we have also observed that the attempts to identify Malik with another netherworld deity or deities are all flawed, though not necessarily fatally. This is to be expected; as Mitchell Dahood put it: "The character and functions of the [Canaanite] gods are subject to such fluctuations that to determine their nature and qualities, or to fix their relations with one another is often impossible."[297]

Just as valuable as the evidence we have examined on Malik himself has been that from Mari and Ugarit concerning the plural entities, malikū and Mlkm, respectively. Their chief contribution has been to estab-

---

[296] Conversely, Patrick D. Miller, Jr. ("Ugaritic and the History of Religions," JNSL 9 [1981] 126) summarizes Baruch Levine's observations on the specifically cultic resemblances between the two (from Prolegomenon to Sacrifice in the Old Testament by G. B. Gray [reprint; NY: Ktav, 1971] xxxiv-xxxv): "B. Levine has observed that the presence of šalamîm in conjunction with 'burnt offerings' places Ugaritic practice clearly in the sphere of Northwest Semitic ritual and close to Israelite practices rather than in association with the practices of other parts of the Near East. . . . Levine even suggests that Ugaritic sacrificial practice at this point may be closer to Israelite than pre-Israelite Canaanite practices."

[297] "Ancient Semitic Deities in Syria and Palestine," Le antiche Divinità semitiche (ed. S. Moscati; Rome: Centro di Studi semitichi, 1958) 72.

lish a clear link with the royal cult of the dead, whether as minor underworld deities or as shades themselves. The twin features of fertility and death, we have argued, are thus to be found in their nature. Their connection, if not identity, with the Ugaritic Rpum will obviously be of much importance as we consider the relevance of the Biblical Rephaim to our study in chapter IV.

With the exception of Spalinger's study ("A Canaanite Ritual"), we have not yet found concrete literary or inscriptional evidence of cultic child sacrifice in Syria-Palestine. As one might have expected from chapter I, the clearest such evidence will be that from the Punic colonies (2.7). First, however, we turn eastward and return to the third millennium, to see what evidence pertinent to the study of Molek and the Molek cult may be found in Mesopotamia.

2.4   THE AKKADIAN EVIDENCE

The evidence from Mesopotamia extends over a greater span of time than that from any other Semitic area, from the Early Dynastic period, through the systemization of the Mesopotamian tradition in Standard Babylonian, to the Late Babylonian admixture of Mesopotamian, Persian and Aramaic elements. As has previously been the case in our study, the oldest evidence is that of the personal names. Such evidence is quickly supplanted in importance, however, by other material which will further develop the portrait which the early Syro-Palestinian evidence has provided of the god Malik.

2.4.1   The Early Dynastic Names

The personal and divine names from the time of Old Akkadian have been collected by I. J. Gelb and J. J. M. Roberts.[298] Only one name comes from the Pre-Sargonic period, Il-su-ma-lik, found at Ur.[299] Roberts doubts that the ma-lik element is a divine name, on the grounds that most of the names in his study have the divine name in initial position.[300] The Eblaite names listed in Appendix A and, indeed, the presence of this very name at Abu Ṣalabikh (2.1.1) make this objection of little force. Roberts is unquestionably correct, however, in observing that the occurrence of the divine name Malik in Pre-Sargonic Mesopotamia is exceedingly rare. While the context of the personal name above does not permit us to say whether the bearer was a native of Ur, by itself the name cannot counter our earlier observation that the many Malik names at Ebla suggest a Syro-Palestinian origin for Malik.

The Mesopotamian material becomes far richer in Sargonic times. Gelb and Roberts agree on seven names, all of which have the divine determinative before Malik: I-gu-^{d}ma-lik; Ìr-am-^{d}ma-lik; Ìr-e-^{d}ma-lik; ^{d}Ma-lik-zi-in-su; Puzur-^{d}ma-lik; Šum-$^{(d)}$ma-lik; and U-zé-^{d}ma-lik. A comparison with Appendix A shows two identical names (except for the determinative), I-ku-ma-lik and Puzur$_4$-ma-lik, and three close variants, Rí/Ré-ì-ma-lik, Šu-ma-lik and I-zi-ma-lik (or Ṣi/Zé-ma-lik). This con-

---

[298] Gelb, Glossary of Old Akkadian (Materials for the Assyrian Dictionary 3; Chicago: University of Chicago, 1957), especially pp. 176-177; Roberts, The Earliest Semitic Pantheon: A Study of the Semitic Deities Attested in Mesopotamia before Ur III (Baltimore: Johns Hopkins, 1972), especially pp. 42-43.

[299] Gelb, Glossary, 177.

[300] Earliest Semitic Pantheon, 105.

firms our understanding of the Ebla names as containing Malik as a divine name and is in line with the suggestion (though it is hardly proof) that Malik was a borrowed deity in Mesopotamia (since it was apparently not customary or necessary at Ebla to mark the name Malik as divine).

Finally, in the Ur III period the divine name itself is attested. In two articles, in 1937 and 1938, Nikolaus Schneider presented four texts (of which three had previously been published elsewhere), each a list of animal offerings, which Schneider judged to be from Drehem in the Ur III period.[301] The texts are in Sumerian, except for an offering in each to $^{(d)}$Ma-al-ku-um/kum-ŠÈ (the divine determinative occurs in one case). In addition, a similar text from Ur mentions Ma-al-ku-um-ŠÈ.[302]

Schneider was doubtlessly right that the syllabic spelling of the name shows that this is no Sumerian deity.[303] Far less certain is his assumption that the texts he presented concerned an Ur III equivalent to Milkom, the Biblical god of the Ammonites (2.5.2). But his observations concerning the stem vowel in the god's name are provocative. First, Schneider suggested that, on the analogy of the variation Ištar, Eštar, Aštar, one can identify Milkom, Melkom and Malkum. Secondly, Schneider proposed that the Akkadian form Malku (or Malik) can be explained as equivalent to the original Molek since Akkadian does not employ an /o/ vowel.[304] Neither argument is particularly convincing, but in one re-

---

[301] "Melchom, das Scheusal der Ammoniter," <u>Bib</u> 18 (1937) 337-343; and "Melchom," <u>Bib</u> 19 (1938) 204.

[302] Gelb, <u>Glossary</u>, 176.

[303] <u>Götternamen von Ur III</u> (AnOr 19; Rome: Pontifical Biblical Institute, 1939) 118.

spect Schneider may have been on the right track, nevertheless. The evidence already examined and, we shall argue, that yet to be presented in this section suggest that the various Akkadian spellings (especially Malik vs. Malku[m]) are attempts to reproduce an originally West Semitic divine name. We should note immediately, however, that the elision of the /i/ for reasons internal to the divine name (i.e., a short /a/) may not be evidenced in the Early Dynastic Mesopotamian material: in all of the cases above, the /i/ may have elided because of the addition of the suffix, -ŠĚ.

We have already observed the great difficulties inherent in attempts to describe the nature of a god on the basis of the use of the divine name in personal names. J. J. M. Roberts agrees that the task is difficult (calling such evidence "rather meager and obviously stereotyped"), but he believes that it may be possible to say something about the origins of Malik:

> The name [Malik] is normally written with the determinative, but this is probably just a device to distinguish the divine name from the same word used as an epithet. Most likely the divine name itself was originally an epithet that split off and became an independent divine name. It is impossible to prove conclusively, but there are indications that the epithet was originally attached to the god Dagan. The two deities appear in several Old Semitic names of the same formation, both have clear and closely related underworld connections, and in the Ur III and Old Babylonian periods mal(i)kum occurs in the plural to designate what appear to be underworld deities.[305]

---

[304] In a later article Schneider reversed the direction of the change, but continued to insist that Malik/Molek was the result of vocalic change, rather than of Masoretic dysphemism ("Patriarchennamen in zeitgenössischen Keilschrifturkunden," Bib 33 [1952] 518).

[305] Earliest Semitic Pantheon, 43.

Roberts's idea that Malik was originally an epithet of another god is likely enough on its face (other examples might be El and Baal), although it is beyond proof (since our oldest evidence, from Ebla, shows Malik as an independent deity). But his proposal that it was Dagan to whom the epithet was originally attached is even more uncertain than Roberts indicates. As we have seen, several gods' names appear in personal name formations identical to those in which Malik appears, and there is no lack of chthonic deities to be interrelated. We shall deal with the evidence of the mal(i)kū immediately below (since, pace Roberts, no attestation appears to exist before the Old Babylonian period). However, the most significant evidence in favor of an identification with Dagan is that already presented from Mari (and used by Talon to suggest a Dagan-Malik identification there). In other words, outside of Old Babylonian Mari, the case for the identification is quite weak.

2.4.2   Old Babylonian Omen Apodoses: the Mal(i)kū

Both CAD and AHW give a representative sampling of the Old Babylonian omen texts which contain references to the mal(i)kū.[306] The texts are all oil omens, and the term in question occurs always in the apodosis. As was the case with the malikū of Mari, the word usually appears in the plural, but there are a few instances with the mimation-ending, presumably singular. Furthermore, there is greater variety in how the term is spelled (vis-à-vis Mari): the /i/ frequently does not appear, as in ma-al-ku; and in at least one case the final consonant of the root appears as /ḫ/ instead of /k/.[307]

---

[306] CAD 10/1:168; AHW 2:596.

The context of the omens shows clearly that the mal(i)kū of Mesopotamia were chthonic in character and negative in nature. They regularly appear in the company of an eṭemmum (ghost) or of kūbu (a type of demon, or an aborted fetus). What has not yet been sufficiently stressed is the place of the mal(i)kū in series of omens, such as those in CT 3.3 and 5.4: the mal(i)kū appear as the climax of a series of bad apodoses.[308] Thus, in 5.4:9, the appearance of six "drops" (tu-tu-ru) means the ma-an-za-az ma-al-ki ("presence [lit., station] of the malkū" [CAD 10/1:238]). In 1. 14 another series climaxes in the apodosis ma-an-za-az ku-bi a-na ma-al-ki-im, while 1. 55 ends a series with the same apodosis as 1. 9.[309] The other text, CT 3.3:41, provides a different pairing, again, at the close of a series: qá-ti ma-al-ki ù e-ṭe₄-em-mi-im ("the hand of the malkū or of a ghost"). The position of the mal(i)kū in these omens would suggest that they were either quite important or of very minor importance relative to the other beings and disasters which might be present in a negative omen. While the judgment of such trends in series of omens is especially vulnerable to cultural bias on the part of the modern reader, our tentative conclusion is that the apodoses decrease in severity. Thus, in CT 5.4:6-9 three "drops" mean that Šamaš

---

[307] See W. von Soden, Grundriss der Akkadischen Grammatik [AnOr 33; Rome: Pontifical Biblical Institute, 1952] 26, for other OB examples of the interchange of these two consonants. It is unlikely that the use of /ḫ/ in the OB examples under study reflects a spirantized pronunciation of the /k/, as was later the case when Akkadian came under Aramaic influence (see 2.4.4).

[308] The texts are numbers II and I (respectively) in vol. 2 of Giovanni Pettinato, Die Ölwahrsagung bei den Babyloniern (2 vols.; Studi semitici 21-22; Rome: Istituto di Studi del vincino Oriente, 1966).

[309] Pettinato (Ölwahrsagung, 2.15) reads ma-ka-li-im in 1. 14 on the basis of another "manuscript."

will demand a "solar disk" emblem (šamšum)[310] in exchange for the life
of the man (so that his very life is apparently directly at stake),
while four mean that he will be held accountable for an offense against
the sun god, and five, for an offense against the moon god. If this
judgment is correct, the mal(i)kū would be, like the malikū of Mari,
lesser netherworld beings. That they were, nevertheless, to be feared
is shown by another (liver) omen apodosis: ma-al-ku a-wi-lam ṣa-ab-tu
("the malkū have seized the man").[311] Their relationship to Malik is uncertain, but a god list from the same period as the omens shows that
they had the same address as he (see immediately below). We turn now to
the Old Babylonian evidence concerning Malik.

2.4.3 Malik in OB-MB and OA-MA God Lists and Names

Our richest Mesopotamian evidence concerning Malik per se is from the
later period of Standard Babylonian (ca. 1000-500 B.C.), in both literary texts and lists. However, much of the material we shall examine in
the category of Standard Babylonian reflects the situation of a considerably earlier period. The best example of this fact is a fragment from
an Old Babylonian god list, which W. G. Lambert identifies as a portion
of the great Weidner list.[312] Of greatest interest to us is the equation

---

[310] See Pettinato, Ölwahrsagung, 1.208-210, for further discussion.

[311] J. Nougayrol, "Textes hépatoscopiques d'époque ancienne conservés au
Musée du Louvre (III)," RA 44 (1950) 32.

[312] "Götterlisten," RLA 3 (1971) 474. The fragment is in Stephen Langdon, ed., The H. Weld-Blundell Collection in the Ashmolean Museum:
1. Sumerian and Semitic Religious and Historical Texts (OECT 1; Oxford: Oxford University, 1923) text 9. For the "Weidner list," see
Ernst F. Weidner, "Altbabylonische Götterlisten," Archiv für Keilschriftforschung (= AfO) 2 (1924) 1-18. Weidner combined the texts
of Schroeder (2.4.4), OECT 1.9 and others.

in OECT 1.9.2:8 between ^dMa-lik and Nergal. Thus, already in the Old Babylonian period, Malik's chthonic character in Mesopotamia is established by the equation of that god (and many others) with the great Mesopotamian king of the underworld.

Interestingly enough, Malik is absent from the AN = Anum and AN = Anu = ša ameli lists of the Old Babylonian period (best known in Middle Assyrian copies), which Lambert calls "the largest and most systematic of the Babylonian god lists."[313] But the god does appear once again in a Middle Assyrian list of the gods of the Anu-Adad temple at Aššur, a list which is nearly identical to one from the time of Sargon II or Sennacherib (in the Neo-Assyrian period).[314]

As for the use of Malik in Akkadian personal names, already in the Old Babylonian period we note a marked decline.[315] Such names do exist, however, as in the Old Assyrian occurrence of Ma-lik-il-šu.[316] Somewhat later, at Nuzi, we find a few personal names containing Malik, as well

---

[313] "Götterlisten," 475. The lists are presented and discussed extensively by Richard L. Litke, "A Reconstruction of the Assyro-Babylonian God-Lists AN:(d)A-nu-um and AN:Anu šá ameli" (unpublished Ph.D. dissertation, Yale University, 1958).

[314] The MA list was published by Karl Fr. Müller, Das assyrische Ritual: 1. Texte zum assyrischen Konigsritual (MVAG 41/3; Leipzig: J. C. Hinrichs, 1937) 16-17; the later list is in Rintje Frankena, Tākultu, de sacrale maaltijd in het Assyrische ritueel (Leiden: Brill, 1953) 5-9. See also Frankena, p. 25, for Malik's presence in a list of the gods of the temple of Aššur (VAT 10126.1:16).

[315] Johann Jakob Stamm's important work on Akkadian personal names (Die akkadische Namengebung [MVAG 44; Leipzig: J. C. Hinrichs, 1939]) considers the ma-lik element in the names it discusses to be the epithet (= "counselor"), not the divine name. What is significant for our purposes, however, is to note that all of the cases where one might argue that the divine name is in use (pp. 215-216,285) are from the OB period.

[316] Hans Hirsch, Untersuchungen zur altassyrischen Religion (AfO Beiheft 13-14; Graz: H. Hirsch, 1961) 43.

as our first Mesopotamian names with Milku/i. The Nuzi names include: Malik-nāṣir (spelled various ways); I-lu-ma-lik; Šarru-malik(AD.GI.GI); and Ṭâb(DÙG.GA)-mil-ki-a-bi/mil-ka-bi.[317] That Malik was a god at Nuzi is confirmed by an additional personal name, published by Theophil J. Meek: Gu-^{d}ma-lik.[318] It is worth stressing that Nuzi, like Ebla and Mari, was outside of the Mesopotamian "heartland." The presence of personal names containing Malik might suggest that the god was viewed more positively there (as he was at Mari and, we argue, at Ebla) than in the heartland.

2.4.4 Malik in Standard Babylonian Literature and Lists

Since the religious literature and lists of the Standard Babylonian (or jungbabylonisch) period are not an attempt at innovation, but rather an effort to gather and systematize traditional Mesopotamian religion, it is no surprize that the evidence relevant to our study contains little that we have not already seen in Mesopotamia. Especially the god lists, although they are often better preserved than earlier versions, provide us with little beyond the equation already known from the Old Babylonian period: ^{d}Malik = Nergal.[319] The single lexical list which contains

---

[317] Ignace J. Gelb, Pierre M. Purves, and Allan A. MacRae, Nuzi Personal Names (OIP 57; Chicago: University of Chicago, 1943) 308. The list includes several other Milku/i names which, according to these scholars, may be Hurrian.

[318] Excavations at Nuzi: 3. Old Akkadian, Sumerian and Cappadocian Texts from Nuzi (Harvard Semitic Series 10; Cambridge, MA: Harvard, 1935) xxxi.

[319] The most important later list with this equation is KAV 63.2:37 (O. Schroeder, "Ein neuer Götterlistentypus aus Assur," ZA 33 [1921] 140). (See also p. 142 for a list of eleven other gods whom the list equates with Nergal.) The divine name Malik alone also occurs in KAV 42.1:32. See Anton Deimal, Pantheon Babylonicum (Rome: Pon-

^{d}Malik (with determinative) explains the name, as we might expect, with ŠU (= ma-al-ku) DINGIR.[320] As has already been noted (2.2.3), one text does present a list of underworld deities paired with their spheres of influence, including: ^{d}ma-lik//šarru ša má-ri$^{(ki)}$.[321] It is difficult to know what to make of this, however, since only five lines earlier the same title is assigned to ^{d}La-ga-ma-al (also equated with Nergal in Weidner, "Altbabylonische Götterlisten," 12).

Of far greater interest than the lists are the literary references to the Mal(i)kū. As suggested above, they stand in clear continuity with the Old Babylonian attestations. Thus, in one text the speaker of a conjuration says: am-ma-ni tu-ub-ba-li napišti^{ti} ana ma-al-ki ("Why do you [witch] want to carry my soul to the m.-s?").[322] The new element in the SB literary texts, as noted already by Healey ("MALKŪ"), is the repeated juxtaposition of the Mal(i)kū with the Anunnaki, and in one text their apparent equation. The latter comes in ll. 7-8 of the so-called "Hymn to Šamaš": a-na t[a]-mar-ti-ka ih-du-ú ilū$^{meš.u}$ ma-al-ku / i-reš-šu-ka gi-mir-šú-nu ^{d}i-gì-gì. W. G. Lambert translates: "At your appearing the counsellor gods rejoice, / All the Igigi gods exult in you."[323] In these lines the malkū appear paired with the Igigi, as the

---

tifical Biblical Institute, 1914) 171, for other SB occurrences of Malik.

[320] Irving L. Finkel, The Series SIG(7).ALAN = Nabnītu (Materials for the Sumerian Lexicon 16; Rome: Pontifical Biblical Institute, 1982) 84.

[321] Ebeling, Tod und Leben, 12.

[322] For the text, see Gerhard Meier, Maqlû: Die assyrische Beschwörungssammlung Maqlû (AfO Beiheft 2; Berlin: G. Meier, 1937) 23. The translation is that of CAD 10/1:169.

[323] Babylonian Wisdom Literature (Oxford: Clarendon, 1960) 126-127.

Anunnaki normally do.[324] The underworld character of both the Mal(i)kū
and the Anunnaki in this period is confirmed by ll. 31-32 of the same
hymn: šap-la-a-ti m[a-a]l-ki ^{d}ku-su$_x$(BU) ^{d}a-nun-na-ki ta-pa-qid /
e-la-a-ti ša [d]a-ád-me ka-li-ši-na tuš-te-šèr.[325] Their chthonic character is also clear from another text, which is worth mentioning for the
connection it provides with the cult of the dead. Ebeling entitles the
text, "Ein König schildert darin das feierliche Begräbnis seines Va-
ters."[326] As in l. 31 of the "Hymn to Šamaš," the Malkū and Anunnaki can
be taken as simply paired, or as in apposition: qi-ša-ati a-na mal-ki /
il$_{a-nun-na-ki}$ / ù ilâni^{meš} a-ši-bu-ut irṣitim^{tim} / [ú]-qa-a-a-iš ("Gifts
for the Malki, the Anunnaki, and the gods who inhabit the earth
[=underworld], I gave"). In either event, it is clear that as late as
the Standard Babylonian period the Mal(i)kū were connected, at least in
the "classical" literature of the time, with feasts by royalty for their
departed forebearers. The persistence of this connection since at least
the kispum celebrations of Mari is striking.

CAD 10/1:168 renders l. 7: "the (nether-world) gods and the m̲.-s
rejoice."

[324] Burkhart Kienast ("Igigū und Anunnakkū nach den akkadischen Quellen," Studies in Honor of Benno Landsberger on his Seventy-fifth
Birthday [ed. H. G. Güterbock and T. Jacobsen; Assyriological Studies 16; Chicago: University of Chicago, 1965] 157-158) suggests
that the Igigi and Anunnaki were usually synonymous from the Old Babylonian period on. In some cases, however, the Anunnaki, but not
the Igigi, are the underworld gods. This latter usage, he believes,
is a vestige of the "chthonischen sumerischen Religion."

[325] Lambert (Babylonian Wisdom Literature, 126-127): "In the underworld
you care for the counsellors of Kusu, the Anunnaki, / Above, you direct the affairs of men." One can just as easily read "Kusu" as
"Kūbu" for another familiar juxtaposition. Reading malkī kūbu as a
construct chain is not necessary, either, but it makes sense if an-
unnakī is to be taken in apposition to malkī, as l. 7 would suggest.

[326] Tod und Leben, 56. The lines quoted below are on p. 58.

Finally, it is fitting that our latest evidence for the Akkadian god M-l-k is of the same sort as the earliest, from Michael Coogan's collection of personal names from Late Babylonian Murašû (cited in 2.2.1). Coogan states, "The West Semitic deity Milk (spelled ^{d}mil-ḫi) occurs in the [West Semitic] name 'abd-milk," and he goes on to cite three Babylonian names, as well: ^{Id}mil-ḫi-AD.URU; ^{Id}mil-ḫi-ta-ri-bi; and ^{I}nu-ú-ḫi^{d}mil-ḫi.[327] He attributes the /ḫ/ in the divine name to the new West Semitic (i.e., Aramaic) practice of spirantization of the /k/.[328]

2.4.5   Summary of Evidence on the Divine Name Malik

Before we turn to the literary evidence of Mesopotamian cultic child sacrifice, it is important that we sum up what can be said about the form and meaning of the divine name Malik, on the basis of the evidence so far examined from Syria-Palestine and that from Mesopotamia. The issue is significant both for what it may say about the conception of Malik in those areas and for the use of the material in the present chapter in understanding the Biblical Molek (see 2.3.5).

That Malik is related to the Semitic root mlk seems beyond dispute. There is considerable disagreement, however, over whether it was first understood according to the West Semitic sense, "prince, king," or the East Semitic, "counselor." The major Akkadian dictionaries are not particularly helpful here. CAD (10/1:168-169) suggests no connection with malākum A, "to counsel," but it also places all of the references we

---

[327] West Semitic Personal Names, 53,64.

[328] Citing Albrecht Goetze, "Accent and Vocalism in Hebrew," JAOS 59 (1939) 452, n. 74.

have found relevant in a listing malku B, "(a god or chthonic demon),"
separate from malku A, "king, (foreign) ruler."[329] Von Soden (AHW
2:595-596), on the other hand, includes nearly all of the material
treated above under malku(m) I, maliku(m), "Fürst, König," but under
definition 3 ("v Göttern") invites comparison with māliku(m), "Ratgeber,
Berater," where, for example, he places the personal name Ilum-ma-lik.

In favor of the understanding "prince, king" is the oldest attested
use of the divine name, at Ebla, where, as we have seen, malikum meant
"king" (2.1.2). (We may add that, whatever the final verdict may be on
the linguistic classification of Eblaite as a whole, lexically, it seems
more inclined toward West Semitic.) Furthermore, all of the instances
we have examined in which Malik is clearly a divine name can be explained given a core sense of "king," while some phenomena (such as the
later alternation with Milku/i forms) are hard to understand if one assumes an original meaning, "counselor." Naturally, it is possible that
Malik goes so far back in the history of the Semites that the alternatives presented here disappear in some Ur-meaning of mlk. But given the
general distrust among scholars of such pre- and proto-historical reconstructions of Semitic, it seems best to stick with conclusions, however
provisional, which can be drawn on the basis of attested occurrences.

Much more evasive of certain solution is the matter of the form of
Malik. If we accept the answer to the question of the core sense as
"king, ruler," two explanations for the form seem possible. First, Malik could be a "primitive noun" (i.e., not de-verbal) like kalbum

---

[329] CAD (10/1:158) also has a brief listing for the verbal use of mlk
meaning "to rule" (malākum B). However, its attestations are limited, as one would expect, to West Semitic areas (Mari and Ugarit).

("dog"), as the absolute form of the Eblaite _malikum_. Second, the name could be a participle from the verbal root _mlk_, "to rule," to be normalized as Mālik.[330]

The lack of plene writing (i.e., *_ma-a-_) at Ebla shows nothing about the vowel's quantity, according to Gelb.[331] But the presence of the /i/ in all the Syro-Palestinian occurrences cited above until late Alalakh (and always at Ugarit) would argue for an originally long /ā/, especially in names from Mari like Ma-li-kum (also Ma-a-li-kum!) and Ab-du-ma-li-ki and in the malikū, where the elision of a short /i/ after a short /a/ might be expected. If the /a/ was originally long, one might explain the Akkadian occurrences without the /i/, none of which is certifiably the result of a short /a/ before the Old Babylonian period (see 2.4.1), as the use of a borrowed common noun (mal[i]kum, "king") for a borrowed god, to avoid confusion with the participial epithet mālik, "counselor," used (at least in SB literature) for several Akkadian gods.[332] Alternatively, the common noun might have been confused with the proper name, given that both were borrowed.

---

[330] A stative, Malik, seems much less likely, since statives generally have a passive force with verbs capable of being transitive. In any case, the absence of the case ending -um is not surprising. Either it dropped off as Malik was used increasingly as a proper name, or, as Gelb suggests ("Šullat and Hamiš," ArOr 18 [1950] 197), the name is an "archaistic form from a proto-Semitic period, in which case endings had not yet been developed."

[331] "Ebla and the Kish Civilization," 15.

[332] Knut L. Tallqvist (Akkadische Götterepitheta [Studia orientalia 7; Helsinki: Societas Scientiarum Fennicae, 1938] 128) lists some nineteen gods for whom māliku was used as an epithet.

This explanation may seem, at least at first glance, to be "too clever by half." If the Eblaite noun malikum was, indeed, not de-verbal (i.e., from the participle *mālikum), then the elision of the /i/ at a later period would occasion no surprize: malikum and malkum would simply be stress variations of the same word.[333] In that case, however, the persistence of the /i/ at Mari would be remarkable.

In sum, the issue of the length of Malik's /a/ is not resolvable, given our present data (so that we cannot, for instance, claim confidently that the OT Molek is phonetically equivalent to Malik). But the larger issue of explaining the interrelationship of the data we have examined so far in this chapter seems clear enough. If Ebla and Mari were indeed part of what Gelb has called the "Kish Civilization," then the continuity which we have observed in both the form (with /i/) and content of Malik, and which is maintained through Ugarit, is no surprise. As to content, the Syro-Palestinian Malik was a significant underworld figure, especially in the popular cult, whose character bore dimensions both of fertility and of death. The discontinuities we have observed in the Akkadian evidence vis-à-vis the Syro-Palestinian, such as the absence of any sign of involvement in fertility and no indication of importance in any cult, well befit a borrowed god, quickly assimilated to Nergal, whose negative characteristics were only enhanced by his foreign origin. While this explanation, once again, cannot claim to be established, it is much to be preferred to any attempt to see the Akkadian Malik as originally independent of the Syro-Palestinian one and more

---

[333] A much later (Late Babylonian) lexical list has both ma-al-ku and ma-li-ku paired with šarru (P. E. van der Meer, Syllabaries A, B' and B: with miscellaneous lexicographical texts from the Herbert Weld Collection [OECT 4; London: Oxford University, 1938] 59).

still to a reconstruction which would see an originally Akkadian Malik, somehow popular at Ebla and (at least by Mari and Ugarit) somehow gaining fertility characteristics. It is therefore the Akkadian forms and conceptions which must be explained as developments of the original Syro-Palestinian Malik. Given especially the evidence of Mari and Ugarit, a most tentative preference for the normalization Mālik may, then, be defended.

2.4.6   Evidence of Cultic Child Sacrifice in Mesopotamia

In the early days of Assyriology the practice of cultic child sacrifice in Mesopotamia was often considered established by both "Accadian" (i.e., Sumerian) and "Assyrian" (i.e., Akkadian) texts. Typical was the essay of A. H. Sayce, in which he claimed to read in one text: "On the high places the son is burnt."[334] By the time of Eissfeldt's monograph on Molk (1935), however, scholars were divided between denying Mesopotamian child sacrifice (e.g., Giuseppe Furlani) and affirming it (e.g., Eduard Dhorme).[335] The most influential judgment was a form of the via media (leaning toward the negative), such as the view we have seen expressed by Friedrich Blome (1.4), that human sacrifice in general was "rare" in ancient Mesopotamia.

---

[334] "On Human Sacrifice among the Babylonians," Transactions of the Society of Biblical Archaeology 4 [1875] 25-31.

[335] Furlani, Il Sacrificio nella Religione dei Semiti di Babilonia e Assiria (Rome: Bardi, 1932), especially p. 147; Dhorme's response to Furlani, "Le sacrifice accadien à propos d'un ouvrage récent," RHR 107 (1933) 107-125, especially 117-119.

In recent years even that guarded affirmation has been challenged.
Wolfgang Röllig states his conclusions on the existence of such evidence
rather baldly: "In Mesopotamien gibt es für das Opfern von Kindern--wie
überhaupt für Menschenopfer--keinerlei sichere textliche Bezeugun-
gen."[336] In fact, the only material which he presents as a possible candidate is the Neo-Assyrian contract curses previously discussed by K.
Deller (1.8). These, it will be recalled, threatened the defaulting
party with the burning of his children to Adad, Adadmilki and Bēlet-ṣēri
in the ḫamru outside of the city. Deller had argued that the burning
was metaphorical and referred in fact to the dedication of a certain
number of the offender's children to the full-time service of the deity.
Thus, he rejected two other possible interpretations: that the curse
clauses "mean what they say," in Morton Smith's words (1.8), pointing to
a practice that was known and carried out as required in ninth- to
seventh-century Assyria; or, that the clauses amount to legal overkill,
designed to ensure compliance with the terms of the contract, but not
really executed in the event of default (a possibility which Deller had
raised). As was indicated in the discussion of Deller and Smith above,
Smith makes a telling point through a close reading of the contracts.
If one were to follow Deller's interpretation, the maker of the contract
would have needed an extraordinary number of children (some twenty-eight
in one instance) in order to be in a position to submit to the prescribed penalty. But without correlative archeological evidence, it is
impossible to say for sure which of the other two interpretations (actual practice or formulaic threat) is correct. As Röllig indicates in his

---

[336] "Kinderopfer," RLA 5 (1980) 601.

RLA article (p. 602), two Bible passages, Jud 11:30ff. (Jephtah's daughter) and 2 Kgs 17:31 (the child-sacrifice cult of the Sepharvites), may speak in favor of the former alternative. Since it is the purpose of this study to illuminate the Biblical material from the comparative, however, we cannot bring these passages to bear on the question at hand without risk of petitio principii in chapter IV.

The most thorough study to date of human sacrifice in the ancient Near East is that of A. R. W. Green, The Role of Human Sacrifice in the Ancient Near East (cited above, 1.1).[337] While most of his study is devoted to archeological evidence, to be examined in chapter III, Green does call attention to certain seals which have been alleged to show the practice of child sacrifice in a cultic context.[338] These are cylinder seals on tablets found in Cappadocia in southern Anatolia from the Isin-Larsa (post-Ur III or Early Old Babylonian) period. While the tablets were produced by Assyrian trading colonies, the seals themselves may "present features that are very different, and perhaps of indigenous origin" (p. 38). Green presents (and accepts, p. 190) W. H. Ward's interpretation of fourteen such seals.[339] The seals show a bull (which Ward and Green take to be a bull-altar), upon which is a "pyramidal pro-

---

[337] Also important is an article by Paolo Xella, "A proposito del sacrificio umano nel mondo mesopotamico," Or n.s. 45 (1976) 183-196. On cultic child sacrifice, however, Xella follows Deller.

[338] The evidence of the seals, like that of the Egyptian temple reliefs studied by Spalinger (2.3.8), could reasonably be considered either with the epigraphic or with the strictly archeological material. Since such evidence is graphic, as opposed to being simply realia, it is treated in the present chapter.

[339] Cylinder Seals and Other Ancient Oriental Seals in the Library of J. Pierpont Morgan (Washington: The Carnegie Institute of Washington, 1910).

tuberance" (interpreted as a flame), and under which in three seals is a
"small human figure," taken to be a child brought for sacrifice:
"Therefore, he [Ward] observes that this could be a bronze bull being
prepared for the immolation of the human victim" (p. 39).

While Green would not claim that the seals necessarily illustrate
Mesopotamian, rather than Anatolian practice, he does stress Ward's use
of southern Mesopotamian seal symbolism to decipher this type. Green
concedes that Ward also relied heavily on the classical authors like
Diodorus Siculus and on the midrashim for his interpretation, but he insists: "As Ward has pointed out, there must have been some basis for
the report of these child sacrifices in Syria, Phoenicia, and Carthage"
(p. 41). In response, we may observe that other evidence, much of it
still to be presented, supports this contention far less equivocally
than do the seals. Also, in any event, the "Bull-Altar" seals cannot be
pressed to show the practice of cultic child sacrifice in Mesopotamia.
The proof of such a practice, in Green's view, must rely on archeological evidence of "foundation sacrifices," which, unfortunately for our
study, are the sole form of Mesopotamian human sacrifice which is not
evidenced in written sources (p. 94).

Finally, Green calls attention to another, more literary source of
information on the subject at hand, but then maddeningly fails to pursue
it. He writes:

> In Mesopotamian records of the post-Sumerian period, some in-
> dications of ritual killing may be extracted from four differ-
> ent classes of material; they are: (1) inferences concerning
> slaves and prisoners, (2) texts dealing with the matter of
> substitution, (3) excerpts drawn from the important New Year
> Festival, and (4) the burning of children upon altars. (p.
> 86; my emphasis)

Green then presents the evidence for points one through three and promptly ends the chapter! Since he speaks in terms of "Mesopotamian records," one assumes that he is not referring to the aforementioned seals. Yet, so far as I can tell, he does not return to the subject of point four.

Before we can turn to the Mesopotamian evidence which Green does explicate, the archeological, we must return to the West, to examine the relevant literary and inscriptional material contemporary with Biblical Israel.

2.5   THE NON-PHOENICIAN, NORTHWEST SEMITIC INSCRIPTIONAL EVIDENCE

Ideally, the most important literary or inscriptional evidence for our entire study would be testimony to Molek or cultic child sacrifice from Palestine itself. Unfortunately, the Palestinian inscriptional evidence is notoriously scanty, forcing us to cast our net wider (as we have done). It is, nevertheless, necessary for us to see just what evidence is available from Palestine and its immediate environs (Transjordan) from the OT period.[340]

2.5.1   The Palestinian Evidence

We have already seen (1.2) how in his article on "Moloch" in PRE3, W. W. Baudissin claimed that Judean jar handles stamped lmlk were indicative of Molek worship, and how he later recanted that claim in his Kyrios. Unfortunately for our study, nearly a century of intensive archeology in Palestine has not brought to light a great deal of inscriptional materi-

---

[340] There is no earlier "Canaanite" inscriptional material (besides Ugaritic [2.3]).

al in Hebrew beyond what was known in Baudissin's time.[341] In fact, the only possible reference to the god Mlk is a personal name on several seventh century seals from Lachish and Beth-Shemesh, 'ḥmlk.[342] The same name is also known from a Samaritan ostracon (likely from ca. 800-775).[343]

2.5.2   The Ammonite Evidence

The Transjordanian material is only marginally more helpful.[344] One would expect the richest evidence to be the Ammonite since the Bible calls the god of Ammon, Milkom. In fact, only one of the four known Ammonite inscriptions mentions Milkom, and even that occurrence requires the restoration of the initial /m/. Line 1 of the ninth-eighth century "ʿAmmān Citadel Inscription" reads: M]lkm.bnh.lk.mbʿt.sbbt[("Milkom has built for you entrances round about . . .").[345]

---

[341] In particular, the name Gdmlk, published in M. A. Levy, Siegel und Gemmen mit aramäischen, phönizischen, althebräischen, himjarischen, nabathäischen und altsyrischen Inhalts (Breslau: Schletter, 1869) 44.

[342] Larry G. Herr, The Scripts of Ancient Northwest Semitic Seals (HSM 18; Missoula, MT: Scholars, 1978) 87,90,109,143. (Other Hebrew personal names containing mlk are in the Bible and will be listed in chapter IV.)

[343] TSSI 1:9.

[344] Pace M. Baldacci ("The Ammonite Text from Tell Siran and North-West Semitic Philology," VT 31 [1981] 363), who speaks of "the large [!] corpus of various inscriptions discovered outside the boundaries of the Israelite kingdom; I am referring to inscriptions in Edomite, Moabite and Ammonite dialects."

[345] The translation is that of the original publisher, S. H. Horn ("The Ammān Citadel Inscription," BASOR 193 [1969] 8). Since then, several other scholars have offered understandings of the text which vary to a greater or lesser degree in nuance from Horn's, but all of which restore M]lkm (besides the articles cited in William J. Fulco, "The ʿAmmān Citadel Inscription: A New Collation," BASOR 230 [1978]

Otherwise, Ammonite features four seal inscriptions worthy of note. Three (from the seventh century) bear the apparent dedication: brk lmlkm ("blessed to Milkom").[346] The other, from the late sixth century, is in Aramaic, but contains, in Herr's words, "a good Ammonite name": ltmk'l br mlkm ("property of Tmk'l son of Milkom").[347]

In sum, the Ammonite material tells us little more than was already known from the Bible: Milkom was an important (if not the chief) Ammonite god in the Biblical period. Whether and in what way Milkom may be related to the OT Molek remains to be examined in chapter IV.

2.5.3 The Moabite Evidence

Moving south to Moab, we find only one inscription of importance to us: the famous Meša stele (ninth century B.C.). In the last century the name of the father of Meša in l. 1 was commonly restored as kmš[mlk], i.e., a "double divine name," including Kemoš (chief god of Moab) and M-l-k.[348] More recent editors have preferred to restore kmš[yt], or the like, a reading which has gained in popularity since the publication in 1963 of the El-Kerak inscription, which contains k]mšyt.mlk.m'b ("Chemosh-yat, king of Moab").[349] The Moabite seal inscriptions feature

---

39-43, see now those by Victor Sasson and William H. Shea in PEQ 111 [1979] 117-125 and 17-25, respectively). The "four known Ammonite inscriptions" are listed in D. Sivan, "On the Grammar and Orthography of the Ammonite Findings," UF 14 (1982) 219-234.

[346] Herr, Seals, 62,74-75. Herr believes that the last two are forgeries. D. Sivan ("Grammar and Orthography," 231) observes, following Avigad: "The phrase brk l is found in the Bible. . . . The use of the phrase points to an isogloss connecting Ammonite with Hebrew."

[347] Herr, Seals, 15.

[348] Thus, Lidzbarski, Handbuch, 415.

kmš in nearly every case, but never mlk.[350]

2.5.4 The Edomite Evidence

Edomite is the least known of the three Transjordanian dialects, being evidenced in little more than assorted seal inscriptions. Still, those seals do supply two personal names which are likely to include the divine name Mlk: Mlklbʿ and Gdmlk.[351]

Far more controversial is the reading of an Edomite royal name, written in the Annals of Sennacherib (i.e., in Akkadian) as ^{Id}A.A-ram-mu ^{l}Ú-du-um-ma-ai ("A.A-rammu the Edomite").[352] Many earlier scholars, including Luckenbill, normalized the name as ^{Id}Malik-rammu. Others, led already by H. Zimmern, have preferred to read the name of the Akkadian consort of the sun god, ^{d}Aya.[353] A third proposal is that of E. Lipiński, who reviewed all of the available evidence for the existence of a god or goddess Ay(a) in West Semitic and concluded that the name under discussion should be read ^{I}Il-a-a-ram-mu and translated, "Mon dieu est exalté."[354] Although a Phoenician seal inscription found in the pal-

---

[349] See G. A. Cooke, *A Textbook of North-Semitic Inscriptions* (Oxford: Clarendon, 1903) 6; and TSSI 2:77.

[350] See Herr, *Seals*, 153-159.

[351] Felice Israel, "Miscellanea Idumea," *RivB* 27 (1979) 173,176. Israel includes both in his index of divine names in personal names (p. 193).

[352] See Daniel D. Luckenbill, *The Annals of Sennacherib* (OIP 2; Chicago: University of Chicago, 1924) 30.

[353] H. Zimmern and H. Winkler, *Die Keilinschriften und das Alten Testament* (3d ed.; Berlin: Reuther und Reichard, 1903) 467. Cf. Rylke Borger, *Assyrisch-babylonische Zeichenliste* (AOAT 33; Kevelaer: Butzon & Bercker, 1978) 202 (sign 579a).

[354] "Recherches ugartiques: 1. Ay, un dieu ugaritique?," *Syria* 44

ace of Nimrud (from the time of the neo-Assyrian empire) shows that
Mlkrm was a West Semitic name in use at the time, one editor of that inscription is at pains to point out that it provides no grounds for reading the theophoric element in the Edomite royal name as ^dMalik.[355] Whatever the verdict in the case of this royal name, the other personal
names discussed above strongly suggest that a god M-l-k was known and
worshipped in Edom, once again, at least in the popular cultus.

2.5.5   The Aramaic Evidence

Although Aramaic reached the height of its influence during the Persian
period as Imperial or Official Aramaic (Reichsaramäisch), literary evidence of Aramaic has been discovered as far back as the tenth-ninth century B.C.[356] The Aramaic evidence is of interest to us because it was
the language of Syria during the monarchical period in Israel, and especially because of the influence which the Syrians had from time to time
on religious affairs in Israel (2 Kgs 16:10-16 being the clearest example). Aramaic material worthy of our attention is not far to seek. One
of the oldest specimens of Old Aramaic is a stele erected by Barhadad of
Damascus at Brēdsch (near Aleppo) to the god Melqart (KAI text 201).
Melqart is best known as the god of Tyre, so that he is properly discussed below, with the Phoenician evidence (2.6.1). For now, we observe
only that the name Melqart is without scholarly doubt derived from mlk
qrt, "King of the City," and therefore of interest to this study, and

---

(1967) 276.

[355] Wolfgang Röllig, "Alte und neue Elfenbeininschriften," NESE 2:48-49.
Röllig vocalizes the Phoenician name as "Milkī-ram."

[356] KAI 2:202.

that this Aramaic stele is the oldest attestation we have of the god's name.[357] Whether this constituted, in Gibson's words, "the veneration by an Aramaean monarch of a Tyrian deity" is arguable (viz., whether Melqart was, indeed, so closely identified with Tyre).[358] What is clear is that a deity with at least an etymological connection to the Syro-Palestinian Malik-Milku/i was worshipped by the king of the Arameans in ninth century Syria.

Unfortunately for this study, references to M-l-k do not abound in Aramaic, even in our hitherto-reliable source of references, personal names. It may be, of course that by the first millennium in Syria, M-l-k had acquired so negative a character that, as we have seen earlier in Mesopotamia, parents no longer used M-l-k as a theophoric element in naming their children. Secondly, M-l-k was apparently not a sufficiently important deity to be included with such notable gods as Nergal, Shamash and El as a treaty witness to the eighth century Sefire inscriptions (<u>KAI</u> text 222), or he may even have been assimilated to Nergal by then. Given our present evidence (or lack thereof), we can say with assurance only that M-l-k was not the significant deity for the Arameans which we have found he was elsewhere in Syro-Palestine, both earlier and among neighboring, contemporary peoples.

Yet even the relative silence of the Aramaic evidence may be helpful in our study. A glance at an Aramaic lexicon shows that Aramaic

---

[357] Gibson (<u>TSSI</u> 2:2) notes that the literary form of the inscription shows that "a Phoenician model [votive text] was clearly being followed." Nevertheless, he shows that the language is Aramaic, not Phoenician.

[358] Ibid.

malkā' meant "the king," while milkā' meant "the counsel."[359] Exposure
to Mesopotamian linguistic elements clearly led to the Aramaic adoption
of the latter lexeme. Yet because Malik-Milku/i was apparently not of
any significance among the Arameans, one can hardly argue that the Aramaic evidence shows that the latter form of the divine name must have
meant "counselor."

2.6 THE PHOENICIAN EVIDENCE

The divine name M-l-k does not occur as such in any Phoenician inscription known to date. This does not mean, however, that there is no relevant Phoenician material. On the one hand, as observed above (2.5.4),
the name of the god Melqart, the chief god of Tyre, is clearly the product of milk and qart, meaning "King of the City." There are also numerous personal and divine names containing the elements Mlk and Mlqrt. On
the other hand, as we saw in connection with Xella's claim that no evidence for molk-sacrifices exists at Ugarit (2.3.7), there is a Phoenician inscription which has been adduced as proof that such sacrifices
were offered in the "Phoenician motherland," as well as in the Punic
colonies (see 2.7 for the latter).

---

[359] Gustaf H. Dalman, *Aramäisch-Neuhebräisches Handwörterbuch zu Targum, Talmud und Midrasch* (reprint; 2d ed.; Hildesheim: Georg Olms, 1967) [orig., 1938]) 238.

2.6.1 Melqart

If the meaning of the name, Melqart, is agreed upon, there is no such consensus on the meaning of the meaning. The dispute centers on how qrt, "city," is to be understood. In the past qrt has been taken by nearly all scholars as a reference to Tyre, where Melqart bore the title, "Ba'al of Tyre" (b'l ṣr).[360] The relatively late appearance of the deity as preeminent at Tyre is commonly connected with an ostensible tenth-century religious reformation conducted by Hiram, Solomon's contemporary, at the time of Tyre's rise to commercial empire.[361] Thus, Melqart, whatever his relationship to other deities such as El and Baal, has been widely understood as an important Canaanite deity in specifically Tyrian form.[362]

An entirely different understanding of the qrt in Melqart is that of W. F. Albright, who argued that "the city" of Melqart's realm was the underworld. Albright adduced three arguments in favor of his reading.[363] First, the Ugaritic texts show that qrt can mean the nether-

---

[360] So a second century B.C. inscription from Malta, CIS 1.122:1.

[361] Julian Morgenstern, "The King-God among the Western Semites and the Meaning of Epiphanes," VT 10 (1960) 139.

[362] The debate over Melqart's relationship to other gods has been long (see already Baudissin, "Moloch," in PRE2) and complex. The most thorough studies in the present century are those of René Dussaud, in which he argues that Melqart is the product of the fusion of Baal and Yam ("Melqart," Syria 25 [1946-1948] 205; see also his "Melqart, d'après de récents Travaux," RHR 151 [1957] 1-21). Other scholars, however, deny the connection with Yam (R. du Mesnil du Buisson, Nouvelles Études sur les Dieux et les Mythes de Canaan [Études préliminaires aux religions orientales dans l'Empire romain 33; Leiden: Brill, 1973] 64) or propose an altogether different identification, as with Tammuz (so Morgenstern, "The King-God," 141).

[363] Archaeology and the Religion of Israel, 81 and 196, n. 29. See also his "A Votive Stele Erected by Ben-Hadad I of Damascus to the God Melcarth," BASOR 87 (1942) 29.

world. Thus, CTA 5.2:15 refers to the infernal destination of Baal's messengers as qrth.hmry, "his [Mot's] city, Hmry." Secondly, Albright appealed to the Barhadad stela, discussed above (2.5.4): "It is scarcely credible that an Aramaean king of Syria in the ninth century would set up a votive stela to the city-god of Tyre in a region so far away from Tyre and would inscribe it in Aramaic." Thirdly, he noted the later identification of Melqart with the Greek god-hero Heracles (Roman Hercules), whose chthonic character is well known.[364]

Few scholars have followed Albright in seeing a chthonic nature in Melqart.[365] Du Mesnil du Buisson contends: "Mais rien de ce que nous savons de Melqart ne peut faire penser qu'il ait été un roi des Enfers; tous les témoignages de l'Antiquité y contradisent."[366] At most, Morgenstern allows that some predecessor form of Melqart may have been chthonic, but he insists that following Hiram's "reformation" Melqart was primarily a solar deity.[367]

In response, we may observe that Melqart's nature is much beclouded; as KAI says (2.36): "Über seinen Charakter ist noch nichts Sicheres zu sagen." This is due above all to the relative paucity of native Phoenician inscriptions in general. Thus, the primary sources of data for old Phoenician theology are all too often later classical discus-

---

[364] See, for instance, Walter Burkert, Griechische Religion (Die Religionen der Menschheit 15; Stuttgart: W. Kohlhammer, 1977) 319.

[365] Colette and Gilbert-Charles Picard ("Hercule et Melqart," Hommages à Jean Bayet [ed. M. Renard and R. Schilling; Brussels, 1964] 576) argue that a late third-century "razor" from Sante Monica depicts Melqart and Hercules as chthonic deities, but they do not mention Albright.

[366] Nouvelles Études, 64.

[367] "The King-God," 141.

sions (such as those by Philo of Byblos) and notoriously ambiguous iconographic media, like coins.[368]

Nevertheless, a few points may be ventured without undue risk. First, there is no question that Melqart reached his greatest popularity at Tyre and, to a somewhat lesser extent, in the Tyrian Punic colonies.[369] But this says nothing about Melqart's nature, nor does it resolve the issue of to what qrt originally referred. In favor of Albright's answers to these two questions stand not only the arguments which he adduced, but also the solar aspects of Melqart's character, admitted by most scholars.[370] As can be shown from both Ugaritic (CTA 6.6:44-46) and Akkadian ("Hymn to Šamaš" 31-32; cf. 2.4.4), the sun god(dess) had an important role in the underworld, indeed, "ruling the shades." Thus, while we cannot by any means speak of Melqart with assurance as King of the Infernal City, such evidence as we possess lends considerable support to such an understanding.[371]

---

[368] See W. Culican, "Melqart Representations on Phoenician Seals," Abr-Nahrain (1960-1961) 41-54, and especially p. 48, regarding the problems of interpretation of coins.

[369] The Picards ("Hercule et Melqart," 570) caution against exaggerating Melqart's popularity at Carthage, especially during the period of the "oligarchy," i.e., before the rule of the Barcide generals, such as Hannibal.

[370] Dussaud ("Melqart," 207) alone mounts a sustained argument against seeing Melqart as a solar deity. See, however, Theodor Klauser, "Melkart," Reallexicon für Antike und Christentum 1 (1950) 1095, for a summary of the countervailing arguments.

[371] Gibson (TSSI 3:116) unintentionally provides further support for Albright's interpretation of qrt by arguing "that at Tyre the leading god was Baal and not Melcarth. . . ." If so, it would make much sense to take the city (qrt) of which Melqart was king as something other than Tyre. However, the above-quoted reference to Melqart as "Lord (Baal) of Tyre" makes Gibson's hypothesis arguable, at best.

A second observation concerning Melqart is also in order. As we have seen repeatedly, the god's name is unanimously read as a construct chain, mlk qrt, or "King of the City." The scholarly discussion has, understandably, focused on the proper interpretation of qrt. Yet we may ask in the light of the preceding sections of this chapter, is the mlk in Melqart no more than the epithet, "king," or does it refer to the deity we have found repeatedly in Syro-Palestine from the third millennium on, Malik-Milku/i? If qrt means Tyre, the former alternative is probably correct, whether the "King" turns out to be El, Baal, Tammuz or some other locally important deity. But if Melqart was indeed a chthonic deity, then the underworld king-god whom we have found clearly at Mari, Ugarit and in Mesopotamia provides a strong impetus to understand Melqart's name as distinguishing that god from any others which might bear mlk merely as an epithet, identifying him specifically as the ancient M(i)lk(u) of the underworld.[372]

Dussaud denies vociferously that any Phoenician god Milk ever existed.[373] However, he dismisses the Ammonite Milkom as being of uncertain etymology, denies the applicability of the OT Molek (since he accepts Eissfeldt's thesis) and is unaware of other comparative evidence. Furthermore, he argues that the theophoric element mlk in names such as Mlkʻštrt is but an abbreviation for Melqart. Dussaud rightly observes, as we have done above, that no independent divine name M-l-k appears as such in Phoenician. But he addresses only indirectly the question of whether Melqart was the Phoenician (or Tyrian) form of M-l-k. The com-

---

[372] I would argue that at all points the Semitic worshippers of Malik-Milku/i were well aware that their god's name meant "king."

[373] "Melqart," 210; "Melqart, d'après de récents Travaux," 1.

parative evidence already presented places great strain on his contention that the Phoenicians knew no M-l-k deity (viz., even in the form
Melqart), and the personal names test his claim further. We turn now to
the evidence of those Phoenician names.

2.6.2   The Evidence of the Phoenician (and Punic) Names

As was the case at Mari and Ugarit, the task of collecting and analyzing
the names has already been performed, this time by Frank L. Benz.[374]
Benz lists some fifty-three personal names containing mlk as a theophoric element, and he suggests (p. 344) that such names contain an "Epithet, of 'El in most cases . . . , becoming a separate deity." He then
seconds Dussaud's proposal that mlk is "probably" an abbreviation of
Melqart (but he does not say whether Melqart is El or that "separate deity"). In sum, Benz is less specific than Dussaud in explaining whether
a distinct deity M-l-k existed in Phoenicia and how Melqart might be related to such a deity. Yet given the nature and quantity of the material, such vagueness (or caution) seems well-advised.[375]

Of much greater interest to this study are those names containing
mlk which Benz calls "compounded divine names" (pp. 344-345). Two are
from Punic inscriptions and are among those mlk combinations which, as
we saw in chapter I, Eissfeldt and his followers have interpreted as
forms of molk-sacrifices: mlk'sr/mlk'mr and mlkb'l. These "names" (so

---

[374] Personal Names in the Phoenician and Punic Inscriptions (Studia Pohl
8; Rome: Pontifical Biblical Institute, 1972). Since Benz does not
distinguish the Phoenician and Punic names, we shall treat them together here.

[375] Benz lists and discusses the names containing Melqart on pp.
347-348.

Benz) will be treated below, with the Punic evidence (2.7). The third "divine name" has also provoked much discussion: Mlk'štrt. The name is a relatively late (Hellenistic) fusion of two Semitic divine names, Mlk and 'štrt, to whom offerings were made at Umm El-'Amed (between Tyre and Akko) and to whom a temple was dedicated at Carthage.[376] As with Melqart, little can be told about the resulting god (other than that it is a male deity, pace Cooke, North-Semitic Inscriptions, 49). Most scholars contend (with Dussaud above) that the mlk component is an abbreviation of Melqart, although Gibson believes that it is an epithet of El, and KAI (2.25), while favoring some epithet, is made cautious by the evidence from Ammon and Ugarit of a deity named M-l-k.[377] The understanding of 'štrt as the goddess's name seems more certain, although the juxtaposition of the god Mlk with the place 'ttrt in Ug5 7 and 8 (as we have argued, 2.3.1) offers a tempting alternative explanation ("Milk of 'Aštaroth"). The presence of 'štrt in other divine compounds (such as 'šmn'štrt, CIS 1.245) argues against this latter possibility, however. Unfortunately, the name Mlk'štrt gives no clue of how its components were interrelated; Mlk as consort or son of 'štrt were early suggestions.[378] Most scholars now opt for a simple compound, like the Ugaritic Ktr-wḤss, although this provides no help in identifying the mlk element.

---

[376] TSSI 3:118-122, and CIS 1.250, respectively. See Benz, Personal Names, 345, and KAI 2.28 for further references to this deity.

[377] TSSI 3:120. On the other hand, Albright (Yahweh and the Gods, 241-242) holds that mlk is not a divine name at all, but rather a common noun, molk, meaning "kingdom, royalty," the etymological predecessor of Punic molk, "princely sacrifice." Thus, the divine name under discussion is to be vocalized as Molk-'aštart, "Royalty of Astarte."

[378] See André Caquot, "Le Dieu Milk'ashtart et les Inscriptions de 'Umm el 'Amed," Semitica 15 (1965) 32, for a review of past proposals.

Of the three proposed understandings of the mlk component, Gibson's reading (an epithet for El) must be deemed the least likely: one would not expect El to be paired with 'štrt, whatever the interrelationship of the two components. If, as we have argued above, Melqart is but the (Syro-)Phoenician form of the god M-l-k in the first millennium B.C., it makes little difference whether one sees mlk in the name under discussion as an abbreviation or as the distinct divine name, M(i)lk. What is most important is that one appreciate the continuity of the mlk in the Phoenician Mlk'štrt with the same god of a full millennium before at Ugarit, as argued by Sergio Ribichini.[379]

2.6.3 Molk-sacrifices in Phoenicia?

Until recently, the only evidence for cultic child sacrifice in mainland Phoenicia came from classical writers, the earliest of whom, Quintus Curtius Rufus, wrote in the first century A.D.[380] The author likely to be historically most reliable, however, is Philo of Byblos (ca. A.D. 100), who was himself Phoenician and who at least claimed to have an ancient source, Sanchuniathon. Philo's testimony is both historical and mythical in nature: he claims that both the Phoenician city fathers, as a matter of custom, and El-Kronos, on one occasion, sacrificed their children in time of threat to their city. The veracity of all reports of Phoenician cultic child sacrifice has been widely doubted, however, given the lack of archeological confirmation and the relative lateness

---

[379] "Un'ipotesi per Milk'aštart," RSO 50 (1976) 43-55, especially 48,55. Ribichini's point stands, even if one disagrees (as we do) with his understanding of 'ttrt in Ug5 7 and 8.

[380] The classical witnesses are quoted and discussed by Mosca, "Child Sacrifice," 8-9,16,22-23,274.

and possible bias of the authors. The strongest arguments that such sacrifices were indeed practiced in Phoenicia have relied heavily on the Punic epigraphic and archeological evidence, coupled with the reasoning that there is an insufficient gap in time before the appearance of such evidence in the colonies to allow for so remarkable a cultic custom to have developed independently of the homeland.

Recently, however, an inscription discovered in the last century in Nebi-Yunis (just north of Ashdod on the Mediterranean coast) has been reappraised and offered as proof that molk was a sacrificial term in Phoenicia, just as Eissfeldt et al. have argued it was in the Punic colonies.[381] The inscription is on the side of the mensa of an offering table (now lost) and is datable to the third-second century B.C. What is remarkable about the inscription is that it, like several Punic inscriptions, begins with [n]ṣb mlk, "stela mlk."[382] Delavault, Lemaire and Picard argue that the parallel is close enough to show that molk-sacrifices were offered by Phoenicians in the homeland.

In response, one should note first that the authors are not claiming that this inscription shows that child sacrifices were offered in the third-second century by Phoenicians. They argue only that mlk is here shown to be a sacrificial term; indeed, by this time the molk-sacrifices were everywhere attenuated by substitution. Secondly, vis-à-vis the anticipated criticism that molk-sacrifices, here allegedly

---

[381] Bernard Delavault and André Lemaire, "Une Stèle 'Molk' de Palestine dédiée à Eshmoun? RES 367 reconsidéré," RB 83 (1976) 569-583; Colette Picard, "Le Monument de Nebi-Yunis," RB 83 (1976) 584-589; Delavault and Lemaire, "Les inscriptions phéniciennes de Palestine," RSF 7 (1979) 24-26.

[382] Cf. especially CIS 1.123a/b = KAI 1.14, no. 61A/B.

made to Eshmun, are otherwise attested only to Baal-Ḥammon (El) and
Tanit, Picard cites the Ugaritic prayer to Baal discussed by Herdner
(2.3.8), Meša's sacrifice recorded in 2 Kgs 3:27 and the OT sacrifices
lmlk. Both of these points are flawed. As to the first, while the parallel of the opening sequence, nṣb mlk, is indeed striking, it must be
pointed out that all of the adduced Punic parallels follow mlk with another, presumably qualifying term, such as b'l (KAI 61A) or 'mr (KAI
61B). This deficiency in the Phoenician inscription was noticed already
by Lidzbarski, who wrote: "In Z. 1 dürfte nṣb mlk zu nṣb mlk b'l oder
mlk 'sr zu ergänzen sein. . . ."[383] Yet, as Delavault and Lemaire observe, the words nṣb mlk appear "au milieu de la première colonne comme
une sorte de titre."[384] Thus, the accidental omission or abrasion of a
following word is unlikely.[385] Secondly, as to the divine recipient of
the sacrifice, Picard's arguments are without force: only the OT references contain the vocable mlk and are thus persuasive candidates for
molk-sacrifices, yet in the context of this study, such use of the Biblical material obviously begs the question. If Eshmun received Phoenician molk-sacrifices, he stands, for now at least, as the sole exception
in a practice otherwise directed solely to Baal-Ḥammon and Tanit. A
third difficulty for those who see here a molk-sacrifice is the strange
word order in the stela: the name of one donor is followed by the god's

---

[383] Ephemeris, 1.286. Lidzbarski argued that the inscription was a for-
gery, a position which Delavault and Lemaire seek to refute ("Une
Stèle 'Molk'," 571-573).

[384] "Une Stèle 'Molk'," 576.

[385] Indeed, none of the accompanying phrases familiar from the Punic mlk
inscriptions is present in the entire Phoenician inscription (unless, as Delavault and Lemaire implicitly argue, h'rkt 'š is equivalent to the Punic btm, "at his own expense" [1.7]).

name and then by a long list of other donors. While the word order in the Punic stelae varies, such a division of the donors' names is unparalleled.

The striking parallel of the opening phrase with Punic specimens remains, and while other understandings of the words are possible (e.g., "royal stela"), none has the _prima facie_ attraction of Delavault and Lemaire's proposal, nor _must_ any replace it, despite its shortcomings. What seems essential, then, is to emphasize the place of this inscription in the context of the rest of the Phoenician evidence. First, in addition to Lidzbarski's concerns with the inscription's very authenticity and the other difficulties noted above, the rule of text criticism, "_unus manuscriptus_, _nullus manuscriptus_," ought to caution against drawing overly-broad conclusions on the basis of this one, late text. Secondly, even if one chooses to reject the entire argument presented above for the existence of a chthonic Phoenician M-l-k god in Melqart, one can argue at most that this stela shows that _mlk_ could be used as a sacrificial term of some sort in Phoenicia by the third-second century B.C. How, when and where that specialization of the term took place, the existence and direction of possible borrowing of the sacrificial usage, and exactly what the term denoted at each time and place are unknown. For now, we can say only that _mlk_ as a sacrificial term is limited to one possible, late first millennium Phoenician attestation and, as we shall now see, to the Punic colonies. On the other hand, the presence of a god Malik-Milku/i is attested in Syro-Palestine (including, we would argue, Phoenicia) and Mesopotamia from the third millennium on (and from the second millennium on with a confirmed chthonic nature).

How the full body of this evidence bears on the OT Molek remains to be
seen, of course. First, we must turn to Eissfeldt's best evidence for
the sacrificial understanding of Molek, the Punic inscriptions.

2.7 THE PUNIC EVIDENCE

2.7.1 The Evidence of the Molk Stelae

The evidence of the Punic inscriptions containing mlk has already been
reviewed in some detail in chapter I (1.4-9).[386] As was recounted there,
Eissfeldt's proposal on the sacrificial meaning of the Punic mlk has
been almost unanimously accepted; only Buber and Charlier have attempted
serious challenges to Eissfeldt's position specifically from the Punic
side of his work (1.7). Mosca's learned, detailed defense of Eissfeldt's position ("Child Sacrifice," chap. IIC) obviates the need for
further review of the Punic material. What follows is a series of observations on the interpretation of the Punic inscriptions, by way of
summary both of what seems assured and of what remains questionable (or
at least not proved).

First, no one has given a cogent response to Eissfeldt's insight
that the variety of syntactical positions in which lmlk appears suggests
that that phrase does not refer to the god to whom the stela and sacrifice were dedicated. When taken together with the observation, made
also by scholars long before Eissfeldt, that reading lmlk as referring
to the god would mean that a stela dedicated to one god commemorated a
sacrifice to another, Eissfeldt's suggestion that lmlk was a sacrificial

---

[386] See also on the iconography of the Punic mlk-stelae: Colette Picard, "Les Représentations de Sacrifice Molk sur les Ex-voto de Carthage," Karthago 17 (1973-1974) 67-138 and 18 (1975-1976) 5-116.

term becomes exceedingly attractive, if not proved beyond a doubt.[387]

Secondly, Eissfeldt's vocalization (following Chabot) of Punic mlk as *molk, on the basis of the Latin stelae from Ngaous which read mol-chomor (or the like) is beyond challenge.[388]

Thirdly, with that said, we must add immediately that little else in Eissfeldt's philological work or his historical reconstruction of the Punic cult (or in the work of his followers) can be counted assured. As to philology, we have already seen what a wide variety of interpretations have been offered for the words and phrases which accompany lmlk, such as 'mr, 'dm and b'l. Although Mosca regards it as the "least controversial of the terms," even the interpretation of 'mr as "lamb" is suspect.[389] While such an understanding might seem assured by the iconography on the Ngaous stelae and by the Latin phrase agnum pro vicario in some late specimens, even so fervent a supporter of Eissfeldt on the interpretation of lmlk as Lipiński objects: "However, the expression -omor points to the participle of the verb 'mr, in English 'to speak' or 'to promise.'"[390]

---

[387] Cooke (North-Semitic Inscriptions, 104) writes regarding CIS 1.123a: "It is curious that the pillar of one deity should be dedicated to another. . . ."

[388] Molk als Opferbegriff, 12-13.

[389] "Child Sacrifice," 58a.

[390] Eissfeldt, Molk als Opferbegriff, pl. 1; Lipiński, "North Semitic Texts from the first millennium BC," Near Eastern Religious Texts Relating to the Old Testament (ed. W. Beyerlin; trans. J. Bowden; Philadelphia: Westminster, 1978) 234. See also Mosca's response to this objection (as formulated by Buber and Charlier) in "Child Sacrifice," 60.

As for historical reconstruction, the Latin stelae do indeed suggest, as Lipiński says, that "it [the Molok sacrifice] was a nocturnal
sacrifice, offered voluntarily to a chthonic deity."[391] But as he further observes: "The inscriptions, at any rate, offer no support for the
view that the Molok sacrifice was often a child-sacrifice: this can
only be concluded from archaeological discoveries and OT accounts."[392]
As we shall see in chapter III, the archeological evidence is present in
abundance. But one must take care in linking such evidence with the
Punic stelae via the OT accounts (since the stelae are not necessarily
linked stratigraphically with the charred bones in the Punic "tophets"),
if the Punic material is then to be used to illuminate the OT Molek.
Furthermore, if the connection of the stelae bearing lmlk with the evidence of cultic child sacrifice does seem likely (and it does), one must
then take care in how one uses both the inscriptional and archeological
evidence to develop a more complete historical picture of the cultic
practice under study. Specifically, as we have already seen (1.9), Mosca's hypothesis that Punic b'l and 'dm meant the upper and lower classes, while brilliant, has, by his own admission, no support in Punic epigraphic evidence. As to the use of the archeological evidence, the
conclusion that the Punic molk-sacrifices were attenuated over time by
animal substitutions, which lies at the base of Eissfeldt's and Mosca's
reconstructions of the history of the rite, is now open to serious challenge, as will be seen in the next chapter.

---

[391] "North Semitic Texts," 234.

[392] Ibid., 235.

In sum, the Punic epigraphic evidence stands apart as an unicum in our study. No indication of a god bearing the name (and not simply the epithet) M-l-k has been discovered, while there is very strong support for Eissfeldt's theory that a Punic sacrifice called mlk existed.[393] As we have seen, with the possible exception of one Phoenician inscription, such a meaning for mlk is restricted to the Punic colonies.[394] No doubt, as Mosca emphasizes, the presence of stelae containing the sacrificial usage of mlk as early as the sixth century B.C. on Malta (CIS 1.123a/b) supports the hypothesis that this lexeme and whatever practice it originally represented were brought with the colonists from Phoenicia. But a connection with the Israelite Molek, which must be established through Phoenicia, remains conjectural.

2.7.2   Iconographic Evidence of Cultic Child Sacrifice

In each section of this chapter we have examined the inscriptional evidence not only for material relevant to a god M-l-k, but also for indications of the practice of cultic child sacrifice. Mindful of Lipiński's warning (quoted above), that the mlk-stelae are not in them-

---

[393] There is one possible, intriguing exception, which might suggest the worship of a Punic god M-l-k. Cooke (North-Semitic Inscriptions, 135-136) discusses a third-second century Punic inscription from Carthage which was found in a necropolis there, written on a sheet of lead: "It was intended, like the Gk. and Roman tabellae devotionis, to be a missive to the gods of the underworld. . . . These tabellae were rolled up and dropped down a tube, which was used also for libations to the dii inferi, into the sepulchre below." Besides the parallel in the use of the tubes with Ugaritic practice (2.3.8), we note that the inscription is directed to rbt ḥwt 'lt mlkt, which Cooke renders: "O ladies Ḥawwath, Elath, Milkath." He then suggests that the three are "the names of infernal deities, forming . . . a triad." Lidzbarski (Ephemeris, 1.30), however, takes mlkt simply as "Königin," and rbt as a singular.

[394] See DISO 154 (s.v. mlk ẉ).

selves proof of such a practice, we must see if other, relevant inscriptional evidence can be adduced for the Punic colonies. Two items of importance have come to light, one of them long known, the other just now entering the scholarly discussion. Like the Egyptian temple reliefs discussed by Spalinger (2.3.8) and the Cappadocian cylinder seals in Green's work (2.4.6), this evidence is iconographic and, thus, could also have been treated in chapter III.

The first item is the stela from Carthage first published in 1923 by Poinsott and Lantier, which appears to portray a priest bearing a child in the same way in which a sacrificial animal is borne in other depictions (see 1.4 for further discussion and references). The second item comes from Spain, where, as we shall see (3.1), no "tophet" has yet been discovered. In 1971 Spanish archeologist Martín Almagro-Gorbea found the remains of a tower of stone from ca. 500 B.C. at Pozo Moro, Spain (about 125 km. southwest of the Mediterranean coast at Valencia).[395] The tower, as reconstructed, stands about five meters tall and 3.65 meters square. Both the red clay on the inside of the tower and a circle of ash, calcinated bone fragments and burnt furnishings show that the tower was used as a cremation furnace.

What has provoked the interest of scholars concerned with cultic child sacrifice is one of the stone relief panels, carved for display on the upper portion of the tower. Charles Kennedy has studied the tower and describes the panel in question as follows:

---

[395] "Les reliefs orientalisants de Pozo Moro (Albacete, Espagne)," Mythe et Personnification (ed. Jacqueline Duchemin; Paris: Société d'Édition «Les belles Lettres», 1980) 123-136, plus 8 plates.

> The relief shows a banquet prepared for a two-headed monster
> with the body of a human. He sits to the left of the scene on
> a throne with a fringed cushion or covering for the seat. The
> two heads of the monster are set one above the other, with
> large eyes, mouths open and tongues extending out and down-
> wards. In its upraised right hand is a bowl. Over the rim of
> the bowl can be seen the head and feet of a small person with
> its head turned to look at the upper head of the monster. The
> monster's left hand holds the left hind leg of a pig which is
> lying on its back on the table in front of the throne. Behind
> the table stands a male figure wearing a long fringed tunic or
> robe. He raises a small bowl in a gesture of offering. The
> right-hand panel is broken, but enough remains to show a third
> figure facing the monster across the table. This figure ap-
> pears to be standing also, its upraised right hand holding a
> sword with a curved blade. The head of the figure, only par-
> tially preserved, is shaped like that of a horse or bull.
> Whether this is supposed to be an actual head or a mask cannot
> be determined. The left hand of the figure reaches forward to
> touch the head of a second small person in a bowl atop a low
> altar located alongside the banquet table.[396]

Kennedy argues from Egyptian, Ugaritic and Biblical comparisons that the
two-headed monster represents Death (pp. 8-12). The "small persons,"
one already dead and one about to be slain, are children being offered
to Death in a sacrificial meal (pp. 14-15). Kennedy goes on to speculate that this sacrificial meal likely entailed cannibalism:

> It cannot be determined from the relief whether those making
> the offering participated in any way in sharing the blood or
> flesh (splanchna) of the child. The supposition would be that
> they did, since the fulfillment of any sacrifice was the sac-
> rificial meal. The gods are called upon to receive their
> share, but the ones who bring the offerings also participate
> in the eating. (p. 15)

Given the rarity of ancient depictions of child sacrifice (Kennedy
can cite only the Poinsott-Lantier stela discussed above), the Pozo Moro
tower relief is of extraordinary interest and importance to this study.
While the tower was apparently not constructed by Punic artisans, the

---

[396] "Tartessos, Tarshish and Tartarus: The Tower of Pozo Moro and the
Bible" (unpublished essay presented to the First International Meeting of the Society of Biblical Literature, Salamanca, Spain, 1983)
8.

influence of Near Eastern models on both the architectural form and the iconography is beyond question.[397] Whether Punic influence extended to the function of the Pozo Moro tower (i.e., as a cremation furnace for child victims of a sacrificial cult) might be suggested by the iconography, but cannot be confirmed by the archeological remains.

Kennedy's last suggestion (concerning cannibalism) aside, an examination of photographs of the relief under discussion supports his interpretation completely. It is therefore legitimate to take note of several points of contact with observations already made in this study. First, the tower relief represents a serious challenge to Weinfeld, Schaeffer and others, who maintain that there is no conclusive indication that cultic child sacrifice was actually practiced among the ancient Semites. The texts may be capable of non-sacrificial interpretation and the archeological remains held ambiguous, but the Pozo Moro tower relief is as close as we are ever apt to come to a photograph of the ancient cult in action, and it shows child sacrifice clearly enough, if nothing else. Secondly, the general context of a sacrificial meal involving a chthonic deity recalls what we have already seen with regard to the malikū at Mari and Ugarit and the character of Malik-Milku/i-Melqart at Mari and Ugarit and in Mesopotamia and Phoenicia. As to the sacrificial meal, we may recall specifically that the meal with the malikū was a facet of the cult of the dead at Mari and Ugarit; similarly, both the iconographic context of this relief (according to Kennedy's interpretation of the adjoining reliefs) and its physical context (on a cremation furnace) are the cult of the dead. As to the divine recipi-

---

[397] Kennedy, "The Tower of Pozo Moro," 7.

ent, while we saw in connection with Ugarit's <u>Mlk</u> that a simply equation with the god Death cannot be proved, the chthonic nature of Malik-Milku/i is beyond dispute, as is the suitability of that god's nature to be assimilated to Death (as in the identification of Malik with Nergal in Mesopotamia).

The fact remains, however, that one would expect the closest ties of the Pozo Moro relief to be with the cultic practice of those who mediated Semitic culture to the native artists, namely, the Punic traders and colonists.[398] As already noted, despite the relief under discussion, we cannot assume that the Pozo Moro tower was itself used for child sacrifice; indeed, the relief does not show that the child victims of which it knew were burned. On the other hand, from the Punic side, it is difficult to determine whether the divine recipients of the sacrifices commemorated by the Punic <u>mlk</u>-stelae were chthonic: if, as most scholars hold, Baal-Ḥammon is to be identified with El, not Baal or Melqart, the entire, vexed issue of El's possibly chthonic traits comes to the fore. In addition, the very purpose of the Punic <u>molk</u> cult itself is an issue. Most scholars have assumed, on the basis of their interpretation of the stelae and of the classical authors (such as Diodorus), that the Punic cult was either a fertility cult or a cult designed to move the god(s) to look favorably on their city, especially in time of crisis (or both). Either explanation is amenable to the inclusion of the cult of the dead in the Punic cult's rationale.

---

[398] It is for this reason that the Pozo Moro tower is being treated with the Punic evidence.

2.7.3 Summary of Punic Evidence

The philological issue of what Molek means, as illuminated by the comparative Semitic evidence, remains open, albeit with a heavy preponderance of the evidence suggesting that Israel's religious milieu had long
known a chthonic god named Malik or Milku/i, while the sacrificial usage
of the root was relatively late and geographically restricted. One can
still argue, of course, that the OT usage of Molek is closest to that of
the Punic molk, forming a lexical (and religio-cultural) isogloss among
Israel, the Punic colonies and (one must argue) Phoenicia. Philologically speaking, the strongest argument in favor of this possibility is,
of course, the shared o-vowel in Punic molk and OT Molek.

On the other hand, the Punic iconographic evidence serves to confirm several observations made in the course of our review of scholarship on Molek and our earlier comparative studies. The reality of cultic child sacrifice among the Semites (if not yet specifically in
Israel) seems demonstrated beyond cavil. Furthermore, the discovery of
the Pozo Moro tower provides supportive evidence for the linkage of Semitic cultic child sacrifice with chthonic deities and meals shared in
the practice of the cult of the dead. Kennedy's suggestions that a similar cluster of phenomena is to be observed in the OT will need to be
tested when we examine the Biblical material.

However, before we turn to the question of Biblical philology or
the importance of the Pozo Moro discovery to the study of the Biblical
practices related to Molek, a distinct body of evidence, the archeological, remains to be reviewed. While it promises to shed light more on
the nature of the Molek cult than on the meaning of the term, we do well

to examine it before we attempt to determine the precise place of the OT Molek in its linguistic and cultural context and seek to reconstruct, as best we can, the Israelite cult which bore that name.

CHAPTER III
THE ARCHEOLOGICAL EVIDENCE

From the first chapter it will have been clear that the interpretation of the OT Molek cult which claims that it entailed actual child sacrifice is, in our view, convincing. It is the purpose of the present chapter to survey the archeological evidence for cultic child sacrifice throughout the Semitic area of the ancient Near East, just as the relevant epigraphic and literary material was sought in chapter II.[399] As was pointed out in the last chapter, the archeological evidence, by its very nature, is far more apt to inform our understanding of the cult than of the term, Molek. Nevertheless, it is essential to examine the realia which serve as the comparative context of the Biblical practice, if we hope to propose a plausible historical reconstruction and explanation for OT Molek and the Molek cult.

As was stated above, the richest source of relevant archeological evidence is the Punic colonies of the western Mediterranean. We shall, therefore, examine this area first. Secondly, we shall return to the Mesopotamian region, where more debatable evidence has been adduced, and

---

[399] The decision to restrict the examination of the archeological evidence (which has to do with the issue of cultic child sacrifice) to Semitic areas is admittedly more arbitrary than that similarly to restrict the study of the literary evidence (which mostly concerned a Semitic term, mlk). However, beyond the obvious need to place some limits on the geographical extent of our study, we may note that neither the attempt of Mader to see a southern provenance for the Israelite cult (in Egypt), nor that of Green to see a northern provenance (in Anatolia and northern Syria) has attracted much scholarly support (see 1.3 and D. J. Wiseman, BSOAS 40 [1977] 441).

finally, to Syria-Palestine, both the main locus of our attention and the most controversial source of material of use to this study.

3.1   THE PUNIC EVIDENCE FOR CULTIC CHILD SACRIFICE

As was the case with the Punic inscriptional material, the archeological evidence has been repeatedly studied and summarized.[400] What is different in regard to the study of the archeological remains, however, is that significant, new discoveries have continued to be made, some of which have forced revisions in previous conclusions. Following a very brief summary of the Punic finds, we shall present this important, new material and then suggest how the Punic evidence may properly be brought to bear on our larger question.

The Punic evidence has been unearthed in a series of sacred precincts or "tophets" (using the OT term) found in the ruins of western Mediterranean colonies. These include: Carthage and Sousse (Roman Hadrumetum) in modern Tunisia; Motya (Sicily); and Tharros, Sulcis, Monte Sirai, Bythia and Nova (Sardinia).[401] Sabatino Moscati's comparative

---

[400] See Mosca, "Child Sacrifice," chapter II A-B.

[401] Mosca ("Child Sacrifice," 104-106) lists the important excavation reports published through the time of his study (1975). Significant reports since then include: for Carthage, L. E. Stager, "Excavations at Carthage," The Oriental Institute Annual Report 1976-77 (Chicago: Oriental Institute, 1977) 34-40; "Carthage: The Punic Project," The Oriental Institute Annual Report 1978-79 (Chicago: Oriental Institute, 1979) 52-59; L. E. Stager, ed., Carthage Excavations, 1976/77: Punic Project, Second Interim Report (Chicago: Oriental Institute, in press); for Motya, A. Ciasca, V. Tusa, M. L. Uberti, Mozia-VIII (Studi semitici 45; Rome: Consiglio Nationale delle Ricerche, 1973) [1971 campaign]; A. Ciasca, "Mozia (Sicilia): il tofet. Campagne 1971-72," RSF 1 (1973) 94-98; A. Ciasca et al., Mozia-IX (Studi semitici 50; Rome: Consiglio Nationale delle Ricerche, 1978) [1972-74 campaigns]; A. Ciasca and A. C. Tusa, "Mozia 1977," RSF 6 (1978) 227-245; A. Ciasca, "Scavi alle Mura di Mozia (campagna 1978)," RSF 7 (1979) 207-227; A. Ciasco and P. G. Guzzo,

study of the various precincts produced the following definition: "un-roofed sacred areas which were enclosed by means of walls and in which were placed urns containing the calcinated remains of children and small animals."[402] In the lowest strata (eighth-seventh century at Carthage) the jars were marked only by cairns of stones, while in later periods (seventh-sixth century on) the burials were commemorated with stelae, some of which, from the sixth-fifth century on, were inscribed. The presence of the animal bones, together with the concentration of strict-ly children's remains in the precincts, makes it unlikely that we have to do with mere cemeteries, as the earliest excavators thought.[403] Fur-

---

"Mozia 1979," RSF 8 (1980) 237-263; for Tharros, E. Acquaro et al., "Tharros-I," RSF 3 (1975) 89-119 [1974 campaign]; "Tharros-II," RSF 3 (1975) 213-225 [1975 campaign]; "Tharros-III," RSF 4 (1976) 197-228 [1976 campaign]; "Tharros-IV," RSF 6 (1978) 63-68 [1977 campaign]; "Tharros-V," RSF 7 (1979) 49-124 [1978 campaign]; "Tharros-VI," RSF 8 (1980) 79-142 [1979 campaign]; "Tharros-VII," RSF 9 (1981) 29-119 [1980 campaign]; "Tharros-VIII," RSF 10 (1982) 37-127 [1981 campaign]; F. Fedele, "Anthropologia fisica e paleoecologia di Tharros: Nota preliminare sugli scavi del tofet, campagna 1976," RSF 5 (1977) 185-193; for Sulcis, S. Cecchini, "Les stèles du tophet de Sulcis," Actes du deuxième Congrès International d'études des Cultures de la Méditerranée Occidentale (Algiers, 1978) 2.90-108; C. Troncheti, "Per la cronologia del tophet di S. Antico," RSF 7 (1979) 201-205; for Monte Sirai, F. Barreca and S. F. Bondì, "Scavi nel to-fet di Monte Sirai, campagna 1979," RSF 8 (1980) 143-145; P. Barto-loni and S. F. Bondì, "Monte Sirai 1980," RSF 9 (1981) 217-230; and for Nova, G. Chiera, Testmonianze su Nora (Collezione di Studi feni-ci 11; Rome: Consiglio Nationale delle Ricerche, 1978); P. Bartolo-ni and C. Tronchetti, La necropoli di Nora (Collezione di Studi fen-ici 12; Rome: Consiglio Nationale delle Ricerche, 1981).

[402] Mosca, "Child Sacrifice," 39, translating Moscati, "Il Sacrificio dei Fanciulli," Rendiconti della pontificia Academia romana di Ar-cheologia 38 (1965-1966) 68. See also Moscati, "Il 'tofet'," Studi sull'Oriente e la Bibbia (Genoa: Studio e vita, 1967), and, more recently, Sandro Filippo Bondì, "Per una Reconsiderazione del To-fet," Egitto e vincino Oriente 2 (1979) 139-150.

[403] H. Benichou-Safar ("À propos des ossements humains du tophet du Car-thage," RSF 9 [1981] 5-9) suggests that those buried in "tophets" were the infants who had died naturally, but had not yet been "ini-tiated" by the proper rite into Punic society. He admits, however,

thermore, there are signs of the popular character of the cult: only
the precinct at Monte Sirai contains or adjoins a temple.

Given this physical evidence, even apart from the inscriptions examined above or the testimony of the classical authors, the Punic practice of cultic child sacrifice seems securely established.   There is,
however, additional evidence, some of it quite recent, which calls into
question the common reconstruction of the Punic cult (as by Mosca), to
say nothing of the more extended use of the Punic evidence to explain
the Biblical Molek.   First, archeologists have long known that the practice of erecting stelae to mark burials in the sacred precincts is not
witnessed in the earliest strata of the precincts.[404] Albright draws a
reasonable conclusion from this fact: "The relatively late date at
which the practice of setting up commemorative stelae in connection with
'tophet' sacrifices was introduced, makes it improbable that they were
derived from Phoenicia proper."[405] If that is the case, and given the
further fact that the earliest commemorative stelae are anepigraphic,
one may well wonder at what point (place and time) the term _molk_ was applied to the Punic cult of child sacrifice.   While the lack of inscribed
stelae hardly disproves that _molk_ was the term used from colonization on
(or, indeed, that it was brought from Phoenicia), this two-century gap

_____

that the bones of the sacrificial animals present a major problem
for his theory (p. 9).

[404] Moscati, "Il Sacrificio dei Fanciulli," 65-66.

[405] Yahweh and the Gods, 238. Palestinian stelae as such (even with
carved reliefs) are, of course, known from long before the founding
of the Punic colonies (see Lawrence Stager and Samuel Wolff, "Child
Sacrifice at Carthage--Religious Rite or Population Control?" BARev
10 (1984) 38, regarding a stela apparently dedicated to Tanit and
Baal Hammon, discovered at Hazor). However, Albright's point stands
with regard to commemorative stelae.

in the continuity of the evidence has not, to my knowledge, previously been noted.[406]

Similarly, the oldest Punic stelae bearing mlk (KAI 61A and B), dated to the seventh-sixth century, were found on Malta, where no sacred precinct has yet been discovered.[407] Again, later and fuller evidence from elsewhere may make a sacrificial understanding probable, but the difficulties of integrating one's interpretations of the realia and the inscriptions into a historical reconstruction which is methodologically sound as well as coherent cannot be ignored.[408]

A still more serious problem for the reconstruction of the history of the Punic cult which has been dominant since Chabot and Eissfeldt has arisen as a result of the excavations at Carthage by the "Save Carthage Campaign."[409] As we have seen in chapter I (1.7,9), the analysis of the contents of burial urns from Carthage and Sousse (primarily the latter) by J. Richard led de Vaux and Mosca to argue that the decreasing ratio of human to animal bones showed that the rite was "attenuated" over time in the direction of more and more animal substitutions. Now the field

---

[406] The Phoenician nṣb mlk inscription, discussed above in 2.6.3, is, as was seen there, both too late (third-second century) and too problematic a text to serve as a significant datum in the reconstruction of the history of Punic mlk as a sacrificial term.

[407] See Moscati, "Il Sacrificio dei Fanciulli," 67, for a summary of the excavations there, including a description of an area intially supposed to be a "tophet."

[408] Malta is not the only important source of stelae bearing mlk in an apparently sacrificial usage which has so far not yielded a sacred precinct. In terms of the quantity of stelae, a still more important site is in Constantine, Algeria (Roman Cirta); see A. Berthier and R. Charlier, Le Sanctuaire punique d'El-Hofra à Constantine.

[409] See now Stager and Wolff, "Child Sacrifice at Carthage," for an extensive summary and photographs of the campaign's finds.

director of the most recent Carthage dig, Lawrence Stager, has proposed
that the evidence from Carthage alone suggests quite the opposite.[410]
Working from preliminary results supplied by the project's osteologist,
J. Schwartz, Stager notes that of eighty urns analyzed from the
seventh-sixth century B.C., fifty (62.5%) contain human bones only,
twenty-four (30%) contain animal bones only and six (7.5%) have a mixture. On the other hand, a second group of fifty urns from the fourth
century yielded the following proportions: forty-four (88%), human
bones only; five (10%), animal bones only; and one (2%), a mixture.
Stager concludes that, while animal substitution was either permitted or
chosen from earliest times at Carthage, Richard's study has misled historians of the Punic rite:

> From this [Schwartz's] analysis, which of course remains ten-
> tative until all of the urn contents have been thoroughly
> studied, I have difficulty accepting the evolutionary scheme
> proposed by many historians of religion who maintain that the
> "barbaric" practice of human sacrifice was gradually replaced
> by the more "civilized" practice of animal substitution. A-
> braham substituting the "ram-in-the-thicket" for his son Isaac
> is usually considered paradigmatic. Such was not the case in
> Carthage: for it is precisely in the 4th-3rd Centuries B.C.,
> when Carthage had attained the heights of urbanity, that child
> sacrifice flourished as never before.[411]

In the "Diskussion" following Stager's article, S. F. Bondì comments
that, also at Tharros, there is "une forte présence d'ossements d'ani-
maux dans les couches anciennes."[412] Thus, the most recent archeological
evidence would suggest that "attenuation" was no more necessarily the

---

[410] "Carthage: A View from the Tophet," Phönizier im Westen (Madrider
    Beiträge 8; ed. H. G. Niemeyer; Mainz am Rhein: Philipp von Zabern,
    1982) 159-160.

[411] "Carthage," 163.

[412] Ibid., 164. See also Bondì, "Reconsiderazione del Tofet," 139.

case than is any specimen of historical "progress."

There are three other points in Stager's article which bear emphasis. First, contrary to Mosca's contention that the burial jars show "the indiscriminate mixing of calcinated human and lamb bones . . . and the presence of bones from several children in a single urn," suggesting that the burning pit or trench was either only periodically cleared of remains or the scene of mass sacrifices (à la Diodorus), Stager says: "The skeletal evidence that has been presented indicates that a conscious effort was made by parents and/or priests to collect from the pyre or altar the particular remains of one or two individuals and to deposit them in an urn."[413] While this says nothing about the popular versus official nature of the _molk_ cult at Carthage, it does suggest that the sacrifices were not restricted to times of communal crisis.[414]

Secondly, Stager observes that by the time of the second set of burial urns examined by Schwartz (fourth century), a significant number contained the bones of two or three children, "invariably," one a premature or newborn child and the other more mature. Stager proposes that such urns evidence cases where parents had vowed an unborn child, only to have it die before or at birth, so that they were compelled to offer their next youngest child.[415] Thus, he argues, the Carthaginian cult was not one of primogenicide. Again, this conclusion will have to be brought to bear on the Biblical evidence in chapter IV.

---

[413] Mosca, "Child Sacrifice," 54; Stager, "Carthage," 159.

[414] Stager and Wolff write: "Our evidence indicates, however, that child sacrifice in times of civic crisis was the exception rather than the rule. We have found no evidence for mass burials" ("Child Sacrifice at Carthage," 44).

[415] "Carthage," 161-162.

Finally, and on a more speculative note, Stager approaches what is in any study of cultic child sacrifice, Punic or Biblical, the ultimate question: Why did the parents do it? Incorporating the observation that animal substitution decreased from the earliest attested practice of the molk cult to the fourth century, Stager notes the "practical benefits" of piety, at least for the wealthy: the number of heirs could be controlled and "the large estates in and around Carthage could be passed on for generations without being greatly subdivided, thus maintaining the wealth and power of the proprietary family."[416] Stager's hypothesis is provocative, albeit, as he says, "possibly premature."[417] Such a "fringe benefit" as he suggests the cult may have provided for wealthy families need not have excluded a more religious motivation for all practitioners of the cult, such as participation in the cult of the dead and/or fertility, which we have found repeatedly linked on the mainland with Malik-Milku/i. We shall pursue this "ultimate question" further as it pertains to the Biblical cult below, in chapter IV.

In sum, the Punic archeological evidence provides ample physical proof that a cult of child sacrifice was practiced from the earliest times of Phoenician colonization in the West.[418] The cult was practised in walled, roofless precincts, sometimes outside of the city walls, and entailed the burning of babies and young children (or young animals) in

---

[416] Ibid., 163.

[417] Feudal Europe, for instance, did not resort to infanticide to deal with its problem of the younger sons of nobles. Second sons customarily became churchmen.

[418] It is important to note that the molk cult has not been shown to be universal among the Punic colonies: no "tophets" or stelae bearing the sacrificial sense of mlk have been found either on Cyprus or in Spain.

acts of individual devotion which were, after a time, commemorated by stelae. While we have referred repeatedly to the Punic practice as the "molk cult," it must be stressed that there is no evidence that molk as a sacrificial term came from Phoenicia; indeed, the earliest burials of the cult's victims bear no inscribed monuments. One can, of course, argue that it is only reasonable to suppose that if the cult itself came from Phoenicia (as reason again, not realia, would suggest), then so did the term. But given the certainty with which some scholars have moved back from the Punic colonies to Phoenicia (and Palestine), the nature of the evidence and of the argument bears emphasis.

It remains true, as we shall see, that the Punic archeological evidence provides the closest parallel to the cult of which the OT appears to speak. In both cases children were sacrificed by fire to a deity in a specific sacred precinct. Moreover, such elements as a strong mixture of the popular and official cults and, as we now know, periods of increased observance of the practice appear to be shared. While we shall have to take care not to assume that the two cults were identical in every respect (including their divine recipient!), there is no question that the Punic evidence provides rich confirmation that cultic child sacrifice by fire was known among the Iron Age Semites whose homeland was Syria-Palestine.

But what of the Semites in general? We shall now examine the archeological evidence concerning the Semites of Mesopotamian provenance.

3.2   THE MESOPOTAMIAN EVIDENCE FOR CULTIC CHILD SACRIFICE

It may be noted from the outset that nothing so spectacular as the Punic
"tophets" has been unearthed in Mesopotamia. In fact, as we have already seen in examining the Mesopotamian texts and seals (2.4.6), there
is much controversy over whether any form of human sacrifice was known
there. Given the often ambiguous character of archeological remains and
the concommitant necessity of interpreting them by the written evidence
(which is itself less than lucid in this case), it is no surprise that
scholars have come to quite different conclusions. Some of the negative
arguments may, indeed, be motivated, as Green suggests, by "the personal
bias of the particular scholar" against admitting that the ancient people who are the focus of one's scholarly career could have engaged in a
practice now considered reprehensible.[419] But there is no doubt that the
evidence is not as clear either way as one could wish.

This last assertion is well illustrated by the diametrically opposed conclusions drawn on the basis of the identical site reports from
Nuzi and Tepe Gawra by Green and Richard Ellis.[420] Green argues, as do
the authors of the site excavation reports, that the archeological evidence shows that children were ritually killed and placed in the founda-
tions and floors of buildings under construction, while Ellis states
flatly: "Neither archaeology nor texts provide any convincing reason to
believe that human sacrifice was ever practised in Mesopotamia, as a
foundation sacrifice or for any other reason."[421] "Foundation sacrific-

---

[419] Role of Human Sacrifice, 189.

[420] Foundation Deposits in Ancient Mesopotamia (Yale Near Eastern Researches 2; New Haven: Yale, 1968).

[421] Ibid., 41.

es" are largely outside the purview of this study since they were evidently practiced at home, rather than at a communal cultic center, as the Molek sacrifices appear to have been. Nevertheless, because there are so few specimens of alleged child sacrifice in Mesopotamia, and because the dispute over the evidence of foundation sacrifices illustrates so well the problems also to be faced in interpreting the archeological material from Syria-Palestine, we shall include a discussion of the alleged foundation sacrifices, as we review the Mesopotamian archeological evidence and comment on the proposed interpretations of it.

The finds at Nuzi and Tepe Gawra are summarized by Green on pp. 59-65 and 65-77, respectively, from the original excavation reports.[422] While he observes that at both sites it was common practice to bury the deceased in the floor of private dwellings, he contends that certain jar burials of infants under and in the walls and floors of houses are suggestive of ritual killings performed for the benefit of the inhabitants. Green bases his case primarily on burials of infants which by the manner or place of their burial seem to show that the remains received special treatment beyond that usually accorded the deceased. Thus, in Nuzi strata III and II (ca. sixteenth-fifteenth centuries B.C.) Green cites several infant burials in upright (rather than the usual inverted) jars, where the jars were placed at floor level or at the base of a wall and then carefully built over (rather than simply buried beneath the

---

[422] Nuzi: Richard F. S. Starr, <u>Nuzi: Report on the Excavations at Yorgan Tepe near Kirkuk, Iraq</u> (2 vols.; Cambridge, MA: Harvard, 1937); Tepe Gawra: E. A. Speiser, <u>Excavations at Tepe Gawra: Levels I-VIII</u> (Philadelphia: University of Pennsylvania, 1935); and Arthur J. Tobler, <u>Excavations at Tepe Gawra: Levels IX-XX</u> (Philadelphia: University of Pennsylvania, 1950).

floor).[423] He stresses especially one case, where a jar containing the
bones of some eleven infants was built over at the base of the wall at
the northern corner of a room (pp. 60-62). The infant remains at Tepe
Gawra have the added feature of being buried in what were clearly sacred
structures, where the most remarkable point is the very concentration of
infants, buried in careful orientation to the altars. The excavator of
strata IX-XX, Arthur Tobler, suggested a provocative explanation for the
Tepe Gawra finds:

> We are, as a result, confronted with the problem of finding a
> reason for the heavy concentrations of both tombs and graves
> around and underneath the Western Temple of Stratum VIII-C;
> the Strata IX, XI, and XI-A Temples; and the Eastern Shrine of
> XIII [all from the Mesopotamian Protoliterate period and ear-
> lier]. The only probable answer is that those temples were
> the seats of chthonic deities who, as the heads of a cult of
> the underworld and the dead, demanded human sacrifice of their
> worshippers.[424]

In response, we may note that at times, Green appears to press his
evidence too hard, implying that a burial with "religious significance"
was, ipso facto, a sacrifice (e.g., p. 71). For the most part, however,
he is well aware of the limitations of his mute material, warning, for
example, that "The mere fact that the interments were contemporaneous
with the construction of walls or pavements does not constitute adequate
proof of ritual killings" (p. 62) and that "There is possible evidence
of ritual killing at Gawra, but certainly all of the sub-pavement and
intramural burials cannot be so classified" (p. 73). Thus, although his

---

[423] Green also calls attention to the first in-house burials in the Pre-
historic period (stratum X) as abnormal for the time: "This is in
contrast to normal type burials and simple inhumations on the outside, unconnected with buildings" (p. 59). He must concede, however, that the new practice may simply reflect the immigration of
the new, Nuzian culture.

[424] Tepe Gawra, 2.124.

work is notable for its strong polemic in favor of the existence of human sacrifice in the ancient Near East, his conclusions regarding foundation sacrifices are measured: "Although other theories are certainly possible, this [ritual killing] seems to be the most reasonable explanation" (p. 77).

In contrast to Green, Ellis takes a decidedly minimalist view of what would constitute proof of foundation sacrifices: "A sacrificial burial made at the construction of the house could now be distinguished from a normal intramural burial only if it exhibited some characteristic features, or if it were built into the structure of the house itself" (p. 35). Granted that, in Ellis's words, there is no sign of "foul play" in the excavation reports, it is Green's best cases, noted above, upon which Ellis concentrates. Ellis argues that since the instances which might be indicative of foundation sacrifices are relatively few, and since even they "did not differ in arrangement or equipment from other burials" (p. 38), there is little cause to posit the existence of so remarkable a practice among the Mesopotamians.

Again in response, it seems that Ellis has read too little out of even that material which he permits to be entered into evidence. He overlooks the indications of abnormal burials listed by Green (above), which, given the great conservatism and even uniformity normally to be found in ancient Near Eastern burials, likely bespeak some special significance (whether or not they indicate sacrifices). Moreover, to suggest that the several "built-in" burials found in such cultically important locations as the foundation and even the corner of buildings may evidence no more than that the deceased died during construction (p. 38)

is to avoid the obvious questions of why such individuals were not buried in the floor (in keeping with normal practice) and why the survivors
were at such pains to care for the remains.[425] In short, while the evidence is doubtlessly equivocal, the practice of foundation sacrifices
seems likely at Nuzi and a distinct possibility at Tepe Gawra.[426]

Of much greater interest to this study than foundation sacrifices
are what Green calls "chapel" sacrifices, first attested in the Habur
region of Syria in the Akkadian (greater Sargonic) period and later at
Ur in the Larsa period (pp. 57-58,77-79). Their significance is only
enhanced when Ellis calls the instances at Ur "the most nearly convincing evidence for [Mesopotamian] human sacrifice" (pp. 38-39), even if,
in the end, he remains unpersuaded. "Chapel" sacrifices are infant burials in private homes (like the Nuzi foundation sacrifices, above), but
in rooms whose religious purpose is apparent from an altar niche at one
end and such cultic paraphenalia as clay platters for food offerings
nearby. The burial jars were set into the floor right in front of the
altar (or, at Ur, before a pillar next to it). What is particularly remarkable at Ur is the distinct separation of the infant burials from the
family vault, found under the floor at the other end of the room. Furthermore, there is regularly one and only one infant buried before each
family altar (although Woolley found a few cases of multiple burials,

---

[425] As the excavator of Nuzi, Stark, repeatedly stresses, not only were
the walls carefully built around the burial jars, but the bodies
were clearly exposed or stripped, so that only bones remained before
the remains were interred (Nuzi, 1.353-354).

[426] Green's case for the latter site, in my opinion, is not as strong as
that for Nuzi. However likely it is that a cemetery outside of the
temple structures existed at Tepe Gawra (Green, p. 73), none has yet
been found, and it is possible that infants were buried in the temples as a matter of course there.

including one of over thirty).

Again, the argument that "chapel sacrifices" were really sacrifices is circumstantial: the excavations report no signs of violence to the bones, and there is no written evidence of such a practice (nor, as a private, rather than official, cultic practice, would we expect any). The strongest point to be adduced, as Green observes, is that regularly (but not "always" [p. 58]) there is a single child buried apart from the family at the foot of the altar. Even Ellis must concede that "this was clearly a special treatment of some sort" (p. 39). Paolo Xella, in a mixed review of Green's work, has no doubts about the evidence for "chapel" sacrifices (or, for that matter, foundation sacrifices): "Green demonstrates convincingly that ritual slayings (above all, foundation sacrifices) are attested at least in the areas of Nuzi, Tepe Gawra, Habur and Ur, even if in different ways."[427]

What is particularly of interest to this study is that both the foundation and the "chapel" sacrifices, if they were practiced at all, were known first and most in what we have elsewhere termed the "periphery" of the Mesopotamian heartland. Green is entirely within the realm of probability when he speculates: "This [the Ur 'chapel' burials] could represent an aspect of southern [heartland] borrowing from the North [periphery], introduced by means of the Amorite invasions" (pp. 82-83). In short, such archeological evidence as there is for cultic child sacrifice in Mesopotamia points to the periphery, indeed, to Syria (Habur) as the area of most frequent practice and likely origin. As we

---

[427] RSF 8 (1980) 151. (Xella's original: ". . . il Green dimostra convincentemente che uccisioni rituali [soprattutto sacrifici di fondazione] sono attestate almeno nelle aree di Nuzi, Tepe Gawra, Habur e Ur, sia pure con modalità differenti.")

saw above with reference to the god Malik-Milku/i, Mesopotamia was open
to influence in religious matters from Syria (just as Mesopotamia, in
turn, influenced Syria, of course). Whether there was a connection between Malik-Milku/i and cultic child sacrifice in Mesopotamia (or Syria)
the sources, written and archeological, simply do not say. Their possible connection in Palestine is, of course, at the heart of the dispute
over the Biblical Molek.

In sum, however strongly one believes that the archeological (and,
for that matter, the written) evidence suggests that the ancient Mesopotamians knew and practiced cultic child sacrifice--and there is good
reason for such belief--the proof of such a practice is not presently at
hand. This is especialy the case, when one places the Mesopotamian evidence side-by-side with the Punic. We turn, finally, to the territory
in between the two, Syria-Palestine, to see how strong an archeological
case exists there for the practice of cultic child sacrifice.

3.3   THE SYRO-PALESTINIAN EVIDENCE FOR CULTIC CHILD SACRIFICE
As was the case with the Mesopotamian archeological evidence, it must be
admitted from the outset that nothing so spectacular as the Punic "tophets" has yet been unearthed in Syria-Palestine. Moreover, in terms of
the cities and areas discussed in chapter II, no promising candidates
for any sort of child sacrifice have been found at Ebla, Mari, Ugarit or
in Phoenicia. This may be due to as-yet-incomplete excavation (Ebla),
to what we now see was poor technique (Ugarit), or to centuries of de-
tritus having been piled on top of any possible evidence through continuous occupation of the sites or the filling-in of the valleys where the

"tophets" were ostensibly located (as Albright and others have suggested was the case in Phoenicia).[428] As a result, our search for possible evidence must focus largely on the region of greatest interest to this study: greater Palestine (i.e., including Transjordan). There, as we have already seen (1.4), archeologists have long known candidates for remains of cultic child sacrifice. In this section we shall not only review such older material, but also examine the alleged evidence which has more recently come to light.

Besides the infant jar burials discovered at Gezer by Macalister and the similar finds at Taanach and Megiddo (1.4), there are two other significant instances where excavators have claimed to have found archeological evidence for cultic child sacrifice, at Jericho and Amman. As for the finds at Gezer (which is, by all accounts, the strongest candidate of the first three sites above), the near-consensus which existed early in this century, that Macalister's evidence showed the practice of ritual child sacrifice, has by now been completely reversed. As we have seen, Macalister's strongest case was built on his discovery of jars containing infants' bones (of which "two at least displayed marks of fire") in the context of stelae and other architectural remains which the excavators called a "high place" (and which, even now, are conceded some "cultic interpretation").[429] Now, however, it is clear that the jars are earlier than the high place, so that the earlier use of the

---

[428] See Gabriel Saadé, Ougarit: Métropole cananéenne (Beirut: Imprimerie catholique, 1979) 18-21, for a summary of the shortcomings of the early excavation reports from Ugarit. More recent reports show improved stratigraphy, but no signs of human sacrifice have as yet appeared. For Albright's suggestion, see Yahweh and the Gods, 238.

[429] Dever, "Gezer," EAEHL 2 (1976) 438.

area (as early as the Ghassulian period) was likely nothing more than as a child cemetery.[430] Nevertheless, the MB IIC cult place is not without interest for this study: Eduard Meyer and Albright have suggested that it (like other "high places") was used for the practice of a cult of dead ancestors.[431]

More recently, Kathleen Kenyon has suggested that she may have found evidence for child sacrifice at Prepottery Neolithic Jericho. Although it was apparently normal to remove the skull of the deceased (and even plaster it) after the body had otherwise decomposed, some children's skulls displayed a difference from the norm: "In the third instance there is an unpleasant suggestion of infant sacrifice, for beneath a curious bath-like structure of mud-plaster there is, besides one complete infant burial, a collection of infant skulls with the neck vertebrae attached, showing that the heads were cut off and not merely collected from burials."[432] Unfortunately, this relatively popular presentation of the find is all Miss Kenyon provides; she hardly treats the Neolithic material at all in the full, multi-volume excavation report, Excavations at Jericho. In any event, the importance of this discovery for our study is limited, given the lack of further evidence bridging the large gap between the Neolithic Period and the Iron Age.

---

[430] Ibid.

[431] Meyer, Geschichte des Altertums (3d ed.; Stuttgart: Gotta, 1953) 1.2.423-424; Albright, "The high place in Ancient Palestine," VTSup 4 (1957) 242-258.

[432] Digging Up Jericho (London: E. Benn, 1957) 72.

A second, very recent discovery is potentially of far greater interest. Airport construction at Amman, Jordan, in the mid-1950's
brought to light a Late Bronze Age structure which the initial excavator, G. Lankester Harding, identified as a temple.[433] Full excavation in
1966 under J. B. Hennessy revealed, in his words: "enormous quantities
of animal, bird and human bones and the abundant evidence of fire. All
levels of occupation were thick with the ashes of small isolated fires
and the altar stone was charred on top."[434] Hennessy concluded that a
"fire cult" was practiced in the temple (p. 162). In a comparative
study of sanctuaries throughout Palestine, Magnus Ottosson cites Hennessy's later statement that the bones were overwhelmingly human, specifically, of human children, and suggests that the temple was employed for
child sacrifice, along the lines of the account of the daughter of Jepthah, from nearby Gilead (Judg 11).[435]

Such a discovery would, of course, rival those of the Punic "tophets" and of the Pozo Moro tower in importance for this study. Unfortunately, subsequent review of the evidence has not been kind to the
Hennessy-Ottosson interpretation. The director of excavations in the
same area in 1976, Larry Herr, notes that, while the human bones from
the temple do show signs of burning, the animal bones do not, and further, that most of the human bones were from adults, not children.
Thus, "the picture is not one of child sacrifice, but more probably that

---

[433] "Recent Discoveries in Jordan," PEQ 90 (1958) 10-12.

[434] "Excavation of a Bronze Age Temple at Amman," PEQ 98 (1966) 162.

[435] Temples and Cult Places in Palestine (Boreas 12; Uppsala: Almquist
and Wiksell, 1980) 104.

of cremation."[436] Herr goes on to suggest that the "large numbers of
fine ceramic vessels, bronze weapons and gold jewelry" from the temple
are "typical tomb furniture of the time" and show the the "temple" [sic]
was really a center for rites connected with the burial and subsequent
cult of the dead, used by nomads or nearby settlers (in Amman). In a
more recent article, Herr goes further, citing the judgment of Robert M.
Little (also of the 1976 expedition) that the human remains appear to be
of Indo-Europeans, and proposing that "Hittites were using the site,
though perhaps not exclusively, for mortuary rites."[437] The crucial issue, from an archeological perspective, is clearly whether the human
bones were of children (so Hennessy) or of adults (so Herr). Little's
recently-published osteological analysis does, indeed, support the latter position.[438] We may note that the Amman airport excavations are of
interest in any case: at the least, they appear to evidence the practice of cremation in connection with the cult of the dead in Late Bronze
Age Palestine.

One might argue that at this point our study of the archeological
evidence for cultic child sacrifice in Syria-Palestine should properly
end, with the conclusion that the evidence is, at best, equivocal for
any cases since the Neolithic period. However, as has been the case
previously in our study, it seems wise to extend the boundaries of our

---

[436] "The Amman Airport Excavations, 1976," ADAJ 21 (1976) 110. On the
crucial matter of the age of the individuals whose bones were found,
see below.

[437] "The Amman Airport Structure and the Geopolitics of Ancient Transjordan," BA 46 (1983) 228. Joseph Calloway supports Herr in the
former's review of Ottosson, JBL 101 (1982) 597-598.

[438] "Human Bone Fragment Analysis," The Amman Airport Excavations, 1976
(ed. L. G. Herr; AASOR 48; Cambridge, MA: ASOR, 1983).

search somewhat, to encompass phenomena closely related to the focus of
our study. In the case of our search for evidence of cultic child sacrifice, the material already presented (especially the Punic) encourages
us to pay particular attention to burial practices, specifically, to any
patterns in the practice of cremation or jar burials. In fact, it is
particularly the former which are of interest; concerning jar burials,
Green writes: "Normal jar-burials are a common find on many sites in
this area [Palestine] from very early down through the Late Bronze
Age."[439] We may add that such burials are by no means uncommon as late
as the Hellenistic Period.[440]

At first glance at prior investigations, we might suspect a search
for evidence of cremation in Syria-Palestine to be hard-pressed to find
anything. Kurt Galling could write in 1937: "Abgesehen von einem Fall
von Leichenverbrennung im Neolithikum in Geser und einem vielleicht
gleichseitigen in Jerusalem, hat es in Syr.-Pal keine Leichenverbrennung
gegeben."[441] On the other hand, with specific reference to Israel, Roland de Vaux argued: "There is no evidence that corpses were cremated

---

[439] Role of Human Sacrifice, 330, n. 21.

[440] My fellow student, Elizabeth Bloch-Smith, who is currently writing a
dissertation on burial customs in ancient Syria-Palestine for the
University of Chicago, was most helpful in this section, sharing her
list of Palestinian sites where evidence of cremations and jar burials has been discovered. Sites with significant finds of infants
buried in jars (without signs of cremation) include: Megiddo--MB
II, LB I, EI I (Guy and Engberg, Megiddo Tombs [OIP 33; Chicago:
University of Chicago, 1938] 57,59,79,137); Tell Zeror--LB to Hellenistic (K. Ohata, ed., Tel Zeror [3 vols.; Tokyo: Society for
Near Eastern Studies, 1966-1970] 3.71-74); Afula--Iron IB (M. Dothan, "Excavations at 'Afula," 'Atiqot 1 [1955] 47); and Dothan--8-7
centuries B.C. (J. P. Free, "The Sixth Season at Dothan," BASOR 156
[1959] 26; "The Seventh Season at Dothan," BASOR 160 [1960] 9).

[441] "Grab," Biblisches Reallexikon (HAT; Tübingen: J. C. B. Mohr, 1937)
238.

in Palestine, except in days long before the coming of the Israelites, or among groups of foreigners; the Israelites never practised it."[442] In the light of the evidence now at hand, both statements (especially Galling's) require modification.

The two cases of cremation remains cited by Galling are, as he says, Neolithic and, therefore, like the case of child sacrifice at Jericho adduced by Kenyon, well before the period of our interest. Nevertheless, it is useful at least to note in passing that Macalister was aware of alternative explanations for his find and moved to counter them. Regarding the "Troglodyte crematorium" which he claimed to have found in a cave just outside Gezer, Macalister stated that the burned bones were not the product of a general conflagration since the strata of ashes varied between black and white, suggesting the alternate dying down and renewal of the flames.[443] Also worthy of note is Macalister's judgment, based on his work at Gezer, that cremation preceded inhumation as a method of burial in Palestine.[444] As will be seen below, this is the exact opposite of the conclusion drawn on the basis of Iron Age finds by other archeologists working elsewhere in Palestine.

Other pre-Iron Age specimens of cremated remains have been suggested from the finds at Late Chalcolithic Jericho, EB IB-III Bab edh-Dhra and MB IIA Tell Beit Mirsim. In the case of Jericho, Kenyon was confident that Tomb A94 contained cremated bones, although she admitted that

---

[442] *Ancient Israel: 1. Social Institutions* (NY: McGraw-Hill, 1961 [French orig., 1958]) 57.

[443] *The Excavation of Gezer*, 1.285. The alleged example of cremation at Jerusalem is in PEQ (1924) 166-167.

[444] Ibid., 75.

it was the only tomb there to show cremation.[445] On the contrary, the excavators at Bab edh-Dhra suggested that burned bones in two "charnel houses" could evidence intentional cremation, but were more likely signs of subsequent fire.[446] Albright found a jar at Tell Beit Mirsim which, in his judgment, contained cremated bones. At the time, this instance was unique in Bronze Age Palestine: "What circumstances led to so unusual a method of disposal of a body, can only be guessed."[447] As we shall see, this case remains unusual, but it is no longer unique, at least in Bronze Age Syria-Palestine.

The earliest Iron Age example from Palestine itself comes from eleventh-century Azor (in Philistia). The excavator, M. Dothan, argues: "It may be assumed that this method of burial was connected with the appearance of a new ethnic element."[448] By far the largest number of Iron Age specimens are in Phoenicia: Khalde (ninth-eighth century); Achzib (eighth-sixth century); Atlit (seventh century); a cave near Sidon (sixth-fifth century); and Tell Rachidieh, near Tyre (sixth century).[449]

---

[445] Excavations at Jericho (4 vols.; Jerusalem: British School of Archaeology, 1960-1981) 1.21.

[446] M. Finnegan, "Faunal Remains from Bâb edh-Dhrâ', 1975," Preliminary Excavation Reports (ed. D. N. Freedman; AASOR 43; Cambridge, MA: ASOR, 1978) 53; D. J. Ortner, "A Preliminary Report on the Human Remains from the Bab edh-Dhra Cemetery," The Southeastern Dead Sea Plain Expedition, 1977 (ed. W. E. Rast and R. T. Schaub; AASOR 46; Cambridge, MA: ASOR, 1981) 129-130.

[447] The Excavation of Tell Beit Mirsim: 2. The Bronze Age (AASOR 17; New Haven: ASOR, 1938) 76.

[448] "Azor," EAEHL 1 (1975) 147.

[449] In addition to the articles in EAEHL, see: for Khalde, R. Saidah, "Fouilles de Khaldé, 1961-1962," Bulletin du Musée de Beyrouth 19 (1966) 64,84-85; for Achzib, M. Prausnitz, "Achzib," RB 67 (1960) 398; for Atlit, C. N. Johns, "Excavations at the Pilgrims' Castle 'Atlit," QDAP 6 (1936) 126-137; for the last two sites, see Saidah,

Of these, the most interesting are the remains found at Atlit: contrary
to the practice both of the Punic colonies and of the other Phoenician
sites, those cremated were not buried in jars, but directly in the sand.
Furthermore, vis-à-vis the Punic practice, the bodies were burned in the
place of their burial, not in a central pit.[450] On the other hand, Johns
observes that some of the pottery found with the burials is otherwise
foreign to Palestine and Cyprus, being known only from Carthage and Motya.[451] Johns argues that the stratigraphy shows a move toward inhumation
in shaft graves in the seventh-sixth centuries, while Saidah (at Khalde)
remarks that cremation and inhumation were practiced side-by-side.[452]

   Northern Palestine ("Israel," in the divided monarchy) has produced
little, if any, evidence of cremation.[453] By contrast, three sites in
the South have yielded such evidence: Tell el-ʻAjjul (tenth-ninth century); Tell Sharuhen, or Fara (South) (tenth-ninth century); and Tell
er-Reqeish (ninth-fourth centuries).[454] Commenting on all three sites,

_____

   p. 85, and the references there.

[450] Johns ("Pilgrims' Castle," 126) writes: "It seems that the bodies
   were laid on a small pyre of branches, surrounded by the usual grave
   furniture of pottery, and so burnt; though in most cases, the fire
   seems to have been extinguished with a covering of sand before the
   body had been entirely consumed."

[451] Ibid., 131-132.

[452] Johns, "Pilgrims' Castle," 134; Saidah, "Khaldé," 84.

[453] E. Bloch-Smith told me that such remains have been found at Kefar
   Yehoshuaʻ in the western Jezreel valley, but I have been unable to
   verify this.

[454] In addition to the articles in EAEHL, see: for Ajjul, W. M. F. Petrie, Ancient Gaza (5 vols.; London: British School of Archaeology
   in Egypt, 1931-1952) 2.pls. 56-58; for Fara, Petrie, Beth-Pelet (2
   vols.; London: British School of Archaeology in Egypt, 1930-1932)
   1.12-13; for Reqeish, W. Culican, "The Graves at Tell er-Reqeish,"
   AJBA 2/2 (1973) 66-68,102-105.

William Culican hypothesizes on the basis of the geographical distribution of the Iron Age evidence (and, to a lesser extent, on the basis of
the pottery) that cremation burials are typical of Iron II Phoenician
culture and, in the case of these three sites, distinguish Phoenician-
influenced remains from earlier, Iron I Philistine material. He admits,
however, that the evidence of Syrian cremations (see below) makes it impossible to "show unequivocally that cremation is to be associated with
Phoenicians."[455]

Three sites in Transjordan have also provided possible evidence of
cremation: Dibon (ninth-sixth century); Nebo; and Sahab (twelfth century).[456] The eight Iron Age tombs at Dibon were all robbed in antiquity,
but nearby one of them was a unique find: a separate "Burnt Bone Deposit," which, according to the excavator, "suggests that the tombs were
systematically robbed and the bones burned, perhaps for fertilizer."[457]
While there is no sign of sacrificial (or, indeed, cultic) activity,
this is the first cremation pit, or separate burned bone deposit, found
in Syria-Palestine. The report of the finds at Nebo is little more than
a student diary, annotated by the excavator, J. Ripamonti, and it is
therefore difficult to comment critically on the interpretations offered

---

[455] "Reqeish," 67,103. Cf. the earlier arguments of Albright, based on
unpublished work by Sukenik, that cremation burials were typically
Philistine ("The Chronology of a South Palestinian City, Tell
el-'Ajjûl," AJSL 55 [1938] 359).

[456] In addition to the articles in EAEHL, see: for Dibon, A. D. Tushingham, The Excavations at Dibon (Dhîbân) in Moab (AASOR 40; Cambridge, MA: ASOR, 1972) 87; for Nebo, S. Saller, "Iron Age Tombs at
Nebo, Jordan," Liber Annuus 16 (1965-1966) 172,178-181; for Sahab,
M. M. Ibrahim, "Archaeological Excavations at Sahab, 1972," ADAJ 17
(1972) 31-32.

[457] Tushingham, Dibon, 87.

therein. We note only that in two caves, in levels specified only as "Iron Age," a black "strip" or "streak" was found which suggested to the excavator that "cremation might have taken place." M. Ibrahim, the excavator of Sahab, is far more careful in his reporting and more cautious in his judgments. He notes that bones with the marks of burning were found in both jars and wooden coffins. He writes: "Fragmentary pieces of carbonised beams probably caused the burnt effect of the bones. This may suggest cremation but the material is still under study.[458]

As was observed above, there is also some evidence of cremation from Syria. P. J. Riis, who collected the material, gives two instances which may be dated to the Bronze Age.[459] These are from thirteenth-century Alalakh (Tell Atchana), excavated by Woolley, and from twelfth-century Ugarit (although, as noted above, it is difficult to assess Schaeffer's archeological claims).[460] Iron Age cremations are evidenced at Hama, Tell Halaf (tenth-ninth century) and Carchemish and Deve Hüyük (ninth-seventh century). Riis also summarizes the early evidence for cremation outside of Syria-Palestine, although he denies that there is any connection with that within. He suggests, on the basis of the items found with the remains at various Syrian sites (such as stelae and stat-

---

[458] "Sahab," 32.

[459] Les cimetières à cremation (Hama: Fouilles et Recherches 2/3; Copenhagen: Fondation Carlsburg, 1948) 36-45.

[460] Woolley, "Excavations at Tal Atchana, 1937," AntJ 18 (1938) 4, and "Excavations at Atchana-Alalakh, 1938," AntJ 19 (1939) 27. Woolley (AntJ 18:4) and Riis (Les cimetières, 39) both cite cremation remains at Ras Shamra as an assured fact, but Woolley gives no citation, while that provided by Riis (Schaeffer, Syria, 1935, 148ff.) does not mention cremations, but only claims a resemblance between the Ras Shamra graves and those from Carchemish and Deve Hüyük (see below). Further attempts to find a claim of cremation graves at Ras Shamra by its excavators have been unsuccessful.

ues), that cremation was a development within the cult of the dead, perhaps intended to purify the dead.[461] In any event, Riis shows that cremation was practiced in widely distributed portions of Syria-Palestine in the Iron Age.

It must be stressed that none of the above-mentioned jar or cremation burials gives indication either of a violent death or (with the possible exception of the Amman "temple") of a sacrificial context. Green is doubtlessly correct when he writes:

> [Syria-Palestine] has contributed very little from which a study of ritual killing of human beings can reasonably be made. Furthermore, the small amount of evidence of this type is so ambiguous, at times, that it is hazardous to attempt a definite conclusion.[462]

Nevertheless, it has been shown that, contra Galling, cremation was known and practiced in Iron Age Syria-Palestine and that the remains were usually buried in jars. To this extent, there is a resemblance to the clear evidence of cultic child sacrifice in the Punic colonies. Furthermore, there have been repeated indications of the practice of the cult of the dead in Syria-Palestine from the earliest times evidenced by burial remains. But, to address de Vaux's claim, was cremation practiced in Israel? Here the image yielded by the archeological evidence is less clear: the pottery which accompanied the burials provides no unambiguous link with Israelites as the objects or the practitioners of cremation. (We may add, a fortiori, that there is likewise no convincing archeological evidence of cultic child sacrifice in Israel.) On the

---

[461] Les cimitières, 44.

[462] Role of Human Sacrifice, 149. Specifically, vis-à-vis our investigation of the Mesopotamian evidence, Green adds that there is no clear evidence of foundation sacrifices in Syria-Palestine.

other hand, pace Culican, there is no reason why Israelites could not have been involved in the Iron II cremation burials at the southern Palestinian sites (indeed, a Hebrew seal was found in the cemetery at Fara where the cremations were located).[463] Also, the practice of the cult of the dead by the Israelites seems clearly evidenced in tombs which are without doubt theirs.[464]

In sum, archeology can show only that human sacrifice in general, and cultic child sacrifice in particular, were almost certainly known and practiced in the Punic colonies, and that they may have been known and practiced elsewhere in Israel's geographical-cultural context (the Semitic peoples of the ancient Near East). What the Israelites did, and why they did it, can only be ascertained (if at all) through a careful reexamination of what remains the best source for the history of Israel's cult, the Hebrew Bible, to which we now turn.

---

[463] Yael Yisraeli, "Sharuhen, Tell," EAEHL 4 (1978) 1082.

[464] See John W. Ribar, "Death Cult Practices in Ancient Palestine," unpublished doctoral dissertation, University of Michigan, 1973; see also Robert E. Cooley, "Gathered to His People: A Study of a Dothan Family Tomb," The Living and Active Word of God: Essays in Honor of Samuel J. Schultz (ed. M. Inck and R. Youngblood; Winona Lake, IN: Eisenbrauns, 1983) 47-58, especially 53-54, for a more reluctant view.

CHAPTER IV
THE BIBLICAL EVIDENCE

As we saw in chapter I, the Biblical references to Molek and to child sacrifice have been mined extensively for centuries in search of information to permit a historical reconstruction of the meaning of the term and the place of the rite in Israelite religion. Without a doubt, the most impressive and influential effort to this end to date has been the work of Eissfeldt, now reexamined and defended at length by Mosca. In brief, they would contend that OT Molek, like Punic molk, was a sacrificial technical term used in ritual child sacrifice and that such sacrifices were an accepted part of orthodox Yahwism until the reformation of Josiah (ca. 622 B.C.). It is the purpose of this chapter not merely to test the Eissfeldt-Mosca hypothesis, but also, as we suggested at the close of chapter I, to see if a superior paradigm for understanding OT Molek and for reconstructing the Molek cult can be obtained through the consideration of a fuller body of relevant comparative evidence, as presented in chapters II and III.

4.1 THE FORM "MOLEK"

The key word in the last sentence is, of course, "relevant." Researchers of Molek have long realized that what evidence will be admissible will depend to a great extent on how one understands the form mōlek philologically. Thus, Eissfeldt (and Mosca) recognized that if one could establish that Molek is a hybrid of an original <u>melek</u> with the vowels of <u>bōšet</u> (Geiger's dysphemism hypothesis [1.2]), the <u>prima facie</u> cognate of Punic <u>molk</u> would be lost. We have already reviewed the arguments of both scholars against Geiger's proposal (1.5,9); in my view, Mosca's, especially, are convincing. It is, indeed, not at all clear why the form <u>mōlek</u> should suggest <u>bōšet</u> to the reader, especially given the lack of analogous forms of dysphemism.[465]

Eissfeldt (implicitly) and Mosca (explicitly) then assume that if <u>mōlek</u> is, indeed, the original form, it must be a *qutl-type noun, cognate with Ugaritic, Phoenician and Punic *mulk, "kingdom, kingship, royalty."[466] This is understandable, since nouns vocalized *qōṭel in MT are regularly o/u-class segolates, from a presumed original *quṭl(u). For both scholars, this assumption (together with the refutation of the dysphemism hypothesis) warrants the exclusion of a great deal of the evidence which prior investigators have adduced (and to which we have added in chap. II). According to Mosca, the failure of the dysphemism of <u>melek</u> as an explanation means the elimination of the various ancient Near Eastern "king" gods (Milkom, Melqart, Adad-milki, etc.) and narrows one's interpretive options to an otherwise-unknown god "Molek" or to a cognate of Punic <u>molk</u>.[467]

---

[465] Matitiahu Tsevat reaches the same conclusion as Mosca regarding the ostensible dysphemism of Molek, and goes beyond him in other respects, in a historical study of the "hypothesis of dysphemism": "Ishbosheth and Congeners: The Names and Their Study," <u>HUCA</u> 46 (1975) 71-85.

[466] Mosca, "Child Sacrifice," 129.

[467] Ibid., 136-137. Mosca concedes that the divine name Muluk appears in a Mari place name, but he argues that since this isolated instance occurs a full millennium before the OT examples, "to connect the two historically (not philologically) is not an argument, but an

The assumption of a *qutl-type noun in Molek is reasonable and understandable, but, like many unexamined assumptions, it may well be
wrong. Indeed, even strong supporters of Eissfeldt's hypothesis have
been uneasy with his explanation of the form of OT Molek. The most common alternative suggestion is one which goes back as far as Andreas Beyer (1680)(1.1), but was explicated most fully by von Soden (1.6): mōlek
as a *maqṭil-type noun from the root hlk. In support of this understanding, von Soden notes that other sacrificial terms, such as môpēt
and ʿôlāh, are of the same type. On the other hand, how a form of hlk
could have taken on the technical sense which it ostensibly did is not
at all clear, even given all the appeals to a parallel in ʿôlāh.

A second possibility would be to argue that, as we have seen especially in the proper names catalogued in chapter II, the Syro-
Palestinian god M-l-k was vocalized in various ways by various population groups, so that OT Molek may simply be the form used among the
Israelites.[468] One could argue that the latter form was used in Syria-
Palestine long before them, in fact, given the Mulik element we found in
a proper name at Ugarit. Such an argument makes due allowance for the
great deal that we do not know about Canaanite and early Israelite religion (however little we may care to admit it), including the vocalization of the Ugaritic M-l-k. This possibility may well be the case, but
unless and until an epigraphic attestation with an o/u-vowel in a clear
use of M-l-k as a divine name is found (such as the form *Mulku which B.
Levine feels able to reconstruct at Ugarit [1.10]), this explanation can

---

act of faith" (p. 245, n. 47).

[468] I.e., that no further philological explanation is possible.

only suggest that the question of Molek's philological explanation must remain open.

There is yet another explanation for the form Molek which, if not so obvious as the segolate proposal, nevertheless deserves serious consideration: mōlek as a Qal active participle of the root mlk, "to rule." The normal form of the Hebrew participle is, of course, vocalized *qōṭēl, with a ṣērē between the second and third radicals. While the interchange of ē and e is not a great obstacle in any case (so that von Soden did not bother to deal with it in his proposal), it may be useful to see how the specific form, mōlek, may have developed. If the earliest recoverable form of the G-stem active participle is *qāṭilu(m), as in Akkadian, the Hebrew participle may well have developed as follows: *māliku > *mōleku > mōlēk. The middle step reflects the so-called "Canaanite vowel shift" (stressed ā > ō) and the "darkening" of the i to e in open syllables, both of which occurred before the case-endings were lost.[469] The MT form, mōlek, would then represent a frozen form, from which the case ending was dropped when the word was used as a proper name (as the evidence in chap. II would suggest was also the case outside of the Canaanite sphere with Malik).

This leaves the problem of the abnormal (for a Hebrew participle) stress on the penultimate syllable. The conventional explanation for the development of the normal stress on the ultima is that the stress shifted from the antepenult of the original (*māliku) to the penult (the eventual ultima) sometime after the "Canaanite vowel shift," but before

---

[469] See Hans Bauer and Pontus Leander, _Historische Grammatik der Hebräischen Sprache des Alten Testaments_ (Halle: Max Niemeyer, 1922) 192,195.

the loss of the case endings.[470] One can, of course, suggest that in the case of Molek the stress was frozen on the /ō/, just as the short /e/ was frozen (instead of the /ē/ which developed later, concommitantly with the loss of the case endings.[471] However, it is the better part of wisdom to admit our limitations here: we simply do not understand the principles of stress in Hebrew well enough to propose reliable reconstructions of pre-Masoretic developments.[472]

The significance of the last two suggested explanations should by now be evident. If Molek can be linked philologically not merely with long-ago Muluk of Mari (who, as suggested in 2.2.1, was likely an independent, local variant), but also with the Mulik and/or Malik evidenced as late and close (to Israel) as Ugarit, the character of the preponderance of relevant comparative evidence will have shifted dramatically. Punic molk will still be important, especially given the archeological evidence, but no longer can the material collected in chapter II regarding the god(s) M-l-k be ruled out of order with the rejection of the dysphemism hypothesis. Specifically, even Milku/i (and related forms, like Melqart and Milkom) reenters the discussion, since we have seen Malik and Milku/i used interchangeably.

---

[470] See, for example, Zellig Harris, Development of the Canaanite Dialects (New Haven: American Oriental Society, 1922) 50.

[471] Ibid., 59-61.

[472] This point is demonstrated at length by Jonathan H. Rodgers, "Semitic Accentual Systems" (unpublished Ph.D. dissertation, Yale University, 1977) 69-163 (on Hebrew). It may be that the Masoretes accented Molek on the penult because it looked most like a *qutl-type segolate.

Finally, it must be noted that the connection of Malik with Molek need not depend on the correctness of our argument that Malik's original form was, more technically, Mālik (2.4.5). Mosca himself observes (in connection with possible explanations for MT ʿaštōret) that a Phoenician vowel shift *ă > stressed ā > stressed ō is attested, and he suggests that the shift "probably developed in some Hebrew dialects."[473] If so, Molek may have developed from a *qaṭl-type segolate, *mal(i)k(u), "king." Thus, if Malik was not originally a participle (*qāṭil form), it may have become such in Hebrew. Be that as it may (such a phonological shift being otherwise unknown in Hebrew),[474] the point stands: the variety of vocalizations evidenced for M-l-k in chapter II make it impossible to exclude a priori a connection between that god (or those gods) and OT Molek.

None of the above establishes the meaning of OT Molek. It shows only that a plausible philological and historical connection may exist with much comparative evidence to which Eissfeldt and Mosca paid scant attention (some of which, to be sure, has surfaced since they did their research). Biblical usage can be determined only through textual study. We now take up that long-awaited task.

---

[473] "Child Sacrifice," 243, n. 31. See, however, Aron Dotan ("Stress Position and Vowel Shift in Phoenician and Punic," IOS 6 [1976] 71-121), who disputes the existence of this development.

[474] See Harris, Development, 61-62, and now W. Randall Garr, "Dialect Geography of Syria-Palestine, 1000-586 B.C." (unpublished Ph.D. dissertation, Yale University, 1983) 42-45.

4.2   M-L-K IN OT PERSONAL NAMES

We may begin our investigation of the Biblical evidence by examining the personal names in the OT which contain the element mlk. Once again, the task of collecting the names has already been performed, this time by G. Buchanan Gray and Martin Noth (among others).[475] It must be conceded immediately that none is vocalized in the MT with an o/u-vowel between the /m/ and the /l/.[476] In fact, according to the MT, all of the mlk-elements are to be understood as the epithet, "king," whether in the absolute form (melek) or with a suffix (malkî, malkām).[477] Thus, Noth argues that the "early" attestations of names with mlk-elements, such as Malkî'ēl (Num 26:45) and Malkî-šûa' (Saul's son), must illustrate the adoption of a Canaanite epithet for their national gods by the Israelites for their national god, Yahweh. On the other hand, attestations from the late monarchy, such as Nətan-melek (2 Kgs 23:11) and Malkîrām (1 Chr 3:18), might well be understood as referring to the borrowed Phoenician god to whom children were sacrificed (so Noth), were it not for the very common occurrence of Malkîyāh(û) (Jer 21:1; 38:1,6; 1 Chr 6:25; 9:12; 24:9). While Noth concedes that mlk, like 'dn, was concretized to a particular god's name from a general epithet applicable to many gods, the presence of Malkîyāh(û) "lässt auch hier die Auffassung

---

[475] Gray, Studies in Hebrew Proper Names (London: Adam and Charles Black, 1896), especially pp. 115-120,146-148; Noth, Die israelitischen Personennamen im Rahmen der gemeinsemitischen Namengebung (Stuttgart: W. Kohlhammer, 1928), especially pp. 114-119,141-143.

[476] The one exception is hammōleket (1 Chr 7:18), but the article on the name suggests that it is probably a gentilic (Noth, Personennamen, 249).

[477] Again, there is one exception: Mallûk (Neh 12:14: K Mlwky; Q Məlîkû), but this has no bearing on our investigation.

von mlk als Titel Jahwes wie in den älteren damit gebildeten Namen als wahrscheinlich erscheinen" (p. 119).

The only names which we may reasonably suspect of concealing the divine name M-l-k are those without a pronominal suffix, to wit: Melek (1 Chr 8:35; 9:41); Regem-melek (Zech 7:2); 'Ăbîmelek (the king of Gerar in the time of Abraham and Isaac; a son of Gideon); 'Ăḥimelek (priest at the time of Saul and David); 'Ĕlimelek (Ruth's father-in-law); 'Ebed-melek (the "Cushite" who aided Jeremiah); and Nǝtan-melek (2 Kgs 23:11). The first name is likely hypochoristic and not a divine name itself. The second is beset by textual problems (cf. LXX Arbeseer ho basileus) and is best set aside. The next three are witnessed (at least as to their consonants) as far back as Ebla, where, we have argued, their malik-element was the divine name (see 2.1.1 and Appendix A). It is impossible to tell, however, whether the mlk-element remained a proper name in Israelite usage, and in at least the case of Aḥimelek the priest, this seems unlikely. Ebedmelek likewise has its equivalent at Ebla (and in post-exilic Babylonia: Abdi-^{d}Milḫi [see 2.4.4]). Noth reads the name as a literal nomen professionis ("servant of the king"), taking melek in its "profane Bedeutung" (p. 118, n. 3), but the Babylonian parallel and the foreign origin of the individual who bore the name in Jeremiah's time make this the best possibility in the OT for a theophoric element related to the Syro-Palestinian deity Malik-Milku/i.[478] Most intriguing of all, however, is the final name listed above. Immediately after relating how Josiah defiled the Tophet, "so that no one

---

[478] The melek-element, then, would either be the product of Masoretic euphemism (analogous to the dysphemism of Meribaal to Mephibosheth), or would further illustrate the confluence of the divine name with the common noun, "king" (cf. Phoenician Milku/i).

might make his son or his daughter pass over by the fire to Molek," Dtr

says that the king "removed the horses which the kings of Judah had giv-

en to the Sun from the entrance of the house of Yahweh, by the chamber

of Netan-melek the eunuch, which was in the courts (parwārim)" (2 Kgs

23:10-11). While guilt-by-association is a procedure to be avoided also

in Biblical studies, the text suggests Netan-melek's complicity (if not

active participation) in those facets of the now-condemned cultus which

took place in the temple proper and raises the possibility that his very

name might incorporate a reference to that part of the cult which was

performed in the valley below.[479] It is to Gray's credit that he recog-

nized the special character of these last two names: "There appears to

me therefore considerable probability that in the two names just consid-

ered we have survivals from Hebrew worship of another god than Yahweh,

and that the names rightly interpreted mean '(the god) Melech has giv-

en,' 'servant of (the god) Melech'" (p. 148). Still, the suggestions

concerning these last two names are speculative, so that if Noth's as-

sertion (that the late monarchical period names with melek most likely

refer to Yahweh) cannot be established, neither can it be refuted.[480]

In sum, both because of the far-richer evidence available elsewhere

in the OT and because of the difficulty in determining the presence of a

distinct divine name, rather than an epithet, in personal names contain-

---

[479] If so, the MT form of his name would be explained in the same way as was that of the other eunuch, Ebedmelek, in the previous note.

[480] Another argument against the presence of the divine name M-l-k in Israelite personal names is the phenomenon we observed above in chap. II: the great decrease in personal names containing Malik-Milku/i once the nature of the god was conceived of as entirely neg-ative. However, since we have yet to establish that OT Molek is a god (to say nothing of having an entirely negative nature), this ar-gument must be set aside for the present.

ing <u>mlk</u>, we are fortunate not to have to rely further on the evidence of
OT personal names in our investigation of Molek.

4.3   THE CULT OF MOLEK IN ISRAELITE LAW

As was shown by our review of the history of scholarship (chap. I), a
vast number of Biblical references have been brought to bear on the Molek question. Each succeeding scholar has found it necessary to argue
either that some previously-neglected Biblical data required inclusion
or that some evidence which had earlier been adduced was, in fact, not
relevant to the problem (or both). The reason for this procedure is not
far to seek: there are but eight occurrences of MT Molek, and they are
found in stereotyped, but not identical, phrases. Scholars have attempted to augment this narrow data base by adducing verses with a formal resemblance to those with Molek (i.e., containing other parts of the
stereotyped phrases), or a material resemblance (i.e., dealing with
child sacrifice, or even human sacrifice in general), or by revocalizing
the MT Molek and <u>melek</u> (Geiger's dysphemism hypothesis and its inverse,
instances of <u>melek</u> which are allegedly euphemized forms of an original
Molek). This study cannot escape the need to augment critically the
eight attestations of MT Molek.

A second problem which has regularly presented itself to those attempting to understand Molek and to reconstruct historically the Molek
cult is the difficulty in ordering whatever material one considers relevant in its historical context. Dating the <u>content</u> of books such as
Leviticus has long been recognized as problematic. More recently, the
need to read materials which became canonical for the entire people of

Israel against the background of those groups which produced and bore
the traditions contained therein in their pre-canonical form has come to
the fore. Therefore, the most objective initial arrangement of the Biblical material to be considered in this study is, in my view, according
to the relatively neutral categories of legal, narrative and prophetic
literature. Historical and other critical judgments concerning individual texts can then be made overtly, after the texts have been presented.

4.3.1 Leviticus 18 and 20

Five of the eight attestations of MT Molek are concentrated in two chapters of Leviticus: one in Lev 18:21 and one per verse in Lev 20:2-5.
All but 20:5 describe the sacrificial act with the verb ntn (18:21 adds
the verb which commonly occurs in D and the prophets, h'byr, as a complementary infinitive). All but 20:5 use zr' ("seed") for the one sacrificed (rather than bn[y]w, "his son[s]," or the like, as elsewhere).
Finally, all five verses have Molek with the definite article, shown
through the vocalization and doubling of the /m/ following the preposition l in all but 20:5, which has the article with /h/.

We have already examined Weinfeld's attempt to show that these
verses do not describe a cult of actual child sacrifice, on the basis of
the context and rabbinic tradition (1.8). Weinfeld is correct that
these verses do not speak of passing through the fire (b'š), as do other
references, and that the context of Leviticus 18 is suggestive of a sexual interpretation (giving one's seed [i.e., semen] to a cultic prosti-
tute), as proposed by part of the later Jewish tradition. But with Mosca and Morton Smith, we have argued that these verses are clearly

describing the same cultic acts that are condemned explicitly elsewhere as sacrificial and that Weinfeld's attempt to divide the Biblical evidence between "reliable" legal-historical sources and "late and tendentious" latter prophets and writings fails. Furthermore, as we saw in our examination of the Punic epigraphic evidence (2.7), the iconography of the Pozo Moro tower utterly refutes Weinfeld's denial of cultic child sacrifice in the Punic colonies and represents a serious challenge to his position as regards the Biblical material. Thus, once again, while Weinfeld's contribution can by no means be ignored, the remainder of this study will focus primarily not on whether or not children were really sacrificed, but on the meaning of "Molek" and the significance of the Molek cult.

Mosca has argued that the evidence in Leviticus 18 and 20 is essentially ambiguous among the positions of Weinfeld and Eissfeldt and the "traditional" position (Molek as a non-Israelite god to whom children were really sacrificed).[481] While this is, indeed, the case with regard to the meaning of ntn (i.e., vis-à-vis Weinfeld, in what sense children were "given"), a careful review of the text and of the arguments of Eissfeldt, Mosca and others reveals that the interpretation of Molek as a sacrificial technical term is sorely beset already in Leviticus. This can be shown, I believe, by an examination of the form, Molek, itself; by the grammar and syntax of the phrases containing that term; and by the context of the verses under study.

---

[481] "Child Sacrifice," 158.

As to the form, Molek, we have already seen that the MT vocalizes it as definite in all five cases, although only 20:5 indicates the article consonantally. Eissfeldt realized that he had to show that Molek was originally indefinite, if the parallel with sacrificial terms such as ləʿōlāh ("as a burnt offering") in Gen 22:2 was to be maintained (pp. 36-38). To this end, he pointed to the LXX, which has a form of archōn (without article) in all cases except 20:5, where the consonantal text requires the article. Eissfeldt and Mosca both claimed that the LXX reflects reliably the presence or absence of the article in its Hebrew Vorlage.[482] While no one has so far undertaken the unspeakably tedious task of a complete test of this assertion, some brief samplings do bear these scholars out. For instance, Mosca notes that the LXX agrees with MT regarding the article on ʿōlāh (p. 153). Unfortunately, it is difficult to test the LXX's treatment of foreign divine names, at least in the Pentateuch, since Baal occurs only four times (always in place names), while Ashtoreth never occurs. More neutrally, however, we may observe that the LXX of the Pentateuch has no article where the MT has a definite form only six times out of 106 occurrences of archōn (not including the instances under discussion). In four cases the LXX has omitted the article from the nomen regens of a Hebrew construct chain (Gen 42:6; Exod 15:15; Num 1:16; 25:18), while in two cases the LXX has a cardinal number with the noun (Num 7:2,3). What is essential to observe, however, is that this entire discussion of the definiteness of MT Molek is a concern only for the Eissfeldt-Mosca hypothesis. Should the article, in fact, be original in all five cases in Leviticus, the analo-

---

[482] Eissfeldt, <u>Molk als Opferbegriff</u>, 37, n. 1; Mosca, "Child Sacrifice," 153. See below concerning the article in 20:5.

gy with le'ōlāh et al. would be lost, but the interpretation of Molek as
a deity would remain entirely possible, given the common occurrence of
the name Baal (outside of the Pentateuch) as habba'al. On the other
hand, the absence of the article is no problem for the "traditional" interpretation, either: personal names (including divine names) usually
do not take the article, and the occurrence of Molek with the article in
20:5 (which we shall argue was likely a slightly later gloss to clarify
a potential ambiguity) could well reflect the usage described above regarding Baal.

A much greater difficulty for the Eissfeldt-Mosca hypothesis arises
out of their argument for the originality of the vocalization of Molek.
It will be recalled that their primary support against Geiger's dysphemism hypothesis is the use of archōn by the LXX, rather than basileus,
the term usually employed to translate Hebrew melek. Their refutation
of Geiger is, as we have said, entirely convincing. But having brought
the LXX archōn into the debate, Eissfeldt and Mosca are hard-pressed to
avoid the conclusion suggested by our discussion of the form, Molek,
above (4.1): that the Hellenistic Jewish translators were simply rendering one active participle meaning "Ruler" by another. Eissfeldt, in
fact, concedes the point (p. 35, n. 2), although he insists that the
translators were ignorant of the true etymology of the word. Mosca, on
the other hand, claims that the translators were consciously rendering a
Hebrew word cognate with the Phoenician/Punic mlk (*mulk), "kingship,
kingdom," in its "more concrete" sense of "ruler" (p. 130). He supports
this assertion (and attempts further to disarm Eissfeldt's critics) by
attempting to show that the cases where the LXX has archōn for MT melek

read more satisfactorily in Hebrew if one assumes an original mōlek,
later euphemized to melek to distinguish it from Molek after the latter
term had become an opprobrium. Thus, in Mosca's opinion, the LXX translators may have forgotten that Molek could be a sacrificial technical
term, but they were on firm etymological ground and had not necessarily
fallen prey to the later notion that Molek was the proper name or title
of a god (as they had, in Eissfeldt's opinion, by using archōn in the
rabbinic and NT sense of "demon").

Mosca's reconstruction is particularly vulnerable at two points.
First, there is no evidence that Phoenician/Punic *mulk ever had the
"more concrete" sense of "ruler."[483] Mosca adduces Hebrew mamlākāh as
semantically analogous (meaning "kingdom, royalty; royal personnage"),
but there is no clear example of the "more concrete" sense ("royal personnage") there, either.[484] Furthermore, if one examines closely the
twelve instances where LXX archōn appears for MT melek, the case for a
conscious rendering of Molek in Leviticus 18 and 20 as one among numerous instances meaning "kingship, kingdom; ruler" is not nearly so strong
as Mosca would have it (pp. 130-133). In Gen 49:20 and Num 23:21 melek
appears as the nomen rectum of construct chains in the sense "royal,"
describing the nomeni regni ("dainties" and "majesty," respectively).[485]

---

[483] DISO 152-154; Richard S. Tomback, A Comparative Semitic Lexicon of
the Phoenician and Punic Languages (SBLDS 32; Missoula, MT: Scholars, 1978) 180-182.

[484] See BDB, s.v.

[485] Regarding Gen 49:20, Mosca stresses that the LXX here, as in Lev
20:5, renders the original Molek with the plural of archōn and suggests that this shows that the LXX thought of Molek as an indefinite, "generalized" concept (p. 249, n. 79). While the plural in
Lev 20:5 remains a problem (Eissfeldt's suggestion of a dittographic
reading of the following /m/ seems as promising a solution as any

Mosca believes that the resulting (MT) readings "delicacies (fit for) a king" and "majesty of a king," are "somewhat forced" (p. 130). However, this overlooks the established usage of melek in construct chains in the sense "royal," such as in Amos 7:13: miqdaš-melek, "royal sanctuary" (parallel to bēt mamlākāh, "temple of [the] kingdom"!).[486] In two other cases, Ezek 28:12 and Isa 10:12, Mosca stresses that the whole kingdoms (of Tyre and Assyria, respectively) and not merely their kings are under prophetic attack. Given that a king (even today) can easily stand for his country, the distinction is overly-fine and not at all conclusive. Two cases, Isa 10:8 and Ezek 37:34, are, even by Mosca's reckoning, ambiguous. Five are in Deuteronomy (17:14,15[twice]; 28:36; 33:5), in which, as Mosca observes, the LXX consistently calls foreign kings basileus and Israelite kings archōn, suggesting a tendentious distinction. He concedes, however, that the distinction could as easily be at the level of the LXX as at that of the Hebrew. This leaves but one good case, Ezek 37:22, where the parallelism of gôy with melek and gôyim with mamlākôt does, indeed, suggest that in place of melek was originally some word meaning "kingdom" (such as the alleged mōlek). However, even here, one must reckon both with the difficulties with Hebrew parallelism

---

[Molk als Opferbegriff, 38, n. 1]), the fact that the LXX changes the number of both members of the construct chain in Gen 49:20 (truphēn archousin for MT maʿădannê-melek) makes conclusions drawn on the basis of changes in number suspect. Regarding Num 23:21, we have followed Mosca's adoption of Albright's emendation of MT terûʿat ("shout") to tōraʿat ("majesty") ("The Oracles of Balaam," JBL 63 [1944] 215). As is shown immediately below, however, the emendation in no way requires that the following word be read as mōlek.

[486] Cf. also 1 Sam 25:36 ("royal feast") and 2 Sam 14:26 ("royal weight"), both of which, however, have hammelek.

in general which have recently been demonstrated,[487] and the context of Ezekiel 37, where the prophet is concerned both with the future unity of the kingdom (Israel) and with the establishment of a single king, whether the latter is to be David (as in the disputed passage, v. 24 [Mosca, "Child Sacrifice," 132-133]), or Yahweh himself (as Ezekiel 34 would suggest).[488] In short, Mosca's contention that "the use of archōn, 'ruler,' as a direct and literal translation of melek, 'king,' is virtually--if not completely--without parallel" (p. 133) is not borne out by the Biblical text. His case (and that of Eissfeldt) against the use of the few cases of archōn = melek to suggest dysphemism in Leviticus 18 and 20 stands, but, on the other hand, he has by no means established a strong case for his contention that the LXX translators read Molek as a common noun meaning "ruler" in Leviticus and "kingdom, kingship" elsewhere in the OT. In conclusion, it seems most probable, as Eissfeldt recognized, that the LXX read Molek in Leviticus as a Qal active participle from the root mlk and translated it with a directly corresponding form. Whether Eissfeldt's further hypothesis (that the LXX had forgotten the original meaning of Molek) will be sustained depends on what our further examination tells us of that original sense. But, as he recognized, the evidence clearly suggests that any change that

---

[487] See James Kugel, The Idea of Biblical Poetry: Parallelism and Its History (New Haven: Yale, 1981); and Michael O'Connor, Hebrew Verse Structure (Winona Lake, IN: Eisenbrauns, 1980).

[488] I agree with Mosca that MT ləmelek is to be deleted from Ezek 37:22. Mosca presents one other case of an ostensibly original mōlek, "kingdom," now MT melek: Josh 11:12 (p. 129). Ironically, it is by far his best case. The reading, "And all the cities of these kingdoms and all their kings," not only makes better sense, it also accounts for the masculine plural suffix on "kings." Unfortunately, the LXX reads basileiōn, not archontōn, so that no direct application to the present debate is possible.

took place in the meaning of Molek was well established by the time of the Greek translators.

Secondly, we turn to the grammar and syntax of the clauses in which Molek is embedded in Leviticus 18 and 20. Two issues, in particular, must be confronted. First, does Hebrew usage tell us the function of the preposition l following the verbs ntn and h'byr? Secondly, does the usage of the clause znh 'ḥry imply anything about the nature of the object of 'ḥry? Mosca (and Eissfeldt before him) stresses that ntn l can be followed not only by the recipient of the "giving," but, given that that semantic range of ntn includes also "set" and "make, constitute," ntn l can mean "to give/constitute as something," specifically in Leviticus, "to give of one's seed as a molk-sacrifice."[489] Of special importance to their case is 1 Chr 21:23, in which ntn l occurs in the context of "giving" (if not specifically sacrificing): l means "as" in the manner just described; and there is no second l with the recipient as object (as is usually the case). Thus, on the basis of ntn l alone, Hebrew usage would suggest that the Eissfeldt-Mosca reading is possible.

But is the same ambiguity present with h'byr l? The presence of the latter verb in Lev 18:21 as a complementary infinitive ensures that the question of the usage of ntn l cannot be divorced from that of h'byr l, which, as we shall see, is by far the most common verb used in the rest of the OT to describe the Molek cult.[490] The construction h'byr l occurs some seven times in the OT (in addition to Lev 18:21):   2 Kgs

---

[489] Eissfeldt, Molk als Opferbegriff, 39-40; Mosca, "Child Sacrifice," 157-158.

[490] See the following section (4.3.2) for a discussion of the meaning and use of h'byr itself.

23:10; Jer 32:35; Exod 13:12; Num 27:7,8; and Ezek 16:21; 23:37. The
first two verses listed have Molek as the object of the preposition and
are thus of no present help to us. In all five of the remaining cases ḻ
takes as its object the recipient of the action. To be sure, Ezek 23:37
also contains a second ḻ employed in the fashion which Eissfeldt and
Mosca suggest was the usage with *ləmōlek in Lev 18:21, i.e., meaning
"as."[491] But in no case (outside of the three in dispute) where only one
ḻ is found with hʿbyr can the meaning of the preposition be "as." Mosca
insists that "any argument based on so small a number of examples is
hardly conclusive" and that to claim that the usage of the preposition
here is established "of course, stands, but as an argument from probability, not necessity" (pp. 194-195). In response, one might observe
that in other cases (including the discussion of znh ʾḥry, immediately
below) a single example is held sufficient to explain the disputed usage. Such was certainly the case in the question of the sense of hʿbyr
bʾš, which Mosca and Morton Smith agree is best illuminated by the one
instance of that clause outside of the Molek issue, Num 31:23. To be
sure, the possibility exists that the usage in Lev 18:21 is unique, but
as at every disputed point regarding the Leviticus references, the
Eissfeldt-Mosca position must argue against a cogent alternative which
is at least probable according to Biblical usage.

---

[491] Even this one instance disappears, however, if one reads lə'oklāh as
an infinitive of purpose, with the "long form" of the infinitive,
rather than the noun, "food," with the preposition (cf. Jer 12:9 and
the parallel verse to Ezek 23:37, 16:20, which has the "short" infinitive in a syntactically identical clause).

What possibility is left open for the Eissfeldt-Mosca interpretation is further restricted by an examination of the other significant
syntactical construction in Leviticus: lznwt 'ḥry hmlk (20:5). Here
there is no dearth of attestations: znh 'ḥry occurs some sixteen times
in the OT. As we have already seen (1.6,7) this clause has often been
considered the ultimate argument against Eissfeldt's hypothesis, both
because it suggests that the article on Molek is original throughout the
Leviticus references and because the object of 'ḥry is regularly an object or being who may be worshipped, not a practice. Eissfeldt and Mosca have displayed considerable ingenuity in countering these arguments.
As to the first (concerning the article), they pointed to Hebrew usage,
in which an article may, indeed, be used with an indefinite noun, if
that noun has previously been mentioned.[492] The second objection was
more complicated. Eissfeldt had already cited Jud 8:27, in which the
Israelites znh 'ḥry the ephod which Gideon had made; thus, Eissfeldt argued, the phrase did not always entail "whoring after" foreign deities,
but could also take "kultisch-mantischen Objekten und Praktiken" as the
object of 'ḥry (p. 39). Mosca refined this argument considerably (pp.
154-157). He noted that in addition to the ten cases with "foreign
gods, idols or demons" (and Gideon's ephod), the objects of the preposition included: "ghosts and familiar spirits" (Lev 20:6); "the nations"
(Ezek 23:30); "that man" (Lev 20:5); and "your heart(s) and your eyes"
(Num 15:39). On this basis, he made three points: first, that znh 'ḥry
could take a wide variety of objects, whose only common denominator was
that at some point they were held to entail idolatry; second, that Molek

---

[492] GKC §126d.

in the sense of mo̱lk-sacrifice could refer to the victim, as well as the practice (cf. 'ōlāh), and so was comparable to Gideon's ephod; and third, that in no case does 'ḥry take as its object a single deity or being (in fact, that the ephod is the most comparable instance to Molek on this point).

Mosca's methodology is faultless here. Unfortunately, a close reexamination of the attestations of znh 'ḥry does not bear out all of his conclusions, especially the first. Eleven of the sixteen instances clearly entail supernatural beings (the ten which begin Mosca's list, plus the "ghosts and familiar spirits" of Lev 20:6, of which we shall have more to say later). The ephod of Jud 8:27 has a supernatural character in its use as a "cultic-mantic" object of veneration.[493] Ezek 23:30 also accuses Israel of consorting with foreign gods, even if that is not the case in a technical, grammatical sense. The context makes this clear: "because you played the harlot with the nations, and polluted yourself with their idols" (RSV). Lev 20:5 is ambiguous (as Mosca also recognizes [p. 250, n. 86]). The key portion reads: wəhikrattî 'ōtô wə'ēt kol-hazzōnîm 'aḥărāyw liznôt 'aḥărê hammōlek. Mosca reads (following the versions): "And I shall cut off him [that man, v. 4] and all who whore after him, so as to whore after the mo̱lk-sacrifice. . . ." One should note, however, that the LXX admits the difficulty of this verse in the clarifications it must introduce: it uses two different words for the two occurrences of znh (homonoeō, "agree," and ekporneuō, "fornicate" [the usual LXX translation of znh], respectively); and it

---

[493] Mosca's contention (p. 250, n. 87) that Gideon did not intend the ephod to be idolatrous (so that objects of znh 'ḥry need not be technically idolatrous) is beside the point: Dtr, not Gideon, chose the phrase znh 'ḥry, and to Dtr, the ephod was idolatrous (môqēš).

renders 'ḥry with eis, whereas in every other case it uses opisō.
Granted these difficulties, another possible understanding becomes attractive: to take Molek as the antecedent of the object pronoun in
'aḥărāyw (whether referring to Molek in v. 4 or as a casus pendens). If
so, the following phrase may have been added as a clarification (Mosca:
"explanatory gloss"), yielding: "And I shall cut off him and all who
whore after him/it, [i.e.,] whoring after (the) Molek. . . ." This latter possibility would eliminate the awkwardness felt by the versions and
would eliminate a usage of znh 'ḥry which is strange, whatever one understands Molek to mean. However, this reading also removes this verse
from the present debate. This leaves one and only one case in which the
object of 'ḥry appears to be non-supernatural in character: "And it
[the tassel with the blue cord] shall be a tassel for you: you shall
see it and remember all the commandments of Yahweh, and you shall do
them and not walk about after your heart(s) and after your eyes, after
which you go whoring" (Num 15:39). Even this case, however, may be no
exception. Martin Noth observes that the tassel originally had
"cultic-mantic" significance:

> It is certain that the "tassels" with their blue cords, at-
> tached to the tassels in some unspecified way (v. 38b), origi-
> nally had a magic, apotropaic significance (cf. the blue lace
> on the high priest's turban according to Ex. 28.37); the al-
> teration in its significance to a means of "remembering" which
> can be "looked upon" in order to remind one of the divine com-
> mandments (v. 39aβb), is artificial (the corners of garments
> do not exactly lend themselves to being "looked upon") and ob-
> viously secondary, an attempt, within the framework of the re-
> ligion of Yahweh, to deprive of its power a custom which had
> originally had a magical significance.[494]

---

[494] Numbers (trans. J. D. Martin; Philadelphia: Westminster, 1968
[German orig., 1966]) 117-118.

If this law is, indeed, engaged in the "baptism" of an originally cultic-mantic act of <u>looking</u> on the tassels, "whoring after the <u>eyes</u>" may well be an oblique reference to the entire, now-forbidden act and its object. If so, one can affirm that, <u>pace</u> Mosca, <u>every</u> instance of <u>znh 'hry</u> is followed either by supernatural beings or by objects which represent them. In this light, the "strictly formal" link between singular "ephod" and singular "Molek" (Mosca's third argument, above) pales in significance. If, on the other hand, one wishes to object to the proposed understanding of Num 15:39, there is but one exception (outside of Lev 20:5) to an otherwise standard usage of <u>znh 'hry</u> with supernatural objects, and the matter becomes, as Mosca would say, one of "probability, not necessity," to be settled on other grounds.[495]

Those "other grounds" are provided conclusively by the third category of our investigation of the Leviticus references, the context. Commentators have always found the structure and composition of Leviticus 18-20 exceedingly difficult to analyze. Source- and form-critics agree that the chapters are composite, but attempts to identify redactional layers have resulted in long lists of alleged editors.[496] Yet the

---

[495] Mosca only hints at what he might have presented as a solution to his difficulty here. We have already noted his point that the <u>molk</u>-victims could be an object, like the ephod. In a footnote he argues that the <u>molk</u>-victims "too, were seen as 'surviving,' but on the divine, not the human, plane" (p. 252, n. 108). Unfortunately, and contrary to his expressed intention, Mosca does not follow up on this suggestion. He might have argued, as have others long before, that the infants were considered divinized upon their sacrifice. However, even if this was the case, it would represent the sole instance where Israel is condemned for "whoring after" what it offers to the god(s), rather than after the gods (or their emblems) themselves.

[496] See, for example, Karl Elliger, <u>Leviticus</u> (HAT 4; Tübingen: J. C. B. Mohr, 1966) 230, 243, 263.

collection of prohibitions in these chapters is clearly not a random
assemblage, permitting the context to be ignored. Weinfeld showed this
to great effect, as he repeatedly emphasized the context of sexual prohibitions in chap. 18, in which the first Molek reference (v. 21) appears.

One division which the text quickly suggests is between chaps.
18-19 and chap. 20. Many of the prohibitions in the first two chapters
appear again in the third, only in a much-rearranged order and with punishments added (usually môt yûmat). This is certainly the case when one
compares 18:21 with 20:1-5. As Weinfeld has emphasized, most of chap.
18 is concerned with forbidden degrees of sexual relations (vv. 6-18)
and other sexual sins (vv. 19-23). Nevertheless, as we have seen, unless one wishes to contend that the practice condemned in Leviticus is
somehow distinct from the cult of Molek as described elsewhere, mizzar'ô
("from his seed") must be equivalent to "his child[ren]" in other passages. Why, then, does 18:21 appear in its present context? Elliger
suggests that the children sacrificed in the cult were the fruit of sexual cultic rites, while Noth believes that the word "seed" may have
served as a "key-word," by which this verse was brought into its present
context.[497] It is no accident that Elliger's explanation closely resem-
bles Weinfeld's reconstruction using the midrashim since it amounts to a
story told to harmonize two texts (or, in this case, 18:21 and its context).[498] On the other hand, Noth's explanation is practically an admis-

---

[497] Elliger, Leviticus, 241; Noth, Leviticus (rev. ed.; trans. J. E. Anderson; OTL; Philadelphia: Westminster, 1977 [German orig., 1962])
136.

[498] Weinfeld, "The Worship of Molech," 144. The usual objection to this
theory is that the sons of Ahaz and Manasseh (2 Kgs 16:3;21:6) were

sion that there is no explanation (or, at least, no substantive connection with the context). In short, the context of 18:21 provides little help to us.

Yet, in my view, this situation should neither surprise nor concern us. The phraseology of the verse itself suggests its composite nature, combining as it does the two verbs used elsewhere in regard to the Molek cult, ntn and h'byr, by means of a lamed of purpose.[499] The witness of the versions implies either that they sensed some awkwardness in this combination, or that they had a variant in (or misread) their Vorlage: the Samaritan Pentateuch has lh'byd, "to cause to serve"; the LXX reads latreuein, "to serve, worship" (presumably from Hebrew lh'byd); while, as Weinfeld has stressed, the Peshitta has lmntnw, "to make pregnant" (possibly from Hebrew lhrby' [so BHK]). The former explanation is preferable in this case. Although a scribal misreading of lh'byd for lh'byr (or vice versa) is easy enough to posit (at least after the adoption of the "Aramaic" block script), the Syriac is clearly an attempt to interpret h'byr (pace BHK), and the other two witnesses may represent such an attempt. Taken together with what we shall see is the stereotypical association of h'byr (not h'byd) with lmlk, the original reading ntn lh'byr seems at least probable.[500] In short, while the conflate nature of Lev 18:21 does not establish its dependence on any other specif-

---

unlikely to have come from such unions (De Vaux, Studies, 87, n. 137).

[499] This is uniformly the usage of the preposition l with an infinitive following ntn in the sense "give" (cf. Gen 28:20; Exod 16:15; Deut 29:3; Neh 9:20).

[500] One might also observe that none of the eight OT occurrences of h'byd is followed by the preposition l.

ic law (including 20:2-5), it does suggest that it is of relatively late
construction, and that a loose relationship with its context (vv.
19-23), which itself appears to be a supplement to the main body of the
chapter (vv. 6-18), is not unexpected. Neither need the sparse contribution of the verse's context concern us, because, as we shall now see,
the context of the Molek references in 20:2-5 is abundantly clear and
rich.

As we have already observed, Leviticus 20 functions in its present
context as a recapitulation of chaps. 18-19, with punishments specified
(as can be seen in nearly any pre-critical or conservative commentary).
Noth suggests that it was originally entirely separate from 18-19, being
a collection of môt yûmat statutes.[501] He identifies vv. 9-21 as the
"kernel," to which the verses preceding and following were added at various (but not widely-spaced) times. What is crucial for our purposes is
to note the evident linkage between vv. 1-5 and v. 6. Noth suggests
that "Verse 6 appends as a secondary addition to this whole section on
'Molech-worship' a threat of punishment for 'turning to mediums and wizards', because this also involved illegitimate cultic practices."[502] Elliger, on the other hand, sees vv. 1-6 as a unit.[503] On this question,
Elliger is the more observant. Verse 6 shares numerous words and phrases with the preceding verses: lznwt 'hry, "to whore after" (v. 5);
wntty 't pny b, "and I shall set my face against" (vv. 3,5); whkrty 'tw
mqrb 'mw, "and I shall cut him off from the midst of his people" (vv.

---

[501] Leviticus, 146.

[502] Ibid., 149.

[503] Leviticus, 268-269.

3,5). This strong formal resemblance leads us to ask if there might not be a material connection between vv. 1-5 and v. 6 stronger than "illegitimate cultic practices." One possibility quickly presents itself, but a brief discussion of v. 6 is required to appreciate it.

Verse 6 specifically condemns "turning to the 'ōbōt and to the yiddə'ōnîm" (cf. 19:31). These entities appear several times in the OT, but the clearest context is 1 Samuel 28, the account of Saul and the "witch" at Endor. Both terms have been extensively discussed (especially 'ôb), both as to Biblical usage and possible cognates.[504] As for the more common 'ôb, the debate has resolved to two alternatives: a cognate of Hittite/Hurrian a-a-pi (a pit connecting one with the underworld), or a cognate of the common Semitic 'ab ("father, ancestor"), especially of Ugaritic ilib ("deified ancestor"). In addition to the philological arguments, Biblical usage adds fuel to the discussion since some attestations suggest that a means of necromancy is involved (e.g., 1 Sam 28:8), while others appear to point to the object of the conjuration, i.e., the ghost of the deceased (e.g., Isa 8:19). Ebach and Rüterswörden, following the initial philological work of Vieyra and Hoffner, have mounted a strong argument in favor of the former understanding, although they press the evidence very hard in some cases (such as Deut 18:11, where 'ôb and yiddə'ōnî are parallelled with the mētîm, the "dead").[505] On the

---

[504] Maurice Vieyra, "Les noms du 'mundus' en hittite et en assyrien et la pythonisse d'Endor," *Revue Hittite et Asianique* 69 (1961) 46-55; Harry A. Hoffner, "Second Millenium Antecedents to the Hebrew 'ôb," *JBL* 86 (1967) 385-401; J. Lust, "On Wizards and Prophets," VTSup 26 (1974) 133-142; M. Dietrich, O. Loretz, J. Sanmartin, "Ugaritisch ILIB und Hebräisch '(W)B 'Totengeist'," *UF* 6 (1974) 450-451; J. Ebach and U. Rüterswörden, "Unterweltsbeschwörung im Alten Testament: Untersuchungen zur Begriffs- und Religionsgeschichte des 'ōb," *UF* 9 (1977) 57-70 and *UF* 12 (1980) 205-220).

other hand, Dietrich, Loretz and Sanmartín and Lust argue forcefully
that the 'ōbōt are the ancestors, although one wonders how Manasseh
could have made ('śh) them (2 Kgs 21:6), or Josiah burned (bʻr) them (2
Kgs 23:24).[506] Because a full adjudication of the question would take us
too far afield, we must be content to make several observations:

(1) the terms clearly have to do with the practice of necromancy,
that is, the seeking (drš) of information from or via the 'ōbōt and
the "knowers" (taking yiddəʻōnîm, by consensus, from ydʻ, "know");

(2) the usual translation of the RSV, "mediums and wizards," is unlikely on both philological and contextual grounds; and

(3) as we shall see, the occurrence of these terms is, to an amazing extent, in the context of passages which clearly have to do
with the cult of Molek.

The last observation will be demonstrated repeatedly, as we examine
the passages relevant to our study in Deuteronomy and Dtr.[507] Lev 20:5-6

---

[505] Should this understanding be correct, one might well suggest a connection with the fiery "pit" which characterized the cults of child
sacrifice in the Punic "sacred precincts" and the Judahite "tophet."

[506] A provocative possibility emerges from the work done by Charles A.
Kennedy on the NT concept of eidōlon ("The Table of Demons: 1 Corinthians 10:20-21" [unpublished manuscript]). Kennedy suggests that
the Pauline "meat sacrificed to idols" was, in fact, meat which had
been shared in family funeral feasts presided over by a sculpted image (eidōlon) of a deceased ancestor, and that such "images" were in
use in the Jewish practice of the cult of the dead (cf. ʻAbod. Zar.
2:3), just as in the Greek and Roman cults. If so, it is tempting
to suggest that the OT 'ōb might have been both the ghost of the ancestor and the stela representing the ancestor, in which he (or she)
was "really present" (to use Christian sacramental terminology).
The overlap of these two senses of 'ōb is also suggested from Ugaritic (CTA 17.1:5): skn iliby, "my ancestral stela." If correct,
this dual meaning would solve the difficulty noted above in Biblical
usage, where 'ōb is sometimes the ghost and sometimes an object employed in necromancy.

[507] For the moment, we note only that this repeated connection is but

represents but the first example: in rapid succession the two verses condemn the one who "whores after" Molek, the 'ōbōt and the yiddə'ōnîm. Here, at last, the portrait of M-l-k suggested by our study of the comparative evidence begins to make sense vis-à-vis the Biblical attestations. The chthonic connection of Molek could not be clearer than it is in the roster of netherworld-entities in Lev 20:5-6. The unifying principle of vv. 1-6 is not merely "illegitimate cultic practices," but the practice of the cult of the dead. This realization makes sense, also, of the condemnation of the guilty party's entire clan (mišpaḥtô) in v. 5: as we saw at Mari and Ugarit, the cult of the dead is a family affair, to secure the blessings (and avert the wrath) of past family for the sake of the family present and yet to be.[508]

Should this connection between the cult of OT Molek and the cult of the dead be sustained by further references (as our third observation concerning the 'ōbōt and yiddə'ōnîm above suggests) and the interpretation of MT Molek as a divine name continue to meet the demands of grammar, syntax and context, we may reasonably posit a connection between Molek and the Syro-Palestinian M-l-k of chap. II. The challenge of the Eissfeldt-Mosca proposal is by no means yet repulsed, however. If the evidence of Leviticus is not equally open to the interpretations placed on it by the "traditional" view and Eissfeldt (and Weinfeld), as Mosca believes (p. 158), we have yet to weigh Mosca's claim that Deuteronomy

one more argument for the integrity of Lev 20:2-6.

[508] The condemnation of the entire family may also have been justified, as in the case of Achan (Joshua 7), by their presumable complicity in covering up a cultic sin which threatened the standing of all Israel before Yahweh. Note that stoning was prescribed in both cases, as well as in Lev 20:27, where the "man or woman in whom is an 'ōb or a yiddə'ōnî" is condemned.

and Dtr favor Eissfeldt and that still another reference (Isa 30:33) establishes his case.

4.3.2 The Law of the Firstborn

Two other portions of the Israelite legal corpus have often been adduced in Molek studies, even though they do not contain the word "Molek": the so-called "Law of the Firstborn" in Exodus; and two verses in Deuteronomy which refer to "burning" (śrp) or "making to pass over" (h'byr) children "by the fire" (b'š). The most important texts regarding the firstborn are Exod 13:2,11-15; 22:28b-29; and 34:19-20, while several references in Numbers are generally considered much later (3:11-13,40-51; 8:17-18; 18:15-16), and two other verses, concerning only animal firstborn, are usually adduced for comparative purposes (Lev 27:26; Deut 15:19). The laws in Exodus and Numbers all express Yahweh's claim on the firstborn sons of the Israelites, and they direct that the firstborn be given to Yahweh, using verbs familiar to us from the Molek-references in Leviticus: h'byr (Exod 13:12) and ntn (Exod 22:28). What has been most provocative for investigators of cultic child sacrifice in Israel, however, is that the form of the law which has often been considered the oldest (Exod 22:28b-29, in the "Book of the Covenant") contains no provision for the redemption of any firstborn, humans included. Thus, many older scholars proposed that the original form of Israel's law called for all firstborn males, human and animal, to be sacrificed (in continuity with the presumed earlier, Canaanite practice), while only later was the substitution of an animal (or, later

still, of money or the Levites) permitted.[509] Eissfeldt argued that even
after redemption was permitted, actual sacrifice of the human firstborn
was allowed and occasionally practiced.[510] He related this conclusion to
the Molek issue by claiming that the "Law of the Firstborn" demonstrated
that child sacrifice was firmly grounded in the pre-Deuteronomic Yahwistic cult (p. 53).

Critics of the use of these verses in Molek studies object on two
grounds: the interpretation of the verses themselves and the relationship of these verses to those which clearly have to do with the Molek
cult. As to the former objection, de Vaux (and, indeed, Eissfeldt)
challenged the notion that any people--Israelite or Canaanite--had ever
practiced the sacrifice of the firstborn with any degree of regularity.[511] Moreover, the literary priority of the forms of the law without
the redemption provision (Exod 22:28b-29; also 13:2) over against those
which have it (Exod 34:19-20; also 13:11-15) is by no means certain.[512]
On the other hand, in both Exod 13:12-13 and (the probably older)

---

[509] See de Vaux, Studies, 70, n. 69, for references.

[510] Molk als Opferbegriff, 51-55. In a later article ("Menschenopfer,"
RGG3 4 [1960] 868) Eissfeldt moderated his position somewhat, conceding that redemption of the firstborn had always been permitted.

[511] Studies, 71. As we have seen (1.1), this objection goes back at
least as far as Witsius (1692).

[512] Perhaps the strongest statement of the case for the priority of Exod
34:19-20 is by Otto Kaiser, "Den Erstgeborenen deiner Söhne sollst
du mir geben: Erwägungen zum Kinderopfer im Alten Testament," Denkender Glaube: Festschrift Carl Heinz Ratschow (ed. O. Kaiser; Berlin: W. de Gruyter, 1976) 46. Kaiser's article provides an impressive collection of data and bibliography, but he fails to
distinguish the sacrifice of the firstborn from the cult of Molek
(as we shall argue is necessary) and is quite radical, in my view,
in repeatedly denying the historical value of passages concerning
the cult of Molek in Leviticus and Dtr as late or too closely mod-
elled on the provisions of Deuteronomy, respectively.

34:19-20, the redemption provision for asses and humans appears after the general statement of Yahweh's claim on all the firstborn, as if appended to the more general provision. Thus, even if one holds that, at least in Israelite law, the redemption provisions were always present, it is at least intuitively clear how they might have been added to an older form, along the lines of Exod 22:28b-29, which knew no such exceptions. However, since we have no Canaanite law codes, such a reconstruction must remain strictly hypothetical, to be supported, modified or rejected on the basis of future archeological discoveries and other OT passages. In sum, the proposal that the "Law of the Firstborn" reflects at least the memory of a pre-Israelite practice of actual, firstborn child sacrifice, if not a historical, Israelite practice, remains problematic.[513]

As for the connection of the "Law of the Firstborn" with the cult of Molek, Mosca has shown that a simple congruence of the two is out of the question: the former had to do with firstborn males, while the latter involved sons and daughters (2 Kgs 23:10) and, if one accepts the record of the Chronicler (Mosca does not), could mean the sacrifice of more than one child of the same family (2 Chr 28:3; 33:6).[514] But his

---

[513] See the assessment of B. S. Childs (Exodus, 195): ". . . the abhorrence of Israel toward the practice [of child sacrifice] at a very early age makes the study of the historical development of any such tradition impossible. The claim on the first-born of animals seems unconnected with any more primitive rite in the Canaanite culture at the time of its appropriation by Israel, but the possibility of latent connotations attached vestigially to such traditions is certainly conceivable."

[514] "Child Sacrifice," 236-237. Mosca hypothesizes that the firstborn son "was no doubt considered the most valuable of potential [molk-]victims," so that 2 Kgs 3:27 and perhaps Mic 6:7 (discussed below, 4.4.2 and 4.5.3, respectively) are pertinent to our topic. This is entirely speculative, however, and is undercut now even by

flat statement that "the so-called 'law of the first-born' lies outside
the scope of the present study" (p. 235) surely goes too far. In the
first place, as Mosca himself notes, the two verbs which are characteristic of references to the Molek cult are also those used in the "Law of
the Firstborn": ntn in Exod 22:28b-29; and hʿbyr in Exod 13:12.[515] The
question is, how to account for this overlap in terminology, if one believes (as we have argued) that the cult of Molek was not conducted in
obedience to some form of the "Law of the Firstborn." Mosca suggests
that ntn and hʿbyr were chosen because "both the mōlek-sacrifices and
the law of the first-born involved the offering or dedication of human
beings to Yahweh, and so the terminology used in connection with animal
sacrifices was inappropriate" (p. 236). He goes on to speculate that
either the terminology was drawn from a common cultic lexicon, or the
cult of Molek borrowed from the "Law of the Firstborn," in order to
avoid the language of animal sacrifices. Mosca's suggestions are beset
by several problems, however. First, in the case of the "Law of the
Firstborn," ntn and hʿbyr do refer to animal sacrifices (i.e., of the
animal firstborn). Secondly, as we shall see (4.4.1), two narratives
which clearly have to do with the sacrifice of the firstborn son, Genesis 22 and 2 Kgs 3:27, use the phrase hʿlh ʿlh ("offer as a burnt offering") to refer to the child sacrifice, although the phrase is used
elsewhere of animal sacrifices. Thirdly, Ezekiel uses other terms from
the vocabulary of animal sacrifices (zbḥ, šḥṭ) in reference to the cult

---

the Punic evidence (see 3.1 and especially Stager and Wolff, "Child
Sacrifice at Carthage," 47-49).

[515] Other versions of the "Law of the Firstborn" make it clear that qdš,
"sanctify," whether in the Piel (Exod 13:2) or the Hiphil (Lev
27:26; Num 3:13; 8:17; Deut 15:19), is synonymous in this context.

of Molek or the sacrifice of the firstborn, or both (cf. Ezek 16:20-21).[516]

Mosca is, nevertheless, unquestionably on the right track in his affirmation that ntn and h'byr, although each covers a wide semantic range, are obviously being employed in some restricted, technical sense in the passages with which we are dealing. Ntn is so common, even in cultic contexts, that specification beyond "give" is difficult, but further refinement does seem possible with h'byr. We have seen that, when it is used with the preposition l, h'byr entails a "making to pass over" to some recipient (4.3.1). The one case in which the recipient is not a divine being is Num 27:7-8, where Moses is instructed to "make to pass over" an inheritance to the daughters of Zelophehad. Thus, we may reasonably suppose that h'byr in cultic usage means more precisely "to transfer ownership or control."[517] Such an understanding closely approaches Weinfeld's "dedicate," but, as we have seen, the common addition of b'š (understood above all according to its use in Num 31:23) in the references to the cult of Molek excludes his non-sacrificial interpretation.[518] It seems likely, therefore, that the cult of Molek and the

---

[516] We shall evaluate Mosca's claim that Ezekiel's words represent a technically imprecise polemic below (4.5.7).

[517] Ntn may well have a similar technical usage; cf. the use of nadānu in Akkadian contracts (Barry L. Eichler, Indenture at Nuzi [Yale Near Eastern Researches 5; New Haven: Yale, 1973] 19,96) and 2 Kgs 23:11. Speiser stresses a clearly related usage in Num 18:7 (and elsewhere) meaning "to dedicate (to cultic service)," in "Unrecognized Dedication," IEJ 13 (1963) 69-73. The proposed technical sense of h'byr appears to have been limited to Israel.

[518] The proposed understanding of the technical, cultic sense of h'byr also would explain the usage of the preposition b in b'š: it is clearly instrumental, detailing the means by which the transfer is accomplished. Hence, we have translated the phrase throughout as "by the fire."

"Law of the Firstborn" share these two verbs not because they entailed
human rather than animal sacrifices (or substitutions for the former),
but because they shared a special emphasis on the transfer of ownership
accomplished by the respective rites. Indeed, Helmer Ringgren notes
just this distinctive aspect of the "Law of the Firstborn" in his history of Israelite religion:

> In this category [sacrifices as gifts] belongs first of all
> the offering of firstlings, which in a certain sense is per-
> haps not a true offering at all. The Old Testament frequently
> enunciates the principle that every first-born of the herd and
> the first fruits of the field belong to Yahweh, and must be
> surrendered to him as a sacred gift (Exod. 13:2; 22:29; 23:19;
> 34:26; etc.). Human beings are the only exception: first-
> born children are to be "redeemed," i.e., a young animal is to
> be substituted for them (Exod. 13:13). The offering of first-
> lings is based on the conviction that everything is given by
> Yahweh and therefore really belongs to him. By dedicating the
> first fruits to him, man recognizes God's claim of ownership
> and guarantees himself the right to use the rest.[519]

The contribution which our appreciation of this important nuance of ntn
and h'byr will make to our understanding of the Molek cult must await
our study of additional passages.

A second reason for caution before too complete a division between
the cult of Molek and the "Law of the Firstborn" is made arises from Ezekiel 20. Verses 26 and 31 appear to be describing the sacrifice of
firstborn children and the cult of Molek, respectively: v. 26 is clearly patterned on Exod 13:12, while v. 31 declares: "by making your sons
pass over by the fire, you are defiled [or defiling yourselves] with all
your idols." We shall wrestle with the interrelationship of these verses (and others) at the appropriate point (4.5.7). For now, we note only
that, while they do not by any means require the identification of acts

---

[519] *Israelite Religion* (trans. D. E. Green; Philadelphia: Fortress,
1966 [German orig., 1963]) 168.

performed in obedience (however depraved) to the "Law of the Firstborn" with the practice of the cult of Molek, these verses do reinforce what Exod 13:12 and Lev 18:21 have already shown: the usage of h'byr in the technical, cultic sense in the cults of Yahweh and of "Molek."

The last term stands, for now, in quotation marks, in recognition of Mosca's aforementioned claim, that the strongest evidence in favor of Eissfeldt's understanding of Molek remains to be examined, in Deuteronomy and Dtr (and, above all, in Isaiah). We turn, then, to the third and final segment of legal material which is pertinent to our investigation, Deuteronomy 12 and 18.

4.3.3   Deuteronomy 12 and 18

Unlike the "Law of the Firstborn," there is no question about whether the two verses from Deuteronomy, described at the beginning of the preceding section (4.3.2), are relevant to the study of Molek. Both 12:31 and 18:10 overlap formally and substantively with 2 Kgs 23:10: "[Josiah] defiled the Tophet which was in the Valley of the Son(s) of Hinnom, so that no one might make his son or his daughter to pass over by the fire lammōlek." As we shall see, both verses also share significant common features with the passages from Leviticus, examined above (4.3.1).

The verse which has both the closer ties to others involved in our study and the richer context is Deut 18:10. The pertinent phrase occurs in a list of "abominations of those nations" (tw'bt hgwym hhm, v. 9) which are not to "be found" among the Israelites, once they settle in the Land. First among these is "one who makes his son or his daughter to pass over by the fire" (ma'ăbîr bənô-ûbittô bā'ēš). There follows a list of seven other forbidden individuals, also designated by participles (vv. 10-11): a "diviner" (qōsēm qəsāmîm); a "soothsayer" (mə'ônēn); an "augur" (mənaḥēš); a "sorcerer" (məkaššēp); a "charmer" (ḥōbēr ḥāber); "one who consults a 'ghost' or a 'knower'" (šō'ēl 'ôb wəyiddə'ōnî; cf. 4.3.1); and "one who inquires of the dead" (dōrēš 'el-hammētîm).[520] The designation of the m'byr as an "abomination" strongly suggests a cultic activity, while the other participles confirm it.[521] Further precision is provided by another common characteristic of the seven items following m'byr: all have to do with activities by which one seeks to gain information from or influence over a divine being or beings.[522] Indeed, the practice of "passing over by the fire" as a part of the cult of the dead is supported (but not proved) by the similar connections of three of the seven activities which follow in the list, including the "diviner" (cf. 1 Sam 28:8), the "one who consults a 'ghost' or a 'knower'" (cf. 4.3.1), and the "one who inquires of the dead" (self-evidently). In this last respect, the information from Deu-

---

[520] The English translations are somewhat conventional (taken from BDB and the RSV) since the exact nuance of some is in dispute (e.g., as we have seen, 'ôb and yiddə'ōnî). See S. R. Driver's commentary for extensive suggestions from comparative philology (Deuteronomy, 223-226).

[521] On the usage of "abomination" in Deuteronomy, see Jean L'Hour, "Les interdits Tô'ēbāh dans le Deutéronome," RB 71 (1964) 481-503. L'-Hour's article is an excellent review of the evidence, but he misses completely the connection (presented immediately below) of the m'byr with the other condemned individuals (490-492).

[522] The last seven items also appear to refer to individuals who practiced the condemned activities over an extended period, although none appears in the "nomen professionis" noun form (*qaṭṭāl). A professional practitioner of the cult of Molek seems unlikely, given that the supply of victims who fit the description "his son or his daughter" was apt to be limited.

teronomy dovetails nicely with that from Leviticus, although it seems best to examine the other passage from Deuteronomy before attempting a critical synthesis, including considerations of dating and tradition history.

Further information concerning the nature of the activities condemned in vv. 10-11 is apparent from the larger context of the chapter. The surrounding verses describe two approved cultic offices: the Levitical priest (vv. 1-8) and the prophet "like unto Moses" (vv. 15-22). As Robert Wilson has emphasized, the latter office was the sole Deuteronomically-approved means of intermediation with Yahweh, suggesting that vv. 9-14 represent a catalog and condemnation of disapproved means.[523] Specifically, given this understanding, the "passing over by the fire" and other activities would represent, in the Deuteronomist's view, activities which the Canaanites practiced vis-à-vis their gods which are not to be performed by Israelites in order to gain information from or influence over Yahweh. The implications of this line of argument for our study are considerable: they suggest that the "cult of Molek" could be incorporated in the cult of Yahweh (albeit, from the Deuteronomist's perspective, not legitimately).

This same conclusion is the most obvious understanding of the other relevant verse from Deuteronomy, 12:31. The verse in its immediate context (vv. 29-31) reads:

> (29) For Yahweh, your God, will cut off the nations which are where you are going, to dispossess them from before you, and you will disposses them and dwell in their land. (30) Take heed to yourself, lest you be drawn after them, after they have been annihilated from before you, and lest you inquire of

---

[523] Prophecy and Society in Ancient Israel (Philadelphia: Fortress, 1980) 161.

their gods, saying, "How have these nations served their gods,
that I, too, may do so?" (31) You shall not do so to Yahweh,
your God, for every abomination of Yahweh which he hates they
have done to their gods. For they have even burned their sons
and their daughters with (the) fire to their gods.

While v. 30, taken alone, might suggest that the Deuteronomist is condemning the Israelite worship of Canaanite gods, the parallel phraseology which ends v. 30 and begins v. 31 shows otherwise: wə'e'ĕśeh-kēn
gam-'ānî ("I shall do so, even I") // lō'-ta'ăśeh kēn lyhwh ("you shall
not do so to Yahweh"). Israel is not to practice the Canaanite cult--of
whose abominations the parade example is that they burn their sons and
daughters--to Yahweh.

In the light of our study of these two verses from Deuteronomy, the
Eissfeldt-Mosca proposal would appear to have received a much-needed
boost. By implication, granted the critical dating of Deuteronomy well
into the divided monarchy, the verses suggest that sacrifices which have
traditionally been classified under the rubric, "the cult of Molek,"
were offered (when made by Israelites) to Yahweh. This conclusion sets
the stage for what is possibly Mosca's most creative proposal. Weinfeld
had observed that both in Deuteronomy and the Deuteronomic History,
h'byr occurs in those references to the cult of Molek in which Israelites are the practitioners, while śrp is used in the two cases where
non-Israelite pagans, whether Canaanites (Deut 12:31) or Sepharvites (2
Kgs 17:31), make the offerings.[524] Weinfeld saw here a tendentious distinction: the non-sacrificial term for "dedicate" was used precisely in
reference to the Israelite cult, while the use of "burn" for what non-

---

[524] Besides Deut 18:10, h'byr occurs in 2 Kgs 16:3; 17:17; 21:6; and
23:10.

Israelites did was polemical exaggeration.[525] Mosca agreed that the two
verbs had been used tendentiously, but, given his differences with Weinfeld over the sacrificial nature of h'byr, he argued that the latter
scholar had misread the direction of the Tendenz. Mosca also observed
that only in the two verses with śrp was the divine recipient of the
sacrifice named. He concluded:

> The implication is obvious: the Deuteronomist uses "burn in
> fire" when straightforward idolatry is involved, but "make to
> pass into the fire" when the same offerings are made by Is-
> raelites to Yahweh himself. While the historian regards both
> Israelite and non-Israelite child sacrifice as heinous "abomi-
> nations," he is fully conscious of the distinction between
> idolatry and the worship of Yahweh as if he were an idol. It
> is this distinction which underlies his selection of either
> śrp b'š or h'byr b'š.[526]

The implications of Mosca's argument for our study are considerable: if Deuteronomy and Dtr employ h'byr only for cultic child sacrifice offered to Yahweh, then presumably the sacrifices which Josiah
sought to eliminate by defiling the Tophet were also being made to Yahweh, since h'byr occurs in the account of his reform (2 Kgs 23:10). If
so, some other explanation than "to [the god] Molek" seems necessary for
lammōlek in that verse, and the full weight of Deuteronomy and Dtr, it
may be argued, should be credited in support of the Eissfeldt-Mosca hypothesis.

Such a conclusion would, of course, be entirely at variance with
the results of our study of the pertinent texts in Leviticus. Unless
one wishes to propose an extremely late date for Leviticus, so that the
ostensible change in the sense of Molek proposed by Eissfeldt and Mosca

---

[525] "The Worship of Molech," 141.

[526] "Child Sacrifice," 173.

took place by then (a possibility which no scholar has advanced), some other explanation for the Deuteronomic evidence seems necessary (again, assuming, as all parties to the discussion do, that Leviticus and D are speaking about the same cultic practice). It is possible, in my view, to show that, despite its initial attraction, Mosca's interpretation of the D material is seriously flawed, and that there is a preferable alternative.

The linchpin of Mosca's argument is the alleged Deuteronomic Tendenz in the use of h'byr and śrp seen by Weinfeld and the interpretation placed upon it by Mosca. The first observation to be made is that both Weinfeld and Mosca have assumed a uniformity in usage between Deuteronomy and Dtr, i.e., that Deuteronomy intended a tendentious distinction and that Dtr correctly apprehended both the Tendenz and its direction and employed it in his own work. While this is by no means impossible, given the presumed continuity in the Deuteronomic movement, it does require that a single example of each verb in Deuteronomy (12:31 and 18:10) be taken as indicative of a Tendenz. Moreover, a closer examination of the two verses shows that the observed distinction in usage is present only in the most technical, grammatical sense. Thus, while in Deut 12:31 it is "these nations" which are said to "burn" (śrp) their sons and daughters, the Israelites are told, "You shall not do so to Yahweh." There is no hint that if they disobeyed, they would be doing other than burning (śrp) their children. The same point could be made, mutatis mutandis, with regard to Deut 18:10. Thus, it may be that Dtr, in describing the history of Israel against the ideal set forth in Deuteronomy, has made a Tendenz of what was, in Deuteronomy, but an alternative usage. To claim a _Tendenz_ in Dtr is also problematic, however, since śrp occurs with reference to child sacrifice only once in the History (2 Kgs 17:31).

On the other hand, it cannot be denied that in the few cases we have in D, h'byr and śrp are distributed as Weinfeld and Mosca say (again, at least in a technical, grammatical sense): h'byr for the Israelite practice; śrp for the non-Israelite. The question remains, however, whether a deliberate distinction has been made and, if so, whether Mosca has correctly apprehended its character (accepting, once again, his refutation of Weinfeld's explanation). Assuming, for the sake of argument, that a _Tendenz_ is present and uniform throughout D, it remains questionable whether it is to be accounted for as designating "idolatry _sensu stricto_" versus "the worship of Yahweh _as if_ _he_ _were_ _an_ _idol_." While, as we have seen, both passages from Deuteronomy suggest that the forbidden practices (when performed by Israelites) were being envisioned as within the cult of Yahweh, the same passages contain hints that no strict division such as Mosca has proposed is possible. For example, the list in 18:10-11 does appear in a context which seems to forbid the use of the designated mantic activities to obtain information from or influence over Yahweh, rather than the approved method of approaching him, the Mosaic prophet. Nevertheless, among the condemned individuals are the "one who consults a 'ghost' or a 'knower'" and the "one who inquires of the [divinized] dead."[527] While these objects of divination were, no doubt, considered under Yahweh, they are clearly not to be identified with him. Secondly, as for Deut 12:31, we have seen the ex-

---

[527] That the dead are divinized is shown by the nature of the objects which drš takes in the sense "inquire of, consult" (cf. BDB, s.v.).

plicit indications that "burning" children was not to be done to Yahweh.
On the other hand, the larger context of the passage suggests that more
must be said. While redaction-critical studies of Deuteronomy have revealed a complex history of composition, it is at least likely that
12:29-31 belongs not with the so-called "law of the centralization of
the cult" (12:2-28), but with the following warnings against temptation
into what is by any reckoning idolatry.[528] Although we have yet to examine in detail the relevant passages from Dtr (4.4.3), we may note that
in all but one case (2 Kgs 16:3), the verses concerning the cult of Molek are in the immediate context of references to idolatrous, Canaanite
cult practices (2 Kgs 17:16; 21:3-5; 23:11).

Such indications of an idolatrous context for the cult of Molek
references in Deuteronomy (and Dtr) do not at all undo the previously-
adduced indications that cultic child sacrifices in Israel were made to
Yahweh.[529] Indeed, even better evidence that this was the case remains
to be presented, from the book of Jeremiah (4.5.6). But the easy com-
mixture in condemnation of practices which Mosca suggests were and were
not idolatrous "sensu stricto" brings the usefulness of his distinction
into question.[530] In brief, was such a distinction operative for the

---

[528] See Gottfried Seitz, Redaktionsgeschichtliche Studien zum Deuteronomium (Stuttgart: W. Kohlhammer, 1971) 107,152-153.

[529] Whether or not such sacrifices were licit before Josiah (as Eissfeldt and Mosca propose) will be examined below.

[530] Mosca would make much of the lack of a specified punishment for cultic child sacrifice in Deuteronomy: "Note that, in Deuteronomy, Israelite idolatry (sensu stricto) is always punishable by
death. . . . However, in Deut. 18:9-14, no specific penalty is attached to "passing one's children into the fire," sorcery,
soothsaying, etc. Deuteronomic tradition clearly regarded such actions as unorthodox and wrong, but not strictly speaking idolatrous"
("Child Sacrifice," 253, n. 120). However, Moshe Weinfeld lists a

Deuteronomist? That is, did the Deuteronomist work with a three-stage system (within Israel) of an orthodox cult to the right God, an abominable cult to the right God and "idolatry <u>sensu</u> <u>stricto</u>"? Combinations of the latter two, such as we have just seen in Deuteronomy 12 and 18, suggest that the Deuteronomic worldview was by no means so subtle. From the Deuteronomic perspective, there were two ways for the Israelite (cf. 30:19): the way of life (orthodoxy) and the way of death (apostasy).[531] To anticipate our discussion of Dtr (4.4.3), even the most obvious candidate for a specimen of the ostensible middle ground, the Northern Kingdom, fails. In Dtr's view, the North's cult is from the first apostate (even idolatrous): 1 Kgs 12:28-33 describes as idol worship the "sin of Jeroboam" which, in Dtr's view, doomed the North and its kings from the start, whatever else they might be or do. As we shall see in that discussion, such a "black-and-white" perspective should come as no surprise, nor should the greater complexity of the actual, historical situation.

There is, I believe, a more satisfactory explanation for the distinction in usage observed by Weinfeld and Mosca. As we have seen, h'byr had a legal/cultic technical usage within the cult of Yahweh, designating the transfer of ownership or control (Exod 13:12; Num 27:7-8).

---

considerable number of sacral offenses which are considered capital crimes in the "Book of the Covenant" and the "Priestly document," but are either not mentioned or forbidden without specification of penalty in Deuteronomy. Whether or not Weinfeld is correct in attributing the differences to "the secular character of the judicial conception of the book of Deuteronomy," it seems clear that the distinction observed by Mosca may be due to larger considerations (Weinfeld, <u>Deuteronomy and the Deuteronomistic School</u>, 240-241).

[531] See A. D. H. Mayes, <u>Deuteronomy</u> (NCB; Grand Rapids, MI: Eerdmans, 1979) 230, regarding 12:29-13:18 as a unit dealing with "the problem of apostasy."

The term also had a technical usage in the "cult of Molek," where the means of the transfer was often specified with b'š. That h'byr was used by the practitioners of the cult and not solely by its detractors seems likely from the verb's wide distribution (besides D, also Leviticus, Jeremiah, Ezekiel and the Chronicler). Thus, D's *Tendenz*, so to speak, may simply have been to restrict the use of the Israelite technical term to Israelite practitioners, while a more purely descriptive term (śrp) was used of non-Israelites. Once again, however, there are but two cases of the latter in D, so that the rationale for the use of śrp is harder to suggest with any degree of confidence.[532] More important will be the use of śrp by Jeremiah (7:31; 19:5), along with h'byr (32:35), to refer to the Israelite cult: is the prophet engaging in polemic (so

---

[532] Weinfeld and Mosca argue that śrp is itself pejorative: "It denotes primarily destruction by fire, not sacrificial burning" (Mosca, "Child Sacrifice," 173). While I agree that śrp is not a sacrificial term and that it often amounts to destruction (see BDB, s.v.), it is not necessarily negative, either. Indeed, it has an intriguing connection to the funerary cult in 1 Sam 31:12: "And all the warriors [of Jabesh-gilead] arose and went all night, and they took the corpse of Saul and the corpses of his sons from the wall of Beth-shan, and they came to Jabesh and burned (śrp) them there" (cf. Jer 34:5; 2 Chr 16:14). Furthermore, it is not at all clear that, in the view of the Deuteronomist and Dtr, "the Canaanites and Sepharvites offer their children to idols, to nothingness . . . the idolators succeed only in 'burning their sons and daughters in fire,' i.e., in destroying them to no purpose" (Mosca, "Child Sacrifice," 173-174). Mosca's interpretation fits Second Isaiah well enough, but not necessarily D. He is well aware (in a footnote to the quotation above) that Meša's sacrifice (2 Kgs 3:27) presents a difficulty; his explanation that the "wrath" which fell on the Israelite army in response to the sacrifice was Yahweh's all-but-begs the question presently at issue. A more satisfactory view of D's position is suggested by Deut 32:8-9 (whatever its place in Deuteronomy's redactional history): all supernatural powers are under Yahweh, and Israel (land and people) is the direct "portion" of Yahweh, but there are other powers, to whom other peoples have been allocated (reading 32:8 with DSS and the versions; cf. Deut 29:25). (V. 17 need not imply that all the various "strange gods" worshipped by Israel were "not-god" in D's perspective.)

Mosca), or is a more innocuous alternation of terms for the same act involved? We shall seek to find out below (4.5.6).

The question remains, however, whether there is room for the chthonic god "Molek," whom we found in Leviticus, in the Israelite cult of child sacrifice (to Yahweh) described in Deuteronomy. Because "Molek" does not occur in either of the references in Deuteronomy (and only once in D), our argument is necessarily defensive in character: to show that an understanding of the references which is in keeping with those from Leviticus is <u>possible</u> (rather than necessary). We begin with the observation, demonstrated at such great length above (chap. II), that an ancient, chthonic, Syro-Palestinian god named Malik-Milku/i was known and worshipped among "those nations" (as exemplified in the culture of Ugarit) which lived in Palestine before the Israelite conquest/ settlement. Thus, Malik-Milku/i was quite likely (if not demonstrably) among "their gods" to whom the Canaanites "burned their sons and their daughters." According to the Deuteronomic ideal (i.e., the book of Deuteronomy), no Israelite was ever to worship such gods (13; 17:2-7), but the History shows that Israel persistently did just that (cf. the references to the idolatrous context of Dtr references to the cult of Molek, cited above). However, there are also indications that the Israelites often (if not always) did so under the aegis of the cult of Yahweh. Thus, Elijah challenges "all Israel" at Mt. Carmel to distinguish between the cults of Yahweh and of Baal and to choose one or the other (1 Kgs 18:21). An even clearer (and, for our purposes, more significant) example is the vast array of Canaanite cult objects which Josiah removed from what remained at all times "the house of Yahweh" in Jerusalem (2

Kgs 23:4-12; cf. 21:4-5). The situation seems clear enough: the people
of Israel and Judah considered themselves at all times good and faithful
worshippers of Yahweh, even while they incorporated large portions of
the Canaanite "old-time religion" into the Yahweh cult, whether through
syncretism of the Canaanite gods with Yahweh, or (as I think more likely) by at least a nominal subordination of the other gods to Yahweh.[533]
Such a situation is confirmed by the direction of the Deuteronomic polemic, as presented above: neither the worship of the Canaanite gods,
nor the practice of their cults (even under ostensibly Yahwistic auspi-
ces) could be tolerated. But von Rad is undoubtedly correct in stressing that at the time (at least for non-Deuteronomists) the issues were
not so obviously clear-cut:

> The simplicity and clarity of this [Deuteronomic] view is un-
> doubtedly only the outcome of a long debate which swayed this
> way and that, and presupposes a slow clarification of what is
> compatible with the cult of Yahweh and what is completely in-
> compatible with it, what is "an abomination to Yahweh."[534]

The importance of apprehending the nature of the historical situation for a correct understanding of the "Molek" references in Deuteronomy is evident. There does, indeed, seem room for a chthonic, Canaanite
deity whose cultus was adopted and adapted by the people of Yahweh. No
doubt, the practitioners claimed to be offering their children to Yahweh. But for Deuteronomy claims that one could practice the cult of Molek as a faithful Yahwist were unacceptable attempts to whitewash the

---

[533] This was, of course, by no means the last example of such a mixture
of older, "pagan" elements with the newer "one, true faith."

[534] *Deuteronomy: A Commentary* (trans. D. Barton; OTL; Philadelphia:
Westminster, 1966 [German orig., 1964]) 123. For an extensive study
from the perspective of the Scandinavian "Uppsala School," see G. W.
Ahlström, *Aspects of Syncretism in Israelite Religion* (Horae Soederblominae 5; Lund: C. W. K. Gleerup, 1963).

old ways and the old gods (again, whether by syncretism or subordination
to Yahweh). The Canaanite cults were abominable in se to Yahweh, even
when offered by Canaanites to their own gods (12:31). Because of such
practices, the Canaanites (and their deities) had been "annihilated"
from before Israel. Therefore, the Israelites had no cause to maintain
(and considerable incentive to reject) the cults of the former deities
of the land, not even for the benefit of the supreme God, now direct
landowner, Yahweh.

We shall have more to say about the historical context of the evidence from Deuteronomy vis-à-vis that from Leviticus in a moment. For
now, it is enough to observe that Deuteronomy is quite amenable to an
understanding of its cult of Molek references which is compatable with
the results of our study of those from Leviticus, although one cannot
claim that the Deuteronomic evidence necessitates such an understanding.
On the other hand, we have seen that the alternative explanations proposed by Weinfeld and Mosca are seriously, if not fatally, flawed. No
doubt, our grasp on the Deuteronomic conception of the "cult of Molek"
will be strengthened considerably when we examine the relevant passages
from Dtr below (4.4.3).

4.3.4   Synthesis of Evidence from Israelite Law

Law is not history, and so the historical information to be obtained
from the legal corpus will necessarily be secured indirectly. Nevertheless, if one assumes that laws were promulgated in ancient Israel, as
they are now, in response to actual, contemporary practices and situ-
ations, then one may look to the legal corpus for considerable help in

historical reconstruction. As was stressed at the outset of our discussion of the Cult of Molek in Israelite Law, two much-mooted issues in the use of the Biblical material are the dating of the <u>content</u> of the laws (i.e., to what historical situation they were addressed) and the nature and theological-political program of those groups which produced the material in question. Both Leviticus and Deuteronomy have been studied extensively along these lines. Leviticus is usually held to be an exilic codification of pre-exilic laws collected by priestly groups associated with the Jerusalem temple (in classical critical terms, the "P" source of the Pentateuch). However, the passages of interest to us all fall within the so-called "Holiness Code" and are, therefore, possibly quite old by critical reckoning.[535] Deuteronomy, on the other hand, is, as we have noted, commonly conceded to have an extensive redactional history of additions to a "core."[536] It is being seen increasingly as the program of a non-Jerusalemite group or groups in the late monarchy, with strong ties to (if not origins in) the northern, "Ephraimite" traditions.[537] Thus, the two works represent roughly contemporary material assembled by groups of quite different standing in the society of the time, the one a part of the Jerusalem "establishment," the other deter-

---

[535] See E. Sellin and G. Fohrer, <u>Introduction to the Old Testament</u> (trans. D. E. Green; Nashville: Abingdon, 1968 [German orig., 1965]) 139-140. As we shall see, I believe that Eissfeldt is wrong in using the references to the cult of Molek in Leviticus to claim that at least those pre-H collections which contained those references cannot be dated earlier than the second half of the eighth century, the time of Dtr's first reference to the cult (<u>The Old Testament: An Introduction</u> [trans. P. R. Ackroyd; NY: Harper and Row, 1965] 237).

[536] See especially E. W. Nicholson, <u>Deuteronomy and Tradition</u> (Oxford: Blackwell, 1967), for a summary of proposals.

[537] See Wilson, <u>Prophecy and Society</u>, 156-157.

mined to work major changes in that establishment from the "outside."[538]

The data which we can obtain from both sources are, therefore, of great historical value. First, as we have already observed, both collections associate the "cult of Molek" with necromancy (or at least divination) by context. Secondly, they both employ the technical term h'byr in reference to the cult. Thirdly, while the references to the cult are in both cases relatively rare, it is clear that both sources saw the cult as a serious threat to orthodox Yahwism: for Deuteronomy it was the very pinnacle (or nadir) of Canaanite abominations; for Leviticus it was serious enough to call for the stoning of the practitioners by the community and the personal intervention of Yahweh if the community failed to act. Thus, we may deduce that the cult was actively practiced, at least in Jerusalem, at least by the late monarchical period.

Other information appears in only one book. Only Deuteronomy explicitly designates the cult as Canaanite in origin, and only that source specifies the means of "transferring ownership or control," viz., "by the fire" (b'š). On the other hand, only Leviticus states that the children were being "given" (ntn) to a god "Molek"; indeed, Deuteronomy implies that the (Israelite) victims were burned to Yahweh. We have suggested how this apparent contradiction may be but different perspectives on the same historical practice, whether Molek was included in the cult of Yahweh by syncretism or by a latitudinarian version of Yahwism which sought to incorporate elements of the "religion of the land" which "pure" Yahwism seemed to neglect (such as the cult of the dead).

---

[538] See also the important contribution of Weinfeld, Deuteronomy and the Deuteronomistic School, 179-189.

We shall have more to say about the particularities of these two programs as we see them reflected and transmuted in the narrative and prophetic literature. Of special interest will be the variance in attitude toward the cult which is evidenced in the latter category (which has led Eissfeldt and Mosca to posit the legality of the cult within Yahwism until Josiah's reform). The legal material leaves no question, however, that by the time of the exile the cult of Molek was unambiguously condemned as the archetypical "abomination" (Deuteronomy), offered to the chthonic deity of old, Molek (Leviticus).

Finally, we may observe that while the very oldest law codes (in Exodus) do not refer to the cult of Molek, they may suggest that cultic child sacrifice was known in earliest Israel, at least among its Canaanite neighbors. Indeed, never far from a discussion of the historical ramifications of the "Law of the Firstborn" is the first of the narratives we shall treat: the "Sacrifice of Isaac" in Genesis 22.

4.4   THE CULT OF MOLEK IN OT NARRATIVE

4.4.1   Genesis 22

As we saw in chapter I, the account of the "Akedah," the near-sacrifice of Isaac, has often been cited in studies of the Molek cult. The reason for this is obvious: Genesis 22 provides one of the few extended references in the Bible to ritual child sacrifice. Even the failure of the narrative to describe an actual offering of a child has been turned to good advantage, as some have alleged a resemblance between the substitution of the ram for Isaac in Genesis 22 and the Punic mlk'mr (understood

as "molk-sacrifice of a lamb").[539] This ostensible resemblance is based
upon the judgment of Gunkel and other form-critics that at the core of
the narrative is an etiology of a cult place where animal sacrifice was
first permitted.[540] The point at issue among those who accept Gunkel's
proposal, and the second possible point of contact with the cult of Molek, is whether the substitution described in Genesis 22 was thenceforth
allowed or commanded. Eissfeldt (following Gunkel) argued that the account merely permitted substitution, so that child sacrifice was licit
(and practiced) in Yahwism until Josiah's reform.[541] Spiegel, on the
other hand, contended that the complete replacement of the older practice by animal substitution is at the heart of the Akedah.[542] Both sides
of this debate agree, however, that the narrative implies at least a Canaanite practice of ritual child sacrifice, and they often appeal to the
"Law of the Firstborn" (4.3.2) as correlative evidence.

The objections to the use of Genesis 22 in Molek studies center, as
they did in our review of the "Law of the Firstborn," on two points, one
having to do with the exegesis of Genesis 22 itself, and the other pertaining to the relationship of the account to verses which clearly have

---

[539] See, for example, Shalom Spiegel, The Last Trial (trans. J. Goldin;
NY: Pantheon, 1967 [Hebrew orig., 1950]) 62-63.

[540] Gunkel argued that the name of the cult place (Jeru'el) had been retained in a "Yahwehized" form in v. 14, as Yahweh-yir'eh (Genesis
[5th ed.; HKAT 1; Göttingen: Vandenhoeck & Ruprecht, 1922]
240-242).

[541] Molk als Opferbegriff, 48. Eissfeldt, in fact, held that at least
later tradition had explicitly connected Genesis 22 with the cult of
Molek: the "Berg" of v. 2 was not simply Jerusalem (an identification made by a redactor contemporary with the Chronicler), but the
Tophet (which, according to Jer 7:31, could be called a "high
place") (pp. 63-64).

[542] The Last Trial, 64.

to do with the cult of Molek. First, several recent commentators have questioned whether the account will yield any information about the place of child sacrifice in the history of Israel's religion. They stress that, whatever the story's original purpose, it presently describes God's ultimate test of Abraham's wavering faith in the Promise. Gerhard von Rad writes:

> Therefore, unfortunately, one can only answer all plaintive scruples about this narrative by saying that it concerns something much more frightful than child sacrifice. It has to do with a road out of Godforsakenness, a road on which Abraham does not know that God is only testing him.[543]

Secondly, the opponents argue, to the extent that the narrative has to do with cultic child sacrifice in Israel, it is to be related to the sacrifice of the firstborn, which, they believe, must be distinguished from the Molek cult. Thus, Mosca suggests: "Although now seen simply in the context of a test, its original purpose may well have been to explain why Yahweh no longer--or never--<u>demanded</u> the sacrifice of the first-born son."[544]

As was the case with the "Law of the Firstborn," it seems to me that both of the objections cited have merit, but that the opponents of the use of the narrative have overestimated the force of their case. As to the narrative itself, there is no question that the present shape of the text severely complicates attempts to reach behind it to discern Israel's understanding of Yahweh's attitude toward child sacrifice. Outside of v. 14, there is no formal indication that the story ever served an etiological function, and that one verse is both beset by text criti-

---

[543] <u>Genesis: A Commentary</u> (rev. ed.; trans. J. H. Marks; OTL; Philadelphia: Westminster, 1972) 244.

[544] "Child Sacrifice," 237.

cal difficulties and of secondary importance in the text as it stands.[545] Secondly, as both von Rad and E. A. Speiser emphasize, the verb nsh ("test, tempt") in v. 1 undercuts any attempt to understand Yahweh as seriously demanding the sacrifice of Isaac.[546] In short, although Genesis 22 does not condemn child sacrifice in so many words, neither can it be used to support Eissfeldt's theory of orthodox child sacrifice in Israel.

As for the relationship of Genesis 22 to the cult of Molek texts, the opponents of any connection are correct that the Akedah has far closer ties to the "Law of the Firstborn."[547] Thus, we would argue (4.3.2), Genesis 22 does not (and did not in any prior form) concern the cult of Molek as such. Indeed, even the resemblance to Punic practice noted above diminishes in importance when one realizes that there is no suggestion of animal substitution in the Biblical cult of Molek.[548]

---

[545] On v. 14 as etiology, see Johannes Fichtner, "Die etymologische Ätiologie in den Namengebungen der geschichtlichen Bücher des Alten Testments," VT 6 (1956) 374; and B. S. Childs, "A Study of the Formula, 'Until This Day'," JBL 82 (1963) 280. Walter Brueggemann argues that the verse is "a place name etiology which has been attached" to the core narrative, vv. 1-13 (Genesis [Atlanta: John Knox, 1982] 185).

[546] Von Rad, Genesis, 239; Speiser, Genesis (AB 1; Garden City, NY: Doubleday, 1964) 164.

[547] Note that while Isaac is technically Abraham's heir, not his firstborn, he is the firstborn of Sarah, and it is the firstborn of the female (ptr rhm) to whom the "Law of the Firstborn" applies.

[548] Another oft-cited connection of Genesis 22 with the Phoenician/Punic practice is the name of the son of El-Kronos whom the god himself sacrificed, according to Philo of Byblos: Ieoud . . . tou monogenous, "Jeüd, the only-begotten"; cf. Gen 22:2: Yeḥidkā, "your beloved one" (see Mosca, "Child Sacrifice," 274 and 276, n. 9, for the text of Philo). However, the Greek text ("only-begotten") suggests a connection with the "Law of the Firstborn," rather than the OT cult of Molek.

On the other hand, it is important to recall that the exegesis of a text differs in some respects from the examination of a text as a historical document, in search of historical information. In this case, unless one wishes to argue that Abraham and Isaac (and the traditions surrounding them) were entirely a late, literary construct, one must admit the force of the argument of S. R. Driver (and others), that the sacrifice of the firstborn must have been a conceivable divine requirement for Abraham, suggesting that it was known (however infrequently) in pre-Israelite or early Israelite Palestine.[549] We have already seen how difficult it is to speak with certainty in this matter, but passages such as Genesis 22 and 2 Kgs 3:27 (4.4.2), along with the Egyptian reliefs discussed by Spalinger (2.3.8), suggest that, at least in emergencies, the sacrifice of the firstborn was known to the Israelites (again, if not necessarily by them). The problems for historical reconstruction presented by the present shape and function of the Akedah story do not allow us to say more than that on the basis of this text.[550] We have already seen, however, that there is another text (Ezek 20:25-26) which must be dealt with in this connection.

---

[549] The Book of Genesis (Westminster; London: Methuen, 1904) 221.

[550] Mosca would explain the history of the account as an original etiology (see the quotation above), which was stripped of that function once the substitution provision was considered Mosaic in origin ("Child Sacrifice," 270, n. 242). This is an attractive suggestion, but impossible to support from the text itself.

4.4.2 <u>Passages of Dubious Relevance in Dtr</u>

The most significant passage which fits this description is 1 Kgs 11:7:
"Then Solomon built a high place for Kemoš, the <u>šiqquṣ</u> of Moab, on the
mountain which is east of Jerusalem and for Molek, the <u>šiqquṣ</u> of the
sons of Ammon."[551] Taken at face value, this verse would appear to establish not merely the divine character of OT Molek, but his identity
with the Ammonite god, Milkom, by virtue of the parallel in vv. 5 and 33
(milkōm <u>šiqquṣ</u> <u>ʿammōnîm</u> and <u>milkōm</u> <u>ʾĕlōhê bənê-ʿammòn</u>, respectively).
Yet the Gordion Knot which is Molek studies will not be so easily
slashed. Mosca argues both from the parallel verses (5 and 33) and from
the LXX renderings in v. 7 (LXX v. 5) that the MT represents a corruption of the original reading, Milkom.[552] While he does not attempt to
explain how the corruption came about, his point is, I believe, well
taken. Two other arguments might be added to those which he offers.
First, 1 Kgs 11:7 is the sole verse in the Bible which suggests that
Milkom of the Ammonites had anything to do with the god of cultic child
sacrifice by fire (assuming, for the sake of argument, the "traditional"
understanding of Molek).[553] Secondly, moving beyond that argument <u>e si-
lentio</u>, the account of Josiah's reform in 2 Kings 23 appears to distinguish between the cult place of Molek in "the Tophet which is in the
valley of the son(s) of Hinnom" (v. 10) and that of Milkom, on "the high
places which were east of Jerusalem, which were to the south of Mount

---

[551] As Mosca observes ("Child Sacrifice," 125), <u>šiqquṣ</u> ("detestable
thing") in this verse is probably a Masoretic dysphemism for <u>ʾĕlōhê</u>
(cf. 1 Kgs 11:33).

[552] "Child Sacrifice," 121-122.

[553] As we have seen (2.5.2), the Ammonite evidence is too sparse to offer any aid.

Corruption" (v. 13). While it is not impossible that one god could have had more than one cult place, both text-critical and substantive considerations lead us to agree that 1 Kgs 11:7 is not of direct relevance to the study of Molek.[554]

A second Dtr narrative which has often been cited in studies of Molek is the story of Jepthah's daughter in Judges 11.[555] Eissfeldt, in fact, cites this passage (together with Genesis 22 and Mic 6:7) to make two points: that child sacrifice was licit in pre-Josianic Israel; and that child sacrifices were occasionally offered (pp. 48-52). While, on the basis of the daughter's "bewailing her virginity" with her companions, one might question the inclusion of this narrative in a discussion of child sacrifice, the possibility that the daughter was an adolescent or younger cannot be excluded (any more than it can be with Isaac in Genesis 22). Nor, as we have already remarked (1.9), is it permissible to exclude this passage because "it contradicts much of what we know about Phoenician-Punic mulk-sacrifices."[556] Rather, the relevance of Judges 11 to our study is questionable on two grounds. First, it lacks any of the stereotyped or technical terminology associated with the cult

---

[554] Two points must be added in passing. First, the removal of this verse from our immediate attention in no way disproves that Molek and Milkom were related, if not identical. Clearly, someone at some point connected them, and the possibility that they did so on the basis of some genuine, historical memory cannot be excluded a priori. Secondly, as was the case with our discussion of the article on Molek in Leviticus (4.3.1), the exclusion of this verse from consideration is crucial only for the Eissfeldt-Mosca hypothesis. The "traditional" interpretation of Molek would be nearly established by the verse's inclusion, but it is not damaged by its rejection.

[555] See especially the discussion of Kamphausen above (1.3).

[556] Mosca, "Child Sacrifice," 161.

of Molek (e.g., h'byr, b'š, lmlk), displaying, rather, some connection
with the "sacrifice of the heir" stories in Genesis 22 and 2 Kgs 3:27 by
virtue of Jepthah's vow: wǝhaʿălîtihû ʿōlāh (v. 31). Secondly, it must
be recalled that by no means did Jepthah intend to vow his only child,
so that even the relationship of the account with the "sacrifice of the
heir" narratives is tenuous. In the end, the long debate over whether
or not Jepthah actually sacrificed his daughter is beside the point, so
far as Molek sacrifices are concerned: there is no sign whatever that
the children offered lmlk were sacrificed by any accident or rash vow.

A third oft-cited text can be disposed of quickly: Hiel of Bethel's rebuilding of Jericho "at the cost of Abiram his firstborn, . . .
at the cost of his youngest son Segub" (1 Kgs 16:34 RSV). At best, the
text is describing foundation sacrifices, rather than anything resembling the cult of Molek, and even this conclusion is by no means certain.[557]

Finally, there is the brief account of Meša of Moab's sacrifice of
"his firstborn son, who was to have reigned after him/in his place" (2
Kgs 3:27). The text is almost universally adduced in studies of Molek,
even by those who reject the relevance of the "Law of the Firstborn" or
of Genesis 22. This is understandable since the sacrifice is by fire
and in a military emergency, inviting comparison with the classical accounts of Diodorus and others regarding the Phoenicians and their colonies.[558] Nevertheless, the ties of this account are especially strong

---

[557] See Green, Role of Human Sacrifice, 169 and notes, for fuller discussion and references.

[558] See Mosca ("Child Sacrifice," 192-193; 261, n. 165) for this argument and others in favor of the relevance of 2 Kgs 3:27 to the Molek
cult.

with the Akedah (especially Gen 22:2): both describe the offering
(h'lh) of the heir as a burnt offering ('ōlāh) in a time of crisis
(whether political or theological).[559] Given our conclusions regarding
the role of Genesis 22 in our study (4.4.1), it is highly questionable
whether 2 Kgs 3:27 is describing the Moabite equivalent of Israel's cult
of Molek. Most significantly, the exclusion of this text from direct
comparison with Molek sacrifices eliminates the closest OT parallel to
the aforementioned classical accounts and offers another indication (together with Stager's recent conclusions regarding the Punic evidence
[3.1]) that the cult of Molek was not practiced only (or even primarily)
in times of national crisis.

Let it be added immediately, however, that the same methodological
situation obtains here as did with regard to Genesis 22, as well as the
"Law of the Firstborn." The elimination of the text from _direct_ relevance to our study does not mean that it is useless to us as a historical source. This text shows, as the other two could only suggest, that
child sacrifice was known among the peoples with whom Israel fought and
lived as neighbors. Along with Genesis 22, it may even imply that the
sacrifice of the firstborn was especially linked with times of emergency, although the rare and isolated character of these texts must be tak-
en into account, and the "Law of the Firstborn," if anything, speaks
against such a theory. In any event, we know that we shall have to look

---

[559] Mosca ("Child Sacrifice," 262, n. 168) argues that the use of 'lh in
2 Kgs 3:27 does not contradict his claim that common sacrificial
terminology was not used for human sacrifice (p. 236): "[The usage]
is to be explained by the popular nature of the original narrative."
However true his claim may be with regard to the cult of Molek, he
fails to note the use of the verb with cognate accusative (h'lh 'lh)
also in Genesis 22.

elsewhere for the rationale behind the cult of Molek.

4.4.3   The Cult of Molek in Dtr and Chronicles

Having "cleared the decks," as it were, of previously-adduced narratives
which are unlikely to be of help to us in our investigation, we may turn
to those which are unquestionably important. While we shall later argue
that there are still other passages which will shed indirect light on
Molek (i.e., those having to do with the cult of the dead [4.6]), in
this section we propose to treat the remaining passages from Dtr and
Chronicles which explicitly deal with cultic child sacrifice by fire: 2
Kgs 16:3 (//2 Chr 28:3); 17:17,31; 21:6 (//2 Chr 33:6); and 23:10.

Because it is the first reference to the cult of Molek in the historical narratives, the statement in Dtr's introduction to the reign of
Ahaz that he "even made his son to pass over by the fire" has borne
enormous weight in many reconstructions of the history of the Israelite
cult. Many scholars have assumed that so noxious a cult (to Dtr) would
not have gone unremarked had it been practiced earlier, so that Ahaz
must have imported the cult. On this reading the source of the cult is
not far to seek: 2 Kgs 16:10-16 recounts in some detail Ahaz's borrowing of a Syrian (or perhaps Assyrian) altar design, so that the adoption
of other cultic elements seems reasonable. On the other hand, other
scholars have argued that since Ahaz's participation in the cult of Molek is but an illustration of how he "walked in the way of the kings of
Israel" (v. 3a), Dtr is claiming that the cult of Molek was already established in the North (and they cite 2 Kgs 17:17, discussed below, in
support). Thus, the "missing link" between the Judahite cult and that

ostensibly practiced in Phoenicia, sought at least since Baudissin (1.2), is supplied. Finally, the context of this verse has often been cited to show that the cult of Molek was, contrary to our earlier contention, practiced in times of national emergency: vv. 5-9 recount the Syro-Ephraimite attack on Jerusalem under Rezin and Pekah.

It is in any event remarkable that the cult of Molek is mentioned so rarely by Dtr. But the supposition that the references are so few because the cult was practiced only under Ahaz and Manasseh before being disrupted by Josiah is only one possible explanation. As we shall see in the discussion of the prophetic corpus, there are signs that the cult was well-established at Jerusalem by the time of Ahaz, and it appears from the duration of the prophets' condemnations of the cult that it was awfully hard to uproot from popular piety for an alleged eighth-century innovation. Indeed, the argument e silentio adduced above may be turned as well (or, I believe, better) to suggest that Ahaz certainly did not introduce the cult, or that would have been mentioned by the unsympathetic Historian.

The possible Northern practice of the cult of Molek is more problematic. As noted, Dtr also appears to claim that the cult was known there in his summary of the sins of the North in 2 Kgs 17:7-18: "and they made their sons and their daughters to pass over by the fire" (v. 17). Because of this verse, the possibility cannot under any circumstances be excluded that the North did practice the cult. Nevertheless, I believe that there is good cause to suggest that they did not. First, arguing once again e silentio, it is remarkable that not one Israelite king is accused of participating in cultic child sacrifice, if any did

so. While it may be argued that "not departing from all the sins of
Jeroboam the son of Nebat" was condemnation enough, Dtr does not always
limit himself to that summary (cf. 1 Kgs 16:31-33; 22:54).[560] Secondly,
it is worth noting that 2 Kgs 17:17 (and the alleged implications of
16:3) are the sole indication in the Bible that Israelites (in the broad
sense) practiced the cult of Molek anywhere except in the Tophet outside
of Jerusalem. Thirdly, and most significantly, both 16:3 and 17:17 are
clearly patterned word-for-word on the condemnation of the Canaanites in
Deuteronomy:

> Deut 12:31: kî gam 'et-bənêhem wə'et-bənôtêhem yiśrəpû bā'ēš
>
> 2 Kgs 16:3: wəgam 'et-bənô he'ĕbîr bā'ēš
>
> 2 Kgs 17:17: wayya'ăbîrû 'et-bənêhem wə'et-bənôtêhem bā'ēš.

The latter verse shows further similarity with the formulations of Deuteronomy by continuing with two divinatory practices from the list which
follows the Molek reference in Deut 18:10: wayyiqsəmû qəsāmîm waynaḥē-
šû. More importantly, both in Deut 12:31 and 2 Kgs 16:3 the practice of
child sacrifice is cited as the parade example of abominations (taking
wgm as "and even," as the context at least in Deuteronomy demands, rather than as "and also"). While, pace Kaiser (4.3.2), such formulaic imi-
tation does not exclude the possibility of a historical referent, I
think it at least equiprobable that Dtr is here, rather, making a purely
theological point: by its "abominations," the North has become no better than "the nations whom Yahweh dispossessed from before the sons of
Israel" (2 Kgs 16:3; cf. Deut 12:29-30), so that it, in turn, has been

---

[560] See Helga Weippert, "Die 'deuteronomistischen' Beurteilungen der Könige von Israel und Juda und das Problem der Redaktion der Königsbücher," Bib 53 (1972) 301-339.

dispossessed. We shall address the question of why Ahaz was described
in terms befitting a Canaanite in a moment.

We shall deal with the ostensible Syrian (or Assyrian) source for
the cult of Molek under our discussion of 2 Kgs 17:31, since some have
also adduced that verse in support of such an origin for the Israelite
cult. For now, it is appropriate to ask: if Ahaz did not introduce the
cult of Molek into the South, why is he the first of only two royal participants indicted by Dtr? While Dtr's tendentiousness is a constant
temptation to over-interpretation (i.e., finding significance in every
distinction the reader may find), some principle of selection seems
likely here. It may be, of course, that Ahaz was simply the first Judahite king to practice the cult. This is uncertain, however, since it
is difficult to imagine that an installation like the Tophet could have
long operated immediately outside of Jerusalem without royal patronage
(if not participation). Mosca has proposed that Dtr (more precisely,
Dtr[1], the Josianic editor, following Cross) chose to mention Ahaz's participation in order to highlight the real reasons for the fall of the
North and the survival of the South:

> With Judah, as with Israel, accusations of "passing children
> into the fire" are not randomly positioned, but carefully in-
> serted at key points in order to reveal the historian's major
> themes. This is especially clear in the case of Ahaz. . . .
> The references to imitating the kings of Israel and to passing
> into the fire are not arbitrary. For the Judaean Ahaz is a
> contemporary of the last Israelite king, Hoshea; and it is
> during Ahaz' reign that Samaria falls to the Assyrians. In
> the juxtapositon of Ahaz and Hoshea, the true reason for the
> Israelite exile stands starkly revealed. Here the expected
> roles are reversed. Hoshea, it is true, "did evil in Yahweh's
> sight, but not as the kings of Israel who preceded him" (II
> Kgs. 17:2). Paradoxically, Ahaz, the Judaean king, "followed
> the paths of the kings of Israel."
>
> The mention of child sacrifice in connection with Ahaz,
> but not Hoshea, is meant to heighten the paradoxical contrast

> between the two kings and the two kingdoms. . . . . By
> contrasting the guilt of Ahaz with the (relative) innocence of
> Hoshea, the Deuteronomist forces us to focus on what he re-
> gards as the true reason for the collapse: the almost Aeschy-
> lean "sin of Jeroboam" which broods over the Northern Kingdom
> throughout its history.[561]

Mosca's solution is most attractive. He is able to suggest how Dtr

subordinated even the "parade abomination" to his larger design in a way

that is subtle, and yet not obscure. Nevertheless, his proposal is not

entirely convincing, or rather, is not quite complete, in my view. For

one thing, the qualification of Hoshea's doing evil as "only not like

the kings of Israel who were before him" is very faint praise and by no

means implies even "(relative) innocence" (although the explicit compar-

ison of both Ahaz and Hoshea to "the kings of Israel" lends some force

to Mosca's suggestion). More importantly, Mosca's solution presupposes

and depends heavily on Cross's theory of two redactions of the History:

the first, Dtr^1, done during the reign of Josiah; the second, Dtr^2, done

during the Exile.[562] Thus, according to Mosca, Dtr^1's setting Ahaz vis-

à-vis Hoshea illustrates the two great themes of the first edition, the

gracious effects of the promise to David in the South and the doom

wrought by the sin of Jeroboam in the North. However, despite an exten-

sive recent defense, it is becoming increasingly clear that the History

underwent additional redactions (at least in part) and that there was at

least one significant, thorough redaction before Josiah's time, quite

possibly at the time of Hezekiah.[563] If this was the case, Cross's "two

---

[561] "Child Sacrifice," 178-179.

[562] Canaanite Myth and Hebrew Epic, 287-298.

[563] The two-edition theory is now defended by Richard D. Nelson, The
Double Redaction of the Deuteronomistic History (JSOT Supplement Series 18; Sheffield: JSOT, 1981). However, see H. Weippert's arti-

grand themes" in his Dtr[1] may fit the "Hezekiah redaction" as well, and Mosca's proposal for the contrast between Ahaz and Hoshea may stand. However, given an earlier redaction, there is another contrast which appears more important: between Ahaz, whose political alliances and theological apostasy (including the divinatory cult of Molek) wrecked only havoc for Judah, and the hero of the redaction, Hezekiah, who spurned foreign alliances and "kept [the] commandments which Yahweh commanded Moses" (2 Kgs 18:6), including consulting a prophet, Isaiah, to determine the divine intention (19:2-7).[564] In other words, under the principle that the king's sin was the nation's, Ahaz's "Canaanite" actions threatened to put Judah at the level of the "nations" (and the North), whom Yahweh dispossessed, courtesy of invading armies (in Ahaz's case, Syria and the North, with Assyria on the horizon). On the other hand, Hezekiah had averted disaster by his orthodox course, so that "he rebelled against the king of Assyria" (and got away with it) and, from the other direction, eliminated the Philistine threat (2 Kgs 18:7-8). As we shall see below, the Josianic redactor transposed the contrast to a higher key, portraying Manasseh as even worse than the Canaanites (and so also Ahaz) and Josiah as incomparable even to the incomparable Hezekiah. Yet from the still later perspective of the exile, it was clear that the "greater Hezekiah" had not been able to undo the effects of the

---

cle ("Die 'deuteronomistischen' Beurteilungen," especially p. 335) and Wilson (*Prophecy and Society*, 157) in defense of an earlier form of the History. The time of Hezekiah seems a good candidate for the earlier edition, especially given the "incomparability formula" in 2 Kgs 18:5: "after him there was none like him among all the kings of Judah, [nor among those] who were before him" (cf. 2 Kgs 23:25).

[564] See Wilson (*Prophecy and Society*, 213-219) for a discussion of Dtr's portrayal of Isaiah as a Mosaic prophet.

abominations of the "greater Ahaz."

The proposed contrast between Ahaz and Hezekiah raises a vexing question, however: what was Hezekiah's stance vis-à-vis the cult of Molek? Once again, our narrative sources present us only with a frustrating silence. We shall see in our study of Isaiah (30:33) that the prophet uses the image of the Tophet rite in an oracle contemporary with Hezekiah, which suggests that Isaiah's audience was quite familiar with the cult practiced there (4.5.4). Yet the Historian's (and Chronicler's) silence remains: Hezekiah is neither credited with the elimination of the Tophet (as is Josiah in Dtr), nor is he accused of participating in the cult. As Mosca observes (p. 218), one can interpret this silence in various ways, including that Dtr (for Mosca, at Josiah's time) found no evidence of Hezekiah's participation, and so presumed him "innocent," or that Dtr knew that Hezekiah had practiced the cult and, for whatever reason, chose not to say so. Again, given an earlier redaction, it is most unlikely that the elimination of the cult of Molek was part of Hezekiah's reform (2 Kgs 18:4), else this would have been mentioned. But, given our proposed understanding of the cult of Molek as a divinatory rite, there is still a word of praise for Hezekiah corresponding to the condemnation of Ahaz for participating in the cult: the aforementioned fact that Hezekiah's only "divination," as it were, was through Deuteronomically-approved channels. While tendentious shaping has doubtlessly played a role here, it is hard to believe that a redactor at least roughly contemporary with Hezekiah could have gotten away with this comparison had Hezekiah personally participated in the Tophet cult. That he might have withdrawn royal participation in, but not royal consent to the cult may seem to us a half-measure, but it is so only in view of Josiah's later actions.[565] In any event, from what we can gather from Isaiah, Tophet's fires burned on.

We noted above that some have taken the context of Dtr's summary introduction to Ahaz's reign in 2 Kgs 16:1-4, i.e., the Syro-Ephraimitic War, to suggest that Ahaz burned his son in a national emergency. We have already seen that such an explanation for the practice of the cult of Molek is unlikely (4.4.2, regarding 2 Kgs 3:27). Neither is it necessarily implied by the account of Ahaz's reign. 2 Kgs 16:1-4 is form-critically distinct from its following context, being, as we have seen, one of a series of "Beurteilungen" with which Dtr structures the History. Verse 5 begins a new unit (marked by 'āz) concerning the highlights of Ahaz's reign (in Dtr's judgment) and adapted from the Book of the Chronicles of the Kings of Judah (v. 19), or whatever other sources Dtr employed. Even reading the chapter as a unit (i.e., in its "canonical shape"), the text implies that the Syro-Ephraimitic threat is a judgment on Ahaz for his acts of apostasy in vv. 2-4, subsequent to those acts (again, note 'āz, v. 5). Ahaz has acted like the Canaanites, and he has brought on the consequences: invasion, with dispossession inevitably to come, if the "abominations" continue unabated (despite the delay worked by the alliance with Assyria).

---

[565] Similarly, Josiah's reform may have been more extensive than Hezekiah's (2 Kgs 18:4-5), but, pace Cross, there is no hint of disapproval of the latter king in Dtr. Indeed, there are hints that Hezekiah did more than Dtr's summary credits him with: in v. 22 the Assyrian Rabshakeh claims that Hezekiah had centralized worship in Jerusalem. Such an omission (or deletion) is best explained, I believe, by a pre-Josianic redaction of the History, followed by one in Josiah's time (see above).

Finally, we may note the parallel verse to 2 Kgs 16:3 in
Chronicles, 2 Chr 28:3. The Chronicler was clearly working from some
form of the Kings text, although there are two intriguing differences:
Ahaz is said to have burned (wyb'r; cf. 2 Kgs 16:3, h'byr) his sons
(bnyw; cf. bnw) in the fire.[566] As noted above (1.2), Geiger explained
the variant verb in Chronicles as the original form used in Biblical
references to the Molek cult (hb'r), which has been euphemized everywhere else to h'byr.[567] We have seen, however, that h'byr has a technical usage in the Israelite cult which suits what we know of the cult of
Molek. The pluralizing of Ahaz's victims (and also of Manasseh's, 2 Chr
33:6), if not attributable to an otherwise-unknown textual variant in
Kings, appears to reflect the Chronicler's animus toward Ahaz.[568] In
Chronicles Ahaz loses the Syro-Ephraimite War (2 Chr 28:5), is attacked
by Assyria when he seeks the aid of Tilgath-pilneser [sic] (v. 20) and
openly sacrifices to the gods of Syria (v. 23)--all additions to or in-
tensifications of the situation as related by Dtr in 2 Kgs 16.[569] Indeed, "sons" is not the only instance of polemical pluralizing: Ahaz is

---

[566] A third addition on the part of the Chronicler, both here and in 2
Chr 33:6 (regarding Manasseh), is the specification of the location
of the cult "in the Valley of the Son of Hinnom." We shall deal
with the Valley (and the Tophet therein) in our discussion of the
relevant passages in Jeremiah (4.5.6), where both occur several
times.

[567] Geiger's proposal is still conceded possibility, if not probability,
by some modern commentators (e.g., Wilhelm Rudolph, Chronikbücher
[HAT 21; Tübingen: J. C. B. Mohr, 1955] 288).

[568] If so, the LXX has continued the process (or harmonized Kings with
Chronicles): the Lucianic recension reads a plural in 2 Kgs 16:3;
the LXX has a plural at 2 Kgs 21:6.

[569] See Rudolf Mosis, Untersuchungen zur Theologie des chronistischen
Geschichtswerkes (Freiburg: Herder, 1973) 186-187, for further discussion.

said to have "walked in the ways of the kings of Israel" in 2 Chr 28:2 (cf. "way" in 2 Kgs 16:3). Thus, while the reading hb'r for h'byr might be the result of a mechanical error (metathesis) either by the Chronicler or his Vorlage, the context suggests a tendentious alteration. The main argument against Tendenz as an explanation is the absence of a similar alteration in the verb in the notice regarding Manasseh in 2 Chr 33:6. However, it will be noted that while the Chronicler's summary of Manasseh is taken almost directly from Kings (which, in turn, almost quotes Deut 18:10), he has inserted additional negative material in the judgment on Ahaz ("he burned incense in the Valley of the Son of Hinnom"), with the result that he divides what we have called the marker of the "parade abomination" (wgm) from its accustomed referent, the practice of the cult of Molek. For whatever reason, the Chronicler has left bad enough alone with Manasseh, but has supplemented his sources' negative view of Ahaz.[570]

Having already treated the reference to cultic child sacrifice in Dtr's summary judgment of the Northern Kingdom (2 Kgs 17:17), we may move to the statement that among those whom the Assyrians imported into the North were the Səparwim, who "burned their sons with (the) fire to 'Adrammelek and 'Ănammelek, the gods of Səparwāyim" (2 Kgs 17:31, reading the last two words with Q). Heretofore, the scholarly debate has centered on the identificaiton of the two gods and the location of Sepharvaim. Proposals for the latter have alternated between Mesopotamia and Syria: most earlier scholars assumed that Sippar in "heartland" Mesopotamia was meant; Albright championed Sibraim, which, according to

---

[570] One obvious possible reason for this is the Chronicler's claim that Manasseh later repented and reformed the cult (2 Chr 33:12-19).

Ezek 47:16, "lies on the border between Damascus and Hamath" (in Syria); more recently, Astour has proposed a return to the east by way of a graphic error in the MT, to Saparda in Media.[571] A similar (and to some degree interlocking) variety of suggestions obtains regarding the divine recipients of the Sepharvites' offerings. Adrammelek is commonly emended to (H)Adad-melek, allegedly cognate with a Syrian-Assyrian Adad-milki.[572] Anammelek, on the other hand, has been read as a corruption both of 'Anat-melek and of 'Anum-melek.[573] The former produces the pair known from Ugarit, Hadad (Baal) and Anat, while the latter suggests a combination of the West Semitic storm god with the East Semitic sky god, Anu. Either reading of the controverted place and divine names yields a strong argument for those who would take this verse along with 2 Kings 16 (regarding Ahaz) to propose a Syrian or Assyrian origin for Israel's cult of Molek, probably imported under the aforementioned Judahite king: the History explicitly states (2 Kgs 17:33) that the peoples listed in v. 24 were worshipping deities from their homelands, and they were presumably doing so according to their native cults.

Recently, two articles have challenged this general (if not detailed) consensus. J. Ebach and U. Rüterswörden argue that Adrammelek makes perfectly good sense without emendation, if one sees it as a com-

---

[571] Albright, *Archaeology and the Religion of Israel*, 220, n. 116; Astour, "Sepharvaim," IDBSup (1976) 807.

[572] We have already seen that this is the suggestion of Albright, Weinfeld and Deller (1.7,8).

[573] For the reading "'Anat-melek," see Weinfeld, "The Worship of Molech," 149, and the literature cited there; for 'Anum-melek, see Albright, "The Evolution of the West Semitic Divinity 'An--'Anat--'Atta," *AJSL* 41 (1925) 86-87, and de Vaux, *RB* 45 (1936) 280.

pound of the epithets 'dr ("powerful") and mlk ("king").[574] They cite
the name Malkandros from Philo of Byblos, which they say is equivalent
to b'l adr, the Punic Ba'al Ḥammon. Similarly, Stephen Kaufmann suggests that the divine names in 2 Kgs 17:31 imply a Phoenician origin
(and a Phoenician location for Sepharvaim): "the only area where 'dr,
'n, and mlk are all at home in the divine onomasticon!"[575] However, Kaufmann's article is far more significant for its negative argument: Kaufmann shows that the logographically-written "Adad-milki," the presumed
Syrian-Assyrian cognate of OT *Adad-melek, need not be read that way at
all. As a result, Weinfeld's hypothesis that Molek was an epithet for
Hadad loses its best evidence, and the argument for the Syrian-Assyrian
source of the cult of Molek is severely undermined.[576]

We have already argued that the account of Ahaz's reign in 2 Kings
16 provides scant support for those who would extract from it grounds
for the historical judgment that the Biblical cult of Molek was borrowed
from Syria or Assyria. Regardless of one's views on the identifications
just discussed, the same must be said of 2 Kings 17. Whether or not the
History is accurate, that the cult was practiced in the Northern Kingdom
(2 Kgs 16:3; 17:17), we have no reason to doubt that it was known in Israel long before the arrival of the Sepharvites. In sum, at best, 2 Kgs

---

[574] "ADRMLK, 'Moloch' und BA'AL ADR: Eine Notiz zum Problem der
Moloch-Verehrung im alten Israel," UF 11 (1979) 219-226.

[575] "The Enigmatic Adad-Milki," JNES 37 (1978) 101, n. 9.

[576] Mosca speculates that the two names may refer to El and Baal, although he agrees with Albright on the Syrian location of Sepharvaim
("Child Sacrifice," 259, n. 158, and 259-260, n. 161). As will be
seen, however, the identifications are not significant for his understanding of 2 Kgs 17:31, as it pertains to the cult of child sacrifice in Israel.

17:31 gives the historian reason to suspect that the Syro-Palestinian
deity Malik-Milku/i was, already by the eighth-seventh century (depending on when one dates this verse), being combined with other deities in
his chthonic cult.[577] On the other hand, as we have seen so often, the
mlk-element of the names may be what the MT says it is: an epithet,
"king," applicable to many deities (including El and Baal, as Mosca suggests). With the identifications so tentative, further certainty is
elusive, and further historical information may be obtained only through
arguments which quickly become circular (such as that all Syro-
Palestinian cultic child sacrifice was to Malik-Milku/i).

Nevertheless, 2 Kgs 17:31 may advance our study if we consider it
theologically, as well as historically. Mosca proposes that Dtr employed both references to cultic child sacrifice is 2 Kgs 17 (vv. 17,
31) in conjunction with the two references in Deuteronomy, which applied
to all Israel, to "show that the circle is now closed so far as the
Northern Kingdom is concerned." Thus, Deut 12:31 claims that the Canaanites "burn" (śrp) their children to their gods; Deut 18:10 forbids the
Israelites to "make to pass" (hʻbyr) their children to Yahweh; 2 Kgs
17:17 recounts that the North did just that; and 2 Kgs 17:31 tells how
the non-Israelite Sepharvites resume the Canaanite practice (śrp). Mosca concludes eloquently:

> The circle is complete. Because the Northern tribes have fol-
> lowed in the "sin of Jeroboam" (cf. II Kgs. 17:21-23), Yahweh
> is so angered that not only does he drive Israel from his
> sight (II Kgs. 17:23)--he even gives their land back to "the
> nations" and allows these nations to resume their idolatrous

---

[577] This possibility is supported by the frequent compounding of Mlk
with other divine names in Phoenician, whether Mlk is understood as
it has been traditionally, as an abbreviation for Melqart, or as the
Malik-Milku/i we have found at Ugarit and elsewhere (see 2.6.1-2).

practices. The covenantal curses are carried out; it is as if the North had never existed.[578]

While we have no quarrel with Mosca's concluding remarks (cf. 2 Kgs 17:23), the proposed cycle is problematic. Even beyond its dependence on a questionable understanding of the usage of h'byr and śrp (4.3.3), it overlooks the fact that Dtr has not remanded the land to non-Israelite gods: the new occupants are on Yahweh's own land and are subject to Yahweh's law (vv. 25-28). Thus, they, too, are subject to dispossession for doing the abominations of the Canaanites to gods not of the land. While it is tempting to see here a thinly-disguised polemic against the Samaritans, it is more likely that Dtr is emphasizing the status of Judah as the sole locus of true Yahwism, while at the same time affirming that all the land of Israel (i.e., the old Davidic empire, excluding vassal states) is the special possession of Yahweh, whoever may happen to inhabit it at any particular time, thereby adding to the theological rationale for Josiah's invasion of the North (2 Kgs 23:15-20).[579] On this reading, Mosca may well be correct that, while the Sepharvites were brought to the North soon after the fall of Samaria in 722/1, the practice of which they are accused in v. 31 reflects the

---

[578] "Child Sacrifice," 176-177.

[579] For an anti-Samaritan understanding of 2 Kings 17, see H. H. Rowley, "The Samaritan Schism in Legend and History," Israel's Prophetic Heritage: Essays in Honor of James Muilenburg (ed. B. W. Anderson and W. Harrelson; London: SCM, 1962) 208-222; see also the refutation of James D. Purvis, The Samaritan Pentateuch and the Origin of the Samaritan Sect (HSM 2; Cambridge, MA: Harvard, 1968) 96. Purvis rightly stresses the harsh and probably supplementary character of vv. 34b-40. Given the above argument for a pre-Josianic recension of Dtr, I would suggest that vv. 1-6 are likely the "annalistic core," from Hezekiah's time, vv. 7-34a from the Josianic redactor (supporting the old Davidic claims, and therefore Josiah's invasion, as suggested above) and vv. 34b-41 by the exilic redactor.

situation in the seventh century, so that the Sepharvites may have
acquired the cult of child sacrifice once in the land (pp. 191-192). On
the other hand, if Sepharvaim was located within the Palestinian (i.e.,
Canaanite) circle of cultural influence, they may have practiced the
cult long before their exile.

Little more remains to be said about Dtr's statement that Manasseh
"made his son to pass over by the fire, and was a soothsayer and an augur, and made an 'ôb and a yiddə'ōnî" (2 Kgs 21:6). Manasseh is obviously being indicted for performing Canaanite abominations (including
the cult of Molek as a divinatory, or even necromantic act) on the basis
of Deut 18:10, an accusation which is made explicit in vv. 2 and 9. We
have already suggested that, like Ahaz, Manasseh is cited for the "parade abomination" of child sacrifice, although other kings may have been
guilty of it, in order to sharpen the contrast with the following reformer king, Josiah. Mosca is quite right in identifying this as the
cause of Manasseh's indictment, and his further suggestion concerning
the role of the child sacrifice references in the Manasseh-Josiah juxtaposition is provocative: "Because Judah outdoes 'the nations' in evil
[under Manasseh], it becomes itself--temporarily--one with them, thus
preparing the way for the new Conquest under the new Joshua
[Josiah]."[580] (We have already suggested that 2 Kgs 17:31 may function
similarly with regard to Josiah's campaign in the North.) There is,

---

[580] "Child Sacrifice," 181. Mosca's further explanation of the Joshua-
Josiah parallel (pp. 182-183) is impressive, although he is forced
to admit that no overt comparisons are to be found (thanks, he says,
to the exilic editor). Also, as we have argued above, Josiah's elevation is not accomplished by the diminution of David or Hezekiah
(cf. 2 Kgs 18:3; 22:2), as Mosca claims, but by praise layered on
top of that given to the latter two figures.

however, no reason to suggest that Dtr has invented the account of Manasseh's participation in the Molek cult (nor does Mosca suggest this); rather, the Historian has expressed it in his own terms and employed it in the service of his larger scheme.[581]

Finally, we come to the one attestation of Molek in all of D: "And he [Josiah] defiled the Tophet, which is in the Valley of the Son (K Sons) of Hinnom, so that no one might make his son or his daughter to pass over by the fire lammōlek" (2 Kgs 23:10).[582] Thus, it is also the sole verse which contains the entire formula whose elements we have been examining: h'byr 't-bnw (w't-btw) b'š lmlk. The verse also is the only one in D to specify the location of the cult in the Tophet in the Valley of the Son(s) of Hinnom, neither of which apparently required any further specification, so far as Dtr was concerned. (As noted above, we shall deal with the Tophet and the Valley when we examine the relevant material in Jeremiah [4.5.6], in which the terms occur outside of direct references to the cult of Molek.)

The most important question which we may put to this verse is, obviously, what it tells us of the meaning of lammōlek. In this case the LXX simply transliterates the word, reading tǫ Moloch.[583] The LXX understanding is clearly the "traditional" one, of Molek as a divine name (since Moloch is not declined); furthermore, the tradition of vocaliza-

---

[581] For a discussion of the Chronicler's version of Manasseh's involvement in the Molek cult, see above, in the discussion of Ahaz.

[582] We have argued above (4.3.2) that the other attestation in D, 1 Kgs 11:7, is a corruption for Milkom.

[583] The LXX reading is usually explained as vowel assimilation, along the lines of MT hōmer = LXX gomor in Ezek 45:13 (Eissfeldt, Molk als Opferbegriff, 35, n. 3). This seems more likely than an independent variant, such as some connection with Muluk of Mari.

tion of the Hebrew followed by the LXX is the same as the MT (given the preceding article). But, from the perspective of Eissfeldt and Mosca, does the LXX rendering then reflect the development in meaning from sacrificial technical term to divine name which they allege? Understandably, neither scholar calls much attention to the change in translation practice (and the presence of the article) vis-à-vis Leviticus.[584] Presumably, at least Mosca would argue that the original Hebrew read ləmōlek here, as in Leviticus.

If, for the sake of argument, we concede this point (although entirely without the grounds on which we did so in Leviticus), we can deal with a more substantive issue raised by this verse. Mosca expresses it incisively, after he has conceded that the "small number of examples" of h'byr l would favor reading the name of a recipient as the object of the preposition (see 4.3.1):

> Still, the dilemma remains. For if the external parallels to h'byr l tend to support the traditional view of mōlek as divine recipient, Deuteronomistic usage of the phrase h'byr b'š favors Eissfeldt's understanding of mōlek as a sacrificial term. In every other reference to "passing into the fire" (Deut. 18:10; II Kgs. 16:3, 17:17, 21:6), the historian has conspicuously avoided naming the recipient of the offering. Why should a divine "Molech" suddenly be introduced in II Kgs. 23:10? The mention of mōlek there is more easily understandable if it is a pleonastic reference to the victim of the rite ("his son or daughter"), rather than a belated attempt to identify the divine recipient.[585]

---

[584] Eissfeldt attributes the change to the LXX's practice of sometimes translating, sometimes transcribing words such as Tophet (p. 36). One must recall, however, that he concedes that the LXX uniformly has the "later" understanding of Molek in mind, even in Leviticus (4.3.1). Mosca does not deal with the LXX of 2 Kgs 23:10.

[585] "Child Sacrifice," 193.

The fact is, however, that _either_ understanding of Molek in 2 Kgs 23:10 is, in a sense, "pleonastic." If we agree that the passages which Mosca lists all refer to the "cult of Molek" (and we do), then Dtr has added something which had in those previous passages been understood, either the name of the divine recipient or the term for precisely the kind of sacrifice being made. Such an addition is in keeping with the rest of the verse, which includes the name of the location of the cult, which had also been understood previously, at least in 2 Kgs 16:3 and 21:6. Therefore, the "sudden introduction" of Molek into 2 Kgs 23:10 does not argue for either view.

The real problem for the "traditional" understanding is to account for the sudden appearance of the ancient, chthonic deity Malik-Milku/i (-Molek), if it had been understood all along that the children were being sacrificed to Yahweh. We have already sought to explain how the cult might be ascribed to either, whether in the understanding of its Israelite practitioners or of its critics (4.3.3,4).[586] But the question remains, why does Dtr choose this one, last reference to the cult in the History to mention the older conception of the recipient? The account of Josiah's reform allows us to suggest, even if not to establish, an explanation. First, it may be noted that all of Josiah's reforming activities which are recounted are directed at foreign cults, not at the heterodox (i.e., non-Deuteronomic) practice of Yahwism.[587] It is there-

---

[586] It also bears emphasis that, if one does not accept Mosca's theory of the nature of Dtr's tendentiousness in the use of the verbs h'byr and śrp, nowhere in Dtr (rather than Deuteronomy) is there any explicit indication that the children were sacrificed to Yahweh.

[587] A possible (even likely) exception is the centralization of worship described in vv. 8-9. However, if this is not a later addition (so James A. Montgomery, The Books of Kings [ed. H. S. Gehman; ICC; NY:

fore no surprize that Dtr chooses this occasion to emphasize the idolat-

rous essence of the cult of Molek. Secondly, as we have seen, the pre-

vious accusations against Ahaz, the North and Manasseh were closely pat-

terned on the phraseology of Deuteronomy, which lacks the name of the

divine recipient. The verse under examination is not so patterned, so

that Dtr was freer to name Molek explicitly here, and thus by implica-

tion to suggest once again that the earlier practitioners had become, at

least theologically, Canaanites.[588]

In sum, there is no denying that, if one allows the revocalization

of lammōlek in 2 Kgs 23:10, the Eissfeldt-Mosca reading has a certain

attractiveness in that verse (which can then be extrapolated over all of

D since Molek occurs only here). However, such a reading requires that

the usage of h'byr l elsewhere in the OT be overlooked, that the nature

of Josiah's listed reforms as of non-Israelite cults be expanded in this

one case, and that the divinatory connection of the several Molek cult

references in D with the clear usage of Molek in Leviticus be set aside.

In short, we have so far seen no evidence which compels us to abandon

---

Charles Scribner's Sons, 1951] 531), then the non-Jerusalemite
priests (khnym) are tainted by the context of v. 5, regarding the
"idol priests" (kmrym) who are also said to have burned incense on
the high places of the cities of Judah.

[588] Matthias Delcor discusses the various foreign cults (but not Molek!)
in 2 Kings 23 and concludes that vv. 5 and 11 describe Mesopotamian
astral cults. Even he concedes, however, that all of the cults have
known Canaanite (including Phoenician and Transjordanian) connections, with the possible exception of the mazzālôt, "constella-
tions," in v. 5 ("Les cultes étrangers en Israël au moment de la réforme de Josias d'après 2R 23: Étude de religions sémitiques
comparées," Mélanges bibliques et orientaux en l'honneur de M. Henri
Cazelles [ed. A. Caquot and M. Delcor; AOAT 212; Kevelaer: Butzon &
Bercker, 1981] 91-123). For a strong argument against an Assyrian
source for any of the cults in 2 Kings 23, see Cogan, Imperialism
and Religion, and John McKay, Religion in Judah under the Assyrians
(SBT 2/26; London: SCM, 1973).

the "traditional" interpretation of "Molek" as a Canaanite deity, whose cult was adopted and adapted by the Israelites. Indeed, much of what we have seen speaks in favor of that understanding and points us, furthermore, to suggest a connection between the chthonic Syro-Palestinian deity Malik-Milku/i, known at Ebla, Mari and Ugarit, and Molek, whose cult likewise appears to have a chthonic (specifically, necromantic) character. We shall test this hypothesis, along with that of Eissfeldt and Mosca, as we examine the third major category of Biblical texts, the prophetic.

4.5 THE CULT OF MOLEK IN THE PROPHETS

Regardless of the judgments one has drawn from the evidence presented to this point, the relevant references have unquestionably been scanty and stylized. Inevitably, the investigator of OT Molek must turn to the prophets, in all their variety of time, location and perspective, for additional insight. As has already been mentioned, Mosca believes that one prophetic passage supplies the clinching argument for Eissfeldt's hypothesis of the meaning of Molek and the place of the cult of Molek in pre-Josianic Yahwism. We shall examine the prophets in roughly chronological order, treating those passages which have been adduced (or which we seek to introduce) in the Molek debate.

4.5.1 Amos

The first two prophets whose books we shall examine are also the only two whose prophetic careers were spent primarily in the Northern Kingdom, Amos and Hosea. What we find in these two books will therefore be of considerable interest as we attempt to answer the question raised in reference to 2 Kgs 17:17: was the cult of Molek practiced in the North?

Three passages from Amos have been brought into the Molek debate: 1:15; 2:1; and 5:26. All require revocalization, but not emendation, of the MT to claim relevance to our study. The first passage is in Amos's "oracles against the nations," at the conclusion of the oracle against Ammon. The MT reads: wəhālak malkām baggôlāh hû' wəśārāyw yaḥdāw ("and their king will go into exile, he and his princes together"). On the other hand, the Lucianic recension of the Greek, along with the translations of Aquila, Symmachus and the Syriac and Vulgate, have mel-chom, which suggests that they read mlkm as Milkom, the Ammonite national god known from 1 Kgs 11:5,22.[589] This reading was supported by some of the older commentators, and retains outspoken defenders.[590]

Given the results of our study to this point, the importance of this verse is, in any case, limited, as we have yet found no historical evidence to link Molek with Milkom or Milkom with the cult of child sacrifice. Nevertheless, because there are several passages where one or more Greek recension has Milkom (or Moloch) for MT "their king," and because such verses have been cited in studies of Molek, we may attempt to

---

[589] The LXX itself (i.e., "Old Greek") is an unlikely option ("and her kings will go into exile, their priests and their rulers together") since it requires either a Vorlage of mlkyh (or the like) for MT mlkm and khnyw for hw', or else substantial interpretation on the part of the translators. The reading "their priests" does help explain the Lucianic understanding, however, and points the way, we believe, to the proper text-critical solution (below).

[590] For the commentators, see the list in W. R. Harper, *Amos and Hosea* (ICC; NY: Charles Scribner's Sons, 1905) 35. A recent (and, in my view, convoluted) attempt to defend not only the originality of "Milkom," but the secondary nature of the MT at other points where it differs from the LXX is Emile Puech, "Milkom, le dieu ammonite, en Amos I 15," *VT* 27 (1977) 117-125.

account for the divergence between our two best witnesses to the original Hebrew, the MT and the LXX.[591] We may note first Zeph 1:5, where
again the MT has "their king" and the Lucianic recension, along with the
other versions listed above, has <u>Melchom</u> or <u>Moloch</u>. We shall return to
this verse below (4.5.5); for now, it is sufficient to mention that <u>mlkm</u>
is clearly a divine name or title in Zeph 1:5. Of far more direct importance to our study of Amos, however, is the nearly identical phrase
(to Amos 1:15) in Jeremiah's oracle against Ammon (49:3 = LXX 30:3):
"for their king (LXX <u>Melchol</u>) into exile shall go, his priests and his
princes together."[592] Given the very similar wording of the oracle
against Moab in 48:7 ("and Kemoš shall go forth into exile, his priests
and his <u>princes</u> with him" [reading with Q]) and the undisputed presence
of "his priests," it is likely that the Greek is the preferable witness
to the original vocalization of <u>mlkm</u> as <u>Milkom</u> in Jer 49:3 (and
49:1).[593] However, the context of Amos 1:15, which antedates any part of

---

[591] The one verse in which the LXX has <u>Me/ilchol/m</u> for MT <u>malkām</u> but
which we shall not treat in any detail is 2 Sam 12:30 (//1 Chr
20:2), in which David takes the crown from the head of "their
king"/"Milkom" upon the conquest of Rabbath-Ammon. Neither reading
yields any information useful to us (since David hardly worshipped
Milkom in any case). More controversial is the following verse,
which reads in the MT: "and he [David] made them [the Ammonites]
pass over by the brickkiln" (<u>bammalbēn</u> = Q; K = <u>bmlkn</u>). Most commentators agree that <u>h'byr</u> must be emended to <u>h'byd</u> ("he set them to
work"); in any event, a connection with the cult of Molek is highly
unlikely since the "victims" were "all the cities of the Ammonites,"
not children. For a thorough review and bibliography (and idiosyncratic solution), see G. C. O'Ceallaigh, "'And <u>So</u> David Did to <u>All</u>
<u>the Cities</u> of Ammon,'" <u>VT</u> 12 (1962) 179-189.

[592] See J. Ziegler, <u>Ieremias</u> (Septuaginta Gottingensis 15; Göttingen:
Vandenhoeck & Ruprecht, 1957) 310-311, for other Greek variants, including <u>Melchom</u> and <u>Moloch</u>.

[593] On the other hand, given the nature of royal patronage (cf. 1 Kgs
2:26-27), one could speak of the "king's priests."

Jeremiah by over a century, is somewhat different. The "oracles against the nations" in Amos suggest that it is people, not gods, who will go into exile (1:5) and that the Ammonite king and princes in 1:15 are comparable to the Moabite "judge" (šōpēṭ) and princes in 2:3. The most likely explanation for the text-critical situation in Amos 1:15, it seems to me, is that the LXX (and succeeding Greek recensions) harmonized the verse from Amos with the similar reference to mlkm of Ammon in Jer 49:3.[594] In effect, the Greek (and Syriac and Vulgate) have levelled the creative reuse which Jeremiah had made of Amos in the former's polemic against other nations and their gods (besides Jer 48:7, cf. 47:15,25; 48:35,46; 49:1; 50:2).

The second significant passage from Amos is the one in which, as noted above (1.7), H. Tur-Sinai and W. F. Albright wish to see a reference to human sacrifice in Moab. Amos 2:1b (MT) reads: ʿal-śorpô ʾaṣmôt melek-ʾĕdôm laśśîd ("because he burned the bones of the king of Edom to lime"). Tur-Sinai would revocalize the last three words to

---

[594] This is Wolff's solution (Joel and Amos [trans. W. Janzen et al.; ed. S. D. McBride; Hermeneia; Philadelphia: Fortress, 1977 (German orig., 1975)] 131-132). Another approach, from the perspective of modern translation theory, is that of Jan de Waard ("A Greek Translation-Technical Treatment of Amos 1:15," On Language, Culture and Religion: In Honor of Eugene A. Nida [ed. M. Black and W. A. Smalley; The Hague: Mouton, 1974] 111-118), who proposes that "the LXX translator of Amos simply divided this broad group of authorities [the śārim] into two more specific subgroups, one religious (hoi hiereis), the other secular (hoi archontes)" (p. 116). While he rightly notes that the LXX of Jer 49:3 and Amos 1:15 do not overlap as much as one might expect, if the two were in some way conflated, he does not explain why the Greek translators chose this "dynamic equivalence" rendering of śārim in only this one case out of the hundreds in the OT. In any event, he agrees that mlkm in Amos 1:15 was not originally vocalized "Milkom." See below on Zeph 1:8 for the suggestion that śārim may denote cultic officials (4.5.5). While this is a possibility in Jer 48:7 and 49:3, it is unlikely in Amos 1:15, given the considerations of context presented above.

read, mōlek 'ādām laššōd ("[the bones of] a human sacrifice out of violence"), while Albright would revise Tur-Sinai's final word to laššēd
("to a demon").[595] This reading does possess an initial attraction since
commentators have long had to admit that the prophet's indictment was
based on an otherwise-unknown incident. Furthermore, Albright's understanding meshes cleanly with the undisputed reading of Ps 106:37 and an
attractive emendation of Hos 3:4 (presented in 4.5.2). All in all, however, the revocalization is unconvincing. Albright's objection that the
MT's phrase "to lime" is redundant ("How can one burn bones without cal-
cinating them?") has little, if any, force, given the tenuous line between superfluity and rich expression, especially in poetry.[596] Mosca
rightly points out that none of the other foreign nations is indicted
for an internal (versus international) violation of divine law.[597] Finally, if Mosca is at all correct in his hypothesis that mlk'dm was a
form of the molk-sacrifice which developed some centuries after the initial Punic colonization (referring to the sacrifice of the children of
commoners), it is amazing that a relatively late, intra-Punic development should be found in the oracle of an eighth-century Judahite prophet
in an oracle concerning Moab. In sum, Mosca is quite correct that the
reading "raises more difficulties than it solves."

---

[595] For references, see 1.7.

[596] Albright's point gets backhanded support from the Targum, followed
by Wolff (Joel and Amos, 162-163), which adds that the "lime" was
further put to use as wall plaster.

[597] "Child Sacrifice," 261, n. 162.

The third and final passage listed above is a notorious crux, and
it has generated a correspondingly extensive literature. As was observed in chapter I (1.1), Amos 5:26 has always received close attention
in studies of Molek, possibly because it is quoted in Acts 7:43 (according to the LXX), the only occurrence of Moloch in the NT. Our present
aim is not to review the range of past proposals, nor to suggest a new
solution to the crux, but only to determine whether and in what way this
verse can supply further information concerning Molek.

The latter part of the verse makes it clear that the prophet is accusing Israel of idolatry ("your images," "your gods which you made for
yourselves").[598] The question is, which gods are the objects of the people's apostacy? The most obvious options devolve from the quite different readings of the MT and LXX. The former has, "And you bear/bore Sikkût, your king, and Kiyyûn, your images, the star of your gods which you
made for yourselves," while the latter reads, "And you took up the tabernacle (skēnē) of Moloch and the star of your god Raiphan, your images, which you made for yourselves." Most recent commentaries and
translations have favored the MT, reading the names of two Assyrian astral gods, Sakkut and Kewan (from Kaiwanu), and explaining the MT vowels
as a dysphemism based on šiqqûṣ, "detestable thing."[599] Such an understanding would effectively eliminate this verse from our present inter-

---

[598] Pace Harper (*Amos and Hosea*, 137-138), who argues that "Amos has in
mind an impure and corrupt worship," not idolatry. (Harper's commentary is invaluable, however, for its summary of scholarship
through 1905.)

[599] See, for example, Wilhelm Rudolph, *Joel--Amos--Obadja--Jona* (KAT
13/2; Gütersloh: Mohn, 1971) 206-207, and Wolff, *Joel and Amos*,
260.

est.[600] However, the MT can scarcely be accepted without some correction. To note but two of the difficulties, "your images" (plural) is
awkward in apposition to "Kiyyûn" (singular), and the line is extremely
long for what one assumes from the context is poetry, whatever one's
views on Hebrew metrics. As a result, even those who favor the proper
names on the basis of the MT, such as the RSV, often turn to the LXX for
assistance with the word order, or for other proposed emendations or de-
letions. We have an additional reason for doing so, as we have already
seen (thanks to Mosca) how unlikely it is that the MT conceals two cases
of dysphemism using šiqqûṣ. Unfortunately, the LXX is also obviously
corrupt. With regard to our concerns, we note that the LXX Moloch simply ignores the suffix on MT malkəkem, while Raiphan is difficult to explain as a rendering of Kiyyûn (or Kîyûn).[601] Charles Isbell would solve
the former difficulty by reading "Milkom" for mlkkm (removing the "dittography" of the /k/), although he does not explain how the Ammonite deity became so attractive to Amos's contemporaries, nor why Milkom would
have been paired with an Assyrian deity, Kewan.[602] The other scholar to
treat the verse at length in recent years, Stanley Gevirtz, reads, "your
(god) MLK," although he is clearly unenthusiastic and does not explain
how a possessive suffix came to be attached to a proper name, contrary

---

[600] The only possible remaining connection to our study would be the
identification of the Assyrian gods with Saturn, to whom Punic
molk-sacrifices were made, according to the Latin stelae (such as
those found at Ngaous).

[601] Raiphan is usually accounted for as a scribal confusion of /r/ for
/k/ and of /p/ for /w/, with the observation that the respective in-
terchanges are more understandable in the paleo-Hebrew alphabet than
the later "Aramaic" block script.

[602] "Another Look at Amos 5:26," JBL 97 (1978) 97-99.

to Hebrew usage.[603]

A comprehensive proposal on this verse lies beyond the scope of this study. Indeed, there is little incentive to pursue such a solution (except for its intrinsic interest). At most, given the LXX reading, "Moloch," one could assert that Molek was worshipped as an idol (tupos) with a "tabernacle" of some sort in the Northern Kingdom, and that the god had some astral connection (assuming the originality of the MT's "the star of your gods"). However, as has been observed, the LXX is unable to account for the possessive suffix, and Isbell's "Milkom" raises the questions noted above (which he does not attempt to answer). The most provocative possibility is supplied by the other divine name as read by the LXX: as Marvin Pope has remarked, "the collocation of MLK and RP-- is significant in the light of the Ugaritic association of RPU and MLK" (cf. 2.3).[604] The contest of Yahweh and Molek/Rapi'u for the worship of all Israel (North and South) would be an appropriate subject for the prophet, according to the legal and historical material which we have already examined.[605] Moreover, the threat to exile the "house of Israel" to a place "beyond Damascus" would then approach Dtr's theme of Israel's dispossession for Canaanite behavior: Israel would be retrojected to the landless status of Abraham in Aram-Naḥaraim.[606] Unfortu-

---

[603] "A New Look at an Old Crux: Amos 5:26," JBL 87 (1968) 274.

[604] "Rephaim Texts," 170.

[605] This assumes that v. 26 refers to the present-future, not the past (since Israelite worship of Canaanite deities before the conquest/settlement is unlikely), unless the prophet is projecting Israel's rebellion backwards, as appears to be the case in Ezekiel 20 (see the commentaries on this much-mooted point).

[606] See Mosca's discussion of the verse ("Child Sacrifice," 257, n. 155) for a similar conclusion.

nately, one can by no means securely establish the pair Molek/Raiphan in the text of Amos 5:26, so that further development of the ramifications of the presence of these names would base speculation on conjecture.

In sum, it seems to me that there are two solutions to this enigmatic passage which commend themselves, neither of which, however, would relate Amos 5:26 to our study. The first is the reading of the two Assyrian divine names. Despite the problems of vocalization, it must be admitted that the association of Sakkuth and Kaiwanu in Assyrian tablets argues forcefully for their pairing here.[607] Moreover, the presence of Assyrian deities does not necessarily date the passage after 722/1 (and thus deny it to Amos).[608] No doubt, the MT has suffered some metathesis of words (cf. RSV) or editorial additions, but an "Assyrian reading" makes much sense in view of the political realities of the time and Amos's threats of exile "beyond Damascus."

The second attractive solution is based on that of Weinfeld, who argues that the verse has to do with the Assyro-Aramean cult of the King ([H]Adad) and Queen (Ištar) of Heaven, as their images were borne in a booth (cf. LXX skēnē) in procession.[609] The suggestive aspect of the proposal, I believe, is the interpretation, "the booth of your king," in v. 26aα. One can agree with Weinfeld that the verse shows the presence of Assyro-Aramean religious influence, or, as we prefer, one can understand Amos's attack to be on Jeroboam I's "golden calf" cult as a form of Baal worship (cf. Hos 13:1-2).[610] According to the latter reading,

---

[607] See Harper, *Amos and Hosea*, 140, for references.

[608] McKay, *Religion in Judah*, 68 and 123, n. 4.

[609] "The Worship of Molech," 149-150.

the prophet would be referring to the god by title, "king."[611] This
reading has the advantage of avoiding all speculation as to the degree
of Assyro-Aramean religious influence in Israel, concentrating instead
on known, Canaanite practices for which, as observed above, Israel (and
Judah) were constantly threatened with exile. Once again, however, the
adjudication of the issue is beyond the scope of this study.

4.5.2 Hosea

The one text from Hosea which is consistently adduced in Molek studies
is 13:2b: lāhem hēm 'ōmərim zōbəḥê 'ādām 'ăgālim yiššāqûn ("to them
they are saying: Those who sacrifice men [will] kiss calves"). All
commentators are agreed that the verse is in the context of a polemic
against Jeroboam's "golden calves" at Dan and Bethel, on the grounds
that they constitute Baal worship. But there is sharp division over the
presence of a reference to human sacrifice. As is so often the case in
Hosea, scholars on both sides of the issue find support in variant forms
of an undoubtedly corrupt text. The various Greek translations uniformly read zbḥy as an imperative ("sacrifice!") suggesting a Vorlage zibḥû.

---

[610] Weinfeld concedes that some fusion of the two is likely. See further on this point our discussion of Zeph 1:5 below (4.5.5).

[611] MT kiyyûn remains a problem. Weinfeld attempts to relate it to Ištar by way of the star-shaped cakes baked by her devotees in Mesopotamia and Israel (cf. Jer 44:19). If kiyyûn is to be related to
"sacrificial cake," perhaps the sense of the verse is something
like: "You take up the booth of your king and the cake of your images, the star of your gods, which you made for yourselves." However, this would be the sole OT occurrence of kawwān in the singular, and Walter Rast's study of the archeological evidence gives
reason to believe that the cakes were representational, rather than
symbolic in shape ("Cakes for the Queen of Heaven," Scripture in
History and Theology: Essays in Honor of J. C. Rylaarsdam [ed. A.
L. Merrill and T. W. Overholt; Pittsburgh: Pickwick, 1977]
167-180).

If the imperative is taken with the first half of the colon, one obtains
a reading along the lines of the <u>RSV</u>: "Sacrifice to these, they say,
Men kiss calves!" This understanding is favored by the sense it makes
of the antecedents of <u>lhm</u> and <u>hm</u>: if <u>lhm</u> denotes the indirect object of
'<u>mrym</u>, one is hard pressed to understand who is addressed.[612] Furthermore, as argued most forcefully by de Vaux, the prophet is attacking the
calf cults of Dan and Bethel, in which we have no (other) indication
that human sacrifice was practiced (nor, in his view, does Hosea otherwise mention such sacrifices).[613] On the other hand, the MT and LXX do
agree that '<u>dm</u> belongs syntactically with <u>zbḥ</u>. This led some earlier
scholars to suggest that '<u>dm</u> might be an appositional genitive, i.e.,
"men who sacrifice."[614] However, given the understanding of the versions
and the normal usage of participles in construct, two recent, major commentaries have argued for a reference to human sacrifice: "They say to
themselves: 'Those who sacrifice men kiss calves'" (Hermeneia); and
"Those who sacrifice people speak to them [the idols]. They kiss the
calves" (Anchor Bible).[615] They believe that the prophet is here decry-

---

[612] For further grammatico-syntactical arguments in favor of this understanding, see Wilhelm Rudolph, <u>Hosea</u> (KAT 13/1; Gütersloh: Mohn,
1966) 235-237. However, it must be noted that the scholars favoring
this view have used the evidence of the versions selectively: the
LXX does read an imperative for <u>zbḥ</u>, but it also takes '<u>dm</u> as the
direct object (<u>thusate anthrōpous</u>). (The Vulgate is ambiguous since
in <u>immolate homines vitulos adorantes</u>, "<u>homines</u>" could be nominative
or accusative.) Also, the syntax of the word order remains proble-
matic: taking <u>lhm</u> with <u>zbḥ</u> instead of with '<u>mr</u> (so <u>RSV</u>) is most unusual.

[613] <u>Studies</u>, 68.

[614] See the references in Green, <u>Role of Human Sacrifice</u>, 349, n. 144.

[615] H. W. Wolff, <u>Hosea</u> (trans. G. Stansell; ed. P. D. Hanson; Hermeneia;
Philadelphia: Fortress, 1974) 219; F. I. Anderson and D. N. Freedman, <u>Hosea</u> (AB 24; Garden City, NY: Doubleday, 1980) 624.

ing the use of legitimate victims of sacrifice (calves) as recipients of sacrifice in a deadly cult which was actually practiced at the time (the last decade of the North's existence, according to Wolff).[616]

It must be emphasized that, at most, this verse describes the practice of human sacrifice in the Northern cult, but not necessarily child sacrifice. In addition, it must be noted that the practice on which the prophet is focusing his ire is not entirely clear in any case: the kissing of idols as an expression of devotion seems to be attested only once, and that indirectly, in 1 Kgs 19:18 (cf. Job 31:27). Thus, whether or not one holds this verse to be a reference to human sacrifice, one must take care in supplying the details of the rite.[617] It is apparent that the primary target of the prophet is Jeroboam's cult places and that human sacrifice is, at most, used as an illustration of the folly and apostasy of worship there. Given the "Ephraimite" traits of both Hosea and the Deuteronomic literature, it is surprizing that if anything resembling the cult of Molek was practiced at Bethel or Dan, the prophet would let it go with such an oblique rebuke.[618] In sum, while the plain

---

[616] Like their opponents, those favoring a human-sacrifice interpretation have not entirely solved the difficulties of the syntax. Wolff's reflexive reading of lhm is rejected by Anderson and Freedman (p. 162), who observe that "they say to themselves" would normally be expressed with blbm. On the other hand, the latter two scholars must argue that hm and zbhy 'dm are in apposition, which is unlikely, given the prosodic character of the verse.

[617] Two scholars, especially, seem to border on the midrashic. Wolff claims that "Human sacrifice is presupposed here, namely, the offering of the firstborn conceived in the sacral forests" (Hosea, 225). Mosca, on the other hand, argues for the originality of the MT as expressing the following irony: "These people have everything backwards. Instead of kissing human beings and sacrificing calves, the fools have reversed the process!" ("Child Sacrifice," 258, n. 155).

[618] For the interrelationship of Hosea and the Deuteronomic movement, see Wilson, Prophecy and Society, 226-231, and the literature cited

sense of the MT appears to suggest that human sacrifice was practiced in the North at the time of Hosea, the poor state of the text, the awkwardness of the MT's syntax and the isolated nature of the reference to human sacrifice (if it is that) prevent us from placing much weight on this verse for purposes of reconstruction.

A second verse from Hosea has been adduced in the aforementioned study of NT eidōlon by Charles Kennedy. As it stands, Hos 3:4 reads: "For the sons of Israel will dwell many days, no king nor prince, nor sacrifice nor stela, nor 'ephod' or 'teraphim'." Customarily, the verse is interpreted to show the two main foci of Hosea's displeasure, the monarchy (cf. 1:4) and the cult (cf. 2:15).[619] After rejecting a proposed emendation by Wolff, Kennedy suggests:

> It might be better to leave the MT as it stands in the second line and amend [sic] the first line to read "without Molech or demon" (shed for sar). This would then produce a set of terms all of which relate to the cult of the dead: Molech, demons, sacrifices, monuments, divining and the representations of the household gods, the teraphim.[620]

Kennedy's proposal has much to commend it. Unlike the first two chapters, Hosea 3 is concerned exclusively with the religious apostasy of Israel, not the political order.[621] Specifically, it is the prophet's intention that the people should "return and seek (bqš) Yahweh" (v. 5), which suggests that, by contrast, to deprive them of other means of divination (i.e., "seeking") fits Hosea's purpose exactly. To connect all

there.

[619] See Anderson and Freedman, *Hosea*, 305; cf. Wolff, *Hosea*, 62.

[620] "The Table of Demons," 16.

[621] This is especially the case if one agrees with Wolff (p. 57) that the words "and David their king" (v. 5) are a later addition.

six items on the list in v. 4 with the cult of the dead, as Kennedy
wishes to do, is more problematic, but by no means impossible. Both
"demons" and "sacrifice" (zbḥ) have that association at least in a later
Psalm (106:37), to be examined below (4.5.8). Albright has argued that
the maṣṣēbôt ("stelae") have such a connection, while the teraphim of
Laban may be understood as related to the ancestor cult in Genesis
31.[622] "Ephod" is capable of a rather broad usage (see BDB, s.v.); it
may be observed, however, that it is regularly paired with teraphim
(Judg 17:5; 18:14,17,18,20; so also in this verse by the absence of 'ēn
between the terms). Indeed, there are clearly three pairings in Hos
3:4, including the first two items: mlk//śr/šd. If one accepts the
emendation of the latter (which, as we have often seen, presents no
large obstacle epigraphically), to understand both items as divine objects of divination commends itself, so that a reading "Molek" is defensible. The MT's melek would then represent the sort of euphemism which,
as we shall see, Eissfeldt and Mosca argue took place in other prophetic
passages.

There is one large obstacle to Kennedy's proposal, however (besides
any qualms one may have about seeing the cult of the dead as a common
denominator of all six items). The pair melek//śār occurs some four
times in Hosea (besides 3:4, 7:3,5; 8:10; 13:10), and śār occurs alone
three times (5:10; 7:16; 9:15). While every other case of śār in Hosea
(except 3:4) is plural, this repeated pairing does make emendation dif-

---

[622] Albright, "The high place in Ancient Palestine," VTSup 4 (1957) 243
(see further on this below, 4.6). Kennedy notes that the conflict
over the stolen teraphim is settled by Jacob and Laban "by a night-
long vigil on a mountain after sacrificing and eating at the stone
monument (LXX stēlē) where both parties swore oaths by the God of
their fathers" ("The Table of Demons," 16, n. 40).

ficult to defend. One could argue, of course, that the very regularity
of the pair melek//śār could account for the "correction" of an original
mōlek//šēd in the consonantal text by an over-zealous scribe. While
much traditional text criticism has employed arguments with such a psychological component as this one, one must admit that this explanation
is pure speculation.[623]

The same judgment applies all the more to the Anchor Bible's understanding of one final verse from Hosea (4:2): "Swearing, lying, murder-
ing, stealing, committing adultery, / They break out--blood
everywhere--and they strike down." Anderson and Freedman write: "The
term dāmîm, we propose, however, probably refers to the shedding of innocent blood by official action, and the crime charged against the nation here, as elsewhere, is the formal sacrifice of human beings, in
particular children who are innocent and unblemished, so as to meet sacrificial requirements."[624] While these scholars rightly observe that
shedding innocent blood is associated with cultic child sacrifice in Ps

---

[623] An entirely different approach to the same end of defending Kennedy's understanding of the six items would be to argue that the original Hebrew paired Molek and śār in some specialized, supernatural
meaning. Both Biblical and extra-Biblical examples of such a specialized usage can be adduced. In the Ugaritic poem, "The Birth of
the Gracious and Beautiful Gods," the god Death bears the "double-
barrelled" name Mt w-Šr, (by hendiadys) "Prince Death" (CTA 23:8).
One need not argue for the identity of Mot and Molek to suggest that
the latter may also have borne the title, śār, or that Hosea may be
speaking of both deities, Molek by name and Mot by title. However,
the meaning of šr in Death's name is disputed (other suggestions are
"Dissolution" and "Evil"). In the Bible we find the late usage (in
Daniel) of śār for national patron-angels (and perhaps even God,
8:11). That this may represent but a specialization of an earlier
usage for supernatural beings is shown by Josh 5:14-15. Nevertheless, all in all, one must admit that Kennedy's proposal and the revision here suggested remain unsubstantiated, however intuitively
attractive they may be.

[624] Hosea, 338.

106:38, little more can be said for their proposal. Although one dare
not put too fine a point on the distinction, the context suggests that
it is not what we would term cultic, but rather secular offenses (including, perhaps, specifically judicial murder) that the prophet has in
mind.

In sum, Hosea provides the investigator of cultic child sacrifice
in Israel with a few tantalizing, possible references, but none upon
which a historical reconstruction of the practice can reliably be based.
Taken together with the similar results of our study of Amos, it must be
admitted that no convincing evidence has yet emerged for the practice of
the cult of Molek (or any cultic child sacrifice) in the Northern Kingdom.

4.5.3 Micah

In contrast to the situation in Amos and Hosea, there is but one possible reference to cultic child sacrifice in Micah, and the debate over
its inclusion in our study in no way depends on an emendation of the MT
or some other text-critical issue. Micah 6:6-7 reads as follows:

> With what shall I come before Yahweh [and] bow to God on high?
> Shall I come before him with burnt offerings, with year-old
> calves?
> Will Yahweh accept thousands of rams, myriads of rivers of
> oil?
> Shall I give my firstborn [for] my rebellion, my offspring
> [for] my life's sin?

The main issues for our purposes are whether v. 7b may be understood as
showing that child sacrifice was practiced in eighth-century Judah and,
if so, whether the rite formed a part of the official Yahwistic cult.[625]

---

[625] For a more general form-critical treatment of the passage, see Paul
Watson, "Form Criticism and an Exegesis of Micah 6:1-8," RestQ 7

The various responses have all shared the observation that there is a
progression of some sort in the proposed offerings of the prophet's sup-
pliant "Everyman." At one end of the spectrum of views on the verse
stands de Vaux, who argued that the sequence is "from possible offers to
impossible offers, from ordinary holocausts to rams by thousands and
torrential libations, and, to continue the progression, the last offer
must appear even more impossible--the sacrifice of the first-born."[626]
Similarly, Buber contends that, while the sacrifices may have been practiced, at no time were they part of Yahwism: ". . . in order to be able
to offer the utmost for expiation, he has to go beyond into the heterodox, but popular sphere."[627] On the other hand, Mosca concurs with Eissfeldt that, while the prophet is rejecting the misuse of all sacrifice,
child sacrifice is nothing other than the most valuable bid in the series: "They seek to conciliate Yahweh not by promising the impossible,
but by offering him a climactic series of gifts that they, at least, regard as both acceptable and effacacious."[628]

We may observe first that, contrary to the assumption shared by de
Vaux, Buber, Eissfeldt and most of the commentaries, this verse can, at
most, supply only indirect information concerning the practice of the
cult of Molek. As we have argued above (4.3.2), with the possible exception of Ezekiel 20, there is no Biblical or extra-Biblical evidence
which indicates that the sacrifice of the firstborn and the cult of Mo-

---

(1963) 61-72 (and the commentaries).

[626] Studies, 69.

[627] Kingship of God, 181.

[628] "Child Sacrifice," 225; cf. Molk als Opferbegriff, 49-50.

lek were coterminus. But with that understood, what of the debate
summarized above? On the one hand, Eissfeldt and Mosca are correct that
Micah in no way singles out child sacrifice as heterodox; moreover, it
is begging the question to assert that such a rite was "impossible" or
at the climax of a prophetic reductio ad absurdum argument against all
sacrifice.[629] Nevertheless, Mosca has overlooked the fact that it is not
"the people" making the successively dearer offers, but the prophet in
their name, in the context of his argument. In short, what makes this
passage so difficult to employ historically is the underlying contrary-
to-fact mood established by the context: none of the sacrifices is de-
sired by Yahweh without the virtues summarized in v. 8, so that the
prophet has no reason to distinguish otherwise desirable from undesira-
ble offerings. In other words, it is impossible to know whether the
prophet obtained his roster of proposed offerings purely from the contemporary cultic life of the people, or included a more theoretical construct of the most valuable sacrifices which one might offer on the basis of the law.[630] In sum, it remains true, as Eissfeldt and Mosca
observe, that Micah in no way signals special disapproval of child sac-

---

[629] The latter claim is advanced by Henry McKeating in The Books of
Amos, Hosea and Micah (Cambridge, NEB; Cambridge: University, 1971)
185.

[630] Three considerations may argue for the latter. First, as we have
seen (4.3.2), there is no (other) indication, again with the possible exception of Ezekiel 20, that the sacrifice of the firstborn was
ever practiced in Israel. Secondly, despite the possibly hyperbolic
accounts of events like the dedication of Solomon's temple (1 Kgs
8:63), "thousands" of rams and "myriads" of rivers of oil were certainly not part of the contemporary sacrificial cultus. Thirdly,
even if one interprets the "Law of the Firstborn" to indicate that
sacrificial primogenicide was permitted in Israel, there is no indication that it ever served as a sin offering on behalf of the pa-
rent; rather, the donation of the firstborn (or first harvested) was
a gift returned to God, signifying his ownership of all.

rifice, but neither is it possible to assert unconditionally that the
rite was part of the Yahweh cult of his day (whatever the prophet
thought of the practice). Fortunately, there is clearer evidence concerning these issues in the book of another eighth-century Judahite
prophet, Micah's contemporary, Isaiah.

4.5.4   Isaiah 1-39

If the truth be told, our examination of the prophets so far has been
disappointing in the paucity and uncertain relevance of the material it
has yielded for our study. While we have already seen that considerable
evidence of interest awaits us in the seventh/sixth-century prophets
Jeremiah and Ezekiel, the question remains whether there is any supplement to Dtr's scanty notices regarding the eighth century. Our last,
best hope is Isaiah, and there we find at least one passage which has
long been adduced in Molek studies (so already Geiger [1.2]), because it
contains possible references both to Molek and the Tophet. Isa 30:33 is
of extraordinary interest to us, because Mosca claims that it provides a
"clear and convincing solution to our dilemma regarding mlk" (p. 195),
specifically, that it establishes Eissfeldt's understanding of Molek as
the correct one.

It is therefore no surprize that Mosca devotes intensive and extensive (twenty-eight pages, plus notes) effort to this verse, or, more
precisely, to the poem in which it occurs (30:27-33). Although we shall
disagree with his conclusions at crucial points, there is no doubt that
his study represents an impressive effort to interpret the canonical
text of a passage which has long been the subject of source- and form-

critical disagreement.[631] In the light of the continuing disagreement
even over the text itself and of his own proposal, it seems best to join
Mosca in temporarily "bracketing" the controverted critical issues, ex-
cept for the observation that we see no reason to deny the passage to
Isaiah and good cause to date it to the "Assyrian crisis" of ca. 701
B.C.[632]

Isa 30:27-33 is, as Mosca shows, a powerful and coherent application of an older song concerning the Divine Warrior (vv. 27-28) to the
crisis of Sennacherib's attack on Jerusalem, in which the prophet describes Yahweh's victory over Assyria, climaxing in the sacrifice of the
king in the Tophet. Mosca begins his exposition with a text-critical
treatment of the entire poem, followed by a proposed translation and a
commentary which stresses Isaiah's use of structural devices like inclu-
sio and word plays which allude both to war and to sacrifice (pp.
207,211). Although one might challenge this or that point, on the whole
Mosca's effort is, as noted, perceptive and acceptable. We move directly, therefore, to the crucial verse, which reads in the MT:

kî-ʿārûk mēʾetmûl topteh /

gam-hîʾ (so Q; K = hûʾ) lammelek hûkān heʿmîq hirḥib //

mədurātāh ʾēš wəʿēṣîm harbēh /

nišmat yhwh kənaḥal goprît bōʿărāh bāh

---

[631] See "Child Sacrifice," 196-197 and 262-263, nn. 176-178, for a review of the debate and references.

[632] See Friedrich Huber, *Jahwe, Juda und die anderen Völker beim Propheten Jesaja* (BZAW 137; Berlin: W. de Gruyter, 1976) 50-54, for a recent treatment of the passage which denies it to Isaiah (and considers the crucial portion of v. 33 a gloss). Cf. B. S. Childs, *Isaiah
and the Assyrian Crisis* (SBT 2/3; London: SCM, 1967) 46-50, for arguments in favor of the oracle's authenticity (except, Childs holds,
vv. 29,32).

("For a burning place has long been prepared; / yea, for the king it is made ready, deep and wide, // its pyre is fire and wood in abundance; / the breath of the LORD, like a stream of brimstone, kindles it" [RSV, altered to fit MT phrasing]). In keeping with scholars at least as far back as Geiger, Mosca would repoint lmlk to ləmōlek. Moreover, he recognizes in the hapax topteh a form of tōpet, "Tophet." Specifically, he believes that it is the sixth example in the poem of a suffixed hē for the third-person, masculine, singular, yielding, "his [the king of Assyria's] tophet."[633] (Thus, Isa 30:33 would be the earliest occurrence of the word in the OT.) Thirdly, like the RSV, Mosca places the major verse division after hûkān and a smaller division before 'ēš, so that he'mîq and hirḥib can be read as Hiphil perfects with mədurātāh as their object, rather than revocalized as infinitive absolutes (Huber) or imperatives (Targum). Finally, Mosca reads the Ketib, gam-hû', and takes it to refer to the king (making the suffix on Tophet prospective).[634] He then translates:

> For his Tophet has long been prepared,
> He himself is installed as a mōlek(-victim).
> (Yahweh) has made its fire-pit deep and wide,
> With fire and wood in abundance.
>
> The breath of Yahweh,
> Like a torrent of sulphur,
> Sets it ablaze![635]

---

[633] This was suggested already by B. Stade, Geschichte des Volkes Israel (Berlin: G. Grote, 1887) 1.610.

[634] Mosca is supported here by de Vaux, Studies, 88, and by W. H. Irwin, Isaiah 28-33: Translation with Philological Notes (BibOr 30; Rome: Pontifical Biblical Institute, 1977) 105.

[635] "Child Sacrifice," 202.

Thus, the poem is the prophet's depiction of the mighty Sennacherib, in-
stalled (hkn), like David (2 Sam 5:12), by Yahweh as mlk--only not as
"king" (melek), but as infant-victim (mōlek). The passage, according to
Mosca, bears numerous points of contact with what is known of the Punic
molk-sacrifices, including the fiery pit outside of the city walls (cf.
Sardis), the musical instruments which accompanied the rite (v. 32), and
the nocturnal character of the sacred occasion (v. 29: kəlêl . . . ḥāg;
cf. the Ngaous stelae: sacrum magnum nocturnum). Finally, since Isaiah
depicts Yahweh as performing the ritual, one can assume that the prophet
had no qualms about its practice; rather, it "was, in fact, part of the
official Yahwistic cultus" (p. 212). In sum, "considering the numerous
other correspondences between the Judean and Phoenician-Punic rites that
can be isolated in the poem, it seems churlish to reject Eissfeldt's
equation of mōlek with mlk . . ." (p. 216). Isa 30:33, then, is the Ar-
chimedean point on which Mosca turns his argument that "das Ende" has
indeed come for any pre-exilic god "Molek."

Although Mosca's proposal is impressive, it is not, in my view,
equally convincing at all points, particularly those which have to do
with the meaning of Molek. As for his adjustments to the vocalization
and division of the MT, his reading of topteh as "his [the king's] Tophet" is certainly to be preferred to the suggestion of certain German
scholars to take the suffix as an interrogative hē on the succeeding
clause.[636] His text is, therefore, accepted. Likewise, his stichometry
is unexceptionable. However, contrary to what is, no doubt, as Mosca
says, "an overwhelming majority of nineteenth- and twentieth-century

---

[636] See Huber, Jahwe, Juda, 52, for references.

scholars" (p. 195), there is good cause <u>not</u> to revocalize MT

<u>lammelek</u>.[637] As we have already seen repeatedly, the mere fact that the

cult of Molek is being talked about hardly demands that the word "Molek"

be present (else we would have far more than eight OT attestations!).

More importantly, retaining the MT vocalization improves the parallelism

and provides an explanation for at least some of the textual confusion

which is evident in the MT. This becomes clear from the following

translation:

> For his Tophet has long been arranged;
> Indeed, for the king it has been established.
> Deep and wide its fire-pit has been made
> With fire and wood in abundance.
> (The remainder of Mosca's translation is fine.)

Thus, in both of the first two cola, Tophet is the subject of a passive

participle. I would contend that once the function of the suffixed <u>hē</u>

on Tophet was forgotten, the word was reinterpreted (and later vocal-

ized) as a feminine biform of Tophet, which would also account for the

switch from the masculine to feminine demonstrative pronoun, <u>hû'</u> >

<u>hî'</u>.[638] While not so crucial as the first bicolon, I would understand

---

[637] Irwin (<u>Isaiah 28-33</u>, 105) agrees that <u>lammelek</u> is to be retained, but he would take "the King" as a reference to Death. Thus, Irwin would agree with Mosca that <u>hû'</u> is the king of Assyria. While we believe that the translation offered immediately below is superior, Irwin's proposal does show that <u>lmlk</u> makes good sense as a reference to the divine recipient of the sacrifice (who would, then, be the subject of the following Hiphil verbs, contrary to Mosca's need to supply "[Yahweh]"). However, if <u>lmlk</u> is read in this way, the vocalization <u>lammōlek</u> seems to me far preferable (without prejudice to the issue of Molek's possible identity with Death [see 2.3.6]), giv-en the presence of "Tophet" immediately before.

[638] This would also account for a change in the vocalization of the suf-fix on <u>mədurāh</u>, although no consonantal emendation was needed (-<u>ōh</u> > -<u>āh</u>). The suffix does argue for the proposed translation, however, since my rendering eliminates the need to skip back to the beginning of the verse for the antecedent of the suffix.

the Hiphil perfects which begin the second half of the verse to continue the passive voice, as impersonal third-person, masculine, singular verbs, employed for variety's sake (cf. GKC §144d).

It should be emphasized that the proposed reading meshes quite well with the sacrificial/military imagery which Mosca has seen elsewhere in the oracle and supports his contention that the passage makes good sense as a unit. But what of his claims concerning the "numerous correspondences" with the Punic molk-rite? Do "numerous correspondences" argue for identity in every detail? Mosca himself admits that the Israelite and Punic cults could have differed, in that only the latter had a statue to which (or even on which) the infants were burned (p. 265, n. 196). Moreover, it seems to me that Mosca has neglected to note that some of the items which make up those correspondences are also held in common with other cultic practices. Musical instruments accompanied many religious acts (cf. the Psalms), and, in particular, the cult of the dead was often a nocturnal pursuit (see 4.6). It remains true that the Tophet/sacrificial precinct is shared only by OT Israel and the Punic colonies (to our knowledge), but even this striking commonality cannot be pressed since we do not know at what point the Israelite and Punic practices began to develop independently of their (presumed) common source. In short, Isa 30:33 is not at all "clear and convincing" evidence for the understanding of OT Molek as a sacrificial technical term.

But what of Mosca's claim that the verse supports Eissfeldt's assertion concerning the orthodoxy of the Molek cult in pre-Josianic Judah? There is no question, it seems to me, that this passage represents the strongest OT support for such a thesis. Isaiah employs the imagery and terminology (Tophet and ma'ābar, v. 32) of the cult of Molek without a hint of condemnation; indeed, he portrays Yahweh himself as making the sacrifice. Moreover, Mosca is correct that the subtle incorporation of references to the cult suggest that Isaiah's audience was actively acquainted with the rite, lessening the force of the possible argument that the prophet was hearkening back to a cult practiced under Ahaz (d. ca. 715 B.C.), but discontinued under the reformer, Hezekiah. In brief, the real force of the argument from this passage is that it is not e si-lentio ("Isaiah never condemns the cult"), but based on a neutral, even positive reference by Isaiah to the cult of Molek. The strongest point which may be brought against the thesis of an orthodox Molek cult, in my view, is similar to the concern we raised regarding Mic 6:7. There the practice of firstborn sacrifice was not specifically condemned, but it, along with other sacrifices, was in a contrary-to-fact mode or context. Here one must recall that the prophet's usage of Molek cult imagery is in any event metaphorical and directed against the enemy of Judah (and, therefore, Yahweh), so that the prophet may be describing the one fit use for the Tophet, which otherwise was as abominable to Isaiah as to D or the later prophets.[639] The latter argument, unfortunately, verges on the psychological and cannot really account for the vast difference in attitude toward the cult between, say, Isaiah and Ezekiel.[640]

---

[639] Compare the use of mythological language in the taunt song against the king of Babylon, Isa 14:12.

[640] It may account, however, for how Isaiah could portray Yahweh as participating in Molek's cult (which Mosca argues is impossible [pp. 216-217]). If Isaiah is not thinking of the sacrifice as offered to Yahweh (as in Deuteronomy), despite the cult's associations with Molek, he may well approve of Sennacherib's being "made to pass over" to the province of a chthonic deity (who was, of course, under Yahweh).

Is it, then, the case that the cult of Molek was part of orthodox Yahwism until Josiah? Such an assertion remains, I believe, overly broad. Whether or not one agrees that there was an edition of the Deuteronomic History produced around Hezekiah's time (as we argued above [4.4.3]), there can be little question that the Deuteronomic movement was by that time gathering force, and their view of orthodox Yahwism certainly did not have room for the cult of Molek. A more sensitive reading of the evidence, in other words, suggests that, at most, the Jerusalem establishment, political and sacral, had a sufficiently latitudinarian view of Yahwism that certain elements of the faith and praxis of the Canaanites were considered acceptable, so long as they did not challenge the supremacy of Yahweh or of his cult. Presumably, Isaiah himself could have shared this view, although one must be still more cautious with him since the one clear reference we have (30:33) is metaphorical, and another passage, to be examined in a moment, may suggest that he took a rather different attitude toward human practitioners of the Molek cult.[641]

Indeed, as must continually be said, dating the content of books such as Leviticus (and even Deuteronomy) is exceedingly difficult, so that the official cult in eighth-century Jerusalem could as easily represent a deviation from an earlier, "purer" form of Yahwism, as a cult

---

[641] Mosca also cites in support of the "orthodox Molek cult" view Isa 31:9b: "oracle of Yahweh, whose flame is in Zion, and whose oven (tannûr) is in Jerusalem." He claims that even if this refers to the Temple (as most scholars believe), "the fact that Isaiah feels free to use such ambiguous language shows his complete lack of concern about the legitimacy of the Topheth and its ritual child sacrifice" (p. 265, n. 201). One may ask, however, "ambiguous" to whom? It is not at all clear that the Tophet was ever viewed as Yahweh's oven.

reformed only later and judged <u>mixtus</u> solely in retrospect. Caution is also called for, because, although texts such as Isa 30:33 and 2 Kgs 16:3 imply that the cult of Molek was long-established in Jerusalem's Tophet, we simply cannot know how long, specifically, whether the cult of Molek was imported (presumably from Phoenicia) under Solomon, or was taken up directly during the conquest/settlement from the Canaanite inhabitants (as we think more likely).[642] In either case, if one gives any credence to the traditions of Israel's existence before the conquest/ settlement, a form of Yahwism without the cult of Molek may well have existed.[643] But did it exist in the South, particularly, at Jerusalem? As we stressed in the introduction to the legal references (4.3), besides a concern about the dating of the contents of the OT literature, one must be sensitive to the presence of various groups within Yahwism as it developed (i.e., to the less-than-monolithic character of "Mosaic Yahwism"), so that the Deuteronomic view (which may well have had northern, "Ephraimite" roots) could have looked with disdain on the southern, Jerusalemite concept of the boundaries of faithful Yahwism. If so, the question is not whether the Jerusalem cultus, including the cult of Molek, was or was not a corruption of an "earlier, 'purer' form of Yahwism," but at what point the Deuteronomic understanding of Yahwism began to influence the Jerusalemite understanding and by what means it did so.

---

[642] These two alternatives are, in substance, Mosca's conclusions (although he would see a Phoenician source in any event) (p. 239), and we agree that the evidence considered to this point favors them. See further our reconstruction of the Molek cult's history in Israel in chap. V for a defense of these alternatives and of our preference for the latter.

[643] This, of course, relates directly to Albright's persistent question: "What was the nature of Mosaic Yahwism?"

Leaving aside, therefore, terms such as "orthodox" for the moment, it seems safe to say that the official Yahwistic cultus of Jerusalem, from at least Solomon through Amon, permitted the practice of the cult of Molek in the Tophet outside of the city, and that the "Jerusalemite" prophets of the time did not think (or choose) to speak out against it as apostate, as their Deuteronomic counterparts certainly would have done.[644]

Our caution regarding Isaiah's personal view of the cult of Molek derives especially from the other verse in chaps. 1-39 which commends itself as a likely reference to that cult: Isa 8:21. While neither cultic child sacrifice nor Molek is mentioned in the MT, there are several signs in the text that the prophet is expressing strong disapproval of exactly the kind of activity which our study to this point has shown the Molek cult to be. Unfortunately, the passage in which the verse appears, vv. 16-22 (or 23), is extremely difficult to interpret in detail, suffering from apparent textual corruption, rare words and questionable line division by the Masoretes.[645] Nevertheless, it seems clear enough that Isaiah is contrasting the "signs and portents" obtained from "Yahweh of hosts who dwells on Mt. Zion" (v. 18) with information secured through necromancy (v. 19), and that he envisions a horrible fate for the practitioners of the latter (vv. 21-22). Of special interest, given our earlier study of Deut 18:10-11 and 2 Kgs 21:6, is the call to the

---

[644] See Wilson, Prophecy and Society, 253-263, for more on the characteristics of "Judean" prophets, especially pp. 256-257 on their greater tolerance (than Deuteronomists) of non-prophetic diviners.

[645] See on these any critical commentary. The issues are summarized by C. F. Whitley, "The Language and Exegesis of Isaiah 8:16-23," ZAW 90 (1978) 28-43.

people by the anonymous apostates (cf. Deuteronomy 13) to "inquire (drš)
of the 'ōbôt and the yiddǝ'ōnîm." The following, parallel line both
clarifies that these beings are the shades of the dead (mētîm) and in-
troduces yet another term for the same, 'ĕlōhîm (cf. 1 Sam 28:13).[646]

The importance of this last point becomes apparent in v. 21. As my
fellow student J. Glen Taylor has shown in an unpublished paper, this
verse and the one following it are replete with the Biblical (and other
ancient Semitic) imagery of Sheol: no dawn (v. 20); the inhabitants
famished and cursing; palpable darkness.[647] Thus, although there is no
grammatical antecedent to the suffix of bāh at the beginning of v. 21,
one has good reason to suspect that it is Sheol to which the people who
consult the dead will pass.[648] Indeed, the context suggests that the

---

[646] Verse 19 is obviously a bicolon all of whose parts concern necromancy, not a dialog between the apostates and the prophet who would, in
v. 19b, have the people "consult their God" (so RSV).

[647] "Notes on Isaiah 8:19-22, and a New Proposal for 8:21-22" (unpublished seminar paper, Yale University, 1982). Taylor emphasizes especially the connections of these verses with Isaiah 14 and 29:1-4.
Cf. also 19:3. For more on the characteristics of the underworld,
see N. J. Tromp, Primitive Conceptions of Death and the Nether World
in the Old Testament (BibOr 21; Rome: Pontifical Biblical Institute, 1969), especially pp. 187-190.

[648] If so, the absence of an antecedent may well be euphemistic. Isaiah
would then be speaking in bitter irony: those who seek knowledge
from the likes of the "knowers" will obtain what they seek, but only
by becoming "knowers" themselves. An entirely different interpretation is to date the passage to the early sixth century and apply it
to the residents of Jerusalem ("Ariel" in chap. 29), who "pass
through the land" in disarray into exile (so Hermann Barth, followed
by R. E. Clements, Isaiah 1-39 [NCB; Grand Rapids, MI: Eerdmans,
1980] 102-103). (Taylor, in the end, argues for both Jerusalem and
Sheol as the referent of bāh.) Without denying for a moment that
the text may have undergone considerable redaction, it seems to me
that the passage makes good sense when applied to the time of Ahaz,
or perhaps Hezekiah (so Taylor), and that at least substantial portions of the passage, including v. 21, are Isaianic (so the commentaries of Duhm [HAT], Wildberger [BKAT] and Kaiser [ATD]).

verb which governs bāh has a specialized usage here: as we shall see
below, with regard to Ezekiel 39 (4.5.6), 'br can refer to the "passing
over" from life to death (cf. English "pass on" and "pass away").

When those who have engaged in necromancy hunger and curse in the
land of the dead ('rṣ, v. 22), they will curse bəmalkô ûbē'lōhāyw, "by
their mlk and their 'lhm."[649] Given our observation above concerning the
usage in this passage of 'ĕlōhîm, "shades, ghosts," in v. 19, one obtains the reading: "And they [the people now in Sheol] will curse by
their king and by their ghosts."   But the primary sense of king, "temporal ruler," is clearly out of place here.   As was often stressed in
chap. II, "king" could be a divine epithet (so often in Ugaritic for El
and Baal), but neither of these gods would appear to fit the chthonic
context (nor was the cult of either a major threat, so far as we know,
in eighth-century Judah, as Baal's certainly was in the North).   The
Targum recognized the difficulty of "king" and translated bmlkw with
ptkryh, "his false god."[650] Yet despite the appropriateness of the
translation in Amos 5:26 and Zeph 1:5 (as noted), it is unlikely that
melek ever took on the specific sense, "idol god."

---

[649] See Whitley, "Isaiah 8:16-23," 31-32, for an explanation of why mlk
and 'lhm cannot possibly be taken as direct objects (so RSV), despite the substantive resemblances which have often been alleged
with Exod 22:27 and 1 Kgs 21:10.   As noted first by Gunkel and especially thereafter by Dahood, 'rṣ can refer to the netherworld.   In
v. 22 the picture is of the shades looking around at ('l; cf. Exod
3:6; Num 21:9) Sheol and seeing nothing but darkness.

[650] Interestingly enough, it used this same rendering for mlkkm in Amos
5:26 (4.5.1) and for mlkm in Zeph 1:5 (4.5.5).   As our discussion of
these two verses shows, the Targum was essentially right in these
cases (even more so, we believe, than in the verse at hand).

A more promising, albeit tentative, solution is to recall the persistent correlation we have observed between the cult of Molek and necromancy (specifically, the 'ōbōt and the yiddə'ōnîm) and between
Malik-Milku/i-Molek and chthonic contexts. Thus, we propose to translate: "And they shall curse by Molek and by their ghosts."[651] The
point, then, would be that, as the people now venerate and divine by Molek and their ancestral shades through child sacrifice and other practices, so they will curse by their names once they are consigned to the
terrors of Sheol in punishment. (If this translation is correct, the
verb 'br in v. 21 would serve as it did in 30:32, in a word play alluding to the Molek cult.)

In contradistinction to this path of doom, the prophet calls his
audience lətôrāh wəlit'ûdāh ("to [the] teaching and to [the] testimony"). As G. B. Gray observes, if v. 20 is Isaianic, of a piece with v.
16, the two terms presumably refer to Isaiah's own oracles to that point
(particularly those spoken in the face of the Syro-Ephraimite threat).
On the other hand, if v. 20 is a later addition (so Duhm, for instance),
the terms, still presumably synonymous, could mean the written law, or
Torah in the sense of Scripture.[652] In any event, this difficult passage
is certainly contrasting the teachings obtained from Yahweh with information to be derived through necromancy. If, as we have suggested, it

---

[651] The suffix on bmlkw would then be the result of dittography with the
initial waw in wb'lhyw, or it may have been added to parallel the
suffix on that word. The reading "Molek or Milcom" is ascribed to
the Targum, Calvin and Junius (only then to be rejected) by J. A.
Alexander, The Prophecies of Isaiah (2d ed.; NY: Charles Scribner,
1870) 195 (reference courtesy of J. G. Taylor).

[652] The Book of Isaiah: I-XXVII (ICC; Edinburgh: T. & T. Clark, 1912)
159.

is in particular necromancy in the cult of Molek which the passage has in mind, then the prophet's own view of the cult was obviously negative. Nevertheless, this passage gives us no cause to revise our assertion above, that the eighth-century Jerusalem cult of Yahweh could have condoned the practice of the cult of Molek by the faithful.

4.5.5 Zephaniah

With Zephaniah we move from the Divided Kingdom to the last decades of pre-exilic Judah. In a way the prophet personifies the transition, being a descendant of the eighth-century reformer, King Hezekiah, active in the reign of his seventh-century counterpart, Josiah (1:1). Although, once again, the prophet's book contains neither Molek (in the MT) nor any references to cultic child sacrifice, close scrutiny may reveal evidence of interest to us. At very least, the book deserves such attention since the prophet evidently had close connections to the royal court in Jerusalem soon before or during the "defilement" of the Tophet by Josiah (2 Kgs 23:10).

The Roman Catholic exegete Liudger Sabottka has taken the lead in suggesting material of use to our study, by proposing that MT melek in three verses (1:5,8; 3:15) be understood as a title of Baal.[653] The first case is the most persuasive. In its context the MT reads:

> (4b) And I will cut off from this place the remnant of Baal [and] the name of the idol-priests with the priests, (5) and those who bow down upon the roofs to the host of heaven, and those who bow down, who swear, to Yahweh and who swear by

---

[653] Zephanja (BibOr 25; Rome: Pontifical Biblical Institute, 1972). Cf. Weinfeld's similar proposal regarding Amos 5:26 (4.5.1). Weinfeld essentially concurs with Sabottka also regarding this verse, by seeing in Zeph 1:5 a reference to (H)Adad ("The Worship of Molek," 149).

their king, (6) and those who depart from following Yahweh and
who do not seek Yahweh and do not inquire of him.[654]

Verse 5 is clearly concerned with syncretism, so that "their king" must
refer to some divine being. Our previous examination of passages from
Amos and Jeremiah (49:1,3) makes understandable the decision of the
Greek Lucianic recension, the Syriac and the Vulgate to read "Milkom,"
although, once again, one is hard-pressed to account for the prophet's
stress on the Ammonite deity (rather than, say, Kemoš of Moab). Sabottka's proposal is attractive precisely at this point (as was Weinfeld's
in Amos 5:26), in that the title "melek" for Baal is well-attested and,
moreover, suggested by the preceding context (v. 4b).[655]

While Sabottka insists (without explanation) that Melek is not to
be related to Molek, the succeeding context may suggest otherwise. The
prophet's concern is with those who fail to "seek" (bqš) and "inquire"
(drš) of Yahweh, implying that at least some of the preceding activities
have entailed the divination of other gods. Our study of the Molek references in Leviticus, D and Isaiah has shown that whatever else may have
been behind the cult of Molek, divination was certainly involved. No
doubt, there was also divination in the cults of Baal and of the host of
heaven, but vv. 5-6, taken together with the apparent equation of Baal
and Molek in Jer 19:5//32:35, suggest that by the end of the seventh

---

[654] I agree with Rudolph (Micha--Nahum--Habakuk--Zephanja [KAT 13/3; Gütersloh: Mohn, 1975] 262) and many other commentators that the
first hnšb'ym ("who swear") in v. 5 should be deleted since nšb' l
is otherwise unknown. But the interpretation is unaffected for our
purposes either way.

[655] Sabottka's further suggestion (following Albright) that the Baal of
v. 4 is Ba'alšamēm, to be identified (following Gray) with Attar,
Milkom, Kemoš and Šlm of Jerusalem has less to commend it, as we
have seen (1.7).

century in Judah the two gods were coalescing, at least in the prophet's
condemnation of their worship (see further on this possibility the examination of the Jeremiah passages below [4.5.6]).[656] If Zeph 1:5b does
represent a reference to Molek, the MT may be explained as as corruption
(mlkm for mlk), or a euphemistic revocalization of a correct, albeit
rare, "their Molek," or a correctly-vocalized play on the meaning of Molek's name.[657] In view of our discussion of Isa 8:21, the second explanation is least likely and the third most likely, but certainty is unat-
tainable.

Sabottka's second candidate for a reference to "King Baal" is Zeph
1:8: "On the day of Yahweh's sacrifice, I will punish the "princes"
(śārîm) and the sons of the king and those who dress in foreign cloth-
ing." Sabottka would understand śārîm as cultic officials, and bənê as
worshippers, of the divine King. Some sacral, rather than secular reference is favored by the absence elsewhere in the book of criticism of
the royal family.[658] Sabottka is correct that śārîm can denote cultic
officials, although the only clear cases which he cites (i.e., besides
Amos 1:15; Jer 48:7; 49:3, discussed above [4.5.1]) have śārîm in con-

---

[656] Rudolph also allows a reference to Baal/Molek in Zeph 1:5 as an alternate possibility to his preferred understanding, an attestation
of Milkom (Zephanja, p. 266), although his claim that the two were
always identified (Jeremiah [3d ed.; HAT 12; Tübingen: Mohr, 1968]
212) is most unlikely, given the results of our study in chap. II.

[657] The second option is proposed by O'Ceallaigh, " And So David Did,"
186, n. 1.

[658] Furthermore, Josiah's son Jehoiakim (presumably his eldest) was but
twelve years old when the reformation began (2 Kgs 22:1,3; 23:36),
so that besides Zephaniah's apparently favorable view of Josiah himself, his sons can hardly have been old enough to draw the prophet's
ire in this oracle (cf. J. M. P. Smith in Smith, W. H. Ward and J.
A. Bewer, Micah, Zephaniah, Nahum, Habakkuk, Obadiah and Joel [ICC;
NY: Charles Scribner's Sons, 1911] 196).

struct with a word which clarifies the sacral function (qōdeš in Isa
43:28; qōdeš and hā'ĕlōhîm in 1 Chr 24:5). As an alternative, we may
mention the possibility that the "sons of the king" are really the bənê
hammōlek, i.e., the victims (or perhaps cult-members) of the cult of Molek.[659] On this reading, the prophet would be contrasting the cultic
sacrifices (and meals) of Molek with a future (or metaphorical) sacrificial feast prepared by Yahweh himself, in which he would "visit wrath
upon" (pqd ʻl) this "abomination."[660] Again, however, we quickly approach pure conjecture. All we can say with certainty is that, pace Rudolph (Zephanja, 262), a secular, literal understanding of "sons of the
king" is beset by even more difficulties than some sacral reading.

The least likely of Sabottka's proposed references, in my view, is
Zeph 3:15: "Yahweh has turned aside your [daughter (of) Jerusalem's]
judgments; he has put away your enemy. The king of Israel, Yahweh, is
in your midst: you shall not fear evil again." Sabottka would divide
the verse after, rather than before melek, yielding, "[Jahwe] beseitigt
deinen Feind, Melek" (p. 124). His reading is unlikely, however, since
the versions unanimously read "enemies," and since neither Baal nor Molek is elsewhere characterized as Israel's enemy.[661]

---

[659] Cf. our discussion of the "son(s) of Hinnom" below (4.5.6). The
"princes" would then be the cult's officials.

[660] Cf. above on Isa 30:33 (4.5.4). See also Isa 34:6; Jer 46:10; and
Ezek 39:17-18 for references to the slaughtering of and feasting on
the enemies of Yahweh on the "day of Yahweh" (cf. our discussion of
Ezekiel 39 in 4.5.6).

[661] Sabottka himself appears to realize that this last suggestion is
less convincing than the others, as he says only that "vielleicht"
the king in 3:15 is a title of Baal (p. 24).

In sum, it is beyond question that Zephaniah contains at least one
reference to a god with the name or title <u>Mlk</u>, whose cult entailed divination. Whether that god is Baal (Sabottka) or Molek (O'Ceallaigh) or
some fusion of the two is not capable of determination. As we have observed, however, the latter option may well be preferable in the light
of other prophetic records of the time. We turn, then, to the one
prophetic book with an indisputable reference to the cult of Molek,
Jeremiah.

4.5.6 <u>Jeremiah</u>

Unlike all of the prophetic references examined to this point, there can
be no question that several verses in Jeremiah have to do with the cult
of Molek. One contains an explicit attestation of Molek in the MT
(32:35), while two others (along with 32:35) decry the sacrifice of
children in the Valley of the Son(s) of Hinnom (7:31; 19:5). As the
following chart shows, the three verses are nearly identical:

<u>7:31</u> / <u>19:5</u> / <u>32:35</u>

And they have built the high places of
the Tophet / Baal / Baal
which is in the Valley / -- / which is in the Valley
of the Son of Hinnom / -- / of the Son of Hinnom
to burn / to burn / to make to pass over
their sons
and their daughters / -- / and their daughters
by the fire, / by the fire, / to (the) Molek,
which I did not command(,)
-- / -- / them,
-- / nor did I say, / --
nor did it enter into my mind(.)
-- / -- / to do this abomination.

The first two verses are immediately followed by the prophet's pejorative redesignation of the locus of the cult and the dreadful implications of that new name for the whole city:

7:32	19:6/11b
Therefore, days are coming--word of YHWH-- when it will no longer be said the Tophet and the Valley of the son of Hinnom, but the Valley of Slaughter, and they will bury in Tophet without room.	Therefore, lo, days are coming--word of YHWH-- when it will no longer be called of this place the Tophet and the Valley of the son of Hinnom, but the Valley of Slaughter. . . . and in Tophet they will bury without room to bury.[662]

All three passages are commomnly assigned to the "prose sermons" of Jeremiah (Mowinckel's "source C"), which have often been alleged to be exilic or post-exilic, Deuteronomically-influenced additions to Jeremiah's original, poetic oracles (Mowinckel's "A") and to third-person, biographical portions, often assigned to Baruch (Mowinckel's "B"). Indeed, with reference to the passages above, most scholars believe that the "Tophet oracle" in chapter 19 (vv. 2b-9, 11b-13) represents an expansion of an original, biographical narrative, concerning the sign-act with the earthen flask (vv. 1-2a, 10-11a, 14-15; 20:1-6).[663] Mosca,

---

[662] The cryptic mē'ên māqôm (liqbor) has been understood in two significantly different ways. Older translators (KJV, Moffatt, J. M. P. Smith read, "till there be no place," while most recent translators (RSV, NEB, NAB, Jerusalem) have, "because there is no room elsewhere." While both readings must add to the Hebrew ("till" and "elsewhere," respectively), and both are possible, the former rendering is, in my judgment, to be preferred. John Bright (Jeremiah [2d ed.; AB 21; Garden City, NY: Doubleday, 1965] 57) defends it by analogy with mē'ên yōšēb in 4:7; 26:9, etc., and points out that the context (7:33; 19:7) envisions unburied bodies defiled and defiling all around them. Indeed, although we do not know where the Molek cult's victims were buried, if the Punic parallels are any guide, simply burying in the Tophet would have been nothing new at all.

[663] E.g., J. P. Hyatt, "The Book of Jeremiah: Introduction and Exegesis," IB 5 (1956) 966-967. One cannot, however, conclude from this that the "Tophet oracle" in chap. 7 is earlier than that in 19 (or 32, for that matter); see Winfried Thiel, Die deuteronomistische Redaktion von Jeremia 1-25 (WMANT 41; Neukirchen-Vluyn: Neukirchener, 1973) 133, n. 78.

therefore, would at first appear to be on firm ground when he speaks of "the distortionary tendency that has been introduced in the intervening decades."[664] Specifically, Mosca holds that the references to the Tophet "as a pagan or paganizing 'high place' (bmh) where Judeans would 'burn' (śrp) their children" (pp. 228-229), as well as the explicit connections with Baal worship in 19:5 and 32:35, bespeak a greater interest in polemical effect than in historical accuracy on the part of the mid-exilic (so Mosca) Deuteronomic redactors.

Recent Jeremiah research has, however, cast doubt on the critical underpinnings of Mosca's case for a "distortionary tendency" in the "C" material.[665] Already in 1951 John Bright mounted an extensive argument against the thesis of any deliberate distortion of Jeremiah's original oracles by the Deuteronomists, who worked, Bright held, "within the lifetime of hundreds who knew him well."[666] Helga Weippert has done a detailed study of four "prose sermon" passages and of the context of selected phrases and has concluded that at least large portions of the

---

[664] "Child Sacrifice," 228. Mosca thus stands in a long line of scholars who have doubted the historical value of the later, supplementary material (even if he is not so extreme as many of them); see already B. Duhm, Das Buch Jeremia (KAT 11; Tübingen: J. C. B. Mohr, 1901) xvii-xviii, who terms such material "zwar keine authentische Geschichte," and J. P. Hyatt, "Jeremiah and Deuteronomy," JNES 1 (1942) 156-173, who argues that the redactors were seeking to make a Deuteronomist of Jeremiah.

[665] It is important to note that even Mowinckel retreated from his original proposal of a distinct "source C," seeking to replace it with a Deuteronomistic "tradition circle" (Prophecy and Tradition [Oslo: Jacob Dybwad, 1946] 62-63; cf. Mosca, "Child Sacrifice," 268, n. 225). It should also be observed that at the same time Mowinckel stressed that the "Deuteronomists" were working from "an independent [of Baruch] parallel transmission of the memories about Jeremiah's sayings."

[666] "The Date of the Prose Sermons of Jeremiah," JBL 70 (1951) 15-35.

so-called Deuteronomic additions are more closely related to undoubtedly Jeremianic oracles than to contemporary Deuteronomic prose (as in the late additions to Dtr), so that they are best explained as deriving from the prophet himself.[667] Even Winfried Thiel, who probably represents the majority of scholars in holding that the "Deuteronomic additions" are both Deuteronomic and additions to Jeremiah's own oracles, insists that minimal historical distortion is present in the former vis-à-vis the latter, particularly in the condemnation of "Götzendienst," such as Molek worship.[668]

But what of Mosca's specific examples of the Deuteronomists' alleged "distortionary tendency"? We have argued above (4.3.3) that śrp need not be pejorative, and its use in 7:31 and 19:5 increases the likelihood that it serves as but a neutral description in Jeremiah. Mosca claims that 7:31 "has acquired fewer pejorative accretions than the two parallel notices" (p. 228), in that it does not claim that the Tophet was "a high place of Baal," but it is 32:35, not 7:31, which contains the neutral technical term, h'byr. However one envisions the interrelationship of the three verses, one is left with a strange mixture of polemic and historical accuracy, given Mosca's reconstruction. While neither Jeremiah nor his redactors gave any quarter to those who claimed to be practicing the cult as good Yahwists (so the end of all three verses), our study to this point has shown that there is no need to suggest that describing the sacrifices as idolatrous was an innovation (by Jeremiah) or revisionist (by an exilic redactor). The verses make perfectly good

---

[667] Die Prosareden des Jeremiabuches (BZAW 132; Berlin: W. de Gruyter, 1973). Unfortunately, Weippert does not treat our passages.

[668] Jeremia 1-25, 133-134.

sense if understood as the protest of those who held that the worship of Molek and Yahweh could not coexist in the cult of child sacrifice, contrary to long-established opinion in Jerusalem.[669] The innovation, if any is present, is more likely in the notion that the worship of Molek amounted to the worship of Baal, although it is understandable that, if Jeremiah and the Deuteronomists indeed had their roots in the North, they would portray all competition to the strictly monotheistic Yahweh worship which they preached as the cult of Yahweh's ancient foe in the North, Baal.[670] On the other hand, the designation of the Tophet as "high places" (bāmôt) may or may not reflect the prophet's (and his redactors') abhorrence of that cultic locale: the usage of bāmāh in Jeremiah and Deuteronomic elements of the D literature is uniformly negative, but the term is an old one, used neutrally elsewhere in Scripture (e.g., 1 Sam 9:19; 1 Kgs 3:4), despite the Canaanite origins of many such sites (cf. Num 33:52), and it may be that the Tophet had contained bāmôt since Jebusite times.[671]

---

[669] Contrast the psychologizing explanation to which Mosca's position drives him: "The prophet's message, however, is clear: since Yahweh does not want such offerings, has never commanded them, they are no better than sacrifices to Baal" ("Child Sacrifice," 230).

[670] See Wilson, *Prophecy and Society*, regarding the northern ("Ephraimite") roots of Jeremiah and the Deuteronomists.

[671] There is some textual difficulty in the three verses under discussion, as to whether the Tophet contained (or was) a bāmāh (singular) or bāmôt (plural). The LXX and Targum, followed by most commentators, read the singular in 7:31, but the uniform use of the plural in the MT of all three verses argues for the originality of bāmôt. Rudolph (*Jeremia*, 56) suggests that this may be a "Plural der Ausdehnung," since there was evidently but one cult place. While this is a reasonable suggestion, the fact is that the OT supplies precious little information about the Tophet itself (Isa 30:33 being probably our best source). The more significant problem is what a "high place" (or "high places") is doing in the Valley! K.-D. Schunck's word study shows that by the time of Jeremiah, bāmāh had

Mosca himself concedes that the three verses examined above cannot
be divorced too thoroughly from the prophet himself, given two apparent
allusions to the cult of Molek in unquestionably "genuine" oracles. The
first, Jer 2:23a, reads:

How can you claim, "I have not defiled myself,
After the Baals I have not gone"?
Observe your conduct in the Valley!
Know what you have done!

In two brief, but incisive articles J. Alberto Soggin has argued that
the "Valley" here is the Valley of the Son(s) of Hinnom and that the
"conduct" cited by the prophet is the cult of child sacrifice, which was
a "peculiar form of worship of the dead."[672] While few would dispute the
identification of the Valley (which, indeed, has been standard since at
least Duhm), Soggin's use of the LXX rendering, "in the cemetery" (en tō
poluandriō), in support of his latter point has been attacked on the
grounds that the LXX is making a connection with 7:32 ("they will bury
in the Tophet"), rather than revealing any special, historical information.[673] While we would contend on the basis of our study that the LXX
was absolutely right in its rendering, even if by serendipity, the whole
question of the "cult of the dead" and its exact relationship to the
cult of Molek deserves separate treatment, which it will receive below
(4.6). For now, we note that already in a "genuine" Jeremianic oracle,

---

come to mean "a small elevation for cultic use" or simply "cult
place" ("bāmāh," TDOT 2 [1977] 141). See further below (4.6) on the
implications of the association of the Tophet with bāmôt.

[672] "'Your Conduct in the Valley': A Note on Jeremiah 2,23a" and "Child
Sacrifice and the Cult of the Dead in the Old Testament," Old Testament and Oriental Studies (BibOr 29; Rome: Pontifical Biblical Institute, 1975) 78-83 and 84-87, respectively.

[673] So Mosca, "Child Sacrifice," 268, n. 228.

the prophet has identified Molek as among the "Baals," probably for the reason suggested above, despite the claims of Jeremiah's audience that they have done nothing wrong.

The same connection of Molek with Baal is apparent in the second "genuine" verse, despite some textual difficulties, although in this case the prophet depicts the people as confessing their idolatry:

> But Baal [MT habbōšet] has consumed
> The produce of our fathers' toil from our youth:
> Their flocks and their herds,
> Their sons and their daughters. (3:24)

While this verse is not so assuredly to be tied to the cult of Molek as was 2:23, "their sons and their daughters" (cf. 7:31; 32:35) makes such a connection likely.

The pertinence of oracles commonly assigned to Jeremiah and to his exilic/post-exilic Deuteronomic redactors raises the thorny question of dating also the historical referent of those oracles. That is to say, do the oracles from the book of Jeremiah tell us whether the cult of Molek survived the "defilement" of the Tophet by Josiah? Jeremiah 1-6 is usually dated to the early years of Josiah's reign (i.e., before his reform), so that the last two verses we examined testify only to the prophet's opposition to the cult of Molek before the reform (and perhaps suggest his influence on the latter).[674] On the other hand, the "Tophet oracles" in chaps. 7, 19 and 32 clearly have to do with the time of Jehoiakim (cf. 26:1), and perhaps also Zedekiah, whenever their literary

---

[674] See Eissfeldt, OT Introduction, 360, and, regarding 2:23, Jacob Milgrom, "The Date of Jeremiah, Chapter 2," JNES 14 (1955) 65-69. A strong effort to date the chapters to Jehoiakim's reign (reckoning the "call" of the prophet in the "thirteenth year of Josiah" [1:1] as at Jeremiah's birth [cf. 1:5]) is made by W. L. Holladay ("A Fresh Look at 'Source B' and 'Source C' in Jeremiah," VT 25 [1975] 409-410), but this proposal has not met with much support.

fixation is to be dated. Yehezkel Kaufmann has argued, however, that
Josiah successfully and permanently rid Judah of all official idolatry,
and that nothing in Jeremiah (or Ezekiel) shows otherwise.[675] He claims
that 2 Kings would have mentioned it if either Jehoiakim or Zedekiah had
restored the cults of Manasseh and that, with respect to the focus of
our interest, the "Tophet oracle" in chapter 19 shows that, "He
[Jeremiah] never accuses his contemporaries of sacrificing children."[676]
Kaufmann's argument e silentio regarding 2 Kings may adequately be answered, we believe, by our study of the passages from Dtr above (4.4.3),
in which we attempted to show that the royal sanction of the Molek cult
was probably not restricted to Ahaz and Manasseh, but was explicitly attributed to them in order to contrast their conduct with that of the re-
formers who succeeded them. To read Jeremiah's "Tophet oracles" as concerning a practice which ceased at least fourteen years earlier (i.e.,
622 - 608 B.C.), but which could still serve as the basis for a threat
directed at the prophet's contemporaries ("Valley of Slaughter") is to
make of the prophet a figure much like Cross's exilic Dtr^2, blaming the
city's destruction on Manasseh (in advance!), as if the conduct of the
current generation was theologically of little relevance for good or
ill.[677] But the prophet himself clearly thought otherwise, as he said
earlier in chapter 7: "For if you truly amend your ways and your doings

---

[675] The Religion of Israel: From Its Beginnings to the Babylonian Exile
(trans. M. Greenberg; Chicago: University of Chicago, 1960)
405-409.

[676] Ibid., 407, n. 2. Kaufmann stresses the apparent emptiness of the
Tophet when Jeremiah delivered his oracle there.

[677] Ibid., 409: "Jeremiah himself is, in the end, compelled to fall
back on the sin of Manasseh (15:4), like the author of Kings."

. . . , then I will let you dwell in this place, in the land that I gave
of old to your fathers for ever" (7:5-7, RSV). In short, Kaufmann errs
by assuming that 2 Kings represents a complete record, by which one can
divide Jeremiah's accusations against his contemporaries (e.g., the worship of the Queen of Heaven) from the "sins of the past which still
haunt the people" (p. 407, n. 2), including cultic child sacrifice. On
the contrary, both Jeremiah and 2 Kings are selective and "tendentious"
(by which I do not intend at this point any quarrel with the accuracy of
what they do include). In sum, neither attempts to retroject the "Tophet oracles'" content into the pre-Josianic past (Kaufmann), nor efforts to see in them historical "distortionary tendencies" attributable
to the "intervening decades" (Mosca) or to the Deuteronomic program
(Hyatt) are, in my view, successful. Jeremiah, supported, as we shall
see (4.5.7), by Ezekiel, confirms that the reform of Josiah did not ex-
punge the cult of Molek in the Tophet from Judah, whatever else its suc-
cesses may have been.

Finally, we must consider the hypothesis of Weinfeld, which is
based especially on passages from Jeremiah, that the cult of Molek may
be identified with the worship of the King (Melek, with dysphemism removed) and Queen (Ištar) of Heaven.[678] Weinfeld observes first the repeated juxtaposition of verses dealing with the Molek cult and those
concerning the King and Queen or host of heaven: Amos 5:26 (see 4.5.1);
Zeph 1:5 (4.5.5); 2 Kgs 21:3,5-6 (//2 Chr 33:3,5-6); 23:4-5,10-12
(4.4.3); Jer 7:18,31; 19:5,13; 32:29,35 (cf. 44:17-19,25). He then argues that the locus (rooftops) and manner (burning incense) of the wor-

---

[678] "The Worship of Molech," 149-154.

ship of the host of heaven match the testimony of neo-Assyrian documents to the same cult in Mesopotamia.[679] However, the manner of worship also fits the cult of Molek, in Weinfeld's view, since, on the basis of Deller's examination of neo-Assyrian contracts (1.7), he believes that the only "burning" which took place in the Biblical cult of Molek was of incense (1.8). He concludes:

> All this shows that the view which holds that children were burned to a deity named Molech rests on an extremely flimsy foundation. Mlk is none other than a king (= Hadad/Baal) alongside the queen Ištar (the queen of heaven), both of whom combined to form at that time the principal deities of the cult of "the host of heaven." (p. 154)

Weinfeld is correct, we believe, in seeing in both the cult of Molek and that of the host of heaven strong Canaanite influence. But the two cannot be identified. Our previous study has shown that one can posit an equation of Baal and Molek by Jeremiah's time in Judah, but that this is a late and possible tendentious phenomenon, and that one cannot maintain the hypothesis that Molek was read Melek before the Masoretes revocalized it. More to the point, although the references to the two cults often occur in close proximity to one another, neither their locus nor their manner of offering is the same. The cult of Molek was practiced always in the Tophet; that of the host of heaven was carried on upon rooftops and in the Temple before Josiah's time (Zeph 1:5; 2 Kgs 21:5), and, so far as we can tell, solely on the rooftops of private homes thereafter. We have already seen the failure of Weinfeld's at-

---

[679] Weinfeld is not arguing that either the cult of Molek or that of the host of heaven derived from Mesopotamia, only that "the Assyrian invasion of the region led to the penetration of the worship of the host of heaven into Judah, opening the door . . . to an Aramean-Phoenician syncretism on a considerable scale" ("The Worship of Molech," 153-154).

tempt to restrict the fuel of Tophet's fires to incense, rather than
children. Moreover, we have seen that Molek is an unlikely candidate
for "King of Heaven" (except, as noted, by late assimilation to Baal),
since he is a chthonic, rather than astral deity (although the two categories are not entirely separate; cf. the sun god, Šm/pš). In sum, the
most likely explanation for the repeated juxtaposition of the references
to the two cults is that both were popular (and, from time to time, official) representatives of Canaanite (or, perhaps, Phoenician) worship
in Judah, to which Deuteronomic writers, especially, took strong exception. (Both also may have had a role as fertility cults; on this, see
chapter V).

Excursus: The Tophet in the Valley

Jeremiah's renaming of the Valley of the Son(s) of Hinnom in 7:32
and 19:6, as well as his apparent allusion to the place by the unmodi-
fied "Valley" (gay') in 2:23, suggest that other indirect allusions to
the locale of the cult of Molek may be discovered in the OT. In addition, we have yet to examine closely the term for the chief installation
of the cult, the Tophet. Because the sure references to both the Tophet
and the Valley are most numerous in Jeremiah, it is at this point in our
investigation that we shall attempt to ferret out any other information
which we can obtain concerning them that may be of help in understanding
exactly what was being done there and why.

In several ways, "Tophet" presents similar interpretive problems to
those encountered in Molek. It occurs but eleven times in the MT (including topteh in Isa 30:33 [see 4.5.4]), and, like Molek in Leviticus
20, its attestations are concentrated, with eight of the eleven occur-

rences in the "Tophet oracles" of Jeremiah 7 and 19.[680] Its etymology
is, if anything, even more uncertain than that of Molek, as we shall see
in a moment. So far as the history of scholarship is concerned, the resemblance of the two terms is clearest in regards to their vocalization:
both have commonly been explained as Masoretic dysphemisms, using bōšet.

The one attestation which might potentially be most useful is the
one which is found entirely outside of the context of cultic child sacrifice, Job 17:6: wətōpet ləpānîm 'ehyeh ("[He has made me] One in
whose face they spit").[681] However, despite the Targum's assumption that
this verse contains a reference to Gehenna, it is most likely that tōpet
in Job is a homonym of the Tophet outside of Jerusalem.[682] Indeed, it is
difficult to see how the two might be related, although Pope has suggested a secondary connection, that the Masoretes may have revocalized
the name of the cult place with the vowels of bōšet to associate it with
"spitting" (Ugaritic wpt).[683] Given Mosca's arguments against the existence of "bōšet dysphemism," it makes more sense, I believe, to propose
that the Masoretes simply replaced the name of the cult place with the
word for "spitting" in Job 17:6, if one insists that "Tophet" is not
original.

---

[680] 2 Kgs 23:10; Isa 30:33; Jer 7:31,32(twice); 19:6,11,12,13,14; Job
17:6.

[681] The translation is that of M. H. Pope, Job (3d ed.; AB 15; Garden
City, NY: Doubleday, 1973) 127.

[682] So BDB, KB, s.v.

[683] Song of Songs (AB 7C; Garden City, NY: Doubleday, 1977) 581. This
etymology assumes, to be sure, that the Hebrew form represents a
borrowing from Aramaic, or at least a dialectical (Northern?) variant, since normally Ugaritic /t/ = Hebrew /š/.

It is, indeed, tempting to hold that Tophet's vowels are not
original, as that removes at least one complication from the vexed issue
of the etymology of the term. We have to do, apparently, with a common
noun, since the article appears on the word six times and a possessive
suffix (given our understanding of Isa 30:33) once, and the three cases
lacking the article all have an attached preposition, from which an
original article could have dropped without change in the consonantal
text, once the usage of the word made of it a proper name.[684] But does
the name have any etymological connection with the rite practiced therein? That is surely the working assumption with which one must begin.
Unfortunately, however, we do not know what the Punic term for the "sacred precinct" was, nor has any obvious candidate emerged from elsewhere, despite the lack of archeological attestation. The most popular
suggestion continues to be that proposed by W. Robertson Smith already
in 1889, that "Tpt is properly an Aramaic name for fireplace," related
to Arabic Othfīya and Syriac Tfāya, "the name for stones on which a pot
is set, and then for any stand or tripod set upon a fire" (cf. Hebrew
'ašpōt, "ashpit, dunghill").[685] Smith supported his proposed etymology
by arguing that the term was borrowed with the practice at the time of

---

[684] Hence, there is no reason why a "Tophet" could not have existed
elsewhere (say, Samaria or Bethel), or why scholars should hesitate
to call the Punic "sacred precincts," "tophets" (so long as they do
not assume that the rites therein were in every respect identical to
those near Jerusalem). However, as we have attempted to show, there
are no sure indications that the cult of Molek (including child sacrifice) was practiced elsewhere in Israel, except for a general accusation levelled at the North (2 Kgs 17:17; see 4.4.3).

[685] Lectures on the Religion of the Semites, 357, n. 1. For a survey of
earlier opinions, see S. D. F. Salmond, "Tophet, Topheth," A Dictionary of the Bible (ed. J. Hastings; NY: Charles Scribner's Sons,
1903) 799.

Ahaz, when Aramean influence was especially strong, and that the vowels are Masoretic alterations. We have argued, however, that both of these suppositions are seriously flawed (4.4.3; 1.9). Albright sought to broaden the appeal of Smith's proposal by tracing the root tpt/špt to Ugaritic tpd, set, place," but Pope has objected to Albright's reading of the crucial passage.[686] Nevertheless, part of Albright's proposal remains possible and appealing: "tpt (tofet) is not necessarily Aramaic but may be dialectical Hebrew like tannôt, 'recite,' in the Song of Deborah." In sum, however, the etymology of Tophet remains unsolved.

We are, therefore, thrust upon the context of the Tophet references for such further information as we can obtain. We examined the oldest OT reference, Isa 30:33, in some detail above (4.5.4). That verse suggested that the Tophet was the cultic installation in which the actual burning of the victims was done, containing (or possibly identical with) a round, dug-out "fire-pit" (following de Vaux and Mosca on mədurāh), in which wood was arranged in preparation for the sacrifice. Most of the other verses add little to this picture, beyond specifying its location, "in the Valley of the Son(s) of Hinnom," and confirming that the Tophet was, indeed, where the Jerusalemites "made to pass over" (2 Kgs 23:10) or "burned" (Jer 7:31; 19:5) their children. The two verses which conclude the combined "Tophet oracle" and sign act of the earthen flask in chapter 19 add that Yahweh will "make" (ntn) the city like Tophet and that he will "defile" (ṭm') like Tophet the houses where cults including that of the host of heaven were practiced (19:12-13). The context shows that these evil consequences will follow on the siege and destruction of

---

[686] Albright, Yahweh and the Gods, 275; Pope, Song of Songs, 581.

the city (vv. 7-9), after which the Tophet will become an overflowing cemetary (v. 11; see discussion above). Thus, to "make" the city like Tophet could mean either that the city as a whole will become an inferno or that it, too, will overflow with the unburied (depending on whether "like Tophet" refers to the cult place before or after the burials of v. 11 occur). Unfortunately, it is hard to say exactly what "defile" means, viz., whether Yahweh is threatening to do to the houses what Josiah did to the Tophet (the details of which are unknown), or whether the prophet means that the effects will be the same, i.e., the denial of future use (only permanently, when Yahweh is the defiler). What hints 2 Kings 23 does provide suggest that burning, desecration of remains and burials could all be used to defile. In sum, it seems clear enough that the prophet is employing the same image which later gave birth to the "Gehenna" of Judaism and the NT (perhaps via Isa 66:24), an amalgam of fire and death and corpses which was, no doubt, far more powerful to those who witnessed the original referent than to anyone since.

Fortunately, we possess considerably more information concerning the Valley of the Son(s) of Hinnom. Not only is the name attested in passages also referring to the Tophet (2 Kgs 23:10; Jer 7:31,32; 19:6) and other verses having to do with cultic child sacrifice (Jer 19:2; 32:35; 2 Chr 28:3; 33:6), but it is found in the list of tribal boundaries in Joshua, forming part of the border between Judah and Benjamin (Josh 15:8[twice]; 18:16[twice]), and in the list of villages occupied by the people of Judah after the Return (Neh 11:30).[687] Furthermore,

---

[687] The name occurs simply as "the Valley of Hinnom" in Josh 15:8 and 18:16 (once each) and in Neh. 11:30. The K of 2 Kgs 23:10 has "sons," while the Q has "son" (hence the variant in parentheses). While "sons" fits better with what we believe is the most promising

there are several references to a "Valley Gate" (ša'ar-haggāy') in the wall of Jerusalem, which presumably led to the Valley Ben-Hinnom (Neh 2:13,15; 3:13; 2 Chr 26:9). Also, we have already seen that Jeremiah makes reference simply to "the Valley" (2:23) and to the newly-named "Valley of Slaughter" (7:32; 19:6).

This is not to say that all of the historical problems with regard to the Valley have been solved. In fact, neither its location nor its etymology is undisputed. Since the revival of Palestinian archeology late in the last century, all three major valleys near Jerusalem have been proposed: the Qidron, on the east; the Central or Tyropoeon (el-Wād) between the Jebusite-Davidic city and the western hill; and the Wādi er-Rabābeh, which sweeps from the west across the south of the city, joining the Qidron at the southeast corner, at the Wādi en-Nār.[688] The first is unlikely, because it is based on a misunderstanding of Jer 19:2 (reading ša'ar haḥarsît as "Eastern Gate," instead of "Potsherd Gate"), and because the Qidron is uniformly called naḥal, not gay'. The choice between the remaining options is more complicated, depending on one's views of the extent of Jerusalem's walls during the Divided Monarchy; in brief, if one holds that only the Jebusite-Davidic city was included (with some expansion northwards), the Tyropoeon is preferable, while if one holds that all or part of the western hill was inside the walls (and so also the Tyropoeon Valley), the western/southern valley

---

explanation of the name (below), to insist upon it in the face of the unanimous opposition of the other references would be arbitrary, at best, and tendentious, at worst.

[688] George Adam Smith, Jerusalem (reprint; NY: Ktav, 1972 [orig., 1877]) 1.173-176, provides a summary of and references to early proponents of all three views.

will be more likely.[689] The results of archeological expeditions at Jerusalem headed by Kathleen Kenyon and others appear to favor the latter
choice, and we shall adopt it for this study.[690]

The etymology of "Hinnom" is also problematic. It is commonly
translated and interpreted as the proper name of the one-time owners
(and left at that), but most recognize this as, effectively, a counsel
of despair. The rabbis sought a connection with "ḥinnām, 'gratuitous-
ly,' the valley which all enter for vanity and worldly lust," but this,
like their connection of Tophet with tāpap (strike, beat [a drum during
sacrifice]), is clearly late and homiletical.[691] The lexica note a possible Arabic cognate, hanna (wailing), but this, likewise, is obviously
a late connection, based on the cult practiced there, and already BDB
recognized it as "improbable."[692] Recently, Marvin Pope has offered a
proposal from Ugaritic which, though it cannot be proved, meshes well
with other results of our study. Pope suggests that the repeated designation of Danel (Aqht's father) as Dnil mt rpi // ġzr mt hrnmy ("Danel,
man of RPI // the hero, man of HRNMY") points to a connection of the
gentilic hrnmy, like the parallel rpi (2.3.2), with the netherworld.[693]

---

[689] The former view is represented in modern scholarship by A. D. Tush-
ingham (Denis Baly and Tushingham, Atlas of the Biblical World [NY:
World, 1971] 158). The latter opinion is shared by most other
scholars (for complete discussion, see J. Simons, Jerusalem in the
OT, 11, n. 1; and The Geographical and Topographical Texts of the
Old Testament [Leiden: Brill, 1959] 13-14).

[690] See map on p. 114 of Lawrence E. Stager, "The Archaeology of the
East Slope of Jerusalem and the Terraces of the Kidron," JNES 41
(1982). Further archeology may, of course, make fools of us all.

[691] Quotation from Pope, Song of Songs, 581.

[692] But cf. KB3, s.v.

[693] "Rephaim Texts," 166. He further cites Arabic harim, "be weak, old,

He notes with approval Albright's comparison of mt hrnmy with the Biblical names Methusael/Methuselah and, on the basis of his own conclusion
that šlḥ in the latter name is a theophoric element referring to the
"channel" to the underworld, proposes that the š'l in Methusael is
Sheol.[694] Thus, Danel and Methuselah, both ancient ancestors in Biblical
reckoning (see Ezek 14:14,20 regarding the former), are called "man of
the netherworld." The connection with our study comes in Pope's suggestion (following Robert Good) that Ugaritic hrnm and OT hnnm (Hinnom) are
"variant names of the netherworld to which the infamous valley of Jerusalem was the entry."[695] In sum, "the biblical son(s) of Hinnom are the
defunct denizens of the netherworld."

Pope's proposed explanation is most attractive, in that it would
help explain the tenacious localization of the Israelite Molek cult in a
certain place near Jerusalem and would reinforce the indications we have
already obtained that the cult had to do with the cult of the dead. As
rabbinic lore shows, there were many entrances to the netherworld, so
that Danel's epithet could refer to one well to the north, such as the
Hrnm = Hermel (in modern northern Lebanon), adduced by Albright.[696] The

---

decrepit," regarding the shades.

[694] Albright, JBL 58 (1939) 97; Pope, Job, 250. Unfortunately, little
is known of the Ugaritic god Šlḥ. It may be that Methusael represents not a reference to Sheol, but a Yahwistic attempt to eliminate
a foreign deity's theophoric element and substitute the more acceptable "of El." Nevertheless, Pope's point may stand concerning the
relationship of hrmn and hnnm (below).

[695] "Rephaim Texts," 166. Pope adduces a third variant in the vexing
haharmôn of Amos 4:3.

[696] "The Traditional Home of the Syrian Daniel," BASOR 130 (1953) 26-27.
For rabbinic views on the locations of the entrances to the netherworld, see b. 'Erubin 19a.

etymology per se is possibly the weakest point of Pope's argument (one could wish for a closer match than harim, or even Albright's hirmil, "old she-camel, old woman"), but if the Valley's name is as ancient as our study has led us to suspect, a cognate convincing to all may be hard to come by.

We have already argued that other occurrences of "valley" (gay') in the OT have to do with the Valley of the Son(s) of Hinnom, including the "Valley of Slaughter" (gê' hahărēgāh) without question and probably the "Valley Gate" and simply "the Valley" in Jer 2:23. We have commented on the latter two above, but have left the first for now. The usage of hărēgāh is to be compared to the "day of slaughter" which Jeremiah wishes for the "wicked" and "treacherous" who were tormenting him (12:3) and especially with the use of the cognate verb, meaning "wholesale slaughter after battle" and "God's slaying in judgment (stern and inscrutable)."[697] The context of both 7:32 and 19:6 clarifies that the prophet envisions the wholesale exposure of corpses of (and thus the defilement of the Valley by) those killed by Judah's enemies at Yahweh's instigation (so explicitly 7:33 and 19:7). In this setting, the use of hrg may well be in deliberate contradistinction to the neutral description of the Valley's wonted activities as śrp, and especially to the sacrificial term h'byr (and perhaps also Ezekiel's šḥṭ and zbḥ, depending on the dating of the respective references). Where now there is occasional, sacrificial slaying, there will be wholesale, unmanageable, profane slaughter.

---

[697] BDB, 247.

However, not all OT occurrences of gay' refer to that of Hinnom, e.g., the Valley of Salt (2 Sam 8:13; 2 Kgs 2:16; 14:7, etc.). Obviously, only those instances which are or might be located near Jerusalem are candidates; while this is generally no problem to determine in the historical books, there are prophetic passages which are harder to adjudicate. Most difficult of all, perhaps, is Isaiah's "Valley of Vision" (22:1,5). The chapter as a whole is replete with textual and interpretational difficulties which cannot be pursued here. The scene is explicitly identified as Jerusalem (vv. 9-10), where no gay' other than Hinnom is known, but, as Simons observes, to identify the "Valley of Vision" with that of Hinnom "leaves the expression itself unexplained."[698] Commentators at least as far back as Marti have, therefore, proposed the emendation of ḥizzāyôn to hinnōm, although this is hard to defend text-critically.[699] Given that Hinnom is the one known gay' outside of Jerusalem, an identification with it seems most likely, even if we still cannot explain what the prophet meant by "Vision."[700] Unfortunately, even if this identification is correct, the context adds little to our understanding. The one point which may be of further interest is Otto Kaiser's contention that "your choicest valleys" ('ămāqayik) in v. 7 in-

[698] Geographical Texts, 439.

[699] Das Buch Jesaja (KAT 10; Tübingen: J. C. B. Mohr, 1900) 169. A. Guillaume adduces an Arabic cognate, ḥadwe, "opposite, over against," yielding, "yonder valley," i.e., either the Tyropoeon or Hinnom, but "vision" is well-enough attested for ḥizzāyôn that this seems improbable. Still less likely is "a deliberate distortion of ḥinnom [sic]" (A. S. Herbert, The Book of the Prophet Isaiah: Chapters 1-39 (Cambridge, NEB; Cambridge: University, 1973) 135.

[700] R. B. Y. Scott's suggestion is provocative, however, in the light of our study: "the reference is probably to divination at an altar in the 'Valley of Hinnom'" ("The Book of Isaiah: Chapters 1-39: Introduction and Exegesis," IB 5 (1956) 290.

cludes Hinnom and the Valley ('ēmeq) of the Rephaim: this may lead us
to suspect that not all prophetic references to Hinnom may be found
through a concordance search under gay'.[701]

Such a search is, however, where one must begin, and it yields two
other significant possibilities.[702] Both are in apocalyptic sections of
prophets, describing God's final war on the enemies of his people. Both
appear to be well after any active practice of the cult of Molek (indeed, neither mentions child sacrifice), but both may still evidence
memories of the significance of the people's "conduct in the Valley."
The first occurs in Ezekiel 39, in the description of the "cleansing of
the land," following God's slaughter of Gog of Magog and his allies.
Verse 11 reads:

> And on that day I shall appoint for Gog a place there, a grave
> in Israel, the Valley of Those-who-pass-over, over against the
> Sea, and it will clog with Those-who-pass-over, and they will
> bury there Gog and all his crowd, and they will call [the
> place], "The Valley of Gog's Crowd."

Verse 15 also contains the last phrase, as the name of the place where
the exposed corpses of Gog's Crowd will eventually be buried. Like all
apocalyptic, this chapter was not intended to be transparent to those
outside the circle of its author(s), but I believe that we can extract
some information significant to our study, nevertheless. The meaning of

---

[701] Isaiah 13-39 (OTL; Philadelphia: Westminster, 1974 [German orig., 1973]) 144.

[702] We do not include among these the gy' ṣlmwt of Ps 23:4, which, pace M. R. Lehmann ("A New Interpretation," 367) is not at all likely to be a reference to a specific place. (Cf. M. Dahood, Psalms I [AB 16; Garden City, NY: Doubleday, 1966] 146-147, who eliminates "val- ley" altogether.) We may add that, while Lehmann's proposed identi- fication of Molek and Mot has some merit (p. 366; cf. 2.3.6), his arguments to that end are sometimes dubious: at one point, he seems to have reversed the positions of the Wadi Qidron and the Valley of Hinnom (p. 365)!

'ōbərim has long been problematic, and it has often been emended to 'ăbārim, under the assumption that it referred either to the place Iyeabarim (Num 21:11; 33:43) or to the mountain(s) of Abarim (Num 27:12; 33:47-48; Deut 32:49), both in Moab, east of the Dead Sea.[703] However, although this might seem suported by qidmat hayyām ("east of the Sea"), the burial place is to be "in Israel," and qidmāh means only "in front of, over against" (and can mean "west of": Gen 2:14).

The crucial observation, in my view, is that of Jonathan Ratosh, that h'brym can be the "ancestors passed away," related to the Rephaim (4.6) and the cult of the dead.[704] Given the status of Gog's Crowd in Ezekiel 39, the rendering of "those who have passed on" (Pope: "the departed"), makes good sense. Moreover, there is good reason to see in the "Valley of Gog's Crowd" a reference to the Valley of the Son(s) of Hinnom. First, if our understanding of both Hinnom and 'ōbərim as presented above is correct, both terms are closely tied to the underworld.[705] Secondly, the Valley Hinnom does lie directly west of the northern end of the Dead Sea, and is connected to the latter by a long,

---

[703] See Walther Zimmerli, *Ezekiel 2* (trans. J. D. Martin; ed. P. D. Hanson and L. J. Greenspoon; Hermeneia; Philadelphia: Fortress, 1983 [German orig., 1969]) 292.

[704] "''ēbr' in Scripture or the Land of h'brym," *Beth Mikra* 47 (1970-1971) 549-568 [in Hebrew]. Summary from Pope, "Rephaim Texts," 173.

[705] Furthermore, it may be that the meaning of the Molek cult's technical term, h'byr, should be reexamined in the light of this chthonic sense of 'br, viz., whether it might mean "to make an 'ōbēr" of the victim. But since there are no specimens of the Hiphil of 'br with this sense besides the ones in question (regarding the cult of Molek), it is methodologically preferable to retain the sense proposed above, "to transfer ownership or control," even though it is tempting to see some combination of the two.

winding wadi.[706] Thirdly, as Zimmerli notes, there may well be a "loose

assonance" intended between hāmôn ("crowd") and Hinnom.[707] Fourthly, it

is worth mentioning, even if not conclusive proof, that the LXX employs

poluandrion ("cemetary") for gay' here, even as it did in Jer 2:23 (and

19:2,6). In sum, we suggest that Ezekiel (or his epigones) is here

playing on the image of the "Valley of Slaughter" idea attached to the

Valley Hinnom by Jeremiah: only in the eschatological battle, it will

be the enemies of Jerusalem, rather than its citizens, who will fill the

graves of the Valley and provide the victuals for the birds and beasts

of the field.[708]

The other apocalyptic specimens of gay' which may be of importance

to us are in Zechariah's depiction of Yahweh's battle against the na-

tions in 14:4-5:

> And his feet shall stand in that day upon the Mount of Olives,
> which is opposite Jerusalem to the east, and the Mount of Ol-
> ives shall be split in half, from east to west, by a very
> great valley. And one-half of the Mount shall depart to the
> north and one-half of it to the south. And you shall flee/And
> shall be stopped up the valley of my mountains, for the moun-
> tains' valley will touch Aṣel/nearby. And you shall flee, as
> you fled from before the earthquake in the days of King Uzzi-
> ah, king of Judah, and Yahweh my God will come, [and] all the
> saints with you.

---

[706] See Pope, "Rephaim Texts," for a demonstration that the Dead Sea is
the Sea in question. Pope would identify the Valley of Gog's Crowd
(or "Gog's Mob") as the entire complex of valleys and wadis bordering Jerusalem, including the Qidron, Hinnom and Rephaim "Valleys."
We shall address the legitimacy of this proposal below.

[707] Ezekiel 2, 317. Zimmerli concludes: "That an etymological aetiolo-
gy is intended here is in any case probable."

[708] Ribichini and Xella reach the same conclusion in their study of Ezek
39:11: "'La Valle dei Passanti'," 439.

The MT is obviously corrupt and confused in places, so that it is difficult to tell precisely what alterations in the topography of Jerusalem
the writer envisions, besides the bifurcation of the Mount of Olives.
The valley (gay') formed by the split is obviously not the same as the
Valley of Hinnom, although, if properly aligned, it might extend the
latter valley directly to the east. If the valley to be stopped up (or
fled, depending on how one vocalizes the wnstm which begins v. 5) and/or
the "mountains' valley" is the Qidron, we have here an unusual use of
gay' instead of naḥal for Qidron, which could support Pope's proposal to
consider the valleys/wadis as a unit (see below). Given the uncertainties of text and reconstruction, however, it seems best to stress instead the role of the Mount of Olives as a conduit for the "saints"
(qədōšîm) approaching Jerusalem. John Briggs Curtis's thorough study of
the Mount's role in the OT and NT is misdirected, I believe, in identifying Molek and Milkom (and thus in claiming that Solomon fostered the
cult of the former on the Mount), but he demonstrates beyond cavil the
chthonic significance of the Mount of Olives.[709] Most importantly, he
comments apropos a mural from Dura-Europos which depicts both Ezekiel's
"valley of dry bones" and Zechariah's split mountain:

> This is the logical combination, for if there was a popular
> reminiscence that the Mount of Olives was sacred to the god of
> the dead and of the underworld, it could be assumed to contain
> an entrance to the realm of the dead. The deep crevasse,
> which is enigmatic in Zechariah, has a real meaning in the mu-
> ral, for here it is the exit from the nether world for the
> dead.[710]

---

[709] "An Investigation of the Mount of Olives in the Judeo-Christian Tradition," HUCA 28 (1957) 137-180. Curtis posits the practice of the
cult of Nergal on the Mount from at least the time of David.

[710] Ibid., 171.

That is to say, in Zechariah 14, Yahweh is depicted as opening that exit, and the "saints come marching in" to the eschatological Jerusalem, by way of a valley parallel to, if not an extension of, the Valley of the Son(s) of Hinnom.

We have already mentioned Marvin Pope's proposal, that other portions of the valleys and wadis bordering Jerusalem besides the Valley Hinnom per se should be considered parts of a single complex for historical purposes.[711] Also, we have seen that Isa 22:7 may suggest that lexical distinctions between gay' and 'ēmeq should not be pressed, if Kaiser's reading is correct. There is further evidence, in my view, in support of this approach, at least regarding gy' (hereafter, "valley") and 'mq (hereafter, "vale"). The best example of the proposed terminological overlap is certainly Jer 31:40a: "And the entire vale of stelae (traditionally, "corpses") and ashes, and all the terraces to (or "upon," with BHK/S) the Wadi Qidron, as far as the corner of the Horses' Gate on the east, shall be holy to Yahweh."[712] It is difficult to avoid seeing in 31:38-40 a quick tracing of the outlines of the city, counter-clockwise, including the Valley Hinnom on the south and the Wadi Qidron on the east. The identification of the "vale" as Hinnom is supported not merely by this sequence, but also by the presence in the vale of memorial stelae and the ashes of sacrificial victims.[713] Whether the stelae marked the burial places of the child victims (as in the Punic

---

[711] Pope's most complete formulations of his views and of their ramifications for our study are in "Rephaim Texts," 174, and Song of Songs, 579-582.

[712] On pgr (stela), see below (4.6). On šdmwt (terraces), see Stager, "Archaeology of the East Slope," 117.

[713] On the latter, see BDB, s.v. dešen.

colonies) or commemorated the ancestors (cf. Ezek 43:7,9, discussed below [4.6]), their presence in the Valley Hinnom would be no surprise,
and nowhere else, to our knowledge, would be apt to have both the stelae
and the ashes.

The most significant topographical feature near Jerusalem which
regularly bears the designation 'ēmeq is the Vale of the Rephaim (Jos
15:8; 18:16; 2 Sam 5:18,22; 23:13; Isa 17:5; 1 Chr 11:15; 14:9,13). It
is almost unanimously identified with the broad beqʻah to the southwest
of the city which merges with the Wādi er-Rabābeh (Valley Hinnom) near
the southwest corner of the city.[714] The vale formed a part of the border between the tribes of Judah and Benjamin and was used by the Philis-
tines as a route of attack against David's Jerusalem. If (when they appear in a Jerusalemite context) "the valley" (haggay') is Hinnom (Jer
2:23) and "the wadi" (hannaḥal) is Qidron (Cant 6:7; Neh 2:15), as seems
likely, "the vale" (hāʻēmeq) is, presumably, first and foremost that of
the Rephaim, despite its evident inclusion of Hinnom in Jer 31:40 and
its possible inclusion of the same in Isa 22:5. This would occasion no
surprise, of course, for, although we have no way of knowing how the
Vale of the Rephaim acquired its name, the name is not likely to be an
Israelite creation, and we have already seen how at Ugarit the rpum and
Rpu were the deified (royal) ancestors and a chthonic deity, respectively, and how they were closely linked, if not identical to, the mlkm and
Mlk, respectively. We shall have more to say about the Biblical Rephaim
and their possible relationship to the cult of Molek below (4.6).

---

[714] Simons, Geographical Texts, 79-80.

More problematic is the "King's Vale" (ʻēmeq hammelek), where Melchizedek met Abraham (Gen 14:17) and where Absalom erected a stela
(maṣṣēbāh) in his own memory (2 Sam 18:18). An older version of the
name appears in Genesis as "the Vale of Shaveh" (Šāwēh), but neither can
be located with any certainty.[715] The combination of a memorial stela
and a vale named hmlk fairly begs for revocalization as Molek, but without further evidence, it is a temptation best resisted.

Finally, we come again to three eschatological passages, this time
from Joel 4. This prophet also speaks of the coming Day when Yahweh
will requite the nations on behalf of Israel, having first gathered them
in the "Vale of Yəhôšāpāṭ" ("Jehoshaphat," or "Yahweh judges"; vv.
2,12), or the "Vale of Heḥārûṣ" ("decision"; v. 14[twice]). It is possible, as Simons says, that the location is "merely visionary," but,
given the concrete reality of Zion, Judah and Jerusalem, there is no
reason why it must be.[716] We have already seen that the eschatological
valleys of judgment in Ezekiel and Zechariah were set in actual locations; indeed, Joel's "Crowds (hămônîm), crowds in the Vale of Decision!" recalls Ezekiel's "Valley of Gog's Crowd" (hămôn gôg). Taking
into account Joel's apparent proclivity to reuse the images and even
words of earlier prophets (e.g., 4:10 vis-à-vis Isa 2:4 and Mic 4:3), it
seems to me that one can argue at least the probability that Joel's vale

---

[715] The traditional "Tomb of Absalom" in the Qidron is, of course, no
help. See Simons, Geographical Texts, 215-216.

[716] Ibid., 465. Simons is inexplicably sounder in his methodology later
on the same page: "In the same way as the 'valley (ʻemeq) of Jehoshaphat', 'the naḥal of the Shiṭṭim' in Joel iv.8 also is doubtless
a visionary element, though this does not alter the fact that the
prophet using this well-known name may have had a concrete feature
in mind."

is the same as the valleys of Ezekiel and Zechariah, i.e., Hinnom or a
place slightly to the east thereof. As with these earlier prophets,
Joel's oracles are too far removed from the practice of the cult of Molek to be of direct help in historical reconstruction, but they do reinforce the impression that the Valley had made an indelible impact upon
the religio-historical consciousness of the inhabitants of Jerusalem:
it had become the appropriate locus for the great and final divine punishment of abominations, whether those of Judah (as in Jeremiah), or
those of the nations (as in Ezekiel, Zechariah and Joel [cf. 4:2-8]),
the very entrance to the netherworld. Again, the Gehenna of Judaism and
the NT was but a small additional step, provoked, we may well suspect,
by the cosmic categories of apocalyptic.

Finally, we may consider also Pope's attempt to include the Wadi
Qidron in this complex of chthonic valleys and vales. Although he is,
in my view, insufficiently sensitive to the distinction which the OT is
at some pains to preserve between "the Wadi" and "the Valley" (simply
asserting, for instance, that "Qidron, Hinnom and Tophet" are all names
for "the Valley" [Song of Songs, 581]), he does mount an attractive case
for the recognition of chthonic (and fertility cult) overtones with specific reference to the Qidron, particularly the section at the northeast
edge of the city, called Wādi al-Jôz, the "Wadi Walnut."[717] Besides the
chthonic and fertility associations of the walnut itself, Pope stresses
the important role of the burial grounds further south, before the Gol-

---

[717] Pope appears to be slightly more accurate in his location of the
wadi in "Rephaim Texts," 174, than in Song of Songs, 579, where he
says that it lies "between the Temple Hill and the Mount of Olives"
(i.e., on the east side of the city). Cf. Simons, Jerusalem in the
OT, 9, n. 3.

den Gate (and elsewhere in the Qidron), in Jewish and Arabic lore
concerning the final resurrection.[718]

In sum, Pope has succeeded, I believe, in showing that the entire
complex of the Vale of the Rephaim, the Valley of the Son(s) of Hinnom
and the Wadi Qidron were long and closely associated with the netherworld and, especially with reference to the latter location, with fertility.[719] There remains no evidence, however, that the cult of Molek
was ever practiced in the Qidron (but see Pope's views on Isa 57:5 below
[4.5.8]), or that the OT ever considered the "entire complex" as a unit.
The importance of maintaining the distinction ourselves, however, pales,
as we recognize all that the cults located at various points shared,
whether considered sympathetically, by their practitioners, or as barely
distinguishable species of the genus, "idolatry," by Josiah and the later prophets.

We may note in closing John Gray's suggestion that the "garden of
the king" (gan hammelek), through which Zedekiah and company fled the
city at its impending fall to Nebuchadnezzar's armies (2 Kgs 25:4; Jer
39:4; 52:7), was "the precinct of the god Melech."[720] The location of

---

[718] Song of Songs, 574-582. Indeed, the Qidron has long served as a
cemetary: pre-exilic graves have been located at Silwan, at the
southern end of the Qidron (for a comprehensive summary of Jerusalem
tomb finds dated to the third millennium B.C. through the Exile, see
L. Y. Rahmani, "Ancient Jerusalem's Funerary Customs and Tombs:
Part Two," BA 44 [1981] 229-235).

[719] That fertility should be connected especially with a wadi is no surprize, since it, in distinction from a "valley," contains a running
stream during the rainy season and, hence, is quickest to evidence
the renewed life of vegitation (cf. G. A. Smith, Jerusalem, 171, and
Pope, Song of Songs, 580).

[720] Legacy of Canaan, 173. Gray further suggests that the "garden of
Uzza," in which Manasseh and Amon were buried, was the same place.

the garden, which is best fixed by Neh 3:15, fits tolerably well with what we know of the Tophet (presumably Molek's "precinct" par excellence), so that revocalization to "the garden of Molek" is not unreasonable, but the evidence is simply insufficient to draw firm conclusions.[721]

4.5.7 Ezekiel

With Ezekiel we move halfway into the exile, as it were, since the book's superscription makes it clear that he was among Judah's elite who were removed to Mesopotamia with King Jehoiachin in 597. The book contains four passages of particular interest to our study, one each from the allegorical histories of Israel in chapters 16 and 23 and two from the somewhat more straightforward history in chapter 20. As we shall see, the passages' context complicates the task of historical evaluation. Nevertheless, Ezekiel's ever-peculiar perspective can reinforce some of our earlier observations and suggest additional information.

Ezek 16:20-21 concerns the fourth in a series of God's gifts which Jerusalem, personified as a harlot, has "taken" (wattiqḥî) and devoted to idolatry (the "harlotry" of the chapter). Much of the prophet's language is familiar from our earlier study, but not all:

> (20) And you took your sons and your daughters, whom you bore to me, and you sacrificed them to them [the ṣalmê zākār, "male images," v. 17] to eat. Were your harlotries too small? (21) You slew my sons and made gifts of them, by making them pass over to them.

---

[721] Cf. Pope's approval of Robert's connection of the "valley" (naḥal) of Cant 6:11 with the king's garden in the Qidron (*Song of Songs*, 580).

The prophet is claiming that Jerusalem's child sacrifice is a step worse
yet (beyond the pale, as it were) than her other idolatry (cf. the chi-
astic "abominations and harlotries" which follows immediately in v. 22,
and also v. 36). His priestly background may be responsible for his use
of ntn (as in Leviticus), along with the more customary h'byr in v. 21.
But what of the choice of "sacrifice" (zbḥ) in v. 20 and "slay" (šḥṭ) in
v. 21?[722] As Mosca observes, this is the first time either has been employed to refer to child sacrifice, and he terms their presence "entirely inappropriate" specimens of "the hyperbole of Exilic reaction to
child sacrifice, . . . intended to equate child sacrifice with animal
sacrifice."[723] It is more likely, in my view, that the priest Ezekiel is
using the language of his personal lexicon, sacrificial terms, to describe the act (we have already seen that no absolute distinction can be
drawn between the language of child and animal sacrifices; cf. 'ōlāh in
Gen 22:2 and 2 Kgs 3:27). Mosca's similar contention that the use of
"to eat" in v. 20 (and "for food" in 23:37)[724] is "tendentious" may also
be otherwise explained as illustrative of Ezekiel's well-known proclivity to literalize the metaphors of earlier prophets: thus, while Jeremiah had spoken of how "Baal has consumed ['kl] . . . their sons and their

---

[722] On these two verbs see Jacob Milgrom, "Profane Slaughter and the
Composition of Deuteronomy," and H. C. Brichto, "On Slaughter and
Sacrifice, Blood and Atonement," HUCA 47 (1976) 1-17 and 19-55, respectively. Both show that both verbs meant, first of all, ritual
slaughter. If Milgrom (pp. 14-15) is correct, that šḥṭ means more
precisely, "to slit the throat" (cf. Brichto's approval, p. 22, n.
5), we may have a clue concerning the method of Molek sacrifices.
See further below on the possibility that Ezek 16:21 implies the sequence: slaying, then burning.

[723] "Child Sacrifice," 232.

[724] See our argument above (4.3.1) that lə'oklāh is also to be rendered,
"to eat."

daughters" (3:24; cf. 5:17 and 4.5.6), Ezekiel straightforwardly speaks
of the images as "eating" the sacrificed children (cf. the "eating" of
the word of Yahweh in Jer 15:16 vis-à-vis Ezek 3:1-3).[725]

The use of ntn and h'byr with "sons and daughters" as direct objects seems sufficient warrant to interpret these verses as having to do
with the cult of Molek. How, then, are we to understand the "male images"? It may be best not to press them for historical data, but rather
to understand "images" as a concretization of the indictment of idolatry
and the emphasis on "male" as a corollary of the "harlotry" metaphor (v.
17: "with them you played the harlot"). Two other possibilities may be
mentioned, however. First, as Eissfeldt observes, the historical referent of these verses is clearly the Canaanite idolatry which constantly
threatened Yahwism.[726] Given the ubiquitous overtones of the fertility
cult in Canaanite religion, one may suspect that the figure of "harlotry" is more than metaphorical, however stereotyped an image for Israelite sin it may have become by Ezekiel's time.[727] If so, by "images of
men" Ezekiel may have intended phallic representations, such as were apparently employed in the fertility cult (and associated with the Molek

---

[725] This understanding is also superior, I believe, to the implication
which Kennedy suggested on the basis of the Pozo Moro tower (2.7),
that child sacrifices were literally eaten by the human participants. Despite the Ugaritic example of Anat and Baal, cited by Pope
("She ate his flesh without a knife; she drank his blood without a
cup" [RS 22.225]), one would like to have clearer, preferably archeological, evidence that ritual cannibalism was practiced in the
ancient Near East, before seeking to integrate such an interpretation into the Molek cult, whose sacrifices appear to have been, like
the 'ōlāh, entirely for the deity.

[726] "Hezekiel Kap. 16 als Geschichtsquelle," JPOS 16 (1936) 287.

[727] See Mosca's objections to any literal understanding of the figure
("Child Sacrifice," 268-269, n. 233).

cult) in Isa 57:8.[728] Secondly, the context may suggest that the images
are the representational stelae of the ancestors, employed in the cult
of the dead. The "fine flour, oil and honey" of v. 19 recall the gifts
to the malikū at Mari, and the association of the ancestors (or their
stelae) with Molek sacrifices would be no surprize at all (see our proposal above concerning the 'ōbôt [4.3.1]). If this understanding is
preferred, one might argue for the revocalization of zākār to zēker,
yielding, "memorial images," but the lack of OT parallels compels caution. One is on safer ground to suggest that the prophet may have been
alluding to the ancestors by playing on the semantic range of zkr.

The other allegorical passage, Ezek 23:36-39, has little to add.
Zimmerli regards the verses (indeed, vv. 36-49) as relatively late and
imitative, and this is supported by the close verbal resemblance of
23:36-39 with 16:20-21.[729] The direction of the dependence is suggested
by the shift in the use of the harlotry figure: whereas earlier examples (Hosea 2, Jeremiah 3, Ezekiel 16) used it to condemn participation
in Canaanite cults, Ezekiel 23 employs it with reference to foreign alliances. The recipients of the child sacrifices are now called gillû-
lîm, "idols" (perhaps a play on gēl, gālāl, "dung"). Verse 39 confirms
that the cult was practiced outside of the temple. It is important to
note that both Oholah and Oholibah (Samaria and Jerusalem, v. 4) are accused of "making to pass over" (h'byr) and "slaying" (šḥṭ) "their sons."
As our previous study of 2 Kgs 16:3 and 17:17 has shown, this may re-

---

[728] So already Ehrlich, Herrmann and Fohrer, according to Zimmerli (Ezekiel 1, 344). See below for additional discussion of Isa 57:5,9 as
referring to the Molek cult.

[729] Ezekiel 1, 491.

flect the historical situation, but it is more likely to be attributable
to the chapter's general tendency to accuse both "sisters" of the same
crimes.[730]

The other two passages, from chapter 20, are not allegorical, but
they present, if anything, even greater interpretive challenges than do
those which are. First, the texts:

> (25) I even gave them statutes that were not good and ordi-
> nances by which they could not live. (26) I defiled them by
> their gifts, by their making every firstborn pass over, so
> that I might devastate them, so that they would know that I am
> Yahweh.
>
> (30) Therefore, say to the house of Israel: Thus says the
> Lord Yahweh: Is it with the conduct of your fathers that your
> are defiled/defiling yourselves, and after their gods
> (šiqqûṣêhem for 'ĕlōhêhem) that you are whoring? (31) When
> you make your offerings, when you make your sons to pass over
> by the fire, you are defiled/defiling yourselves with all your
> idols to this day. So shall I be inquired of by you, house of
> Israel? By my life--word of the Lord Yahweh--I shall not be
> inquired of by you!

As the final verse suggests, the passages are in the context of the coming of the elders of the people already in exile to Ezekiel, in order to
inquire of (drš) Yahweh, just as we have seen Deuteronomy demands. Yahweh responds (through the prophet) with an extended review of Israel's
history, climaxing with accusations of the Deuteronomic "parade abomination" (tô'ăbōt, v. 4) of child sacrifice, both in the historical survey
(v. 26, preceding the formula in v. 27) and with regard to the contemporary "house of Israel" (v. 31). For past and present crimes--above all,
child sacrifice--Yahweh refuses to be inquired of: the prophet is only

---

[730] It is also possible that the authors are dependent on some form of
the Deuteronomic History, including 2 Kgs 17:17; note the designation of child sacrifices as tô'ăbōtêhen, "their abominations" (v.
36).

to deliver messages from Yahweh to the people, not vice versa.[731]

Again, the use of terms such as h'byr and b'š leaves little doubt that the accusations are of the practice of the Molek cult. But three important questions remain. First, whatever does the prophet mean by saying in Yahweh's name that Yahweh had given "statutes not good" and "ordinances by which they could not live"? Secondly, what are we to make of v. 26, which appears to link the "Law of the Firstborn" (4.3.2) with the cult of Molek after all? Thirdly, do vv. 30-31 mean that the cult of Molek was practiced in Mesopotamia by the exiles? We shall take up these questions seriatim.

The first question has, understandably, provoked much discussion. Within chapter 20, v. 25 is obviously set in contradistinction to v. 11 ("I gave them my statutes, and my ordinances I made known to them, in which, if a man does them, there is life") and the periodic repetition of that positive valuation in vv. 13 and 21. Evidently, it is the prophet's view that after sufficient rebellion and profanation, the good laws, which were the way of life, were succeeded by not-good laws, which were the way of not-life. But "were succeeded" conceals the agent: Ezekiel explicitly states that Yahweh gave both sets of laws. To be sure, the notion of a "demonic" side to Yahweh is not an innovation, either within Ezekiel, or within the Bible (Ezek 3:20; 14:9; cf. the "hardening of hearts" in Exod 7:3; 10:1; Isa 63:17; also 2 Sam 24:1; 1 Kgs 22:20-23; Isa 6:9-10).[732] Nevertheless, Zimmerli rightly states: "Even

---

[731] See further on this theme, Robert R. Wilson, "An Interpretation of Ezekiel's Dumbness," VT 22 (1972) 91-104.

[732] A somewhat outdated, but interesting discussion from an older "history of religions" perspective is Paul Volz, Das Dämonische in Jahwe (Tübingen: J. C. B. Mohr, 1924).

so the statement that Yahweh makes his law . . . the occasion of punishment is unique in the Old Testament."[733] What we appear to have in v. 25
is Ezekiel's peculiar combination of a Deuteronomic understanding of
history (past sins accounting for present disaster/punishment) with a
priestly emphasis on the crucial role of the giving of the Mosaic law
(especially sacrificial law: "gifts," v. 26) for Israel's subsequent
history.[734]

What is more significant for our present concerns is the second
question, which has to do with the specimen of not-good laws by which
Yahweh sought to "defile" his rebellious people. As Mosca observes, v.
26 need not necessarily have to do with the Molek cult at all, since it
uses only terms known from the "Law of the Firstborn" (hʿbyr, kl-pṭr
rḥm).[735] However, it is hard to see how v. 26 can be divorced from the
reference to child sacrifice in v. 31, which includes bʾš, a code word
for the Molek cult. In the end, Mosca suspects a conflation, and proposes that whether or not v. 26 originally had to do with the Molek
cult, it "still bears witness to the fact that the Exilic or post-Exilic
community retained some memory of children having once been offered to
Yahweh" (p. 233). There is no reason, however, to posit such distance
between this verse and the prophet or the actual practice of the
cult.[736] While I agree with Mosca that a "conflation" of sorts is pres-

---

[733] Ezekiel 1, 411.

[734] So Wilson, *Prophecy and Society*, 284. The passage also emphasizes
Ezekiel's absolutely monotheistic view of Yahweh as omnipotent (cf.
Isa 45:7).

[735] "Child Sacrifice," 232.

[736] Zimmerli considers the core of the chapter to be vv. 2-26 and 30-31
(less the reference to child sacrifice in 31; see below) and notes

ent, a more satisfactory explanation, I believe, is to see in v. 26 Ezekiel's counterpart to Jeremiah's insistence that child sacrifice was
something "which I did not command, nor did it enter into my mind"
(7:31; 19:5; 32:35). Both prophets' remarks are in response to the people's claim that Yahweh had, indeed, legislated child sacrifice, which
they were offering him in the cult of Molek. Jeremiah does not give the
people's basis for this claim, but he responds to it with a flat denial.
Ezekiel, on the other hand, tells us that the people were applying (or
misapplying; cf. 4.3.2) the most closely applicable law, the "Law of the
Firstborn" in Exodus.[737] Then, in a baroque twist worthy of the prophet,
Ezekiel turns the theological tables on the practitioners: very well,
Yahweh did give the law they were citing, but it was given so that obedience would not bring life, but would "devastate" them.[738] If Israel
would not obey God's good laws for life, they would obey his bad laws
for death, but they would obey.[739]

---

that the original prophecy was delivered in 591 B.C. (*Ezekiel 1*,
404-406).

[737] On the basis of the use of p̱t̲r r̲ḥm, rather than b̲kw̲r, one suspects
that they were citing Exod 34:19 (and treating the redemption provision in v. 20 as permissive, as with an ass, not directive), rather
than 22:28, the verse usually cited by commentators, but one cannot
be sure. It is also possible that the cult's practitioners were
citing a law which does not appear in the final canon, as seems to
be the case in Jer 26:11, where the prophet is hailed before the
court for "prophesying against the city" (cf. Exod 22:27) (as suggested by my advisor, R. Wilson). That Ezekiel did not believe any
more than Jeremiah that Yahweh had really commanded child sacrifice
seems clear enough from chapter 16.

[738] Or "desolate," with Moshe Greenberg (*Ezekiel 1-20* [AB 22; Garden
City, NY: Doubleday, 1983] 369), but not "horrify" (so most others), as if Yahweh meant thereby to work repentance.

[739] The resemblance of God's giving "laws not good" to his hardening the
heart of Pharaoh may have one additional, theological ramification.
The prophet may be recalling not merely the "Law of the Firstborn,"

Thirdly, there is the matter of the verse which is of the greatest
potential value in the chapter, as we seek to reconstruct the history of
the Molek cult, especially in the sixth century. While it is difficult
to place exactly on the time line of Israel's history the accusations in
much of the chapter, vv. 30-31 are explicitly addressed to Ezekiel's
contemporaries, and it is above all the practice of child sacrifice by
fire on which Yahweh grounds his refusal to be inquired of, as the elders sought in v. 2.[740] Is Ezekiel, then, accusing his fellow exiles of
child sacrifice? This apparent implication (and its unlikelihood) has
led several commentators to reject the words, "when you make your sons
to pass over by the fire," in v. 31 as a late, "clumsy" (so Zimmerli)
addition, imitating v. 26.[741] This suggestion overlooks the absence in

---

but the reason which one level of the tradition gave for Yahweh's
claim on the firstborn: his slaying the firstborn of Egypt (Exod
13:15). Specifically, the P writer in Exodus warned his countrymen
against disobedience by using the phrase "did not listen" of both
Pharaoh and the Israelites in the course of the plague narrative
(7:13 and 6:9, respectively), and then by showing what happens to
one who does not listen: God hardens his heart (7:2) and sends
plagues (on this point, see R. R. Wilson, "The Hardening of Pharaoh's Heart," CBQ 41 [1979] 31-32). The priest Ezekiel may be drawing out the conclusions of this tradition for his rebellious contemporaries: God has hardened their hearts (by giving "laws not good")
and now, climactically, is responsible for slaying their firstborn,
only by their own hands!

[740] An initial attempt to schematize Ezekiel's overview of the history
of Israel would appear to place vv. 25-26 in the wilderness period
(vv. 18,28). (If so, Ezekiel may be identifying the "bad laws"
which were given after the good ones were violated with the second
giving of the law after the golden calf incident, as recorded in Exodus 34, including v. 19!) However, there is no evidence that child
sacrifice was practiced in the wilderness, or, for that matter, that
Israel was threatened with exile from the land before they possessed
it (v. 23). Obviously, the prophet has retrojected both, in keeping
with his theme that Israel has been rebellious from the outset (indeed, already in Egypt, v. 8), rather than becoming so only in the
land (cf. Hosea, Jeremiah). In fact, as we have argued, v. 26 suggests recent, if not contemporary, activity.

Ezekiel of the sharp distinction between the exiles of 597 and those left behind (cf. Jeremiah 24); rather, Ezekiel's attention constantly alternates between Palestine and Mesopotamia, and "house of Israel" includes the Israelites in both places. May we, then, conclude that Ezekiel knew of an openly-practiced cult of Molek in Jerusalem, presumably in the Tophet? The "allegorical histories" of chapters 16 and 23 are inconclusive since both are even harder to schematize than chapter 20, and neither alludes to anything like the reform of Josiah. Chapter 20, however, especially v. 31 ("to this day"), appears to support an affirmative conclusion, particularly given the evidence of Jeremiah in favor of the practice of the cult after Josiah.[742]

One last historical issue may be mentioned. Many scholars have taken the sequence of verbs in Ezek 16:21 ("slew . . . gave by making to pass over") as an indication that the victims were first killed, then burned.[743] While both the use of the consecutive, narrative tense and the analogy of animal sacrifice (and of Genesis 22) argue in favor of this conclusion, this one verse is too little evidence for one to be apodictic. Our best hope in this connection is from the analogy of the

---

[741] Ezekiel 1, 412. Cf. K. W. Carley, The Book of the Prophet Ezekiel (Cambridge, NEB; Cambridge: University, 1974) 133; W. Eichrodt, Ezekiel (OTL; Philadelphia: Westminster, 1970) 274.

[742] Pace Mosca ("Child Sacrifice," 233), who regards "to this day" as "prophetic exaggeration," and argues: "It seems most improbable that the Topheth was rebuilt after its destruction by Josiah. . . ." He is likely closer to the mark, when he continues, "or that the mōlek once outlawed, was ever again countenanced in orthodox prophetic or priestly circles" (although one suspects that arguments over whose views were orthodox continued right up until one side was vindicated in 587/6!).

[743] So, for example, G. A. Cooke, The Book of Ezekiel (ICC; Edinburgh: T. & T. Clark, 1951) 169.

Punic archeological evidence, specifically, the osteological material from the "Save Carthage Campaign," now being analyzed by Jeffrey Schwartz (3.1).

4.5.8   The Cult of Molek after the Fall of Jerusalem

"He defiled the Tophet which is in the Valley of the Son(s) of Hinnom, so that no one might make his son or his daughter to pass over by the fire to Molek"--so wrote the Josianic editor of the Deuteronomic History of what he, no doubt, assumed was the end of the cult of Molek in Israel (or at least Jerusalem). But was the cult revived after Josiah? As we have seen, some of the strident condemnations by the prophets Jeremiah and Ezekiel might be explained as reflective of the pre-Josianic practice (e.g., Ezekiel 16/23), but others, and the sheer number of the references, suggest that the Tophet did not stay defiled for long. A more difficult (and controversial) question is whether the cult of Molek was practiced during or after the exile. In this section we shall treat the remaining references which most likely have an exilic or post-exilic date, in hopes of discovering whether or not they speak of a contemporary cult of child sacrifice.[744]

The first post-exilic passage to be treated is not from the prophetic corpus, but is rather the sole clear reference to cultic child sacrifice in the Writings (outside of Chronicles). Ps 106:37-38 reads in its context:

---

[744] At least in its Punic setting the cult of child sacrifice was a very long time dying off. Despite the best efforts of the Roman authorities to suppress it, Tertullian could write (ca. A.D. 197): "to this day that holy crime persists in secret." Thus, Mosca suggests that the Punic cult continued, at least in outlying areas, until sometime in the third century, A.D. ("Child Sacrifice," 20).

(34) They did not destroy the peoples as Yahweh had told them.
(35) They mixed with the nations and learned their practices.
(36) They served their idols, and they [idols] became a snare
       to them.
(37) They sacrificed their sons and their daughters to demons;
(38) They shed innocent blood--
       the blood of their sons and their daughters,
       whom they sacrificed to the idols of Canaan--
       and the land was polluted with the blood.
(39) They became defiled with their practices, and they went
       whoring by their deeds.

The psalm is a recital of Israel's rebellions, effectively in counter-
point to the recounting of Yahweh's saving acts in Psalm 105.[745] Verses
38-39 (regarding child sacrifice) are clearly intended to describe the
behavior of the people following the conquest/settlement (vv. 34-35),
without any hint of an intervening exile. Most attempts to date the
Psalm have, in fact, focused on vv. 46-47, which are usually taken to
imply an exilic or post-exilic date.[746] Thus, despite its likely exilic
or post-exilic date of composition, Psalm 106 does not bespeak a contemporary practice of cultic child sacrifice.

Nevertheless, the psalm may be of some interest to our study. The
Deuteronomic flavor of Psalm 106 has long been noted, and it is confirmed in the particular verses which are the focus of our attention.[747]

---

[745] See A. Weiser, The Psalms (trans. H. Hartwell; OTL; Philadelphia:
Westminster, 1962 [German orig., 1959] 679-680, for more on the implications of this juxtaposition.

[746] A handy chart of the dates proposed by various scholars is in S. I.
L. Norin, Er spaltete das Meer (Coniectanea Biblica, OT Series 9;
Lund: C. W. K. Gleerup, 1977) 121, n. 37. Weiser (Psalms, 680) insists that "vv. 46f. do not necessarily presuppose the Babylonian
exile," while Weiser (p. 679) and M. Dahood (Psalms III [AB 17A;
Garden City, NY: Doubleday, 1970] 67) note the apparent quotation
of the psalm in 1 Chr 16:35-36, so that an extremely late date
(e.g., Maccabean) is excluded.

[747] See H.-J. Kraus, Psalmen (4th ed.; BKAT 15/2; Neukirchen-Vluyn:
Neukirchener, 1972) 728, regarding the Deuteronomic connection.
Zimmerli (Ezekiel 1, 405) calls attention also to the resemblances

Just as we found in our study of Deut 12:31, cultic child sacrifice is presented as the "parade abomination" of the Canaanites, the one specimen of their "practices" (v. 35b) "learned" by the Israelites which the psalmist chooses to cite, in order to explain the subsequent political subjections of Israel. The view of the Deuteronomists, Jeremiah and Ezekiel that child sacrifice was really to Canaanite deities (all protests about their being to Yahweh to the contrary) is repeated by vv. 36-37. Indeed, depending on whether one is willing to date this psalm in the exile, and, if so, how early in the exile, it may be argued that Psalm 106 reinforces our suspicion, explicated in our reconstruction of the cult below (chap. V), that there was too little time for the switch in the meaning of Molek alleged by Eissfeldt and Mosca to have taken place. The latter point, however, cannot be pressed with regard to this passage, nor need it be, in view of the force of the other evidence.

The remaining references which we shall treat in this section are from the so-called "Third Isaiah": Isa 57:5,9 and 66:3. Like Psalm 106, there is much disagreement as to whether the verses are to be dated to the exile or after it.[748] But these verses cannot be ignored, because they contain at least two unmistakable references to cultic human sacrifice and one possible mention of Molek.

---

of this psalm to Ezekiel. Specifically, we may note, only Ps 106:37 and Ezek 16:20 use zbḥ in reference to child sacrifice.

[748] See Eissfeldt, OT Introduction, 341-346, for a summary of views on the dating and integrity of "Third Isaiah," and in particular p. 345 regarding proposed dates for 57:1-6, which range from before 587 to the fourth or third century B.C., and for 66:1-4, which vary from slightly before the first return of exiles in 538 to the later limits specified for 57:1-6.

The designation "human," rather than "child," in the preceding sentence is necessitated by the third verse listed above, Isa 66:3a. For the most part, the half-verse consists of paired participles, the first in each pair denoting an orthodox cultic practice and the second a forbidden act. Interpreters have wrestled with how to understand the interrelationship of the pithy phrases; Muilenburg's translation will make the problem clear:

> Who slaughters an ox, who kills a man,
> Who sacrifices a lamb, who breaks a dog's neck,
> Who presents a cereal offering, who offers swine's blood,
> Who makes a memorial offering, who blesses an idol.[749]

As Claus Westermann observes, the verse is less likely to be a radical condemnation of previously-acceptable cult practices ("A is as bad as B"), than a "polemic against a form of syncretism."[750] However, since the verse does not specify child sacrifice (to say nothing of the Molek cult), one cannot be sure that it is pertinent to our study. Nevertheless, the cultic context does show that human sacrifice (not murder) is being spoken of, and some of the other condemned acts suggest that the verse may be important to us, after all. As Muilenburg notes, at least one ancient historian connected Punic child sacrifice with cultic canine killing: "According to Justin (History of the World XIX.1.10), Darius forbade the Carthaginians to offer human victims in sacrifice or to eat the flesh of dogs."[751] In addition, Isa 65:4 explicitly links the con-

---

[749] "The Book of Isaiah: Chapters 40-66: Introduction and Exegesis," IB 5 (1956) 761.

[750] Isaiah 40-66 (trans. D. M. G. Stalker; OTL; Philadelphia: Westminster, 1969 [German orig., 1966]) 413-414.

[751] "Isaiah 40-66," 762.

sumption of pork with the practice of the cult of the dead.[752] ("Blesses
an idol" is too general to point to any specific practice.) In sum,
while the general character of the reference forbids its being pressed,
Isa 66:3 may well testify to the continued practice of the Molek cult in
Judah, either by those left behind in the Exile (given a pre-538 date)
or by the inhabitants of the land (whether returnees or not) in the
post-exilic period.[753]

There is no question that Isa 57:5 speaks of child sacrifice, although it employs a verb (šḥṭ) which is elsewhere used only by Ezekiel
(16:21; 23:39) in reference to the practice. The chief questions for
our purposes are whether the passage is alluding to the cult of Molek
and whether an exilic or post-exilic practice is in view. Mosca contends that the first question may be answered affirmatively since "the
clefts of the rocks" are reminiscent of the burials of the earliest Punic molk-victims in niches in the bedrock, while "the use of nḥlym, 'wadis,' is probably intended to call to mind the valley (gy') of Ben-
Hinnom, where the Topheth had been located. . . ."[754] While it is
possible that an allusion to the ill-famed Valley is present, it is far
more likely, I believe that both the plural "wadis" and the "clefts of
the rocks" (in parallel!) have to do with the hidden loci where the

---

[752] See further on this connection below (4.6) and especially R. de
Vaux, "Les Sacrifices de porcs en Palestine et dans l'Ancien Orient," Von Ugarit nach Qumran: Festschrift O. Eissfeldt (ed. J. Hempel and L. Rost; BZAW 77; Berlin: Töpelmann, 1958) 263-265.

[753] De Vaux's comment that "It is hardly likely that sacrifices 'to Moloch' continued so late" (Studies, 69, n. 68) is, of course, no argument.

[754] "Child Sacrifice," 234.

now-outlawed cult continued to flourish in secret.[755] That it was the
cult of Molek is confirmed by v. 9, which I would read:

> You journeyed to [or drenched yourself for][756] Molek [MT me-
> lek] with oil;
> You multiplied your ointments;
> You sent your messengers far away,
> You cast [them] down to Sheol.

While some have seen in lammelek a reference to a human monarch, the
cultic context of the chapter suggests that a deity's name or title is
present, and the explicit chthonic destination of the envoys argues
strongly for the original presence of Molek.[757] The identity of the
"messengers" should be obvious in this light: they are the cult's child
victims, mentioned in v. 5.[758] If this understanding is accepted, it

---

[755] In other words, the appropriate parallel is not with the earliest
Punic strata, but with the latest practice of the molk-cult, when
the Romans sought to suppress it. Cf. Jonas C. Greenfield's comment
concerning s'py hsl'ym in this verse: "these are clefts in the rock
in which a person can hide out or carry out a foul act rather than
overhanging cliffs" ("The Prepositions B.....Taḥat.....in Jes 57:5,"
ZAW 73 [1961] 228, n. 13). See Pope, Song of Songs, 580-581, for
arguments favoring the identification of "wadis" with Qidron-Hinnom
and for an exposition of the fertility-cult overtones in Isa
57:3-10. Pope has suggested to me privately that the "clefts of the
rocks" are the family tombs cut in the rocks (cf. discussion of Isa
65:4 below [4.6]). This fits what we know of the Molek cult quite
well, although it is incapable of demonstration.

[756] See John J. Scullion, "Some Difficult Texts in Isaiah cc. 56-66 in
the Light of Modern Scholarship," UF 4 (1972) 113, for a summary of
the philological discussion of the rare tāšuri and references.
While the bracketed translation suits the parallelism better, either
rendering makes sense in the context of the whole verse. (See also
P. Wernberg-Moller, "Two Notes," ZAW 8 [1958] 307-308, for the
translation, "You lavish oil on Melek. . . .")

[757] Mosca translates, "You journeyed to the mōlek with oil" (p. 233),
but does not explain how one "journeys to" a sacrifice (and with
oil, yet another offering).

[758] As Mosca rightly notes (p. 234). Our understanding of Molek obviates the need, however, to see in the verse a polemical move such as
he claims is present: "The 'envoys' . . . would be the children,
the victims who never reach the idols for whom they are intended;

will aid us greatly in our subsequent attempts to explain how the victims functioned in the necromantic transaction which the practitioners
sought to accomplish through the Molek cult's sacrifices.[759]

But do these verses point to the post-exilic existence of the cult
of Molek? Mosca claims that "the stereotyped nature of the other charges in Isa. 57:3-13" suggests that the prophet "is simply selecting from
the now standard repertoire of pre-Exilic sins" (p. 234). While there
are, indeed, certain resemblances with pre-exilic oracles, it seems to
me more likely that the prophet is employing their language from time to
time to condemn those contemporary practices which, in his view, brought
down the wrath of Yahweh in the first place.[760] This is supported by the
usage of the favorite Deuteronomic expression, "under every green tree":
Isa 57:5 witnesses to a breakdown of the D usage, which always (save
once) accompanies the phrase with some form of "on every high hill."[761]

---

instead, the offerers succeed only in sending their own children
down 'to Sheol.'" No doubt, the prophet would have agreed (cf. v.
13), but there is no sign of such a disjunction within v. 9 and no
need, given our interpretation, for such a refined intention.

[759] Still another indication of the chthonic context of Isaiah 57 is in
v. 13: "let your qibbûṣ-es save you." While qibbûṣ is a hapax in
the OT, it recalls the nuptial blessing of Keret, discussed above
(2.3.3), in which Keret is blessed btk.rpi.arṣ / bpḫr.qbṣ.dtn ("in
the midst of the Rephaim of 'earth' / among the assembly of the
gathering of Ditanu") (CTA 15.3:3-4, 14-15). Pope is correct, I believe, in seeing in both occurrences a collective reference to one's
ancestors (private communication).

[760] Westermann (Isaiah 40-66, 325) agrees, although he puts the matter
as follows: "When the exile was over, the pre-exilic prophets' oracles of doom [including 56:9-57:13] were given a fresh significance
for the present. The charges were made to refer to the conduct of
the transgressors, the 'godless', from whom the devout or righteous
were increasingly obligated to sever themselves."

[761] So Deut 12:2; 1 Kgs 14:23; 2 Kgs 16:4 (= 2 Chr 28:4); 17:10; Jer
2:20; 3:6; Ezek 6:13. The one exception is Jer 3:13.

Furthermore, we have seen that v. 5 is most naturally understood as referring to the practice of cultic child sacrifice away from the publically-visible Tophet in the Valley immediately outside Jerusalem (which is never called a "wadi" [naḥal]). On the other hand, the dating of all of Isaiah 56-66 remains in dispute (as noted above), so that we cannot be dogmatic.

In sum, the exilic/post-exilic references to the cult of Molek are few and much-debated. The cult had certainly lost any licit status which it ever possessed by the time of the exile, so that further practice of the cult was likely quite secretive. Persian support for the religious law of the Jews (cf. Ezra 7:26), which by the time of the Return must have assumed much of the shape of the canonical Pentateuch, almost guarantees that the Tophet was not restored to its pre-exilic function. Nevertheless, the verses examined in this section have suggested that what one suspects to have been the case did, in fact, happen: the "old-time religion" of Molek continued, albeit in the "clefts of the rocks in the wadis," before slowly fading away.

We might now move immediately to sum up our findings in the form of a reconstruction of the history and function of the cult of Molek in ancient Israel. We shall essay that task below, in chapter V. First, however, we shall attempt to flesh out the relatively meager information which the Bible directly contributes concerning Molek with a brief investigation of what, we believe, this study has shown to be the most promising source of additional light on the subject (besides any future, dramatic archeological finds): the testimony of the Bible to the practice of a cult of the dead in Israel. Such an investigation will not merely add depth to the Biblical Molek references, but will also further demonstrate the importance of the extra-Biblical material examined in chapter II and will link the relevant Biblical and extra-Biblical material all the more closely.

4.6   THE CULT OF MOLEK AND THE CULT OF THE DEAD

The preceding portion of the chapter has dealt with all of the Biblical references which have to do directly with the cult of Molek. Yet, as we have repeatedly observed, both the extra-Biblical and Biblical evidence suggests that the cult is to be considered within the Israelite practice of the "cult of the dead." In this final section we intend to define more precisely what that term entails in this study and to examine selected texts and topics which may further illuminate the cult of Molek, albeit indirectly. Therefore, the following discussion is necessarily more cursory and more speculative than that which has preceded. Nevertheless, it is necessary, if we hope to advance the study of the Molek issue through this investigation and, specifically, if we hope to propose a defensible answer to what we called above the "ultimate question": Why did the parents do it?

The cult of the dead in ancient Israel has itself been the subject of longstanding and intensive study.[762] In his 1973 thesis John W. Ribar outlines the history of scholarship since the mid-nineteenth century, including figures such as Edward Tylor, Herbert Spencer, Julius Lippert,

---

[762] Thus, the following treatment can in no way hope to be comprehensive. In particular, sociological and anthropological aspects have had to be neglected. For a brief overview of the competing theories and bibliography, see L. Y. Rahmani, "Ancient Jerusalem's Funerary Customs and Tombs: Part One," *BA* 44 (1981) 171-177.

Bernhard Stade, Friedrich Schwally, Adolphe Lods, and, most recently, W. F. Albright.[763] He notes that the early scholars often assumed, on the basis of comparative anthropological evidence, that a cult of the dead flourished in Israel, while many more recent writers have rejected such claims as unsubstantiated by sufficient Biblical data. Indeed, he argues, the subject was moribund until Albright revived it with his proposal, based on Palestinian archeological, as well as comparative evidence, that the Israelite bāmāh was "primarily, though not exclusively, a mortuary shrine" (p. 7).[764]

Two obstacles prevent our moving immediately to passages of interest to our study. First, considerable scholarly objection remains to the thesis that a cult of the dead was practiced in Palestine, even by the Canaanites. W. Boyd Barrick has mounted a forceful challenge to Albright's understanding of bāmāh, while Robert E. Cooley has concluded on the basis of his examination of MB-LB tombs that "cultic practices were

---

[763] "Death Cult Practices," 4-8. A particularly rich, older study of which Ribar was apparently unaware is Lewis B. Paton, Spiritism and the Cult of the Dead in Antiquity (NY: Macmillan, 1921).

[764] Ribar's own study raises questions about Albright's methodology and interpretation of data, but its aim concurs with Albright's conclusion: Ribar attempts to show, using the results of excavations of Palestinian tombs, that "we can make [a] fairly sound case for one component of a 'cult of the dead,' viz., offerings for the dead on a repeated basis" (pp. 2-3). Ribar's chief data are "holes cut in the ceilings or walls of burial tombs and caves [which] may well have provided for the introduction of offerings for the dead within on a repeated basis after the initial interment," as well as evidence for variant forms of such access structures (pp. 45-46). He also cites as corroborative evidence for the existence of the cult of the dead the following Bible passages: Isa 57:6 (cf. 4.5.8); Deut 26:14; and Ps 106:28 (see below). He concludes by suggesting that the custom of kispum-like food offerings for the dead may have been brought with those who migrated to Palestine from Mesopotamia and North Syria in the MB period, and by noting that the practice seems to have disappeared during the Iron I period in Israel.

not a part of the activity for the dead.[765] Secondly, as Ribar has also recognized, arguments over the existence and meaning of a "cult of the dead" in Israel can all-too-easily descend into logomachy; a working definition is needed.

The second obstacle is the more easily surmounted. While we have somewhat glibly referred to the "care and feeding of the ancestors" above, a more adequate statement is now needed. First, we must make clear that, as used in this study, "the cult of the dead" is not restricted to the relatively short-term requirements of burial and attendant practices which follow immediately upon a death (i.e., the "rites of passage"). A "cult of the dead" is established in response to the belief that the dead have a continuing claim upon the living, either because of the deplorable state of the dead without care, or because the dead are perceived as having some power to influence events in the world of the living, for good or ill (or out of both piety and fear). However, as Ribar observes, "rationales for death cult activities and the beliefs connected with them are variable and are not necessarily to be regarded as constituative elements."[766] We therefore join him in defining a "cult of the dead" according to the following "formal criteria": "activities (especially offerings) which (1) are oriented toward the dead, (2) periodically conducted, [and] (3) at sites specially associat-

---

[765] Barrick, "The Funerary Character of 'High Places' in Ancient Palestine: A Reassessment," VT 25 (1975) 565-595; Cooley, "Gathered to His People," 54. Cooley's views are more fully presented in "The Contribution of Literary Sources to a Study of the Canaanite Burial Pattern" (unpublished Ph.D. dissertation, New York University, 1968).

[766] "Death Cult Practices," 9-10.

ed with the dead."[767]

That some activity within the limits of our definition went on in
Biblical Israel seems clear enough from the passages cited by Ribar (see
note above), as well as Deut 14:1 and 18:11 (see 4.3.3); Isa 8:19-22
(4.5.4; cf. the other occurrences of 'ōbôt and yiddə'ōnîm discussed in
4.3.1) and 65:4 (below; cf. also Isa 66:17); and, especially, 1 Sam
28:8-25 (4.3.1). Indeed, given the cultural context, it would be star-
tling if Israel did not have a cult of the dead in some form. Miranda
Bayliss has sketched the cult in its Mesopotamian dress, while, within
Syria-Palestine, Marvin Pope has explored the Ugaritic version.[768] In
both areas, both archeological and literary evidence support the existence of the cult. Of course, one must always be sensitive to the possibility that Israel went its own way at a given point. We are, therefore, much indebted to H. C. Brichto for his thorough study, which shows
conclusively, I believe, that traces of a belief in the ancestors' afterlife and of a felt necessity to provide for their needs are pervasive
in the Scriptural record.[769]

What, then, of the aforementioned scholarly reservations concerning
the existence of the cult? G. E. Wright, for instance, asserts with
reference to Deut 26:14: "This scarcely has reference to the offering
of sacrifice to the spirits of the dead, as some have attempted to af-

---

[767] Ibid., 10.

[768] Bayliss, "The Cult of Dead Kin in Assyria and Babylonia," Iraq 35
(1973) 115-125; Pope, "The Cult of the Dead at Ugarit." See now
also P. Matthiae's claim to have found evidence of a royal cult of
the dead at Ebla: "A Hypothesis on the Princely Burial Area of Middle Bronze II Ebla," ArOr 49 (1981) 61-62.

[769] "Kin, Cult, Land and Afterlife--A Biblical Complex," HUCA 44 (1973)
1-55.

firm, because such a custom simply did not exist in Israel."[770] Part of the problem may be semantic: "to" in Wright's "to the spirits" could mean "for the benefit of," as well as "in worship of." Note in particular that our definition above does not require that the dead be worshipped (although they may be), only provided for.[771] Furthermore, the presence of a cult of the dead "at sites specially associated with the dead" is not refuted by the aforementioned criticisms by Barrick and Ribar of Albright's theory concerning the funerary function of the bāmāh. Barrick effectively faults Albright for improperly schematizing his archeological data and for unnecessary, pro causa emendation of the Biblical text, while Ribar stresses that Albright failed to demonstrate the funerary connection of his Palestinian archeological evidence, although that connection was clear enough in his comparative data. In short, while bāmāh, it seems, was not necessarily associated with the cult of the dead, neither scholar suggests that the cult of the dead could not be observed at whatever sort of installation a "bāmāh" actually was. Thus, while bāmôt in Jer 7:31; 19:5; and 32:35 cannot be used as one more indication of the chthonic connection of the Molek cult, neither is their presence in these verses improper, or an indication to the contrary.[772]

---

[770] "The Book of Deuteronomy: Introduction and Exegesis," IB 2 (1953) 487. De Vaux also objects to the hypothesis of a cult of the dead in Israel, on the grounds that "acts of worship directed toward the dead . . . never existed in Israel" (Ancient Israel, 1.60).

[771] More to the point, perhaps, the traditional Roman Catholic distinction between latreia (worship of God) and douleia (veneration of the saints) may be relevant here (only by analogy, of course): however much popular piety may tend to blur the line between them, a distinction is possible.

[772] The same may be said regarding maṣṣēbāh in such verses as 2 Sam

Whatever the whole truth may be about the nature of the Israelite cult of the dead, there is, as noted, sufficient support for its exis- tence in some form to permit us to turn now to specific evidence which may be of value in our larger investigation. We may begin with two of the verses cited above, both of which are closely associated with pas- sages treated earlier in this chapter: Ps 106:28 (cf. Ps 106:37-38) and Isa 65:4 (cf. Isa 57:5,9 and 66:3). Both are, as we have seen, probably of exilic or post-exilic date. The former reads:

> They yoked themselves to the Baal of Peor;
> They ate [the] sacrifices of [the] dead.

As we saw in our examination of vv. 37-38, this psalm is a confessional catalog of Israel's past sins. This time, however, there is no doubt as to the historical referent: it is the apostasy of the Israelites at Shittim with the Moabites, recorded in Numbers 25. The crucial point for our purposes is the correspondence between zibḥê 'ĕlōhêhen in Num 25:2 and zibḥê mētîm in Ps 106:28. Commentators have often interpreted the latter by the former, arguing that the author of the psalm is stig- matizing the Moabites' gods as "dead." However, as Dahood notes, "No biblical text calls the gods mētîm, 'the dead,' but II Sam xxviii 13 and Isa viii 19 use the term 'ĕlōhîm, 'gods,' to describe the deceased."[773] The question is, how to understand the construct chain in both cases. Since the dead were neither sacrificed nor sacrificers, some sense like that of the RSV, "sacrifices offered to [or for] the dead," seems pref- erable, and, indeed, there are other indications in Numbers 25 that the

_____

18:18.

[773] Psalms III, 74.

Israelites joined the Moabites in a marzēaḥ, or funeral feast.[774] The value of this verse for our purposes is to show that from earliest times, Israel was familiar with and at least periodically shared in the funeral feasts known to us also from our investigation of the Mari and Ugaritic evidence in chapter II. While we cannot assume that the feasts were always and everywhere identical, the close association of the Israelite cult of Molek with other facets of the cult of the dead, such as necromancy, suggests that we look closely for further Scriptural references to the cult of the dead which may shed light on our topic.

While marzēaḥ occurs in the MT only in Amos 6:7 and Jer 16:5, and neither of these verses is particularly helpful to us, the second verse listed above (Isa 65:4) also clearly has to do with a meal shared in the context of the cult of the dead, and it is of interest. Somewhat like Isa 66:3 (4.5.8), Isa 65:3-5a contains a series of participles, in this case all in apposition to hā‘ām, "the people." Verse 4 reads:

> Who sit in the tombs, /
> And in secret places pass the night; //
> Who eat swine's flesh, /
> And broth [so Q; K = fragment] of unclean things is [in] their
> vessels.

The activities are clearly those of a cult of the dead, including spending the night in the rock-cut tombs, presumably equivalent to the "secret places," and consuming ritual meals there.[775] The first bicolon is

---

[774] So already *Sipre Numbers* 131. See Pope, *Song of Songs*, 217-218, for further explanation and exposition. Anderson and Freedman (*Hosea*, 632) offer an entirely different understanding, revocalizing Ps 106:28 to zibḥê mētim, "human sacrifices," parallel to zibḥê ’ādām in Hos 13:2 (4.5.2). However, they do not take note of the more logical parallel in Num 25:2 and simply reject both "sacrifices to the dead" and "sacrifices for the sake of the dead" without explanation.

[775] Other activities, as shown by v. 3, were "sacrificing in the gar-

usually taken to refer to the practice of incubation, sleeping in a sacred place in hopes of receiving a special revelation through a dream
(so already the LXX: di' enupnia). This is a reasonable guess, although neither colon mentions "sleep" as such.[776] The first bicolon does
suggest, however, that both halves of the second are functionally synonymous. De Vaux has studied the evidence regarding the ritual use of
pork in the ancient world and has concluded: "Le porc est considéré
comme un animal 'chtonien', que sa nature destine à être offert aux di-
vinités infernales . . . le cochon est réservé pour des rites plus ou
moins secrets qui s'accomplissent rarement. . . ."[777] Thus, the Israelite law had much more in mind than hygiene when it forbade the eating of
pork; it was condemning in particular participation in the Canaanite
cult of the dead. The verse at hand demonstrates that the law was not
universally observed, even as late as the exilic/post-exilic period.
The "unclean things" of the final colon are usually taken not as meat
unclean in se (like pork), but as that which has become unclean by remaining uneaten until the third day after sacrifice (cf. Lev 7:18;

---

dens" and "burning incense upon the bricks." The former activity
could conceivably be an oblique reference to the cult of Molek, giv-
en Gray's proposal on the "Garden of the King" (4.5.6), although, as
we have said, it is doubtful that the Tophet was used for child sacrifice after the fall of the city. The latter practice could refer
to the cult of the host of heaven (cf. Weinfeld, "The Worship of Molech," 153), although that was usually practiced on rooftops (so
that some have emended "gardens," gannôt, to "rooftops," gaggôt).

[776] For a study of the interrelationship of dreams and shades with the
cult of the dead, see Friedrich Schmidtke, "Träume, Orakel und Totengeister als Künder der Zukunft in Israel und Babylonien," BZ n.s.
11 (1967) 240-246. Note that, however one understands the activity
in this bicolon, it does point to the practice of the cult of the
dead at night, as we stressed vis-à-vis Mosca in the discussion of
Isa 30:33 above (4.5.4).

[777] "Les sacrifices de porcs," 261.

19:7). Kennedy, in his article on the Pozo Moro tower, has suggested that the meat in the broth mentioned in the verse at hand may have been further contaminated by being consumed at funeral feasts, since the corresponding Greek and Roman meals were held on the third day after a death. In sum, he argues: "The backsliding Israelites are compounding their crimes against God by eating proscribed meat at a forbidden time, a doubly damning repast."[778]

It is evident, then, that the cult of the dead, including the funeral feast, was known and practiced by Israel before the conquest/settlement, after the Return (or at least in the exilic period) and, on the basis of passages already examined (such as 1 Samuel 28 and Isa 8:19-22), also during the pre-monarchical and monarchical periods. Furthermore, we have seen that that practice is roundly condemned in the Deuteronomic and the exilic/post-exilic literature.[779] We have repeatedly seen that the cult of Molek is linked to the cult of the dead. Yet the connection of the former with concepts or practices attached to the latter (other than necromancy) remains vague. Are further ties indicat-

---

[778] "Tartessos, Tarshish and Tartarus," 13. This reading is, in my view, preferable to that for which Kennedy eventually opts, in view of the Pozo Moro scene (2.7), that the "broth of abominable things" may have been made of sacrificed children's flesh. While such an explanation would solve many problems regarding the role of child sacrifice in the Molek cult, we have argued above (4.5.7) that the mythological text from Ugarit cited by Pope, and now the mythological scene from Pozo Moro, do not constitute sufficient evidence that the victims were "consumed" by anyone except the divine recipient.

[779] See, however, Brichto ("Kin, Cult, Land," 28-29) for the argument that all Scripture prohibited participation in the cult of the dead "in connection with foreign families and their ancestral cults," but sanctioned (not prescribed) it with regard to the Israelites' own ancestors. He may have a point, as we shall argue in the final chapter, with regard to the views of the pre-exilic Jerusalemite "establishment."

ed by the Biblical or extra-Biblical evidence?

The important role of the funeral feast in the cults of the dead at Mari, Ugarit and, as we now see, Israel, suggests that we look first for any indication that an equivalent of the malikū, the "guests" at the feasts held at the first two places, were also known in Israel. While we face, once again, the difficulty of sorting out occurrences of a form of mlk, there are two attestations of the plural of melek which are suggestive of an OT equivalent of the malikū. The first is in the so-called "Isaiah Apocalypse," Isa 24:21: "And on that day Yahweh will punish the host of heaven [lit.: "height"] in heaven and the kings of the earth upon earth."[780] Since this "host" is supernatural and, as we have seen, the recipients of illegitimate worship, it makes sense to suppose that the parallel malkê are the same. The case for an equivalent of the malikū might well be considered established, if the following nomen rectum were hā'āreṣ, which has repeatedly been shown to include the sense, "underworld." However, the following word is hā'ădāmāh. It is possible that in such (probably) late literature as this, the latter word for "earth" has taken over the entire semantic range of the former, but lacking concrete evidence, one is thrown back on the parallelism alone, so that the understanding of this verse must remain open.

The second candidate is much stronger, Ezek 43:7b,9:

> (7b) But the house of Israel shall not defile my holy name again, neither they, nor their kings, by their harlotry and by the stelae [trad.: "corpses"] of their kings [in] their bāmôt.

---

[780] As Kaiser shows, mārôm, "height," is "a favorite paraphrase in apocalyptic writing for heaven" (Isaiah 13-39, 194).

(9) Now they shall/let them send away their harlotry and the
stelae of their kings far from me, and [then] I shall dwell in
their midst forever.

While it is possible to read mlkm as "kings" in all three occurrences
here, the presence of pigrê suggests that a different (or additional)
sense may be intended. David Nieman first saw that there were instances
where the usual rendering of peger as "corpse" (cf. Akkadian pagru) did
not make sense, e.g., Lev 26:30 ("the pigrê of your idols"). On the basis of the Ugaritic usage of pgr (as equivalent to skn), he suggested
"stela" as the meaning in Lev 26:30 and the two verses at hand.[781] Since
then, Kurt Galling has proposed the modification that peger refers to
stelae erected in memory of one deceased, not in idolatrous worship.[782]
As we have seen repeatedly, the association of stelae with the cult of
the dead is well-established, and we may well suspect, given the evidence from Mari and Ugarit, that the mlkm associated with such stelae
were the (perhaps royal) ancestors feted in the funeral feasts. There
is, however, another option for the rendering of pgr in Ugaritic and Hebrew: a pagru-offering, similar to that in Akkadian, especially that
associated by Talon (2.2.3) with Dagan, Mari's bēl pagrê.[783] If this is
the correct interpretation, the link with the malikū is even closer:
Ezekiel would be stressing the mutual exclusivity of the practice of the
(royal?) cult of the dead ("pagru-offerings to/for your malikū") and

---

[781] "PGR: A Canaanite Cult-Object in the Old Testament," *JBL* 67 (1948)
55-60.

[782] "Erwägungen zum Stelenheiligtum von Hazor," *ZDPV* 75 (1959) 11.

[783] See Jürgen H. Ebach, "PGR = (Toten-)Opfer? Ein Vorschlag zum Ver-
ständnis von Ez. 43,7.9," *UF* 3 (1971) 365-368. This understanding
has been accepted by Dietrich, Loretz and Sanmartín ("PGR im Ugaritischen," *UF* 5 [1973] 289-291) and by Dijkstra and de Moor
("Problematical Passages in the Legend of Aqhâtu," *UF* 7 [1975] 175).

Yahweh's presence in Jerusalem.[784] In either case, some understanding of melākîm as other than (or in addition to) the present-future (v. 7bα) or past (vv. 7bß,9) kings of Israel is further supported by the fact that these are the only occurrences of melek in Ezekiel 40-48; otherwise, the vision is of a land ruled (under God) by a nāśi', "prince." In sum, while the attestations are precious few, there are at least two passages in which the OT may testify to a belief in chthonic beings, commemorated in the cult of the dead, who bore a designation cognate with that of the malikū of Ugarit and Mari.[785]

Such slim evidence would scarcely be worth pursuing were it not for the considerably richer store of Biblical references to the beings who our study of the Ugaritic material indicated were closely associated with or identical to the malikū: the Rephaim. As has often been noted, the Biblical attestations of "Rephaim" fall into two general categories: some, particularly in Deuteronomy and Joshua, appear to reflect an ethnic usage for pre-Israelite inhabitants of Palestine (or for one group

---

[784] As Zimmerli stresses, 43:7a reflects the expansion of Yahweh's "throne" and "footstool" from the ark (or temple) to all of Jerusalem (cf. 48:35) (Ezekiel 2, 415). Thus, the argument over whether the last word in v. 7 should be vocalized bāmôtām, "their high places" (so Albright), or bəmôtām, "at their deaths" (so Zimmerli et al.), cannot be settled on the grounds that only the temple is under discussion, where the presence of "high places" would be unlikely. Although the reading remains uncertain (and may even represent a dittography with the following bətittām), the MT makes sense and, if our understanding of mlkm in these verses is correct, may be a reference to the bāmôt in the Valley Hinnom, spoken of by Jeremiah (7:31; 19:5; 32:35).

[785] Abraham Malamat raises the possibility of a specifically royal Israelite cult of the dead, with ceremonies similar to the Akkadian kispu, in a footnote at the end of an article on OB and OT genealogies ("King Lists of the Old Babylonian Period and Biblical Genealogies," JAOS 88 [1968] 173, n. 29). He adduces 1 Sam 20:5,18ff. and 1 Sam 20:6,29 as suggestive of such a practice on the part of Saul and David, respectively.

among them [Gen 15:20]); others, especially in Isaiah and the Writings,
clearly mean the dead in general (Prov 9:18) or the royal dead (Isa
14:9).[786] At first glance, based on this distribution, it might appear
logical to posit a development from the former to the latter sense. We
have already seen, however, that the actual situation is a far more complex one: while scholars of Ugaritic have similar (and not unrelated)
disputes over the core sense(s) of Ugaritic Rpum, we found that at least
some (or even, as we are inclined to believe, all) of the references to
the Rpum have to do with the shades (2.3.3). While we can no more attempt a definitive treatment in this study of the Biblical Rephaim than
we could of their Ugaritic counterparts, we can explore specific matters
related to the Rephaim which our study to this point has led us to consider of special interest.

First, we may note the complex of names and concepts surrounding
the one specimen of the Rephaim whom the Israelites are said to have encountered alive: "Og the king of Bashan, who dwelt in Ashtaroth and in
Edrei," the last of the "remnant of the Rephaim" (Deut 1:4; Josh 13:12;
cf. Josh 9:10; 12:4).[787] Og was the northernmost victim of Israel's

---

[786] See, for example, R. F. Schnell, "Rephaim," IDB 4 (1962) 35.

[787] Gen 14:5 relates that in Abraham's time Chedorlaomar of Elam "came
and smote [the] Rephaim in Ashtaroth-Qarnaim," and Gen 15:18-20
promises to Abraham's descendants "this land, from the river of
Egypt to the great river, the River Euphrates," which is further described as then belonging to a series of peoples, including the Rephaim. However, Genesis 14 is a notorious historical crux (the
"Melchizedek chapter"), and, while Ashtaroth-Qarnaim appears to be
identifiable with two neighboring cities in Bashan (cf. Amos 6:13),
the identity (and historical status) of several of the peoples is in
question, including "the Zuzim in Ham" and the "Emim (see below) in
Shaveh-kiriathaim." As for Gen 15:20, this is the only time in
which the Rephaim appear in the "catalog of Canaanite nations," and
in this case they are the sole name in the list without the gentilic
ending, suggesting that their presence in Gen 15:20 may be secon-

Transjordanian campaign, defeated immediately after "Sihon king of the Amorites, who dwelt at Heshbon" (Num 21:33-35). The only other detail we have concerning Og (in contrast to the considerable material regarding Sihon), besides the brief notices of this defeat, is that Og's bedsted of iron, measuring nine by four cubits, was still to be seen at Rabbah in Ammon.[788] The most important datum for our purposes, however, is Og's location, as king of Bashan, in Ashtaroth and Edrei. It will be recalled that the Ugaritic god Rapi'u ruled from the same cities, while M-l-k was said to dwell at Ashtaroth (2.3.1,2). Marvin Pope has suggested that the chthonic character of both gods (or of the one, if they are the same) is reinforced by their geographical associations. Specifically, he notes, the land of Bashan (presumably related to Ugaritic btn, "serpent," often a chthonic symbol) often has underworld overtones in the Bible, most clearly in Ps 68:16 and Jer 22:20 and quite possibly in Amos 4:1.[789] Similarly, he contends, Og's historicity is questionable, given the fabulous legends which rabbinic lore preserved about him and (more persuasively, to my mind) the attestation of his name in a Phoenician tomb inscription, threatening violators with the wrath of

---

dary.

[788] Most scholars agree with the classic study of Paul Karge (Rephaim: die vorgeschichtliche Kultur Palästinas und Phöniziens [2d ed.; Paderborn: F. Schöningh, 1925] 638-641), that "Og's bed" was, in fact, one of the giant dolmens which were erected as tombs as late as the Iron Age (see R. W. Dajani, ed., "Archaeological News: Discovery of an Iron Age Burial in Dolmens," ADAJ 11 [1966] 102-103). If one holds with those scholars (below) who contend that the Rephaim (and similar groups) were long gone from Palestine by the time of Israel's arrival (if there ever was such a people), reports of their giant stature may well have devolved from the great fields of dolmens.

[789] "The Cult of the Dead," 170-171.

"the Mighty Og."[790] In sum, while there is no denying the existence of a
historical land named Bashan, containing the cities Ashtaroth and Edrei,
these place, like Jerusalem, had strong mythological associations (in
the case of Bashan and its cities, chthonic ones).[791]

While, as the several dissertations on the subject have shown, the
Rephaim present a topic which defies easy generalities, a few points
pertinent to our investigation can be made. First, it should be noted
that, for the most part, the Rephaim are not simply pre-Israelite inhabitants of Palestine, but predecessors of those who held the land when
Israel arrived. Deut 2:10-11,20-21 describes the Rephaim who once occupied Moab as "Emim" (the Moabite name), while those who preceded the Ammonites were the "Zamzummim." Both names may point particularly to
their posthumous status, if "Emim" is related to 'êmāh, "terror, dread,"
and "Zamzummim" to zmm, "murmur" (cf. məṣapṣəpîm in Isa 8:19; 29:4). In
any event, Israel never encountered either group. The same cannot be
said of the Anakim, alleged in Num 13:33 to be descendants of the half-
divine Nephilim (Gen 6:4), whom the spies reported seeing in southern
Canaan (Num 13:28) and whom Joshua all-but-annihilated in his southern
campaign (Josh 11:21-22); these also, according to Deut 2:11, were

---

[790] Ibid., 174. (See text and discussion by W. Röllig in NESE 2:2-4.)
For an alternate explanation and philological discussion of "Og"
(which concurs in denying the likelihood of any historical king by
that name), see Chaim Rabin, "Og," Eretz-Israel 8 (1968) 251-254
[Hebrew], 75*-76* [English summary].

[791] Thus, L'Heureux's argument against reading the pair 'ttrt / hdr'y as
cities in Ug5 2:2-3 on the grounds of their distance from Ugarit,
and Margulis's difficulties with a dual dwelling for Og (2.3.2),
present no problem. We have to do here with mythological, as well
as historical space, in which, for instance, Zion can be described
as a city far in the North (so Ps 48:3). Bashan and its cities,
while they had a known location, were also as close as the all-too-
proximate netherworld.

"known as Rephaim."[792] Some confusion in the tradition is evident, however, since the already-defeated Og "alone was left of the remnant of
the Rephaim." It is prudent, in my view, to posit that, while the possibility of an ethnic group bearing the name "Rephaim" (and of a historical Og) cannot be excluded absolutely, the name (and its synonyms)
seems primarily to have been applied to those long-gone from the Palestinian scene. It seems clear that Israel borrowed the term from those
who themselves had applied it to their predecessors in the land (whether
they were historical or, with Karge, mythical), or, in view of at least
a substantial portion of the Ugaritic evidence regarding the Rpum, to
their own ancestors. In either event, Israel (and the Deuteronomists)
was at some distance from the original use of the word.

Secondly, as noted, the occurrences of "Rephaim" in the (latter)
prophets and the Writings identify the Rephaim with the dead in general.
While the relationship between the two Biblical uses remains problematic, one suspects that the name initially applied to the dead ancestors/
predecessors of the nations dispossessed by Israel (plus Moab), but was
later employed in a much broader sense to include also Israel's dead.[793]
Thus, the process of "democratization" of the Rpum, which we saw evidenced in one Ugaritic text (CTA 6.6:45), was taken a step further,
across ethnic lines.[794]

---

[792] The name 'nqym is usually related to 'nq, "neck," perhaps meaning
"the ones with a long neck, i.e., giants" (so L'Heureux, Rank among
the Gods, 115, citing Karge, Rephaim, 641-644).

[793] Rp'm had the same broader application to all the dead in Phoenician
inscriptions, as seen by H. W. F. Saggs, "Some Ancient Semitic Conceptions of the Afterlife," Faith and Thought 90 (1953) 71.

[794] As noted above, Isa 14:9 seems to recall the earlier, more restricted usage of "Rephaim" for the royal dead.

What, then, was the nature of Israel's relationship with the Rephaim? In the study cited above, Brichto shows that tending to the
needs of at least one's own ancestors was considered a pious duty, necessary for the well-being of one's forbears in Sheol. Scripture says
little, if anything, about an attitude of fear toward them (necessitat-
ing propitiation), although such beliefs are clear enough elsewhere, as
we have seen. There is, however, one hitherto-overlooked text which may
be of extraordinary value to us. The Chronicler tells us concerning the
sad end of King Asa of Judah: "In the thirty-ninth year of his reign,
Asa became sick in his feet, severely sick, but even in his sickness he
did not inquire of Yahweh, but by the healers" (2 Chr 16:12).[795] The
reformer-king, whose sole earlier flaw had been turning to Damascus,
rather than Yahweh, for help in war, is in the end faulted for "inquir-
ing" (<u>drš</u>) "by healers" (<u>bārōpə'îm</u>), rather than of Yahweh. Previous
commentators have noted with discomfort this unique deprecation of physicians and have moved quickly to stress Asa's failure to seek help from
Yahweh.[796] The use of a technical term for divination, however, suggests
that the real situation had nothing to do with earthly physicians.
Rather, like his predecessors at Mari and Ugarit, King Asa was seeking
information (and the boon of healing) from his ancestors, the Rephaim.[797] Thus, a cultic role for the ancestors, as providers of ben-

---

[795] Whether "feet" is intended literally or euphemistically here is irrelevant for our purposes.

[796] So, for example, E. L. Curtis and A. A. Madsen, The Books of Chronicles (ICC; NY: Charles Scribner's Sons, 1910) 390; J. M. Myers, II
Chronicles (AB 13; Garden City, NY: Doubleday, 1965) 95. See, however, Morris Jastrow, "Rô'ēh and Ḥōzēh in the Old Testament," JBL 28
(1909) 49, n. 23, for the proposal advocated here (only as a second
choice, in Jastrow's case).

efits, as well as the recipients thereof, is indicated for Israel, at least in the Jerusalem of the Divided Kingdom. That they were sought out for purposes besides healing, and by means of a notorious cult in the Valley of the Son(s) of Hinnom, has been shown above, in our examination of references to the cult of Molek.

---

[797] See 2.3.3 for a discussion of the vocalization and etymology of Rephaim. As noted there, this verse's significance was suggested to me by M. H. Pope.

CHAPTER V

THE CULT OF MOLEK IN ANCIENT ISRAEL

In view of the history of scholarship on the Molek issue, it is perhaps fitting that we sum up first the findings of our investigation vis-à-vis Eissfeldt's classic hypothesis and Mosca's defense of it. As for their most influential proposal, that OT Molek was originally a technical term for a type of child sacrifice, we have found that the Punic cognate they adduced probably reflects an intra-Punic (or, at most, a Phoenician-Punic) development and that the Biblical attestations of Molek are to varying degrees intolerant of the suggested sense. Rather, their well-advised rejection of Geiger's dysphemism hypothesis has led them to overlook a substantial and growing body of evidence that an ancient Syro-Palestinian deity Malik, later Milku/i or Molek, played an important role in the popular cultus of Ebla and was worshipped as a chthonic god in Mesopotamia, Mari, Ugarit--and Israel. Philologically, we have seen that the various names all devolve from the root mlk in its West Semitic sense, "to rule as king," and that Malik and Molek are likely to be participial forms, meaning, "Ruler," rather than forms of a segolate, such as *malk or *mulk. Moreover, it is clear that the god was closely related to the deified, often royal ancestors, known variously as the malikū and the Rephaim, who were feted in the cult of the dead and sought out in necromancy for information and other benefits.

Ironically, it is Eissfeldt's less-approbated proposal, that the Molek cult was licit in Israel until Josiah's reform, that has won qualified approval in our study. While, as Mosca also saw, Eissfeldt wrongly included evidence regarding the "Law of the Firstborn" and the "Akedah" in the discussion, we did find, on the basis of admittedly slim evidence, that the cult of Molek was practiced in Jerusalem with the full approval and even participation of the royal and sacerdotal establishment until Josiah, when the originally-Northern Deuteronomic movement succeeded in its long-term aim of, among other things, having the cult declared an abomination and its cult place defiled.

We may conclude this "reactive" portion of our summary by taking up Mosca's methodological challenge (1.8) to account for the rise of the rejected understandings of Molek. First, as for Weinfeld's (and the rabbis') non-sacrificial reading, Mosca is quite possibly correct that this interpretation took its impetus from "the ambiguity of ntn, the use of zr‘, 'seed, semen,' and the possibility of equating Hebrew h‘byr with Aramaic ‘bbr, 'impregnate'," early in the post-exilic period ("Child Sacrifice," 240). On the other hand, we have reason to question the alleged "birth of a god" Molek, sometime "between the Josianic reform and the closing centuries of the pre-Christian era." As we have seen, the alleged Tendenz of Jeremiah and Ezekiel, in describing the previously-orthodox cult as idolatry, has been overdrawn by Mosca; the prophets were, rather, concerned with the boundaries of orthodox Yahwism, which had previously, in Jerusalemite circles, permitted the cult of the (lesser) deity, Molek. Philologically, Mosca's proposed development of the sense of hammōlek from "mulk-victims" to "the kingdom (of idolatry)" to "the (archetypal) 'Molech'" founders on the middle step: Mosca's best evidence for it, the LXX's <u>archōn</u>, does not mean "kingdom," but "ruler." Most serious of all, perhaps, is the extreme difficulty which both Eissfeldt and Mosca have in dating the alleged switch in the meaning of the Hebrew word: Eissfeldt does not even try, while Mosca's range is, as can be seen above, quite broad. If, as Eissfeldt realized, the LXX treated MT Molek as a deity (or demon), the range of time for the switch narrows considerably, and if the conclusions of our grammatical and contextual study of the Leviticus references (4.3.1) are accepted, the span into which the change must be fitted shrinks nearly to the vanishing point. In sum, the development of the non-sacrificial interpretation from the sacrificial (whether in its traditional form or according to Eissfeldt-Mosca) is explicable. The "traditional" view (as modified below) is understandable as the original sense, based on the full body of evidence presented above, and so needs no explanation as to its "development." Eissfeldt's hypothesis grew, as we have observed, from the correlation of the most comparable archeological evidence (to the Biblical cult) with an apparently intra-Punic usage of <u>molk</u>, after most of the other Semitic literary and inscriptional material had been improperly excluded by the proper rejection of Geiger's theory. In the end, however, we see that the proposals of both Geiger and Eissfeldt must be held as modern inventions of unquestionably brilliant minds.

What, then, can be said in a more positive vein? While we have far less information than we would like, in order to propose a reconstruction of the history of the cult of Molek in Israel, an attempt at such a presentation seems the best way to sum up the results of our study and perhaps to suggest the direction of future investigations. First, as to the source of the Israelite cult, we must take note of the unanimous view of Biblical passages which comment on the subject that the practice was a Canaanite institution. While one cannot exclude the possibility that Israel always had the cult, both the Biblical testimony and the apparently Syro-Palestinian origins of the god suggest that to hold the Biblical view as a polemic directed at the Canaanites has no support in historical data.[798] The hypothesis of the Canaanite origins of Israel's Molek cult has much to commend it, as it accounts for the apparent similarities between the Israelite conception of the god and of attendant phenomena (e.g., the Rephaim) and their Ugaritic counterparts. On the other hand, one must admit that there is then a disturbing lack of attestations for a very long period, until the reign of Ahaz. One might, then, favor the theory of a Phoenician origin for the cult, borrowed by Israel in the time of Solomon, during a time of great influence on the Israelite cultus by the Tyrians under Hiram. If Tyre was the cult's source, its god, Melqart, "king of the City," would be the counterpart of Molek, and the common point of origin with the cult of the Punic colonies would be identified.[799] Such a source is favored by our

---

[798] Naturally, this point cannot be divorced from the vexed issue of Israel's origins. The Biblical view presumes that Israel had its national origins outside of Palestine and then took possession of the land (whether by conquest, more gradual infiltration, or some combination thereof). The recently-proposed "revolt theory" of Mendenhall and Gottwald makes somewhat more difficult a clean distinction between the Canaanites and the forerunners of Israel. In any event, it would appear, there was ample opportunity for Canaanite religious influence on Israel, given the Canaanite enclaves which remained for a considerable period (above all, Jerusalem) and the apparent absorption of Canaanite population elements into Israel.

[799] One might then argue that the Punic specialization of molk took place because El(Baal-Ḥammon) and Tanit, not Melqart, were the Punic

tentative conclusion that the Molek cult in Israel was practiced only in
the Tophet in the Valley Hinnom outside of Jerusalem; conversely, if one
holds that the cult was known in the North after the division of the
kingdom, a tenth-century Phoenician source is most unlikely, since, pace
Dtr, it appears that Jeroboam I was attempting a return to "pure Yahwism," unsullied by Solomonic innovations. Even if the Jerusalem Tophet
was the cult's sole locus, however, an older, Canaanite origin is possible, as is a specifically Jebusite source for this particular form of
the chthonic deity's worship, taken over by Israel at some point following David's conquest of the city. In this latter case, Israel would be
adding but one more form of inquiry of the ancestors to an already
long-established practice (cf. 1 Samuel 28). In sum, barring the archeological discovery of the Tophet at Jerusalem (or one elsewhere in
Palestine), we have insufficient evidence to go beyond the conclusion we
reached in our examination of the Biblical references: that the cult of
Molek was Canaanite in origin, well-established by the time of Ahaz, and
was practiced at least at Jerusalem until the fall of the city in 587/6
B.C., with the exception of the reign of Josiah and possibly of Hezekiah. It is also likely, as we have argued (4.5.8), that an attempt to
revive the cult was made sometime during the Exile or soon after the Return, although not in the Valley Hinnom, and that, as in North Africa,
the practice persisted in secret, increasingly-isolated places, before
disappearing considerably later.

---

recipients of the sacrifices, and the traditional "to the Ruler" was
misunderstood in time.

What, then, was the place of the cult in Israelite religion? Given
the extreme unlikelihood of anything approaching a universal (i.e.,
every-family) practice of the cult (and its distinction from any practice of first-born sacrifice), the Molek sacrifices were surely irregu-
lar and voluntary (cf. the nēder, tôdāh and nədābāh offerings). It is
possible that, as was apparently true of the Punic offerings, the sacrifices were performed in fulfilment of vows made to the deity (whether
Yahweh, Molek or the ancestors), and one may conjecture that, by the nature of the gift and the connections which scholars such as Pope have
seen between the cults of love and death, the vows usually had to do
with fertility.[800] (In any event, as we have seen, the cult of Molek was
apparently not, at least primarily, associated with securing the help of
the god[s] in time of military emergencies.)

Also problematic is the issue of who participated in the cult. On
the one hand, the evidence so far available from Ebla associates Malik
with the popular, rather than official cult, and the OT prophets, at
least, give no indication that only the kings were involved. On the
other hand, the evidence from Mari and Ugarit suggests that the cult of
the ancestors was of special concern to the royal house, and the apparent localization of the Israelite cult in the royal cult of Jerusalem
may argue for a similar delimitation of the Molek cult in Israel, despite the apparent "democratization" of the cult of the ancestors. The
historical evidence is, again, insufficient for us to posit either view

---

[800] A fertility connection is also suggested by the concern of the ancestors, demonstrated by Brichto, for the fertility of their proge-
ny, and thus the perpetuation of their own name and care. However,
how this aim was served by the sacrifice of certain of those descendants is less than clear.

with certainty; obviously, one's answer will be related to the question
posed above, concerning whether Israel adopted the cult before or after
the institution of the monarchy.

We are in a somewhat better position, I believe, vis-à-vis the history of the Molek cult over against the development of Yahwism. Apparently, the cult was adopted and adapted by Molek's subordination to Yahweh, at least at Jerusalem. As indicated in our study of the cult of
the dead (4.6), the ancestors (Rephaim, or perhaps Melakim), who formed
at least an indirect object of the Molek cult's attentions, could have
been the forbears of the land's prior owners, whose care was now taken
over by the Israelites (whether out of piety or fear), or they could
have been (or included also) their own ancestors, who were now to be
cared for in the style of the ancestors of the Canaanites. The Deuteronomists, having seen the deleterious effects on piety and theology of
the syncretism of Yahweh and Baal in the North, objected strenuously to
the Jerusalemite accomodation, and their views were vindicated by Nebuchadnezzar's armies in 587/6. The extent of the Deuteronomists' victory
can be seen not only in the references to the cult of Molek in particular, and the shape of the canon in general, but in the absence in post-
exilic Judaism of anything like a counterpart to the archangel Mālik of
Islam, who governs the damned on behalf of Allah (Sura 43:77).[801]

So why did the parents do it? Like Mosca, we must prescind from
psychology at the distance of millennia ("Child Sacrifice," 273). Outside of the reasonably clear connections of the cult with necromancy and

---

[801] "'Malek,' they will call out, 'let your Lord make an end of us!'
But he will answer: 'Here you shall remain'" (<u>The Koran</u> [trans. N.
J. Onwood; Penguin classics; 3d ed.; Baltimore: Penguin, 1968]
150).

the much vaguer possibility of a fertility function, this "ultimate question" remains unanswered.[802] The data are all-too-few, and much mystery remains. Even those steeped in the theology of the Father's sacrifice of the Son as the Lamb for the sins of the world (reversing the mlk'mr, as it were) must be taken aback at the thought of the slaying and transfer by fire of one's own child for any conceivable purpose. One can only be thankful that "das Ende" came for Molek long enough ago to produce so much obscurity.

---

[802] In an unpublished paper made available to me by Marvin Pope, Robert Good suggests that the child sacrifices may have been the ritual "re-enactment of the death of the fertility god, using a real child, . . . as a means of reifying the god's passage through puberty." Unfortunately, we simply know too little of Molek to say whether he did or did not have fertility attributes, or whether he was considered a "dying-and-rising god."

Appendix A
CATALOG OF EBLAITE PERSONAL NAMES CONTAINING *MA-LIK*

Name	Published or Listed in[1]	Times Attested
A-ba-ma-lik	MEE 1,2	3
A-BAN-ma-lik	ARET 3.367[2]	1
A-bù/bu$_x$-ma-lik	ARET 3; MEE 1; Pettinato, Archives, 260	11
A-da-ma-lik	ARET 3.100	1
A-dam-ma-lik	ARET 3; MEE 1,2	5
A-ga-iš-ma-lik	ARET 3.100	1
A-ḫa/Aḫ-ra-ma-lik	ARET 2,3	14
A-kà-al-ma-lik	Pettinato, RSO 50:5	1
A-lum-ma-lik	ARET 3.888	1
A-ma-lik	ARET 2,3; MEE 1,2	10
A-ma-ma-lik	ARET 3	2
A-na-ma-lik	MEE 1,2	2
A-píl-ma-lik	Pettinato, RSO 50:3	1
A-si-ma-lik	ARET 3; Pettinato, Archives, 209	3
A-šu-úr/šur$_x$-ma-lik	ARET 3; MEE 1,2	9
Bar-za-ma-lik	ARET 3; MEE 1	3
Bù-AN-ma-lik	ARET 3.945	1
Bù-da-ma-lik	ARET 2,3; MEE 1,2; Pettinato, Archives, 224	23

Bu$_x$-ma-lik	ARET 3.665	1
Da-ḫi-ir/ḫir-ma-lik	ARET 3;	4
	Fronzaroli, SEb 3:70	
Da$_5$-zi-ma-lik	Fronzaroli, UF 11:279	1
Dab$_6$-zi-ma-lik	ARET 3.366	1
Dar-^{d}ma-lik	Pettinato, Archives,	1
	88,110	
Du-bí/bù-ḫi/ḫu	ARET 3; MEE 1,2;	18
	Pettinato, Archives, 161	
Du-bí-ma-lik	ARET 3	?[3]
Du-bí/bù-uš-ma-lik	ARET 3	?
Du-bù-da-ma-lik	ARET 3	?
Du/Ṭu-bù-ma-lik	ARET 3; MEE 2	8
Du-bù-(x)-ma-lik	ARET 2.14	1
Du-na-ma-lik	ARET 3.467	1
Du-za-ma-lik	MEE 2.26	1
Dur-ma-lik	MEE 1.6527	1
Eb/Ib-du-ma-lik	ARET 2,3; MEE 1,2	7
En-àr-ma-lik	MEE 1.782	1
En-bù/pù-ma-lik	ARET 3; MEE 2;	4
=Ru$_{12}$-bu-ma-lik	Hecker, "Eigennamen," 167	
EN-gi-ma-lik	ARET 2	2
EN.IR-ma-lik	MEE 2.3	1
En-ma-lik	MEE 2.37	1
En-na-ma-lik	ARET 2,3; MEE 1,2;	43
	Pettinato, Or 44:370;	
	Pettinato, RSO 50:4	

En-și/zi-ma-lik	ARET 2,3; MEE 1,2;	47
	Pettinato, Or 44:370;	
	Pettinato, OrAnt 18:	
	129-187 (passim);	
	Pettinato, Archives,	
	208-209	
=Ru$_{12}$-și-ma-lik	Hecker, "Eigennamen," 167	
Gi-ma-lik	ARET 2.30	1
Gi-ra-ma-lik	ARET 3; MEE 1,2	4
GIBIL/GIBIL$_4$-ma-lik	ARET 2,3; MEE 1,2;	17
	Fronzaroli, SEb 1:76	
Gú-na-ma-lik	ARET 3.266	1
Gú-za-ma-lik	Pettinato, Archives, 207	1
Ḫar-da-ma-lik	ARET 3.160	1
Ḫir-ma-lik	Fronzaroli, UF 11:277	2
I-da-ma-lik	ARET 2,3; MEE 1;	13
	Lipiński, "Formes," 195	
I-ḫir-ma-lik	ARET 3.322	1
I-ḫuš-ša-ma-lik	Pettinato, OrAnt 18:157	1
I-ib-ma-lik	ARET 2,3; MEE 1,2	11
I-ku-ma-lik	ARET 3.467	1
I-lu$_5$/lul-za$_x$-ma-lik	ARET 3; MEE 2	15
I-rí-ik-ma-lik	ARET 3; MEE 1,2;	12
	Archi, SEb 2:22-23;	
	Fronzaroli, SEb 3:46;	
	Archi, BA 44:147;	
	Archi, SEb 4:230	

I-šar-ma-lik	ARET 3	7
I-ti-kà/ki-ma-lik	ARET 3; MEE 1	3
I-ti-ma-lik	ARET 3; MEE 2;	8
	Pettinato, Archives, 210	
I-zi-ma-lik	MEE 1;	2
	Fronzaroli, UF 11:279	
Ib-BU-ma-lik	ARET 2.28	1
Ib-dur-ma-lik	ARET 3	2
Ib/Ip-ḫur-ma-lik	ARET 2,3; MEE 1;	10
	Pettinato, Or 44:371	
Ib-ir-ma-lik	ARET 3.135	1
Ib-na-ma-lik	Pettinato, Archives, 260	1
Ig/Ik-bù-ul-ma-lik	ARET 3; MEE 1,2	12
Iḫ-ra-ma-lik	MEE 1,2	2
Íl-a-ma-lik	ARET 3.468	1
Íl-ba-ma-lik	ARET 3; MEE 2;	20
	Pettinato, Or 46:231;	
	Pettinato, OrAnt 18:	
	129-175 (passim)	
	Archi, BA 44:148	
In-ma-lik	ARET 2; MEE 2;	11
	Archi, BA 44:148	
Ìr-an/[d]-ma-lik	ARET 2,3; MEE 1,2;	70
	Pettinato, OrAnt 18:	
	129-159 (passim);	
	Pettinato, Archives, 222;	
	Archi, BA 44:146;	

	Archi, SEb 4:80	
Ìr-da-ma-lik	ARET 2,3; MEE 1,2	17
Ìr-ḫuš-za$_x$-ma-lik	ARET 3.940	1
Iš$_{11/x(y*)}$-a-ma-lik	ARET 2,3; MEE 2;	10
	Pettinato, Archives, 224	
Iš-al-ma-lik	MEE 1.6519	1
Iš-ba-al-ma-lik	ARET 3.562	1
Iš-la-ma-lik	MEE 1,2	2
Iš-ta-ma-ma-lik	Gelb, SMS 1/1:22	1
KA-ma-lik	ARET 3	?
Kéš/KEŠDA-ma-lik	ARET 3; MEE 1;	6
	Pettinato, OrAnt 18:184	
Ku-ir-ma-lik	ARET 3.930	1
Ku-ma-lik	ARET 3.244	1
Lu-a-ma-lik	MEE 2.29	2
Lu-la-ma-lik	MEE 2.22	1
Ma-aš/áš-ma-lik	ARET 3; MEE 1	2
Na-a-ma-lik	MEE 1.716	1
NE-gi-ma-lik	ARET 2.14	1
NE-zi-ma-lik	ARET 3; MEE 2	19
Ni-ba$_4$-ma-lik	MEE 2.19	1
NI-NE-na-ma-lik	ARET 3.335	1
Puzur$_4$(-ra)-ma-lik	ARET 2,3; MEE 1,2;	43
	Pettinato, OrAnt 18:172;	
	Pettinato, Archives, 138,140	
Rí-dam-ma-lik	ARET 3; MEE 1,2	8
Rí/Ré-ì-ma-lik	ARET 2,3; MEE 1,2;	34

	Fronzaroli, SEb 1:6;	
	Archi, SEb 2:24;	
	Archi, BA 44:148	
Sa-ab-za-ir-ma-lik	MEE 2.3	1
Sí/Zi-mi-na-ma-lik	MEE 1; Archi, SEb 2:39	4
Si/Ší-ti-ma-lik	ARET 2,3; MEE 1,2	8
Sur-ba-ma-lik	ARET 3.531	1
Şi/Zé-ma-lik	ARET 2; MEE 2	6
Ša-du$_8$-ma-lik	ARET 3	?
Ší-ir-ma-lik	MEE 2.19	1
Šu-bù-ul-ma-lik	MEE 1.4939	1
Šu-du$_8$-ma-lik	ARET 3.100	1
Šu-ma-lik	ARET 3; MEE 2;	34
	Fronzaroli, SEb 1:6	
Šu-ra-ma-lik	ARET 3.828	1
Ta/Ti-kéš-ma-lik	MEE 1,2;	3
	Pettinato, Archives,	
	88,94,110	
Téš-da-ma-lik	ARET 3	2
Tù-bil-ma-lik	Pettinato, Archives,	1
	88,110	
Zi-la-ma-lik	ARET 3	2

NOTES TO APPENDIX A:

[1]This is a suitable point at which to protest the proliferation of citation systems already ·in Eblaite studies, a situation which is rapidly becoming as confused (and confusing) as that in Ugaritic. Even within Pettinato's own works, one must contend with the inventory (TM) number, the catalog number and the number assigned a given text for the purposes of any given volume (such as MEE 2). Other scholars tend to cite, in addition, the article in which a text

was initially published. One hopes that a standard system of references may soon be agreed upon.

[2]The text number is given with the volume in cases of <u>hapax</u> <u>legomena</u> from ARET or MEE.

[3]Names marked "?" are in the index of divine names in ARET 3, but are not found in the index of personal names. It is therefore impossible to confirm that they actually occur in a text.

Appendix B

CATALOG OF AMORITE DIVINE AND PERSONAL NAMES CONTAINING M-L-K FORMS

"Malik" Names:

Ma-li-kum

Ma-a-li-kum

Ma-li-ki

Ma-li-ka-tum

Ma-li-ka

Ma-lik-su-mu-ú

Ma-lik-za-du-um

A-ḫi-e-ma-lik

E-wi-ma-lik

Ḫa-lí-ma-lik

Ḫa-ri-ma-lik

Ḫa-ri-ma-li-ki

Ḫa-ab-du-ma-lik

Ab-du-ma-lik

Ab-du-ma-li-ki

An-du-ma-lik

Ì-lí-ma-lik

I-lu-ma-li-ka-yi[ki]

A-mi-ma-lik

Ḫi-im-di-ma-lik

Ḫa-ar?-šum?-ma-lik

"Milku/i" Names:

Me-il-ku

Mi-il-ki-im

Mil-ka-tum

Mi-i/el-ga-num

Mi-il-ku-ni-im

Mi-il-ku-nim

Mi-il-ku-ma

[d]Mi-il-kum

Mi-el-ki-i-[la]

Mil-ki-lu

Mi-il-ki-lu

Mi-il-ki-lum

Mi-il-ki-la-el

Mi-il-ki-li-el

Mi-il-ki-lí-il

[Mi]-el-ki-li-il

Mi-il-ki-li-e-lum

Mi-il-ki-lu-i-la

Mi-il-ki-ta-ga

Mi-il-ku-da-nu-um

Mi-il-ku-ma-il

Ia-tar-ma-lik

Da-du-ma-lik

Ia-am-zu-ma-lik

Ia-ri-im-ma-lik

Ri-ip-a-ma-lik

Ši-ma-li-ik-ti

Ia-šu-ub-^{d}ma-[lik]

La-aḫ-wi-ma-lik

La-aḫ-wi-ma-li-ku

"Malki" Names:

^{d}Ma-al-ki

Bi-it-ta-ma-al-ki

Ì-lí-mil-ku

Ki-mi-il-ki-el

Ka-u-ka-mi-il-ku

"Muluk" Names:

Mu-lu-ga-an

A-bi-mu-lu-ki

^{d}Mu-lu-uk^{ki}

I-lu-um-mu-lu-uk^{ki}

^{d}Mu-lu-ka-yi^{ki}

Ḫa?-al-da-mu-lu-uk

I-tar-mu-lu-uk

La-ar-mu-lu-uk

NOTE TO APPENDIX B: Names are listed in the order of Gelb's Computer-aided Analysis, 321-323.

Appendix C

CATALOG OF PERSONAL NAMES FROM UGARIT
CONTAINING M-L-K FORMS

Syllabic Cuneiform	Alphabetic Cuneiform
^{m}A-bi-milku(LUGAL)	Abmlk
^{m}Abdi(ARAD)-milku(LUGAL)	Aḫmlk
Abdi(ARAD)-milku(LUGAL)-ma	Aḫtmlk
A-ḫa-tu$_{4}$/^{f}Aḫat(NIN)-milku(LUGAL)	Iḫmlk
A-ḫi/Aḫi(ŠEŠ)-milku(LUGAL)	Ilmlk
Ia-du-milku(LUGAL)	ʻbdmlk
Ia-pa-milku(LUGAL)	ʻdmlk
Ia-ri-milku(LUGAL)	Ymlk*
Ili/Ilu(AN)-milku(LUGAL)	Ypʻmlk
Ili(AN)^{li}-mu-lik	Kṯrmlk*
Baʻal(^{d}IM)-ma-lak*	Mlkbn
^{f}Ma-li-kí-lu	Mlky
^{f}Mi-il-ka-a/ia	Mlkyy
^{f}Mi-il-ki-in-a-ri	Mlkytn
^{m}Mi-il-ki-lu	Mlknʻm
Milku(LUGAL)-aḫu(ŠEŠ)	Pmlk
Nûrī-^{d}ma-lik	Pdrmlk*

Šapaš(^{d}UTU)-milku(LUGAL)*   Qnmlk

                                    Ršpmlk*

                                    Šmmlk

                                    Špšmlk*

(* marks names unlikely to contain the divine name M-l-k)

SELECT BIBLIOGRAPHY OF WORKS CITED

Ahlström, G. W. Aspects of Syncretism in Israelite Religion. Horae Soederblominae 5. Lund: C. W. K. Gleerup, 1963.

Aisleitner, Joseph. Wörterbuch der Ugaritischen Sprache. Berlin: Akademie, 1963.

Albright, William F. Archaeology and the Religion of Israel. 3d ed. Baltimore: Johns Hopkins, 1953.

_____. "The Chronology of a South Palestinian City, Tell El-ʿAjjûl." AJSL 55 (1938) 337-359.

_____. "The Evolution of the West-Semitic Divinity ʿAn--ʿAnat--ʿAtta." AJSL 41 (1925) 86-87.

_____. The Excavation of Tell Beit Mirsim: 2. The Bronze Age. AASOR 17. New Haven: ASOR, 1938.

_____. "The high place in Ancient Palestine." VTSup 4 (1957) 242-258.

_____. "The Oracles of Balaam." JBL 63 (1944) 207-233.

_____. Review of Molk als Opferbegriff, by O. Eissfeldt. JPOS 15 (1935) 344.

_____. "The Traditional Home of the Syrian Daniel." BASOR 130 (1953) 26-28.

_____. Yahweh and the Gods of Canaan. Garden City, NY: Doubleday, 1968.

Alexander, Joseph Addison. The Prophecies of Isaiah. 2 vols. 2d ed. NY: Charles Scribner, 1870.

Almagro-Gorbea, Martín J. "Les reliefs orientalisants de Pozo Moro (Albacete, Espagne)." In Mythe et Personnification, edited by J. Duchemin. Paris: Société d'Édition "Les Belles Lettres", 1980.

Alt, Albrecht. "Die Opfer in den phönikischen Inschriften von Karatepe." TLZ 75 (1950) 571-576.

_____. "Die phönikischen Inschriften von Karatepe." WO 1 (1949) 272-287.

_____. "Zur Talionsformel." ZAW 52 (1934) 303-305.

Anderson, Francis I., and David Noel Freedman. <u>Hosea.</u> AB 24. Garden City, NY: Doubleday, 1980.

Archi, Alfonso. "Ancora su Ebla e la Bibbia." <u>SEb</u> 2 (1980) 17-40.

_____. "Further Concerning Ebla and the Bible." <u>BA</u> 44 (1981) 145-154.

_____. "Kiš nei Testi di Ebla." <u>SEb</u> 4 (1981) 77-87.

_____. "A Mythologem in Eblaitology: Mesilim of Kish at Ebla." <u>SEb</u> 4 (1981) 227-230.

_____, and Maria Giovanna Biga. <u>Testi amministrativi di vario contenuto (Archivio L. 2769: TM.75.G.3000-4101).</u> ARET 3. Rome: Missione archeologica italiana in Syria, 1982.

Aro, J. Review of <u>Textes admisitratifs</u>, by M. Birot. <u>OLZ</u> 56 (1961) 603-605.

Astour, Michael. "The Nether World and Its Denizens at Ugarit." In <u>Death in Mesopotamia</u>, edited by B. Alster. RAI 26. Mesopotamia 8. Copenhagen: Akademisk, 1980.

_____. "Sepharvaim." IDBSup (1976) 807.

_____. "Two Ugaritic Snake Charms." <u>JNES</u> 27 (1968) 13-36.

Baldacci, M. "The Ammonite Text from Tell Siran and North-West Semitic Philology." <u>VT</u> 31 (1981) 363-368.

Baly, Denis, and A. D. Tushingham. <u>Atlas of the Biblical World.</u> NY: World, 1971.

Barrick, W. Boyd. "The Funerary Character of 'High Places' in Ancient Palestine: A Reassessment." <u>VT</u> 25 (1975) 565-595.

Barton, George A. "Moloch (Molech)." <u>The Jewish Encyclopedia.</u> NY: Funk and Wagnalls, 1916.

Baudissin, Wolf Wilhelm. <u>Adonis und Eshmun.</u> Leipzig: J. C. Hinrichs, 1911.

_____. <u>Jahve et Moloch: sive de ratione inter deum Israelitarum et Molochum intercedente.</u> Leipzig: Fr. Guil. Grunow, 1874.

_____. <u>Kyrios als Gottesname im Judentum und seine Stelle in der Religionsgeschichte.</u> 4 vols. Giessen: Alfred Töpelmann, 1929.

_____. "Moloch." <u>PRE2</u>, edited by J. J. Herzog, G. L. Plitt and A. Hauck. Leipzig: J. C. Hinrichs, 1882.

_____. "Moloch." <u>PRE3</u>, edited by A. Hauck. Leipzig: J. C. Hinrichs, 1903.

_____. Review of Études sur les Religions Sémitiques, by M.-J. Lagrange. ZDMG 57 (1903) 812-837.

Bauer, Hans, and Pontus Leander. Historische Grammatik der Hebräischen Sprache des Alten Testaments. Halle: Max Niemeyer, 1922.

Bayliss, Miranda. "The Cult of Dead Kin in Assyria and Babylonia." Iraq 35 (1973) 115-125.

Bea, Aug. "Kinderopfer für Moloch oder für Jahwe?" Bib 18 (1937) 95-107.

_____. "Moloch in den Maritafeln." Bib 20 (1939) 415.

Benichou-Safar, H. À propos des ossements humains du tophet du Carthage." RSF 9 (1981) 5-9.

Bennett, W. H. "Molech, Moloch." A Dictionary of the Bible, edited by J. Hastings. NY: Charles Scribner's Sons, 1903.

Benz, Frank L. Personal Names in the Phoenician and Punic Inscriptions. Studia Pohl 8. Rome: Pontifical Biblical Institute, 1972.

Berthier, André, and René Charlier. Le sanctuaire punique d'El-Hofra à Constantine. Paris: Arts et métiers graphiques, 1955.

Beyer, Andreas. "Additamenta." In De Dîs Syris, by J. Selden. 3d ed. Amsterdam: Lucam Bisterum, 1680.

Biggs, Robert D. Inscriptions from Tell Abū Ṣalābīkh. OIP 99. Chicago: University of Chicago, 1974.

_____. "Semitic Names in the Fara Period." Or n.s. 36 (1967) 55-66.

Birot, Maurice. Textes administratifs de la salle 5 du Palais. ARM 9. Paris: Imprimerie Nationale, 1960.

Blome, Friedrich. Die Opfermaterie in Babylon und Israel. Rome: Pontifical Biblical Institute, 1934.

Bottéro, Jean. Textes économiques et administratifs. ARM 7. Paris: Imprimerie Nationale, 1957.

Brichto, Herbert Chanan. "Kin, Cult, Land and Afterlife--A Biblical Complex." HUCA 44 (1973) 1-55.

_____. "On Slaughter and Sacrifice, Blood and Atonement." HUCA 47 (1976) 19-55.

Bright, John. "The Date of the Prose Sermons of Jeremiah." JBL 70 (1951) 15-35.

_____. Jeremiah. 2d ed. AB 21. Garden City, NY: Doubleday, 1965.

Brongers, H. A. Review of De Molochdienst, by K. Dronkert. Nederlands Theologisch Tijdschrift 8 (1954) 243-245.

Brueggemann, Walter. Genesis. Atlanta: John Knox, 1982.

Buber, Martin. Kingship of God. Translated by R. Scheimann. 3d ed. NY: Harper and Row, 1967 [German orig., 1956].

Buccellati, Giorgio. The Amorites of the Ur III Period. Pubblicazioni del Seminario de semitistica, Ricerche 1. Naples: Istituto Orientale de Napoli, 1966.

Burkert, Walter. Griechische Religion. Die Religionen der Menschheit 15. Stuttgart: W. Kohlhammer, 1977.

Cagni, Luigi, ed. La Lingua di Ebla. Seminario di Studi Asiatici, Series Minor 14. Naples: Istituto Universitario Orientale, 1981.

Calloway, Joseph A. Review of Temples and Cult Places, by M. Ottosson. JBL 101 (1982) 597-598.

Caquot, André. "Nouveaux documents ougaritiens." Syria 46 (1969) 241-265.

_____, and Maurice Sznycer. Ugaritic Religion. Iconography of Religions 15/8. Leiden: Brill, 1980.

Carcopino, Jérôme. "Survivances par substitution des sacrifices d'enfants dans l'Afrique romaine." RHR 106 (1932) 592-599.

Carley, Keith W. The Book of the Prophet Ezekiel. Cambridge, NEB. Cambridge: University, 1974.

Cazelles, Henri. "Encore un texte sur Mâlik." Bib 38 (1957) 485-486.

_____. "Molok." DBSup 5 (1957) 1337-1346.

_____. "Ugarit." Annuaire de l'École Pratique des Hautes Études, Ve Section: Sciences Religieuses 88 (1979-1980) 231-234.

Chabot, J.-B. "Note sur une inscription punique de Carthage." CRAIBL (1922) 112-114.

Charlier, René. "La nouvelle série de stèles puniques de Constantine et la question des sacrifices dits 'Molchomor', en relation avec l'expression 'BSRM BTM'." Karthago 4 (1953) 3-48.

Childs, Brevard S. The Book of Exodus. OTL. Philadelphia: Westminster, 1974.

_____. *Isaiah and the Assyrian Crisis.* SBT 2/3. London: SCM, 1976.

_____. "A Study of the Formula, 'Until This Day'." *JBL* 82 (1963) 279-292.

Clements, Ronald E. *Isaiah 1-39.* NCB. Grand Rapids, MI: Eerdmans, 1980.

Cogan, Morton. *Imperialism and Religion: Assyria, Judah and Israel in the Eighth and Seventh Centuries B.C.E.* SBLMS 19. Missoula, MT: Scholars, 1974.

Coogan, Michael David. *West Semitic personal names in the Murašû documents.* HSM 7. Missoula, MT: Scholars, 1976.

Cooke, George Albert. *The Book of Ezekiel.* ICC. Edinburgh: T. & T. Clark, 1951.

_____. *A Textbook of North-Semitic Inscriptions.* Oxford: Clarendon, 1903.

Cooley, Robert E. "The Contribution of Literary Sources to a Study of the Canaanite Burial Pattern." Unpublished Ph.D. dissertation, New York University, 1968.

_____. "Gathered to His People: A Study of a Dothan Family Tomb." In *The Living and Active Word of God: Essays in Honor of Samuel J. Schultz,* edited by M. Inck and R. Youngblood. Winona Lake, IN: Eisenbrauns, 1983.

Cooper, Alan. "Divine Names and Epithets in the Ugaritic Texts." In *RSP3,* edited by S. Rummel. AnOr 51. Rome: Pontifical Biblical Institute, 1981.

_____. "MLK 'LM: 'Eternal King' or 'King of Eternity'." In *Love and Death in the Ancient Near East: Essays in Honor of Marvin H. Pope,* edited by J. Marks and R. Good. Guilford, CT: Four Quarters, in press.

Cramer, Martin Friderick. *De Molocho Ammonitarum Idolo.* Wittenberg: Officina Vidua Gerdensiae, 1720.

Cross, Frank Moore. *Canaanite Myth and Hebrew Epic.* Cambridge, MA: Harvard, 1973.

Culican, William. "The Graves of Tell er-Reqeish." *AJBA* 2/2 (1973) 66-105.

_____. "Melqart Representations on Phoenician Seals." *Abr-Nahrain* 2 (1960-1961) 41-54.

Curtis, Edward Lewis, and Albert Alonzo Madsen. *The Books of Chronicles.* ICC. NY: Charles Scribner's Sons, 1910.

Curtis, John Briggs. "An Investigation of the Mount of Olives in the Judeo-Christian Tradition." HUCA 28 (1957) 137-180.

Dahood, Mitchell. "Ancient Semitic Deities in Syria and Palestine." In Le Antiche Divinità Semitiche, edited by S. Moscati. Rome: Centro di Studi Semitiche, 1958.

_____. Psalms I. AB 16. Garden City, NY: Doubleday, 1966.

_____. Psalms III. AB 17A. Garden City, NY: Doubleday, 1970.

Dajani, R. W., ed. "Archaeological News: Discovery of an Iron Age Burial in Dolmens." ADAJ 11 (1966) 102-103.

Dalman, Gustaf H. Aramäisch-Neuhebräisches Handwörterbuch zu Targum, Talmud und Midrasch. Reprint. 2d ed. Hildesheim: Georg Olms, 1967 [orig., 1938].

Daumer, G. Fr. Der Feuer- und Moloch-dienst der alten Hebräer als urväterlicher, legaler, orthodoxer Kultus der Nation. Braunschweig: Fr. Otto, 1842.

Dawood, N. J., trans. The Koran. 3d ed. Penguin classics. Baltimore: Penguin, 1968.

Deimal, P. Anton. Pantheon Babylonicum. Rome: Pontifical Biblical Institute, 1914.

_____. Šumerisches Lexikon. 4 vols. Rome: Pontifical Biblical Institute, 1930-1950.

Delavault, Bernard, and André Lemaire. "Les inscriptions phéniciennes de Palestine." RSF 7 (1979) 1-39.

_____. "Une Stèle 'Molk' de Palestine Dédiée à Eshmoun? RES 367 Reconsidéré." RB 83 (1976) 569-583.

Delcor, Matthias. "Les cultes étrangers en Israël au moment de la réforme de Josias d'après 2R 23: Étude de religions sémitiques comparées." In Mélanges bibliques et orientaux en l'honneur de M. Henri Cazelles, edited by A. Caquot and M. Delcor. AOAT 212. Kevelaer: Butzon & Bercker, 1981.

Deller, Karl Heinz. Review of Les sacrifices de l'Ancien Testament, by R. de Vaux. Or n.s. 34 (1965) 382-386.

Dhorme, Eduard. "Le dieu Baal et le dieu Moloch dans la tradition biblique." Anatolian Studies 6 (1956) 57-61.

_____. Review of Molk als Opferbegriff, by O. Eissfeldt. RHR 113 (1936) 276-278.

_____. "Le sacrifice accadien à propos d'un ouvrage récent." RHR 107 (1933) 107-125.

Dietrich, M., and O. Loretz. "Totenverehrung in Māri (12803) und Ugarit (KTU 1.161)." UF 12 (1980) 381-382.

_____, and J. Sanmartín. "Einzelbemerkungen zu RS 24.251." UF 7 (1975) 127-131.

_____. "Der 'Neujahrspsalm' RS 24.252 (=UG.5, S.551-557, NR.2)." UF 7 (1975) 115-119.

_____. "PGR im Ugaritischen." UF 5 (1973) 289-291.

_____. "Stichometrische Probleme in RS 24.245 = UG.5, S. 556-559, NR. 3vs." UF 7 (1975) 534-535.

_____. "Ugaritisch ILIB und Hebräisch ꜣ(W)B 'Totengeist'." UF 6 (1974) 450-451.

Dijkstra, Meindert, and Johannes C. de Moor. "Problematical Passages in the Legend of Aqhâtu." UF 7 (1975) 171-215.

Dossin, Georges. "Signaux Lumineux au Pays de Mari." RA 35 (1938) 174-186.

Dotan, Aron. "Stress Position and Vowel Shift in Phoenician and Punic." IOS 6 (1976) 71-121.

Driver, Samuel Rolles. The Book of Genesis. Westminster. London: Methuen, 1904.

_____. A Critical and Exegetical Commentary on Deuteronomy. ICC. NY: Charles Scribner's Sons, 1903.

Dronkert, Karel. De Molochdienst in het Oude Testament. Leiden: Brill, 1953.

Du Mesnil du Buisson, Robert. Nouvelles Études sur les dieux et les mythes de Canaan. Études préliminaires aux religions orientales dans l'Empire Romain 33. Leiden: Brill, 1973.

Duhm, Bernhardt. Das Buch Jeremia. KAT 11. Tübingen: J. C. B. Mohr, 1901.

Dussaud, René. "Melqart." Syria 25 (1946-1948) 205-230.

_____. "Melqart, d'après de récents travaux." RHR 151 (1957) 1-21.

_____. "Milk, Moloch, Melqart." RHR 49 (1904) 163-168.

_____. "Précisions épigraphiques touchant les sacrifices puniques d'enfants." CRAIBL (1946) 371-387.

_____. Review of Molk als Opferbegriff, by O. Eissfeldt. Syria 16 (1935) 407-409.

_____. Review of Molk als Opferbegriff, by O. Eissfeldt. AfO 11 (1936) 167-168.

_____. Review of "Le vocabulaire sacrificiel punique," by J. Février. Syria 34 (1957) 393-395.

_____. "Trente-huit textes puniques provenant du Sanctuaire des ports à Carthage." Bulletin Archéologique du Comité (1922) 243-260.

Ebach, Jürgen H. "PGR = (Toten-)Opfer? Ein Vorschlag zum Verstandnis von Ez. 43,7.9." UF 3 (1971) 365-368.

_____, and Udo Rüterswörden. "ADRMLK, 'Moloch' und BAʿAL ADR: Eine Notiz zum Problem der Moloch-Verehrung im alten Israel." UF 11 (1979) 219-226.

_____. "Unterweltsbeschwörung im Alten Testament: Untersuchungen zur Begriffs- und Religionsgeschichte des ʾōb." UF 9 (1977) 57-70 and UF 12 (1980) 205-220.

Ebeling, Erich. Tod und Leben nach den Vorstellungen der Babylonier. Berlin: W. de Gruyter, 1931.

Edzard, Dietz Otto. Verwaltungstexte verschiedenen Inhalts (aus dem Archiv L. 2769). ARET 2. Rome: Missione archeologica italiana in Siria, 1981.

Eichler, Barry L. Indenture at Nuzi: The Personal Tidennūtu Contract and its Mesopotamian Analogues. Yale Near Eastern Researches 5. New Haven: Yale, 1973.

Eichrodt, Walther. Ezekiel. Translated by C. Quin. OTL. Philadelphia: Fortress, 1970 [German orig., 1965-1966].

Eissfeldt, Otto. "The Beginnings of Phoenician Epigraphy according to a Letter written by William Gesenius in 1835." PEQ 74 (1947) 68-86.

_____. "Hesekiel Kap. 16 als Geschichtsquelle." JPOS 16 (1936) 286-292.

_____. "Menschenopfer." RGG3 4 (1960) 868.

_____. Molk als Opferbegriff im Punischen und Hebräischen und das Ende des Gottes Moloch. Beiträge zur Religionsgeschichte des Altertums 3. Halle: Max Niemeyer, 1935.

_____. Neue keilalphabetische Texte aus Ras Schamra-Ugarit. Sitzungsberichte der deutschen Akademie der Wissenschaften zu Berlin 6. Berlin: Akademie, 1965.

_____. The Old Testament: An Introduction. Translated by P. R. Ackroyd. NY: Harper and Row, 1965.

_____. Ras Schamra und Sanchunjaton. Beiträge zur Religionsgeschichte des Altertums 4. Halle: Max Niemeyer, 1939.

Elliger, Karl. Leviticus. HAT 4. Tübingen: J. C. B. Mohr, 1966.

Ellis, Richard S. Foundation Deposits in Ancient Mesopotamia. Yale Near Eastern Researches 2. New Haven: Yale, 1968.

Février, James G. "Essai de reconstruction du sacrifice Molek." JA 248 (1960) 167-187.

_____. "Molchomor." RHR 143 (1953) 8-18.

_____. "Le rite de substitution dans les textes de N'Gaous." JA 250 (1962) 1-10.

_____. "Les rites sacrificiels chez les Hébreux et à Carthage." REJ 4/3 (1964) 7-18.

_____. "Le vocabulaire sacrificiel punique." JA 243 (1955) 49-63.

Fichtner, Johannes. "Die etymologische Ätiologie in den Namengebungen der geschichtlichen Bücher des Alten Testaments." VT 6 (1956) 372-396.

Finkel, Irving L. The Series SIG(7).ALAN = Nabnītu. Materials for the Sumerian Lexicon 16. Rome: Pontifical Biblical Institute, 1982.

Finkelstein, Jacob Joel. "The Genealogy of the Hammurapi Dynasty." JCS 20 (1966) 95-118.

Finnegan, Michael. "Faunal Remains from Bâb edh-Dhrâ', 1975." In Preliminary Excavation Reports, edited by D. N. Freedman. AASOR 43. Cambridge, MA: ASOR, 1978.

Fisher, Loren R. "A New Ritual Calendar from Ugarit." HTR 63 (1970) 485-501.

Frankena, Rintje. Takultu, de sacrale maaltijd in het Assyrische ritueel; met een overzicht over de in Assur vereerde goden. Leiden: Brill, 1953.

Fronzaroli, Pelio. "Un Atto reale di Donazione dagli Archivi di Ebla (TM.75.G.1766)." SEb 1 (1979) 3-16.

_____. "The Concord in Gender in Eblaite Theophoric Personal Names." UF 11 (1979) 275-281.

_____. "Problemi de Fonetica eblaita, 1." SEb 1 (1979) 65-89.

_____. "Il Verdetto per A'mur-Damu e sua Madre (TM.75.G.1430)." SEb 3 (1980) 65-78.

_____. "Un Verdetto reale dagli Archivi di Ebla (TM.75.G.1452)." <u>SEb</u> 3 (1980) 33-52.

Fulco, William J. <u>The Canaanite God Rešep</u>. American Oriental Series 8. New Haven: American Oriental Society, 1976.

Furlani, Giuseppe. <u>Il sacrificio nella religione dei Semiti di Babilonia e Assiria.</u> Rome: Bardi, 1932.

Galling, Kurt. "Erwägungen zum Stelenheiligtum von Hazor." <u>ZDPV</u> 75 (1959) 1-13.

_____. "Grab." <u>Biblisches Reallexikon.</u> HAT. Tübingen: J. C. B. Mohr, 1937.

Garbini, Giovanni. "<u>Mlk 'mr</u> e <u>mlk b'l</u>. A proposito di CIS I 123B." <u>RSO</u> 43 (1968) 5-11.

_____. "Une nouvelle interpretation de la formule punique BŠRM BTM." <u>Comptes rendus du group linguistique d'études chamito-sémitiques</u> 11 (1967) 144-145.

Garr, W. Randall. "Dialect Geography of Syria-Palestine, 1000-586 B.C." Unpublished Ph.D. dissertation, Yale University, 1983.

Gaster, Theodore H. <u>Myth, Legend and Custom in the Old Testament.</u> NY: Harper and Row, 1969.

Geer, Russel M. <u>Diodorus Siculus: Library of History.</u> LCL 10. Cambridge, MA: Harvard, 1954.

Geiger, Abraham. <u>Urschrift und Übersetzungen der Bibel.</u> 2d ed. Frankfurt am Main: Madda, 1928 [orig., 1857].

Gelb, Ignace J. <u>Computer-aided Analysis of Amorite.</u> Assyriological Studies 21. Chicago: Oriental Institute, 1980.

_____. <u>Glossary of Old Akkadian.</u> Materials for the Assyrian Dictionary 3. Chicago: University of Chicago, 1957.

_____. <u>Thoughts about Ibla: A Preliminary Evaluation, March, 1977.</u> SMS 1/1. Malibu, CA: Undena, 1977.

_____, P. M. Purves and A. A. MacRae. <u>Nuzi Personal Names.</u> OIP 57. Chicago: University of Chicago, 1943.

Gese, Hartmut, Maria Höfner and Kurt Rudolph. <u>Die Religionen Altsyriens, Altarabiens und der Mandäer.</u> Die Religionen der Menschheit 10/2. Stuttgart: W. Kollhammer, 1970.

Gevirtz, Stanley. "A New Look at an Old Crux: Amos 5:26." <u>JBL</u> 87 (1968) 267-276.

Ghillany, F. W. Die Menschenopfer der alten Hebräer. Nurenberg: Johann Leonhard Schrag, 1842.

Good, Robert M. "Supplementary Remarks on the Ugaritic Funerary Text RS 34.126." BASOR 239 (1980) 41-42.

Goodwin, Thomas. Moses et Aaron: seu Civiles et Ecclesiastici Ritus Antiquorum Hebraeorum. 4th ed. Ultrajecti: Balthasaris Lobé, 1698 [English orig., 1616].

Görg, M. "Noch Einmal: Edrei in Ugarit?" UF 6 (1974) 474-475.

Gray, George Buchanan. The Book of Isaiah: I-XXVII. ICC. Edinburgh: T. & T. Clark, 1912.

_____. Studies in Hebrew Proper Names. London: Adam and Charles Black, 1896.

Gray, John. "Canaanite Religion and Old Testament Study in the Light of the New Alphabetic texts from Ras Shamra." In Ug7, edited by C. F. A. Schaeffer. MRS 18. Paris: Paul Geunther, 1978.

_____. "The Desert God Aṭtr in the Literature and Religion of Canaan." JNES 8 (1949) 72-83.

_____. The Legacy of Canaan. 2d ed. VTSup 5. Leiden: Brill, 1965.

Green, Alberto Ravinell Whitney. The Role of Human Sacrifice in the Ancient Near East. ASOR Dissertation Series 1. Missoula, MT: Scholars, 1975.

Greenberg, Moshe. Ezekiel 1-20. AB 22. Garden City, NY: Doubleday, 1983.

Greenfield, Jonas C. "The Prepositions B.....Taḥat.....in Jes 57:5." ZAW 73 (1961) 226-228.

Greenstein, Edward L. "Another Attestation of Initial h > ' in West Semitic." JANESCU 5 (1973) 157-164.

Greissing, Valentin. zbḥ bnym lmlk h.e. Immolatio Liberorum Molocho Facta. Wittenberg: Christian Schrödter, 1678.

Gröndahl, Frauke. Die Personennamen der Texte aus Ugarit. Studia Pohl 1. Rome: Pontifical Biblical Institute, 1967.

Gsell, Stéphane. "Stèles votives à Saturne découvertes près de N'Gaous (Algérie), par Jeanne et Prosper Alquier." CRAIBL (1931) 21-26.

Gunkel, Hermann. Genesis. 5th ed. HKAT 1. Göttingen: Vandenhoeck & Ruprecht, 1922.

Harding, G. Lankester. "Recent Discoveries in Jordan." PEQ 90 (1958)
     7-18.

Harper, William Rainey. Amos and Hosea. ICC. NY: Charles Scribner's
     Sons, 1915.

Harris, Zellig. Development of the Canaanite Dialects. New Haven:
     American Oriental Society, 1922.

Healey, John F. "Death, Underworld and Afterlife in the Ugaritic
     Texts." Unpublished Ph.D. dissertation, University of London, 1977.

_____. "MALKŪ : MLKM : ANUNNAKI." UF 7 (1975) 235-238.

_____. "MLKM/RP'UM and the kispum." UF 10 (1979) 89-91.

_____. "Ritual Text KTU 1.161--Translation and Notes." UF 10
     (1978) 83-88.

_____. "The Underworld Character of the God Dagan." JNSL 5 (1977)
     43-51.

Hennessy, J. B. "Excavation of a Bronze Age Temple at Amman." PEQ 98
     (1966) 155-162.

Herbert, A. S. The Book of the Prophet Isaiah: Chapters 1-39.
     Cambridge, NEB. Cambridge: University, 1973.

Herdner, Andrée. "Nouveaux textes alphabétiques de Ras Shamra--XXIVe
     campagne, 1961." In Ug7, edited by C. F. A. Schaeffer. MRS 18.
     Paris: Paul Geunther, 1978.

_____. "Un nouvel exemplaire du Rituel." Syria 33 (1956) 104-112.

_____. "Une prière à Baal des Ugaritains en danger." CRAIBL
     (1972) 693-703.

Herr, Larry G. "The Amman Airport Excavations, 1976." ADAJ 21 (1976)
     109-111.

_____. "The Amman Airport Structure and the Geopolitics of Ancient
     Transjordan." BA 46 (1983) 223-229.

_____. The Scripts of Ancient Northwest Semitic Seals. HSM 18.
     Missoula, MT: Scholars, 1978.

Hirsch, Hans. Untersuchungen zur altassyrischen Religion. AfO Beiheft
     13/14. Graz: H. Hirsch, 1961.

Hoffner, Harry A. "Second Millennium Antecedents to the Hebrew 'ôb."
     JBL 86 (1967) 385-401.

Hoftijzer, Jacob. "Eine Notiz zum Punischen Kinderopfer." VT 8 (1958)
     288-292.

Holladay, William L. "A Fresh Look at 'Source B' and 'Source C' in Jeremiah." VT 25 (1975) 394-412.

Horn, S. H. "The Ammān Citadel Inscription." BASOR 193 (1969) 2-13.

Horwitz, William J. "The Significance of the Rephaim: rm.aby.btk.rpim." JNSL 7 (1979) 37-43.

Huber, Friedrich. Jahwe, Juda und die anderen Völker beim Propheten Jesaja. BZAW 137. Berlin: W. de Gruyter, 1976.

Huffmon, Herbert Bardwell. Amorite Personal Names in the Mari Texts: A Structural and Lexical Study. Baltimore: Johns Hopkins, 1965.

Hyatt, James Philip. "The Book of Jeremiah: Introduction and Exegesis." IB 5 (1956) 777-1142.

_____. "Jeremiah and Deuteronomy." JNES 1 (1942) 156-173.

Ibrahim, Moawiyah M. "Archaeological Excavations at Sahab, 1972." ADAJ 17 (1972) 23-36.

Irwin, William Henry. Isaiah 28-33: Translation with Philological Notes. BibOr 30. Rome: Pontifical Biblical Institute, 1977.

Isbell, Charles D. "Another Look at Amos 5:26." JBL 97 (1978) 97-99.

Israel, Felice. "Miscellanea Idumea." RivB 27 (1979) 171-205.

Jastrow, Morris. "Rô'ēh and Ḥôzēh in the Old Testament." JBL 28 (1909) 42-56.

Jensen, Peter. "Die Götter kəmôš und melek und die Erscheinungsformen Kammuš und Malik des assyrisch-babylonischen Gottes Nergal." ZA 42 (1934) 235-237.

Jirku, Anton. "Gab es im AT einen Gott Molek (Melek)?" ARW 35 (1938) 178-179.

Johns, C. N. "Excavations at the Pilgrims' Castle 'Atlit." QDAP 6 (1936) 121-152.

Kaiser, Otto. "Den Erstgeborenen deiner Söhne sollst du mir geben: Erwägungen zum Kinderopfer im Alten Testament." In Denkender Glaube: Festschrift C. H. Ratschow, edited by O. Kaiser. Berlin: W. de Gruyter, 1976.

_____. Isaiah 13-39. OTL. Philadelphia: Westminster, 1974 [German orig., 1973].

Kamphausen, Adolf. Das Verhältnis des Menschenopfers zur israelitischen Religion. Bonn: Röhrscheid und Ebbecke, 1896.

Karge, Paul. Rephaim: die vorgeschichtliche Kultur Palästinas und Phöniziens. 2d ed. Paderborn: F. Schöningh, 1925.

Kaufmann, Stephen A. "The Enigmatic Adad-Milki." JNES 37 (1978) 101-109.

Kaufmann, Yehezkel. The Religion of Israel: From Its Beginnings to the Babylonian Exile. Translated by M. Greenberg. Chicago: University of Chicago, 1960.

Kennedy, Charles A. "The Table of Demons: 1 Corinthians 10:20-21." Unpublished manuscript.

_____. "Tartessos, Tarshish and Tartarus: The Tower of Pozo Moro and the Bible." Unpublished essay presented to the First International Meeting of the Society of Biblical Literature at Salamanca, Spain, 1983.

Kenyon, Kathleen. Digging Up Jericho. London: E. Benn, 1957.

_____. Excavations at Jericho. 4 vols. Jerusalem: British School of Archaeology, 1960-1981.

Kienast, Burkhart. "Igigū und Anunnakkū nach den akkadischen Quellen." In Studies in Honor of Benno Landsberger on his 75th Birthday, edited by H. G. Güterbock and T. Jacobsen. Assyriological Studies 16. Chicago: University of Chicago, 1965.

Klauser, Theodor. "Melkart." Reallexikon für Antike und Christentum, edited by T. Klauser. Stuttgart: Hiersemann, 1950.

Knudtzon, J. A. Die El-Amarna-Tafeln. 2 vols. Leipzig: J. C. Hinrichs, 1910-1915.

Kornfeld, Walter. "Der Moloch: Eine Untersuchung zur Theorie O. Eissfeldts." WZKM 51 (1952) 287-313.

Kraus, Hans-Joachim. Psalmen. 4th ed. BKAT 15/2. Neukirchen-Vluyn: Neukirchener, 1972.

Lagrange, Marie-Joseph. Études sur les Religions Sémitiques. 2nd ed. Paris: Lecoffre, 1905.

Lambert, W. G. Babylonian Wisdom Literature. Oxford: Clarendon, 1960.

_____. "Götterlisten." RLA 3:473-479.

Langdon, Stephen, ed. The H. Weld-Blundell Collection in the Ashmolean Museum: 1. Sumerian and Semitic Religious and Historical Texts. OECT 1. Oxford: University, 1923.

Lehmann, Manfred R. "A New Interpretation of the Term šdmwt." VT 3 (1953) 361-371.

Levine, Baruch. "The Cult of Molech in Biblical Israel." Leviticus
    Commentary. Jewish Publication Society of America, forthcoming.

Levy, M. A. Siegel und Gemmen mit aramäischen, phönizischen,
    althebräischen, himjarischen, nabathäischen und altsyrischen Inhalts.
    Breslau: Schletter, 1869.

L'Heureux, Conrad E. Rank among the Canaanite Gods: El, Baal and the
    Repha'im. HSM 21. Missoula, MT: Scholars, 1979.

L'Hour, J. "Les Interdits Tô'ēbāh dans le Deuteronome." RB 71 (1964)
    481-503.

Lidzbarski, Mark. Ephemeris für semitische Epigraphik. 3 vols.
    Giessen: Alfred Töpelmann, 1900-1915.

_____. Handbuch der nordsemitischen Epigraphik. 2 vols. Reprint.
    Hildesheim: Georg Olms, 1962 [orig., 1898].

Lipiński, Edward. "North Semitic Texts." In Near Eastern Religious
    Texts Relating to the Old Testament, edited by W. Beyerlin. OTL.
    Philadelphia: Westminster, 1978.

_____. "Recherches Ugaritiques: 1. Ay, un dieu ugaritique?"
    Syria 44 (1967) 253-282.

Litke, Richard L. "A Reconstruction of the Assyro-Babylonian God-Lists,
    AN:(d)Anum and AN:Anu šá amēli." Unpublished Ph.D. dissertation,
    Yale University, 1958.

Little, Robert M. "Human Bone Fragment Analysis." In The Amman Airport
    Excavations, 1976, edited by L. G. Herr. AASOR 48. Cambridge, MA:
    ASOR, 1983.

Löwengard, M. Jehova, nicht Moloch, was der Gott der alten Hebräer,
    1843.

Luckenbill, Daniel David. The Annals of Sennacherib. OIP 2. Chicago:
    University of Chicago, 1924.

Lust, J. "On Wizards and Prophets." VTSup 26 (1974) 133-142.

Macalister, A. The Excavation of Gezer. London: J. Murray, 1912.

McKay, John William. Religion in Judah under the Assyrians. SBT 2/26.
    Napierville, IL: Alec R. Allenson, 1973.

McKeating, Henry. The Books of Amos, Hosea and Micah. Cambridge, NEB.
    Cambridge: University, 1971.

Mader, Evaristus. Die Menschenopfer der alten Hebräer und der
    benachbarten Völker. Biblische Studien 14/5-6. Freiburg: Herder,
    1909.

Malamat, Abraham. "King Lists of the Old Babylonian Period and Biblical Genealogies." JAOS 88 (1968) 163-173.

Margalit, Baruch. "The Geographical Setting of the AQHT Story and Its Ramifications." In Ugarit in Retrospect, edited by G. D. Young. Winona Lake, IN: Eisenbrauns, 1981.

Margulis, Baruch. "A Ugaritic Psalm (RS 24.252)." JBL 89 (1970) 292-304.

Marti, Karl. Das Buch Jesaja. KAT 10. Tübingen: J. C. B. Mohr, 1900.

Matthiae, Paolo. Ebla: An Empire Rediscovered. Translated by C. Holme. Garden City, NY: Doubleday, 1981 [Italian orig., 1977].

_____. "A Hypothesis on the Princely Burial Area of Middle Bronze II Ebla." ArOr 49 (1981) 55-65.

May, H. G., ed. Oxford Bible Atlas. 2d ed. London: Oxford, 1974.

Mayes, A. D. H. Deuteronomy. NCB. Grand Rapids, MI: Eerdmans, 1979.

Meek, Theophil J. Excavations at Nuzi: 3. Old Akkadian, Sumerian, and Cappadocian Texts from Nuzi. Harvard Semitic Series 10. Cambridge, MA: Harvard, 1935.

Meer, P. E. van der. Syllabaries A, B(1) and B: with miscellaneous lexicographical texts from the Herbert Weld Collection. OECT 4. London: Oxford, 1938.

Meier, Ernst. Review of Der Feuer- and Moloch-dienst, by G. F. Daumer, and of Die Menschenopfer der alten Hebräer, by F. W. Ghillany. Theologische Studien und Kritiken 16 (1843) 1007-1053.

Meier, Gerhard. Maqlû: Die assyrische Beschwörungssammlung Maqlû. AfO Beiheft 2. Berlin: G. Meier, 1937.

Meyer, Eduard. Geschichte des Altertums. 3d ed. Stuttgart: Gotta, 1953.

Milgrom, Jacob. "The Date of Jeremiah, Chapter 2." JNES 14 (1955) 65-69.

_____. "Profane Slaughter and the Composition of Deuteronomy." HUCA 47 (1976) 1-17.

Miller, Patrick D., Jr. "Ugarit and the History of Religions." JNSL 9 (1981) 119-128.

Mommert, Carl. Menschenopfer bei den alten Hebräern. Leipzig: E. Haberland, 1905.

Montgomery, James A. The Books of Kings. Edited by H. S. Gehman. ICC. NY: Charles Scribner's Sons, 1951.

Moor, Johannes C. de. New Year with Canaanites and Israelites. Kampen: J. H. Kok, 1972.

_____. "Rāpi'ūma--Rephaim." ZAW 88 (1976) 323-345.

_____. "The Semitic Pantheon of Ugarit." UF 2 (1970) 187-228.

_____. "Studies in the New Alphabetic Texts from Ras Shamra, I." UF 1 (1969) 167-188.

Moore, George F. "Biblical Notes: 3. The Image of Moloch." JBL 16 (1897) 161-165.

_____. "Molech, Moloch." Encyclopaedia Biblica, edited by T. K. Cheyne and J. S. Black. NY: Macmillan, 1902.

Morgenstern, Julian. "The King-God among the Western Semites and the Meaning of Epiphanes." VT 10 (1960) 138-197.

Mosca, Paul G. "Child Sacrifice in Canaanite and Israelite Religion: A Study in Mulk and mlk." Unpublished Ph.D. dissertation, Harvard University, 1975.

Moscati, Sabatino. "Il sacrificio dei fanciulli." Rendiconti della Pontificia Accademia Romana de Archeologia 38 (1965-1966) 61-68.

Mosis, Rudolf. Untersuchungen zur Theologie des chronistischen Geschichtswerkes. Freiburg: Herder, 1973.

Movers, F. C. Die Phönizier. Bonn: Eduard Weber, 1841.

Mowinckel, Sigmund. Prophecy and Tradition. Oslo: Jacob Dybwad, 1946.

Muilenburg, James. "The Book of Isaiah: Chapters 40-66: Introduction and Exegesis." IB 5 (1956) 381-773.

Mulder, Martin Jan. Kanaänitische Goden in het Oude Testament. Exegetica: Oud- en Nieuw-Testamentische studiën 4,4-5. The Hague: Voorheen Vankeulen Periodieken, 1965.

Müller, Hans-Peter. "Religionsgeschichtliche Beobachtungen zu der Texte von Ebla." ZDPV 96 (1980) 1-19.

Müller, J. G. "Moloch." PRE1, edited by J. J. Herzog. Stuttgart: Rudolf Besser, 1858.

Müller, Karl Fr. Das assyrische Rituel: 1. Texte zum assyrischen Königsritual. MVAG 41/3. Leipzig: J. C. Hinrichs, 1937.

Münter, Friedrich. Religion der Karthager. 2d ed. Copenhagen: Johann Heinrich Schubothe, 1821.

Myers, Jacob M. II Chronicles. AB 13. Garden City, NY: Doubleday, 1965.

Nakata, Ichiro. "Deities in the Mari Texts: Complete inventory of all
the information on the deities found in the published Old Babylonian
cuneiform texts from Mari and analytical and comparative evaluation
thereof with regard to the official and popular pantheons of Mari."
Unpublished Ph.D. dissertation, Columbia University, 1974.

Neiman, David. "PGR: A Canaanite Cult-Object in the Old Testament."
JBL 67 (1948) 55-60.

Nelson, Richard D. The Double Redaction of the Deuteronomistic History.
JSOT Supplementary Series 18. Sheffield: JSOT, 1981.

Nicholson, E. W. Deuteronomy and Tradition. Oxford: Blackwell, 1967.

Nielsen, Ditlev. Ras Šamra Mythologie und Biblische Theologie.
Abhandlungen für die Kunde des Morgenlandes 21/4. Leipzig:
Deutschen Morgenländischen Gesellschaft, 1936.

Norin, Stig I. L. Er spaltete das Meer. Coniectanea Biblica, OT Series
9. Lund: C. W. K. Gleerup, 1977.

Noth, Martin. Die israelitischen Personennamen im Rahmen der
gemeinsemitischen Namengebung. Stuttgart: W. Kohlhammer, 1928.

_____. Leviticus. Rev. ed. Translated by J. E. Anderson. OTL.
Philadelphia: Westminster, 1977 [German orig., 1962].

_____. Numbers. Translated by J. D. Martin. OTL. Philadelphia:
Westminster, 1968 [German orig., 1966].

Nougayrol, J. "Textes hépatoscopiques d'époque ancienne conservés au
Musée du Louvre (III)." RA 44 (1950) 1-44.

Nowack, W. Hebräische Archäologie. Freiburg: J. C. B. Mohr, 1894.

O'Ceallaigh, G. C. "And So David Did to All the Cities of Ammon." VT
12 (1962) 179-189.

Ortner, Donald J. "A Preliminary Report on the Human Remains from the
Bab edh-Dhra Cemetery." In The Southeastern Dead Sea Plain
Expedition, 1977, edited by W. E. Rast and R. T. Schaub. AASOR 46.
Cambridge, MA: ASOR, 1981.

Ottosson, Magnus. Temples and Cult Places in Palestine. Boreas 12.
Uppsala: Almqvist and Wiksell, 1980.

Pardee, Dennis. "A Philological and Prosodic Analysis of the Ugaritic
Serpent Incantation UT 607." JANESCU 10 (1978) 73-108.

_____. "The Preposition in Ugaritic." UF 8 (1976) 214-322.

Parker, Simon B. "The Feast of Rāpi'u." UF 2 (1970) 243-249.

_____. "The Ugaritic Deity Rāpi'u." UF 4 (1972) 97-104.

Paton, Lewis Bayles. Spiritism and the Cult of the Dead in Antiquity. NY: Macmillan, 1921.

Pettinato, Giovanni. The Archives of Ebla, with an afterward by M. Dahood. Garden City, NY: Doubleday, 1981 [Italian orig., 1979].

_____. Catalogo dei Testi Cuneiformi di Tell Mardikh-Ebla. MEE 1. Naples: Istituto Universitario Orientali di Napoli, 1979.

_____. "Culto Ufficiale ad Ebla durante il regno di Ibbi-Sipiš." OrAnt 18 (1979) 85-132.

_____. Die Ölwahrsagung bei den Babyloniern. Studi Semitici 21-22. Rome: Istituto di Studi del vincino Oriente, 1966.

_____. Testi Amministrativi della Biblioteca L. 2769. MEE 2. Naples: Istituto Universitario Orientale di Napoli, 1980.

_____. "Testi cuneiformi del 3. millennio in paleo-cananeo rinvenuti nella campagna 1974 a Tell Mardikh = Ebla." Or n.s. 44 (1975) 361-374.

_____. Testi Lessicali Bilingui della Biblioteca L. 2769. MEE 4. Naples: Istituto Universitario Orientali di Napoli, 1982.

_____. Testi Lessicali Monolingui della Biblioteca L. 2769. MEE 3. Naples: Istituto Universitario Orientali di Napoli, 1981.

Picard, Colette. "Le Monument de Nebi-Yunis." RB 83 (1976) 584-589.

_____, and Gilbert-Charles Picard. "Hercule et Melqart." In Hommages à Jean Bayet, edited by M. Renard and R. Schilling. Collection Latomus 70. Brussels, 1964.

Pitard, Wayne T. "The Ugaritic Funerary Text RS 34.126." BASOR 232 (1978) 65-75.

Plataroti, Domenico. "Zum Gebrauch des Wortes MLK im Alten Testament." VT 28 (1978) 286-300.

Poinsott, Louis, and Raymond Lantier. "Un sanctuaire de Tanit à Carthage." RHR 87 (1923) 32-68.

Pope, Marvin. "The Cult of the Dead at Ugarit." In Ugarit in Retrospect, edited by G. D. Young. Winona Lake, IN: Eisenbrauns, 1981.

_____. Job. 3d ed. AB 15. Garden City, NY: Doubleday, 1973.

_____. "Notes on the Rephaim Texts from Ugarit." In Essays on the Ancient Near East in Memory of Jacob Joel Finkelstein, edited by M. Ellis. Memoirs of the Connecticut Academy of Arts and Sciences 19. Hamden, CT: Archon, 1977.

_____. Song of Songs. AB 7C. Garden City, NY: Doubleday, 1977.

Puech, Emile. "Milkom, le dieu ammonite, en Amos I 15." VT 27 (1977) 117-125.

Purvis, James D. The Samaritan Pentateuch and the Origin of the Samaritan Sect. HSM 2. Cambridge, MA: Harvard, 1968.

Rabin, Chaim. "Og." Eretz-Israel 8 (1968) 251-254 [Hebrew], 75*-76* [English summary].

Rad, Gerhard von. Deuteronomy: A Commentary. Translated by D. Barton. OTL. Philadelphia: Westminster, 1966 [German orig., 1964].

_____. Genesis: A Commentary. Rev. ed. Translated by J. H. Marks. OTL. Philadelphia: Westminster, 1972 [German orig., 1972].

Rahmani, L. Y. "Ancient Jerusalem's Funerary Customs and Tombs." BA 44 (1981) 171-177, 229-235 and BA 45 (1982) 43-53, 109-119.

Rast, Walter E. "Cakes for the Queen of Heaven." In Scripture in History and Theology: Essays in honor of J. C. Rylaarsdam, edited by A. L. Merrill and T. W. Overholt. Pittsburgh: Pickwick, 1977.

Ratosh, Jonathan. "'ʿēbr' in Scripture or the Land of hʿbrym." Beth Mikra 47 (1970-1971) 549-568 [Hebrew].

Ribar, John Whalen. "Death Cult Practices in Ancient Palestine." Unpublished Ph.D. dissertation, University of Michigan, 1973.

Ribichini, Sergio. "Un'ipotesi per Milkʿaštart." RSO 50 (1976) 43-55.

_____, and Paolo Xella. "Milkʿaštart, mlk(m) e la tradizione siropalestinese sui Refaim." RSF 7 (1979) 145-158.

Riis, P. J. Les cimetières à cremation. Hama: Fouilles et Recherches 2/3. Copenhagen: Fondation Carlsberg, 1948.

Ringgren, Helmer. Israelite Religion. Translated by D. E. Green. Philadelphia: Fortress, 1966 [German orig., 1963].

Roberts, J. J. M. The Earliest Semitic Pantheon: A Study of the Semitic Deities Attested in Mesopotamia before Ur III. Baltimore: Johns Hopkins, 1972.

Rogers, Jonathan Henry. "Semitic Accentual Systems." Unpublished Ph.D. dissertation, Yale University, 1977.

Röllig, Wolfgang. "Alte und Neue Elfenbeininschriften." In NESE, edited by R. Degen, W. W. Müller, W. Röllig. 3 vols. Wiesbaden: Otto Harrassowitz, 1972-1978.

_____. "Kinderopfer." RLA 5 (1980) 601-602.

Rost, Leonhard. Review of Molk als Opferbegriff, by O. Eissfeldt.
Deutsche Literaturzeitung 57 (1936) 1651-1652.

Rowley, H. H. Review of De Molochdienst, by K. Dronkert. BO 10 (1953)
195-196.

_____. "The Samaritan Schism in Legend and History." In Israel's
Prophetic Heritage: Essays in Honor of James Muilenburg, edited by
B. W. Anderson and W. Harrelson. London: SCM, 1962.

Rudolph, Wilhelm. Chronikbücher. HAT 21. Tübingen: J. C. B. Mohr,
1955.

_____. Hosea. KAT 13/1. Gütersloh: Mohn, 1966.

_____. Jeremia. 3d ed. HAT 12. Tübingen: J. C. B. Mohr, 1968.

_____. Joel--Amos--Obadja--Jona. KAT 13/2. Gütersloh: Mohn,
1971.

_____. Micha--Nahum--Habakuk--Zephanja. KAT 13/3. Gütersloh:
Mohn, 1975.

Saadé, Gabriel. Ougarit: Métropole Cananéenne. Beirut: Imprimerie
Catholique, 1979.

Sabottka, Liuder. Zephanja: Versuch einer Neuübersetzung mit
philologischem Kommentar. BibOr 25. Rome: Pontifical Biblical
Institute, 1972.

Saggs, H. W. F. "Some Ancient Semitic Conceptions of the Afterlife."
Faith and Thought 90 (1953) 157-182.

Saidah, R. "Fouilles de Khaldé: Rapport préliminaire sur la première
et deuxième campagnes (1961-1962)." Bulletin du Musée de Beyrouth 19
(1966) 51-90.

Salmond, S. D. F. "Tophet, Topheth." A Dictionary of the Bible, edited
by J. Hastings. NY: Charles Scribner's Sons, 1903.

Sayce, A. H. "On Human Sacrifice among the Babylonians." Transactions
of the Society of Biblical Archaeology 4 (1875) 25-31.

Schaeffer, Claude F. A. "Sacrifice à M-l-k, Molech ou Melek." In Ug4,
edited by C. F. A. Schaeffer. MRS 15. Paris: Imprimerie Nationale,
1962.

Schlögl, Nivard. "Das Wort molek in Inscriften und Bibel." WZKM 45
(1938) 203-211.

Schmidtke, Friedrich. "Träume, Orakel und Totengeister als Künder der
Zukunft in Israel und Babylonien." BZ n.s. 11 (1967) 240-246.

Schneider, Nikolaus. <u>Götternamen von Ur III.</u> AnOr 19. Rome: Pontifical Biblical Institute, 1939.

_____. "Melchom." <u>Bib</u> 19 (1938) 204.

_____. "Melchom, Das Scheusal der Ammoniter." <u>Bib</u> 18 (1937) 337-343.

_____. "Patriarchennamen in zeitgenössischen Keilschrifturkunden." <u>Bib</u> 33 (1952) 516-522.

Schnell, R. F. "Rephaim." <u>IDB</u> 4 (1962) 35.

Schroeder, Otto. "Ein neuer Götterlistentypus aus Assur." <u>ZA</u> 33 (1921) 123-147.

Schunck, K.-D. "bāmāh." <u>TDOT</u> 2 (1977) 139-145.

Schwally, Friedrich. "Berichte: Semitische Religion im allgemeinen, israelitische und jüdische Religion." <u>ARW</u> 19 (1919) 347-382.

Scott, R. B. Y. "The Book of Isaiah: Chapters 1-39: Introduction and Exegesis." <u>IB</u> 5 (1956) 151-381.

Scullion, John J. "Some Difficult Texts in Isaiah cc. 56-66 in the Light of Modern Scholarship." <u>UF</u> 4 (1972) 105-128.

Segal, J. B. Review of <u>Studies in OT Sacrifice</u>, by R. de Vaux. <u>JTS</u> 17 (1966) 418-420.

Seitz, Gottfried. <u>Redaktionsgeschichtliche Studien zum Deuteronomium.</u> Stuttgart: W. Kohlhammer, 1971.

Selden, John. <u>De Dis Syris.</u> 3d ed. Amsterdam: Lucam Bisterum, 1680.

Sellin, Ernst, and Georg Fohrer. <u>Introduction to the Old Testament.</u> Translated by D. E. Green. Nashville: Abingdon, 1968 [German orig., 1965].

Simons, Johannes. <u>The Geographical and Topographical Texts of the Old Testament.</u> Leiden: Brill, 1959.

_____. <u>Jerusalem in the Old Testament.</u> Leiden: Brill, 1952.

Sivan, D. "On the Grammar and Orthography of the Ammonite Findings." <u>UF</u> 14 (1982) 219-234.

Smith, George Adam. <u>Jerusalem.</u> Reprint. NY: Ktav, 1972 [orig., 1877].

Smith, J. M. P., W. H. Ward and J. A. Bewer. <u>Micah, Zephaniah, Nahum, Habukkuk, Obadiah and Joel.</u> ICC. NY: Charles Scribner's Sons, 1911.

Smith, Morton. "A Note on Burning Babies." JAOS 95 (1975) 477-479.

Smith, William Robertson. Lectures on the Religion of the Semites. 2d ed. London: Adam and Charles Black, 1894.

Snaith, Norman H. "The Cult of Molech." VT 16 (1966) 123-124.

Soden, Wolfram von. Grundriss der akkadischen Grammatik. AnOr 33. Rome: Pontifical Biblical Institute, 1952.

_____. Review of Molk als Opferbegriff, by O. Eissfeldt. TLZ 61 (1936) 45-46.

Soggin, J. Alberto. "Child Sacrifice and the Cult of the Dead in the Old Testament." In Old Testament and Oriental Studies. BibOr 29. Rome: Pontifical Biblical Institute, 1975.

_____. "'Your Conduct in the Valley': A Note on Jeremiah 2,23a." In Old Testament and Oriental Studies. BibOr 29. Rome: Pontifical Biblical Institute, 1975.

Spalinger, Anthony. "A Canaanite Ritual found in Egyptian Reliefs." Journal of the Society for the Study of Egyptian Antiquities 8 (1978) 47-60.

Speiser, E. A. Excavations at Tepe Gawra: 1. Levels 1-8. Philadelphia: University of Pennsylvania, 1935.

_____. Genesis. AB 1. Garden City, NY: Doubleday, 1964.

_____. "Unrecognized Dedication." IEJ 13 (1963) 69-73.

Spencer, John. De legibus Hebraeorum ritualibus et earum rationibus. 2d ed. Hagae-Comitum: Arnold Leers, 1686.

Spiegel, Shalom. The Last Trial. Translated by J. Goldin. NY: Pantheon, 1967 [Hebrew orig., 1950].

Stade, Bernhard. Geschichte des Volkes Israel. Berlin: G. Grote, 1887.

Stager, Lawrence E. "The Archaeology of the East Slope of Jerusalem and the Terraces of the Kidron." JNES 41 (1982) 111-121.

_____. "Carthage: A View from the Tophet." In Phönizier im Westen, edited by H. G. Niemeyer. Madrider Beiträge 8. Mainz am Rhein: Philipp von Zabern, 1982.

_____. "The Rite of Child Sacrifice at Carthage." In New Light on Ancient Carthage, edited by J. G. Pedley. Ann Arbor: University of Michigan, 1980.

_____, and Samuel R. Wolff. "Child Sacrifice at Carthage--Religious Rite or Population Control?" <u>BARev</u> 10 (1984) 30-51.

Stamm, Johann Jacob. <u>Die akkadische Namengebung</u>. MVAG 44. Leipzig: J. C. Hinrichs, 1939.

Starr, Richard F. S. <u>Nuzi: Report on the Excavations at Yorgan Tepe near Kirkuk, Iraq.</u> 2 vols. Cambridge, MA: Harvard, 1937.

Strong, James. "Molech." In <u>Cyclopaedia of Biblical, Theological, and Ecclesiastical Literature</u>, edited by J. McClintock and J. Strong. NY: Harper and Brothers, 1894.

Tallqvist, Knut Leonard. <u>Akkadische Götterepitheta</u>. Studia Orientalia 7. Helsinki: Societas Scientiarum Fennicae, 1938.

Talon, Philippe. "Un nouveau panthéon de Mari." <u>Akkadica</u> 20 (1980) 12-17.

_____. "Les offrandes funéraires à Mari." <u>AIPHOS</u> 22 (1978) 53-75.

Tarragon, Jean-Michel de. <u>Le culte à Ugarit: D'après les textes de la pratique en cunéiformes alphabétiques.</u> Cahiers de la Revue Biblique 19. Paris: Gabalda, 1980.

Taylor, J. Glen. "Notes on Isaiah 8:19-22, and a New Proposal for 8:21-22." Unpublished seminar paper, Yale University, 1982.

Thiel, Winfried. <u>Die deuteronomistische Redaktion von Jeremia 1-25.</u> WMANT 41. Neukirchen-Vluyn: Neukirchener, 1973.

Tobler, Arthur J. <u>Excavations at Tepe Gawra: 2. Levels 9-20.</u> Philadelphia: University of Pennsylvania, 1950.

Tomback, Richard S. <u>A Comparative Semitic Lexicon of the Phoenician and Punic Languages.</u> SBLDS 32. Missoula, MT: Scholars, 1978.

Tromp, Nicholas J. <u>Primitive Conceptions of Death and the Nether World in the Old Testament.</u> BibOr 21. Rome: Pontifical Biblical Institute, 1969.

Tur-Sinai, Naphtali Herz. <u>Ha-Lashon ve-ha-Sefer.</u> 3 vols. Jerusalem: Bialik Institute, 1948-1955 [Hebrew].

Tushingham, A. D. <u>The Excavations at Dibon (Dhībân) in Moab.</u> AASOR 40. Cambridge, MA: ASOR, 1972.

Vaux, Roland de. <u>Ancient Israel.</u> 2 vols. NY: McGraw-Hill, 1961.

_____. "Religion de l'Ancient Testament." <u>RB</u> 62 (1955) 609-610.

_____. Review of <u>Molk als Opferbegriff</u>, by O. Eissfeldt. <u>RB</u> 45 (1936) 278-282.

_____. "Les Sacrifices de porcs en Palestine et dans l'ancien Orient." In Von Ugarit nach Qumran: Festschrift O. Eissfeldt, edited by J. Hempel and L. Rost. BZAW 77. Berlin: Töpelmann, 1958.

_____. Studies in Old Testament Sacrifice. Cardiff: University of Wales, 1964.

Vieyra, Maurice. "Les noms du 'mundus' en hittite et en assyrien et la pythonisse d'Endor." Revue Hittite et Asianique 69 (1961) 47-55.

Virolleaud, Charles. "Les nouvelles tablettes alphabétiques de Ras-Shamra (XIXe campagne, 1955)." CRAIBL (1956) 60-67.

Volz, Paul. Das Dämonische in Jahwe. Tübingen: J. C. B. Mohr, 1924.

Waard, Jan de. "A Greek Translation-Technical Treatment of Amos 1:15." In On Language, Culture and Religion: in honor of Eugene A. Nida, edited by M. Black and W. A. Smalley. The Hague: Mouton, 1974.

Ward, W. H. Cylinder Seals and Other Ancient Oriental Seals in the Library of J. Pierpont Morgan. Washington: Carnagie Institute of Washington, 1910.

Watson, Paul. "Form Criticism and an Exegesis of Micah 6:1-8." RestQ 7 (1963) 61-72.

Watson, Paul Layton. "Mot, the God of Death, at Ugarit and in the Old Testament." Unpublished Ph.D. dissertation, Yale University, 1970.

Weidner, Ernst F. "Altbabylonische Götterlisten." Archiv für Keilschriftforschung 2 (1924) 1-18.

Weinfeld, Moshe. "Burning Babies in Ancient Israel. A Rejoinder to Morton Smith's Article in JAOS 95 (1975), pp. 477-479." UF 10 (1978) 411-413.

_____. Deuteronomy and the Deuteronomistic School. Oxford: Clarendon, 1972.

_____. "The Molech Cult in Israel and Its Background." In Proceedings of the Fifth World Congress of Jewish Studies, edited by P. Peli. Jerusalem: World Union of Jewish Studies, 1969 [Hebrew, with English abstract].

_____. "The Worship of Molech and of the Queen of Heaven and its Background." UF 4 (1972) 133-154.

Weippert, Helga. "Die 'deuteronomistischen' Beurteilungen der Könige von Israel und Juda und das Problem der Redaktion der Königsbücher." Bib 53 (1972) 301-339.

_____. Die Prosereden des Jeremiabuches. BZAW 132. Berlin: W. de Gruyter, 1973.

Weiser, Artur. The Psalms. Translated by H. Hartwell. OTL. Philadelphia: Westminster, 1962 [German orig., 1959].

Wernberg-Møller, P. "Two Notes." VT 8 (1958) 305-308.

Westermann, Claus. Isaiah 40-66. Translated by D. M. G. Stalker. OTL. Philadelphia: Westminster, 1969 [German orig., 1966].

Whitley, C. F. "The Language and Exegesis of Isaiah 8, 16-23." ZAW 90 (1978) 28-43.

Wilke, Fritz. "Kinderopfer und kultische Preisgabe im 'Heiligkeitsgesetz'." In Festschrift zur 57. Versammlung deutscher Philologen und Schulmänner in Salzburg, 1929. Vienna: Rudolf M. Rohrer, 1929.

Wilson, Robert R. "The Hardening of Pharaoh's Heart." CBQ 41 (1979) 18-36.

_____. "An Interpretation of Ezekiel's Dumbness." VT 22 (1972) 91-104.

_____. Prophecy and Society in Ancient Israel. Philadelphia: Fortress, 1980.

Winer, Georg Benedikt, ed. "Molech." Biblisches Realwörterbuch. Leipzig: Carl Heinrich, 1838.

Wiseman, D. J. The Alalakh Tablets. London: British Institute of Archaeology at Ankara, 1953.

_____. Review of The Role of Human Sacrifice, by A. R. W. Green. BSOAS 40 (1977) 441.

Witsius, Hermann. Miscellaneorum Sacrorum. Trajecti ad Rhenum: Franciscum Halman, 1692.

Wolff, Hans Walter. Hosea. Translated by G. Stansell. Edited by P. D. Hanson. Hermeneia. Philadelphia: Fortress, 1974 [German orig., 1965].

_____. Joel and Amos. Translated by W. Janzen et al. Edited by S. D. McBride. Hermeneia. Philadelphia: Fortress, 1977 [German orig., 1975].

Woolley, C. Leonard. "Excavations at Atchana-Alalakh, 1938." AntJ 19 (1939) 1-37.

_____. "Excavations at Tal Atchana, 1937." AntJ 18 (1938) 1-28.

_____. Ur Excavations: 2. The Royal Cemetery. London: Kegan, Paul Trench, 1954.

Wright, George Ernest. "The Book of Deuteronomy: Introduction and Exegesis." IB 2 (1953) 311-537.

Xella, Paolo. "A proposito del sacrificio umano nel mondo mesopotamico." Or n.s. 45 (1976) 185-196.

_____. "KTU 1.91 (RS 19.15) e i sacrifici del re." UF 11 (1979) 833-838.

_____. Review of The Role of Human Sacrifice, by A. R. W. Green. RSF 8 (1980) 149-153.

_____. I testi rituali di Ugarit. Pubblicazioni del Centro di Studio per la Civiltà Fenicia e Punica 21 [Studi Semitici 54]. Rome: Consiglio Nationale delle Ricerche, 1981.

_____. "Un Testo Ugaritico Recente (RS 24.266, Verso, 9-19) e il 'Sacrifico dei Primo Nati'." RSF 6 (1978) 127-136.

Ziegler, Joseph. Ieremias. Septuaginta Gottingensis 15. Göttingen: Vandenhoeck & Ruprecht, 1957.

Zimmerli, Walther. Ezekiel 1. Translated by R. E. Clements. Edited by F. M. Cross and K. Baltzer. Hermeneia. Philadelphia: Fortress, 1979 [German orig., 1969].

_____. Ezekiel 2. Translated by J. D. Martin. Edited by P. D. Hanson and L. J. Greenspoon. Hermeneia. Philadelphia: Fortress, 1983 [German orig., 1969].

Zimmern, H., and H. Winkler. Die Keilinschriften und das Alte Testament. 3d ed. Berlin: Reuther und Reichard, 1903.